21
ARCHAEOLOGY OF THE SPANISH MISSIONS OF TEXAS

Edited with an Introduction by
Anne A. Fox

GARLAND PUBLISHING, INC.
NEW YORK & LONDON, 1991

Introduction © 1991 Anne A. Fox
All rights reserved

All rights reserved

Library of Congress Cataloging-in-Publication Data

Archaeology of the Spanish missions of Texas / edited with an introduction by Anne A. Fox.

p. cm. — (The Spanish borderlands sourcebooks ; 21)

Includes bibliographical references.

ISBN 0-8240-2097-9 (alk. paper)

1. Spanish mission buildings—Texas. 2. Texas—Antiquities. 3. Spaniards—Texas—Antiquities. I. Fox, Anne A. II. Series.

F387.A73 1991

976.4'02—dc20   90-22360

Printed on acid-free, 250-year-life paper.
Manufactured in the United States of America

SPANISH BORDERLANDS SOURCEBOOKS

Presenting Over Four Hundred and Fifty Scholarly Articles and Source Materials Documenting Interactions Between Native Americans and Europeans from California to Florida

Each Volume Edited with an Introduction by a Major Scholar

General Editor
David Hurst Thomas
American Museum of Natural History

A GARLAND SERIES

Contents

Sources ix

Introduction xiii

Mission Construction and Administration

Selections from *The San Xavier Missions: A Study in Historical Site Identification* (1969)
Kathleen Kirk Gilmore 3

Selections from *A Lipan Apache Mission: San Lorenzo de la Santa Cruz,* 1762–1771 (1969)
Curtis D. Tunnell 21

Selections from *Guidelines for a Texas Mission: Instructions for the Missionary of Mission Concepción in San Antonio, Texas* ([1976]1990)
Benedict Leutenegger 75

Report Submitted by Rev. Father General, Fray Ignacio Maria Lava to the Father President, Fray José Manuel Pedrajo, Minister at Mission San José (1983)
Marian Habig, Benedict Leutenegger, and M. Carmelita Casso 123

Related Structures

Archaeological Monitoring of the San José Acequia (41 BX267), Wastewater Facilities Improvements Program, San Antonio, Texas (1988)
I. Waynne Cox   *133*

Archaeological Investigation of the San Juan Dam, 41 BX 266, Bexar County, Texas (1989)
David B. Hafernik, I. Waynne Cox, and Anne A. Fox   *143*

Selection from ***Archaeological Survey and Testing at Rancho de las Cabras,*** Wilson County, Texas (1981)
James E. Ivey and Anne A. Fox   *153*

Mission Sites Archaeology

Selections from ***A Description of the Stratigraphy, Features and Artifacts from an Archeological Excavation at the Alamo*** (1967)
John W. Greer   *189*

Selections from ***The History and Archeology of Mission San Juan Capistrano, San Antonio, Texas:*** Volume I (1968)
Mardith K. Schuetz   *217*

Selections from ***An Archeological Investigation of Mission Concepción, San Antonio, Texas*** (1977)
Dan Scurlock and Daniel E. Fox   *297*

Archeological Research at 41SA25, Mission Dolores de los Ais (1977)
James E. Corbin   323

SOURCES

CORBIN, JAMES E.
    1977   *Archeological Research at 41SA25, Mission Dolores de los Ais. A Preliminary Report submitted to the Texas Historical Commission.* Austin: Texas Historical Commission. Reprinted by permission.

COX, I. WAYNNE
    1988   *Archaeological Monitoring of the San José Acequia (41 BX 267), Wastewater Facilities Improvement Program, San Antonio, Texas.* Pp. 1–9. Archaeological Survey Report, No. 175. San Antonio: Center for Archaeological Research. Reprinted by permission of the Center for Archaeological Research, Texas Archaeological Society.

GILMORE, KATHLEEN KIRK
    1969   *The San Xavier Mission: A Study in Historical Site Identification.* State Building Commission Archaeological Program Report, No. 16. Pp. 4–9, 63–70. Austin: State Building Commission. Reprinted by permission of the author.

GREER, JOHN W.
    1967   *A Description of the Stratigraphy, Features and Artifacts from an Archaeological Excavation at the Alamo.* Pp. 3–14. State Building Commission Archeological Program Report, No. 3. Austin: State Building Commission. Reprinted by permission.

HABIG, MARIAN, BENEDICT LEUTENEGGER, AND M. CARMELITA CASSO,
EDITORS AND TRANSLATORS
1983   Report Submitted by Rev. Father General, Fray Ygnacio
                 Maria Lava to the Father President, Fray José Manuel
                 Pedrajo, Minister at Mission San José. In *The San José
                 Papers. The Primary Sources for the History of Mission
                 San José y San Miguel de Aguayo from Its Founding in
                 1720 to the Present. II: August 1791–June 1809.* Pp. 12–
                 18. San Antonio: Old Spanish Missions Historical Research
                 Library. Reprinted by permission.

HAFERNIK, DAVID B., I. WAYNNE COX, AND ANNE A. FOX
1989   *Archaeological Investigation of the San Juan Dam, 41 BX
                 266, Bexar County, Texas.* Pp. 1–9. Archaeological Survey
                 Report, No. 179. San Antonio: Center for Archaeological
                 Research. Reprinted by permission of the Center for
                 Archaeological Research, Texas Archaeological Society.

IVEY, JAMES A. AND ANNE A. FOX
1981   *Archaeological Survey and Testing at Rancho de las
                 Cabras, Wilson County, Texas.* Pp. 1–30. Archaeological
                 Survey Report, No. 104. San Antonio: Center for
                 Archaeological Research. Reprinted by permission of the
                 Center for Archaeological Research, Texas Archaeological
                 Society.

LEUTENEGGER, BENEDICT, O.F.M., EDITOR AND TRANSLATOR
1976   *Guidelines for a Texas Mission: Instructions for the
                 Missionary of Mission Concepción in San Antonio
                 Texas.*Transcript of Spanish Original with English
                 Translation and Notes. Completely Revised (1990) by
                 Sister Carmelita Casso and Sister Margaret Rose
                 Warburton. San Antonio: Old Spanish Missions Historical
                 Research Society. Reprinted by permission.

SCHUETZ, MARDITH K.
1968   *The History and Archaeology of Mission San Juan
                 Capistrano, San Antonio, Texas.* Pp. 1–3, 69–132. State
                 Building Commission Archaeological Program Report, No.
                 10. Austin: State Building Commission. Reprinted by
                 permission of the author.

SCURLOCK, DAN AND DANIEL E. FOX
    1977   *An Archeological Investigation of Mission Concepción, San Antonio, Texas.* Pp. 30–52. Office of the State Archaeologist Report, No. 28. Austin: Texas Historical Commission. Reprinted by permission.

TUNNELL, CURTIS D. AND W. W. NEWCOMB, JR.
    1969   *A Lipan Apache Mission,* Part I: The Archeological Investigation: The Site and Structures. Pp. 3–51. Bulletin of the Texas Memorial Museum No. 14. Austin: The Texas Memorial Museum. Reprinted by permission.

INTRODUCTION

This volume includes excerpts from selected publications that the author considers milestones in the development of Texas mission archaeology. The choices have often been difficult to make, but have been chosen to illustrate specific points of view or aspects of archaeological fieldwork. Since a compendium of mission site reports, end to end, would prove redundant and wasteful of precious space, it has been decided to use sections from a variety of types of reports. While this may not please the authors, it will be easier on the reader and allows more variety in subject matter. In most cases, artifact sections have not been included, since the intended emphasis is on the development of techniques for mission excavations. It would be accurate to say that artifactual recovery and identification techniques have progressed at much the same pace as have those of excavation. Anyone interested in that aspect of the problem is referred to the complete reports listed in the References section below.

In order to perform intelligently in the field, the archaeologist must first understand the mission system and how it operated in Texas. As an aid to this understanding, the first section is devoted to the construction and administration of Texas missions, as explained in the archival record and demonstrated through archaeology.

One of the first difficulties facing mission archaeologists in Texas has been to locate and identify the intended site. Although many Texas mission sites are well known and properly identified, equally as many have been identified only within the past twenty years or so, and a handful are still unlocated. Kathleen Gilmore in her search for the San Xavier mission complex in 1967 evolved an interesting and practical method for identifying mission sites. Her method and its application are included here (Gilmore 1969).

One of the early concerns of archaeologists was to determine the methods of construction used by the Franciscans. Curtis Tunnell in his 1962 excavations at the site of Mission San Lorenzo de la Santa Cruz in Central Texas, through careful observation and recording, compiled a detailed account of the construction methods and materials used on this site. His descriptions, included in this volume (Tunnell and Newcomb 1969), have since been invaluable in helping archaeologists

working on Central Texas mission sites to identify and understand structural traces in the ground.

Another aspect of the mission establishment that is important for the archaeologist to understand is what activities were taking place at the site and how and by whom they were administered. We are fortunate to have available a translation of a set of mid-eighteenth-century guidelines "meant for a missionary who has never been in charge of a mission and is all alone and does not know whom to consult for advice" (Leutenegger 1976:2). A portion of this interesting document is included here.

The Texas missions operated under nearly impossible conditions. They were truly frontier institutions, far from any source of supply, dependent for most of the year largely on the industry of their inhabitants and the ingenuity of the Franciscans who had to feed, clothe, and minister to the spiritual lives of the Indians under their care. Supplies from Mexico were delivered once a year by pack train. The accounts of these shipments provide insights into the life of the mission, and are particularly interesting when examined in the light of the instructions for the missionary described above. The particular inventory included here for Mission San José near San Antonio (Habig, Leutenegger, and Casso 1983), dating near the end of the mission period, is surprisingly similar in content to inventories of shipments earlier in the century. Articles such as buttons, beads, and religious jewelry turn up regularly in excavations. Items obviously intended for the Franciscans indicate that they had a few of their accustomed amenities, even on the frontier.

Many of the missions, particularly in the drier parts of Central and West Texas, depended on irrigated farming to produce sufficient food. The construction of a dam and acequia was an important first step in the development of a mission, and the actual location of the site was generally dependent on an available water supply sufficient to irrigate the fields as well as to provide water for the inhabitants.

Since San Antonio once had five mission establishments, remains of these waterways lie beneath the surface throughout the city and the surrounding area. Concern for recording and preservation of the acequia systems has led to archaeological monitoring of sewer line construction and other public works projects. In the process, the histories of most of the mission acequias have now been compiled, and local archaeologists are becoming proficient in recognizing acequia traces in the ground. An example of such a monitoring project is included here, along with an account of the recording of a mission dam (Cox 1987; Hafernik, Cox, and Fox 1989), one of the few such structures that have survived floods and flood control efforts on the San Antonio River.

Directly related to the missions of the San Antonio River valley were extensive livestock raising activities which provided sustenance and raw materials for mission inhabitants and a source of income as well. Included here is a portion of the report on the first of five seasons of work at the ranch of Mission San Francisco de la Espada (Ivey and Fox 1981).

Although the basic organization and administration of a mission was much the same throughout the Texas mission system, details of construction varied according to the raw materials available. In all cases, the first temporary buildings were of jacal construction, using upright poles set into wall trenches and roofing with thatch. In Central and West Texas where stone was readily available, stone and adobe were used for more permanent structures. In the woodlands of East Texas, upright log construction continued in use throughout the life of the mission.

Included in the final section of this volume are excerpts from four site investigations that illustrate different approaches to mission excavation. These differences are due partly to variation in the impetus for the project, partly to the conditions at the site, and perhaps also partly to the relative amount of experience that had been accumulated in mission archaeology at the time.

When the Witte Museum did test excavations at the Mission San Antonio de Valero (later to become the Alamo) in 1966, there was little knowledge or understanding of what might be found in the way of undisturbed Spanish deposits on a downtown site that had been continuously in use since mission times. A rather random location of test units revealed that a great deal of information could be gained from the site. John Greer's fieldwork opened the door to numerous later investigations, which have revealed in-place structures and artifacts that otherwise might never have been recovered (Greer 1967 this volume).

The following year, the Witte Museum and the Archdiocese of San Antonio sponsored excavations by Mardith Schuetz at Mission San Juan Capistrano, just south of San Antonio. With no experience in working with standing structures, Schuetz evolved a method for controlling and recording the removal of fill from mission rooms that had been occupied into the late nineteenth century (Schuetz 1968 this volume). This extensive project really opened the minds of the public as well as those in the archaeological profession to the possibilities of mission period archaeology in San Antonio. In a separate volume, Schuetz (1969) demonstrated the value of carefully documented archival research, in close relationship to archaeological investigation, in reconstructing mission history.

In answer to a need for specific architectural information, in 1971 the Texas Historical Commission sent an archaeological crew under the direction of Dan Scurlock to Mission Nuestra Señora de la Purissima Concepción de Acuña in San Antonio. The resulting information was a welcome addition to our accumulating knowledge of Spanish building practices. Later archaeological investigations, both at Concepción and elsewhere, leaned heavily on these reported details (Scurlock and Fox 1977 this volume).

The first professional excavation in an East Texas mission site was conducted by students at Stephen F. Austin State University in 1977 under the direction of James E. Corbin. The site had been previously identified as that of Mission Dolores de las Ais, located on Mission Hill near Nacogdoches, Texas. The site is completely buried and has been bisected by a highway. The preliminary report included here (Corbin 1977) demonstrates how much valuable information can be extracted from what might be considered a destroyed site. The final report, not reprinted here (Corbin, Kalina, and Alex 1980), describes the site and the recovered artifacts in greater detail.

Anne A. Fox

REFERENCES

CLARK, JOHN W., JR.
    1978   Mission San José y San Miguel de Aguayo: Archeological Investigations, December, 1974. *Archeological Report No. 29*. Texas Historical Commission, Austin.

CLARK, JOHN W., JR., AND ELTON R. PREWITT
    1979   Archeological Test Excavations in Areas to Be Affected by a Proposed French Drain West of the Granary, Mission San José State Historic Site (41BX3), Bexar County, Texas. *Reports of Investigations No. 3*, Prewitt and Associates, Austin.

CORBIN, JAMES E., ARLIN KALINA, AND THOMAS C. ALEX
    1980   Mission Dolores de las Ais. *Papers in Anthropology No. 2*, Stephen F. Austin State University, Nacogdoches.

EATON, JACK D.
    1980   Excavations at the Alamo Shrine (Mission San Antonio de Valero). *Special Report No. 10*, Center for Archaeological Research, The University of Texas at San Antonio.

FOX, ANNE A.
    1988   Archaeological Excavations at Mission Concepción, Fall of 1986. *Archaeological Survey Report No. 172*, Center for Archaeological Research, The University of Texas at San Antonio.

FOX, ANNE A., FERRIS A. BASS, JR., AND THOMAS R. HESTER
    1976   The Archaeology and History of Alamo Plaza. *Archaeological Survey Report No. 16*, Center for Archaeological Research, The University of Texas at San Antonio.

FOX, ANNE A., AND THOMAS R. HESTER
    1976   Archaeological Test Excavations at Mission San Francisco de la Espada. *Archaeological Survey Report No. 22*, Center for Archaeological Research, The University of Texas at San Antonio.

GILMORE, KATHLEEN K.
    1967   A Documentary and Archeological Investigation of Presidio San Luis de las Amarillas and Mission Santa Cruz de San Saba, Menard County, Texas, a Preliminary Report. *Report No. 9*, State Building Commission Archeological Program, Austin.

    1974   Mission Rosario, Archeological Investigations 1973. *Archeological Report No. 14*, Part 1, Texas Parks and Wildlife Department, Historic Sites and Restoration Branch, Austin.

    1975   Mission Rosario, Archeological Investigations 1974. *Archeological Report No. 14*, Part 2, Texas Parks and Wildlife Department, Historic Sites and Restoration Branch, Austin.

IVEY, JAMES E.
  1983   Archaeological Testing at Rancho de las Cabras, Wilson County, Texas, Second Season. *Archaeological Survey Report No. 121*, Center for Archaeological Research, The University of Texas at San Antonio.

IVEY, JAMES E., AND ANNE A. FOX
  1981   Archaeological Survey and Testing at Rancho de las Cabras, Wilson County, Texas. *Archaeological Survey Report No. 104*, Center for Archaeological Research, The University of Texas at San Antonio.

JONES, COURTENAY J., AND ANNE A. FOX
  1983   Archaeological Testing at Rancho de las Cabras, Wilson County, Texas, Third Season. *Archaeological Survey Report No. 123*, Center for Archaeological Research, The University of Texas at San Antonio.

MOUNGER, MARIA A.
  1959   Mission Espiritu Santo of Coastal Texas: An Example of Historic Site Archeology. Masters thesis, University of Texas, Austin.

SCHUETZ, MARDITH K.
  1966   Historic Background of the Mission San Antonio de Valero. *Archeological Program Report No. 1*, State Building Commission, Austin.

  1970   Excavation of a Section of the Acequia Madre in Bexar County, Texas, and Archeological Investigations at Mission San José in April, 1968. *Archeological Report No. 19*, Texas Historical Survey Committee, Austin.

  1974   The Dating of the Chapel at Mission San Juan Capistrano, San Antonio, Texas. *Special Report No. 12*, Texas Historical Commission, Office of the State Archeologist, Austin.

SCURLOCK, DAN, ADAN BENAVIDES, JR., DANA ISHAM, AND
   JOHN W. CLARK, JR.
   1976   An Archeological and Historical Survey of the Proposed Mission Parkway, San Antonio, Texas. *Archeological Survey Report No. 17,* Office of the State Archeologist, Austin.

MISSION CONSTRUCTION AND ADMINISTRATION

THE SAN XAVIER MISSIONS:

A Study in Historical Site Identification

by

KATHLEEN KIRK GILMORE

STATE BUILDING COMMISSION

ARCHEOLOGICAL PROGRAM

Report Number 16   March, 1969

PRINCIPLES OF HISTORICAL SITE IDENTIFICATION

Historical site identification has long concerned many people. The routes traveled by Cabeza de Vaca, Coronado, and other early explorers, and the location of early missions and settlements in Texas, and the location of Biblical sites in the Holy Land, have, for example, intrigued the interest and imagination of many. There has been little published material, however, that considers a theoretical basis for making accurate field identification of "lost" historical sites.

The procedure for identifying historical sites usually has been to establish the approximate location from documentary sources and to look for archeological sites in that vicinity without detailed archeological study of the site. It is not sufficient, however, that an archeological site occur at an appropriate place; it must also be the right kind of archeological site.

Herbert E. Bolton, the historian, tentatively identified in the early 1900s a number of missions and several Indian villages in Texas. By using historical documents and the fact that Indian pottery was present he located a Neches village of the seventeenth century at an archeological site subsequently found to be entirely prehistoric (Newell and Krieger, 1949: 8). The controversy over the location of Fort St. Louis (Bolton, 1924: 171; Cole, 1946: 473) on the Texas Gulf Coast was finally resolved when artifacts of French and Spanish origin, dating from the late seventeenth and early eighteenth century, respectively, were found in excavations on Garcitas Creek by the Texas

Memorial Museum (Newcomb, 1961: 62).

Phillips, Ford and Griffin (1951: 347-421) in attempting to locate sites visited by the De Soto Expedition in 1541 set up a hypothesis of a 1541 date and tested this working hypothesis against the De Soto narratives and the interpretation of them by the De Soto Commission. By setting up an archeological formula of what to expect at a site that may have been visited by the De Soto Expedition they found many discrepancies in the De Soto Commission's locations because the Commission did not take into full account the chronological position of the archeological remains at certain sites.

Johnson and Jelks (1958: 405) tentatively identified the Pearson archeological site with a Tawakoni village visited by Friar Calahorra in 1760 by correlating Calahorra's diary of the trip with modern geography and by comparing the artifacts found with those of other archeological sites. They did not work out any standard principles to be followed but stated that accurate historical site determination in Texas depends upon two sets of data: historical documents and archeological finds. Later Duffield and Jelks (1961) questioned the reliability of the correlation by stating that the cultural remains found at the site cannot be dated precisely enough to say whether or not the Pearson site was the Tawakoni village visited by Calahorra. The authors list four criteria to be satisfied before the field location of a historical site can be accurately identified: 1) geographic location, 2) environment including topography and vegetation, 3) physical evidence of occupation, and 4) correspondence of cultural traits.

Massey (Starnes, 1966: 103) excavated in areas proposed by Bolton for the sites of the San Xavier missions, and believed he had

verified Bolton's locations, although no artifacts of Spanish Colonial origin were found.

To systematically search for "lost" historical sites and to attempt to identify them with assurance as to place and time of existence, a model of what the site should look like in the field can be constructed by using certain principles.

Method and Theoretical Basis

To construct a model of what a site should look like in the field four areas of information should be investigated: geography, topography, physiography, and physical cultural remains. The information is obtained from research in documents relating to the problem, from archeological data about related sites, and from ethnographic accounts. This information is evaluated and a reasonably good concept of what the site should look like in the field is formulated. No one of the principles or areas of information can be used alone to identify a site. All must be reasonably well reconciled with the field data before the site identification can be made with assurance. This is especially true of the physical cultural remains, because it is conceivable that a location could be found which would fit criteria of the first three and not the last. Bolton (Newell and Krieger, 1949: 12) found Indian pottery at the site he proposed for the seventeenth century Neches village, but it was not seventeenth century pottery, nor were any eighteenth century artifacts found. This same mistake was made by Massey (Starnes, 1966:103) at the San Xavier missions where he found nineteenth century artifacts and assumed they originated in the eighteenth century.

Information about physical cultural remains is obtained from archeological data from excavated sites of the same time period. These data provide a comparison or a comparable set of data to form a model of what might be expected. Typological studies based on broad arrays of data from archeological sites also provide a chronological basis for the expectation of physical cultural remains. Archeological data also aid in evaluating contradictory elements of the documentary and ethnographic data, but most important is the formulation from archeological data of a model of the cultural remains to which the findings at the site must be reconciled.

In investigating Spanish Colonial sites many documentary sources are contradictory or ambiguous. Most Spanish Colonial documents were written with several aims in mind - to please the authorities, to support the writer's position, and to secure financial aid and approval. Consequently, those points agreed on by the most writers should be given the most weight. An example of this is Barrio's report of his survey of the San Xavier missions on July 12, 1749 (see Historical Background: 19), in which he places Mission San Francisco below (east of) Mission San Ildefonso. All other references place San Ildefonso below San Francisco, so it may be assumed Barrio either made a mistake or was uninformed. The controversy over the size of the San Xavier River (see Historical Background) is an example of the subjectivity of the statements, the nature of the statement depending on the bias of the author.

Changes brought about by time in the meaning of words, in equivalents of measurements, in topography, and in physiography must also be taken into consideration. The Spanish land league of the mid-eighteenth

century is generally considered to be equivalent of 2.63 English miles
(Johnson and Jelks, 1958: 416), but in other countries the measurement
for the league was different (Haggard and McLean, 1941: 78). To further
complicate the problem, early travelers seldom were exact in recording
their routes, and generally only estimated the direction and distance
they traveled. The measurement used for the vara was different for each
province in Spain as well as in Mexico and other Latin countries, and to
determine the exact equivalent it would be essential to know where the
surveyor originated, because he used the vara with which he was familiar
(*Ibid.:* 70).

GEOGRAPHY

All references in documentary sources to geographic location
are noted and evaluated in terms of modern geography and are plotted on
a map. It is essential that at least one of the references be to some
identifiable landmark which can be used as a base point for other references. Measurements may then be made to and from this point using, if
necessary, several English equivalents of the measurement given, and
the most reasonable and least ambiguous conclusions used as part of the
preliminary model.

TOPOGRAPHY

From the written record, all topographic features and their
locations are noted and plotted on a map if possible, and a reasonably
good idea of the topographic nature of the area is formed. Some changes
may have taken place in drainage patterns and in the general morphology
of the land because of modern industry such as gravel pits or roads.

Erosion also may have caused changes in the area.

PHYSIOGRAPHY

Evidence of the physiographic nature or natural environment of the location is obtained from documentary sources. This includes plants, animals, soils, climate and the like. Changes may have taken place by clearing of the land, by overgrazing, by the extinction of certain plants and animals, or by changes in general ecology.

PHYSICAL CULTURAL REMAINS

When the first three principles have been followed and the site is searched for, there must be a model of the cultural remains that are expected to be found, and unless those found fit the model then the location of the site is tenuous. This part of the model is made not only from documentary data, but also from ethnographic sources and from archeological data.

CONCLUSIONS

Field location of Mission Complex

In 1914 Bolton (1915: 227-230) identified the sites of the San Xavier missions to his satisfaction from the historical documents, using in particular a survey made in 1750 by Eca y Musquiz (Appendix III). Mission San Francisco Xavier he placed on Kolb's Hill (Frank Felton farm), and Mission Candelaria on San Andres Cemetery Hill (Jimmy Robertson farm). The garrison he located three-fourths mile west from the mission in the valley which terminates at Cemetery Hill. The location of San Ildefonso was not so easy for him to determine as there were two rises above the junction of the San Gabriel River and Brushy Creek. One rise, according to Bolton, was correct for the distance to Brushy Creek. He selected another rise one-third mile west of the first one as a more likely spot because the distance between the two rivers is three-fourths mile "which corresponds with the 1800 varas [5000 feet; 1 Texas vara = 2.78 feet] given as the width of the plain opposite Mission San Ildefonso." This spot he indicated as the probable site of Mission San Ildefonso. Bolton (*Ibid.*: 230) states, "It [the site of San Ildefonso] may be slightly incorrect but at most it cannot be more than a few hundred yards out of the way." He gives no indication of knowing these were the sites except by Musquiz' measurements.

In 1936 granite markers were placed near the assumed sites of the missions. How it was decided where to place the markers is unknown. The marker for San Francisco Xavier is on Highway 908 at the entrance

to the Frank Felton farm (Kolb's Hill). The monument is inscribed as follows:

SITE OF THE
MISSION SAN FRANCISCO
XAVIER DE LOS DOLORES

ESTABLISHED BY FRANCISCAN MISSIONARIES IN
1746 WITH THE HOPE OF CIVILIZING AND
CHRISTIANIZING THE COCO, MAYEYE, ORCOQUIZA,
KARANKAWA AND OTHER TRIBES OF INDIANS**
THE MARTYRDOM OF PADRE JOSE GANZABAL AND
THE CIRCUMSTANCES CONNECTED THEREWITH CAUSED
THE DEPARTURE OF THE INDIANS AND THE FRIARS
AND THE REMOVAL OF THE MISSION TO THE SAN
MARCOS RIVER IN 1755 * REESTABLISHED IN 1757
ON THE SAN SABA RIVER FOR THE CONVERSION OF
THE LIPAN APACHES WITH THE NEW NAME OF
MISSION SANTA CRUZ DE SAN SABA

The marker for Mission San Ildefonso is about one and one-eighth miles east of the marker for San Francisco Xavier on the same highway, and is inscribed as follows:

SITE OF THE
MISSION
SAN ILDEFONSO

ESTABLISHED BY FRANCISCAN MISSIONARIES IN 1749
WITH THE HOPE OF CIVILIZING AND CHRISTIANIZING
THE COCO, MAYEYE, ORCOQUIZA, KARANKAWA, AND
OTHER TRIBES OF INDIANS ** THE MARTYRDOM OF
PADRE JOSE GANZABAL AND THE CIRCUMSTANCES
CONNECTED THEREWITH CAUSED THE DEPARTURE OF
THE INDIANS AND THE FRIARS AND THE REMOVAL
OF THIS MISSION TO THE SAN MARCOS RIVER IN
1755 * REESTABLISHED IN 1762 ON THE NUECES
RIVER FOR THE CONVERSION OF THE LIPAN APACHES
WITH THE NEW NAME OF MISSION SAN LORENZO DE LA
SANTA CRUZ

The marker for Mission Nuestra Candelaria is one and one-half miles west on Highway 908 from the marker for Mission San Francisco and one mile north across the San Gabriel River on a farm road. The inscription is as follows:

SITE OF THE
MISSION NUESTRA SENORA
DE LA CANDELARIA

ESTABLISHED BY FRANCISCAN MISSIONARIES IN
1749 WITH THE HOPE OF CIVILIZING AND
CHRISTIANIZING THE COCO, MAYEYE, ORCOQUIZA,
KARANKAWA, AND OTHER TRIBES OF INDIANS **
THE MARTYRDOM OF PADRE JOSE GANZABAL AND
THE CIRCUMSTANCES CONNECTED THEREWITH CAUSED
THE DEPARTURE OF THE INDIANS AND THE FRAIRS
AND THE REMOVAL OF THIS MISSION TO THE SAN
MARCOS RIVER IN 1755 * REESTABLISHED IN
1762 ON THE SABINAL RIVER FOR THE CONVERSION
OF THE LIPAN APACHES WITH THE SAME NAME OF
NUESTRA SENORA DE LA CANDELARIA

Castañeda in his competent work *Our Catholic Heritage in Texas*, Vol. III (1939) documents the history of the San Xavier Missions. He apparently did not attempt to identify the sites but assumed Bolton was correct. He does mention, however, that numerous documents were not available to Bolton in 1914.

A recent history of the missions (Starnes, 1966) includes archeological testing by Dr. W. C. Massey of Texas Christian University. These tests were in areas identified by Bolton as sites of the respective missions. The listing of artifacts by Starnes is completely useless for any recognition or identification. The writer examined the artifacts from Massey's excavations, but none could be identified as Spanish Colonial in origin. The sherds recovered were white paste earthenware and slip-decorated ware both made in the nineteenth century.

Musquiz (Appendix III) states that he began his survey at the junction of the San Xavier River and Arroyo de las Animas, on the bank of the San Xavier River. He must have been at a point where the river runs northward as he measured the east bank and not the west bank because "it [west bank] sloped toward a range of hills toward which the flood reaches

when the river overflows out of its bed at some 160 varas (444 feet) which is the distance to said hills." At present there are six places within one and one-half miles of the junction where the river flows northward, only one of which has a range of hills 160 varas distant (I on map, Figure 14). It is possible the river has changed its course in 200 years, but it does seem improbable that the survey was begun precisely at the junction in view of the fact that upstream from the junction there are no hills for a distance of about one mile. Musquiz also states at this spot of the first measurement he is one-half of one-fourth league (1,738 feet) from Mission San Ildefonso. If this were so it would place the mission, which was on a hill whose slopes were planted with crops, on the flood plain of the river. The flood plain was known to be subject to floods as piles of debris were noted. It is not likely that the Spanish would risk having a mission in a location so obviously subject to these floods. Musquiz writes that San Ildefonso was 1800 varas (5,000 feet) from the river and three-fourths league (10,414.8 feet, 1.98 miles) from Mission San Francisco Xavier. San Ildefonso could not be one-eighth league (1,738 feet) from the junction of the two rivers even allowing for drastic changes in the drainage. This measurement, "one-half of one-fourth league from San Ildefonso," must be an error, probably in copying from Musquiz' original report. It is more likely that he reported instead three-fourths league if his first measurement of the river was made at the spot labeled "I" on the map (Figure 14). From this spot also he apparently measured the plain to the fence of Mission San Francisco as 5000 varas (13,889 feet). Perhaps Brushy Creek deserved its present name 200 years ago, and Musquiz' surveying party was unable to reach the precise confluence

of the two rivers. If these assumptions are correct Mission San Ildefonso should have been on the hill which is 6,000 feet south of the San Gabriel River and 10,000 feet from a hill toward the west, placing it on the Lyendecker farm.

Musquiz went up the stream to Apache Pass and then measured down the stream to where the garrison and Missions Candelaria and San Francisco were located. The measurements fit very well with present topography, the possible location of two missions being on hills, Mission Candelaria on the Jimmy Robertson farm and Mission San Francisco on the Frank Felton farm. The measurement for the location of the garrison is in the flood plain near the river. As the three missions were all on hills and there was constant danger from the Apaches coming across the river it is difficult to believe the garrison would not also have been on a hill. Here may have been another mistake in copying. A transposition from the figure "9" to the figure "6" would not be too difficult, and perhaps Musquiz' figures originally were 1971-1/2 varas to the garrison from the mission, as the measurement of the plain between the two was 1961-1/4 varas. This would place the garrison 10 varas (27.78 feet) from the creek where the measurement of the plain began. If this were so the hill cut by Highway 908 (Figure 14) near Worley's store may have been the site of the garrison.

The site selected by Felipe Rábago for the proposed presidio or fort may have been that of Mission Candelaria. The top of this hill has an elevation that would allow the surrounding country side to be seen, as noted by Rábago. It is questionable whether the mission was actually relocated, as the formal fortifications were never built, or whether the Fathers merely agreed to relocate. Candelaria must have remained the

mission closest to the garrison as Ceballos went to it after his escape.

At all four of the areas suggested as possibilities for the missions and presidio sherds of eighteenth century majolica have been found on the surface. On the hill on the Jimmy Robertson farm also were found sherds of Indian pottery and a butt plate fragment from a French flintlock gun. These artifacts coincide with those that could be expected for sites of the time period according to the model. Further searching should be done in these areas to attempt to delimit areas of concentrations of artifacts, and it would be necessary for test excavations to be made to accurately identify the precise location of the other two missions and the presidio.

Archeological investigation has shown that one mission was surely located on the Frank Felton farm. In all probability this was Mission San Francisco, but this cannot be stated with assurance until excavations have been made to establish the precise locations of the rest of the mission complex.

It was the lack of a concept of what could identify a Spanish Colonial site that led both Bolton and Massey to assume they had found the precise locations of the missions. They neglected a most important part of the model, that of what physical cultural remains could be expected at a mid-eighteenth century Spanish Colonial site in Texas.

Effectiveness of Method

In an attempt to identify correctly and precisely a particular historical site, the San Xavier complex of missions, a model of what the site should look like in the field was formulated from documentary, ethnographic, and archeological sources by using four criteria or principles:

geography, topography, physiography, and physical cultural remains. After the model had been constructed an area which could be reconciled with it within reasonable limits was searched for in the field. In this particular instance the method was effective and successful because the field data compared favorably with the model, leading to the conclusion that the site of a mission had been found.

Briefly the model stated that:

The San Xavier missions were

1) Northeast of San Antonio about 130 miles in a straight line projection; 250 miles from Natchitoches;
2) Between two streams, on hills south of one of the streams;
3) In an area of mild climate and moderate rain fall with occasional drought; and
4) Should have Spanish Colonial and Indian artifacts present, and at one area a structure 75 feet by 84 feet.

The field data indicate that:

The San Xavier missions were found to be

1) 130 miles northeast of San Antonio; 250 miles west of Natchitoches;
2) Between the San Gabriel River and Brushy Creek in Milam County, Texas;
3) In an area on the western (dry) edge of the humid east Texas region; and
4) Artifacts of Spanish Colonial and Indian origin were

found, and at one site indications of a structure
77 feet by 84 feet were found.

The effectiveness of any method is dependent upon sufficient data. That is, an identification cannot be made with confidence by any means unless ample data are available. The method here is designed to reduce subjectivity and to indicate--by systematically using the four principles or criteria--the probability that a particular site is the correct one. The more replete the correlation is between the model and the field site with respect to the criteria, the more probable is the correctness of the identification.

At the San Xavier Mission sites the field data in no way violated any part of the model, and in fact agreed with all criteria beyond the realm of chance. Therefore it is concluded that a mission site was found and the method is effective.

REFERENCES

Bolton, Herbert E.
    1915   **Texas in the Middle Eighteenth Century.** 1962 Edition. Russell and Russell, New York.

Cole, E.W.
    1946   LaSalle in Texas, **Southwestern Historical Quarterly,** Vol. 49, No. 4, pp.472-50, Texas State Historical Association, Austin.

Duffield, Lathiel, and Edward B. Jelks
    1961   **The Pearson Site.** Department of Anthropology, The University of Texas, Archeology Series No. 4, Austin.

Haggard, J.V., and M.D. McLean
    1941   **Handbook for Translators of Spanish Historical Documents.** Semco Color Press, Oklahoma City.

Johnson, LeRoy, Jr., and Edward B. Jelks
    1958   The Tawakoni - Yscani Village, 1760: A Study of Archeological Site Identification. **The Texas Journal of Science,** Vol. 10, No. 4, The Texas Academy of Science, Austin.

Newcomb, W. W., Jr.
    1961   **The Indians of Texas.** The University of Texas Press, Austin.

Newell, H. Perry, and Alex D. Krieger
    1949   The George C. Davis Site, Cherokee County, Texas. **American Antiquity,** Vol. 14, No. 4, Pt. 2.

Phillips, Phillip, J. A. Ford, and J. B. Griffin
    1951   Archeological Survey in the Lower Mississippi Valley, 1940-1947. **Papers of the Peabody Museum of American Archeology and Ethnology,** Harvard University, Vol. 25.

Starnes, Gary Bert
    1966   The **San Gabriel Missions, 1746-1756.** M. A. Thesis, Texas Christian University, Ft. Worth.

BULLETIN
OF THE TEXAS MEMORIAL MUSEUM

14

July 1969

A Lipan Apache Mission
San Lorenzo de la Santa Cruz · 1762–1771

PART I

THE ARCHEOLOGICAL INVESTIGATION

By Curtis D. Tunnell

PART II

THE ETHNOHISTORICAL INVESTIGATION

By W. W. Newcomb, Jr.

PART III

SUMMARY AND CONCLUSIONS

THE TEXAS MEMORIAL MUSEUM
24th & Trinity, Austin, Texas 78705/The University of Texas at Austin

PART I

THE ARCHEOLOGICAL INVESTIGATION

CURTIS D. TUNNELL

SITE OF THE MISSION
SAN LORENZO DE
LA SANTA CRUZ
FOUNDED BY FRANCISCAN MISSIONARIES
AMONG THE LIPAN APACHE INDIANS
IN 1762 • ABANDONED IN 1769

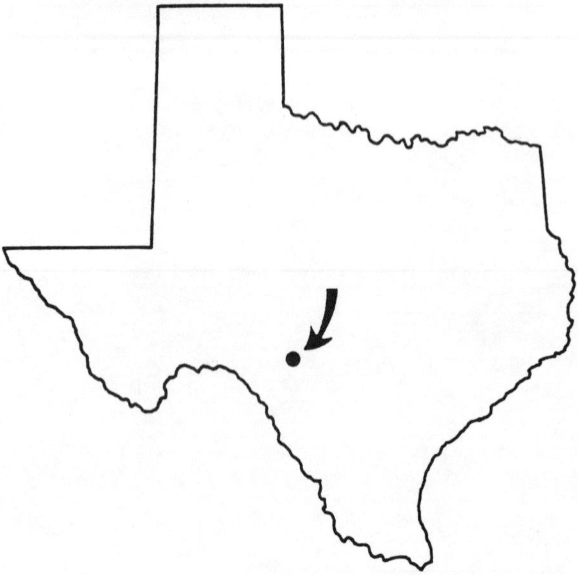

The Site

The ruins of Mission San Lorenzo de la Santa Cruz are located on a low ridge which runs parallel to the east bank of the Nueces River just below the mouth of a spring-fed tributary, at the north edge of the city of Camp Wood, Real County, Texas, at approximately 29° 40' 40" N. latitude and 100° 01' 00" W. longitude. The spring-fed Nueces is never dry here near its headwaters, and despite severe periodic flooding, the highest recorded floods have never covered the mission ruins. A large spring rises from the limestone bedrock some 500 feet northeast of the mission and flows into the Nueces about 200 feet west of the quadrangle wall. Flowing at a constant rate of approximately 2,000 gallons per minute, it serves as the water source for the city of Camp Wood. The spring influenced the selection of this site for the mission and furnished an abundant supply of fresh water during its occupation.

The excellence of this locality as a habitation spot is demonstrated by evidences of a series of occupations. (1) Archaic and Neo-American burned rock middens, many feet in thickness, are scattered around the vicinity, and a few artifacts from these aboriginal occupations were found beneath the floors of some of the mission structures. (2) The mission occupied the ridge during the 1760's, leaving hundreds of tons of construction materials and midden debris to mark its existence. (3) The ruins of the burned out mission apparently saw intermittent occupation by small Indian groups (possibly some Lipans occasionally returned to the familiar spot) in the late eighteenth and early nineteenth centuries; a hearth in the fill of Structure 8 belonged to one such visit. (4) A temporary United States military outpost (Camp Wood) occupied part of the mission site intermittently between 1857 and 1861 (Webb, 1952, I: 285). Artifacts from these camps were found around and in the fill of some of the mission structures and on the surface of the ridge farther to the south. (5) Local legend tells of a sheepherder and his family who camped among the mission ruins in the latter part of the nineteenth century; a hearth and other artifacts in the upper fill of Structure 10 possibly represent this occupation. (6) Early Anglo-American house foundations and debris are found to the north and south of the mission site. (7) Houses on the outskirts of the present city of Camp Wood are scattered around the old mission ruins and the spring-fed tributary.

The primary concern here is with the Franciscan Mission, San Lorenzo de la Santa Cruz, established on this site by the Spanish in the latter half of the eighteenth century. By 1962, 200 years after its establishment, the walls of Mission San Lorenzo had fallen into irregular low mounds of crumbled adobe. Cactus, scrubby grass, and mesquite brush covered the uneven surface. Aside from a granite monument alongside State Highway 55, east of the site, there was little to indicate its presence.

The southern portion, comprising about 70 per cent of the site, had been thoroughly leveled by machinery when a Texas Memorial Museum field crew began work at Mission San Lorenzo in the fall of 1962. Its surface was strewn with crushed adobe bricks and Spanish colonial artifacts, and large numbers of undressed limestone building blocks had been gathered from the surface and stacked in long piles. Since no walls or foundations were visible among the debris it was feared that most of the site had been destroyed, but fortunately most of the floors were intact. The northern 30 per cent of the site, on another property, was undisturbed, and the lower walls and floors of the mission structures in this area were protected by low mounds of melted adobe and native vegetation.

Excavation Procedure

A grid system, oriented with magnetic north, was established over the entire site, and the nu-

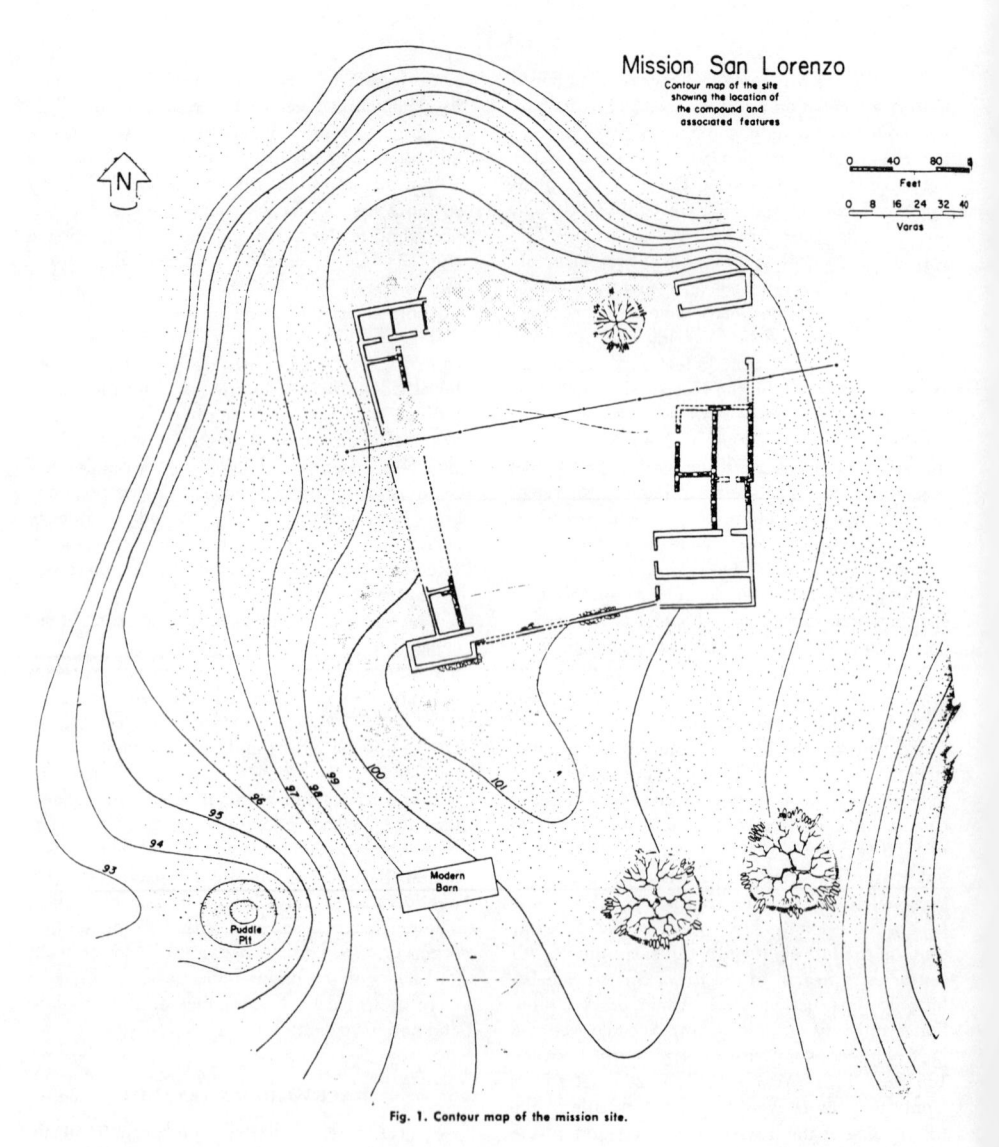

Mission San Lorenzo
Contour map of the site
showing the location of
the compound and
associated features

Fig. 1. Contour map of the mission site.

merous grid stakes proved to be an invaluable aid in mapping the structures, features, and walls of the mission quadrangle. A contour map of the site showing the topographic features in the immediate vicinity was drawn (Fig. 1). All elevations at the site were measured in relation to an "X" mark cut in the level surface of the threshold stone in the west entrance of Structure 2. This datum mark was assigned an arbitrary elevation of 100.0 feet.

Along the property line the low rubble mounds had been cross-sectioned by the machinery, and a little work on the first day of excavation revealed the presence of adobe wall bases and adobe floors in the profile. After making an exhaustive surface collection from the site, a small ditching machine was used to locate wall foundations in the bulldozed area. Shovels were then employed to follow the foundations and thereby outline structures.

When the complete outline of a structure had been revealed, small test pits about one foot square were dug along the inside of the walls to determine the depth to the floor. The structure fill was always less than one foot in depth in the bulldozed area of the site. This fill was removed down to the burned roof material and the contents were collected from a one-fourth-inch mesh screen and bagged. Samples of the roof materials were then collected and the fill of the floor was processed and bagged separately. When multiple floor levels were encountered, the fill between the floors was processed as a separate provenience unit.

In the non-bulldozed portion of the site a similar excavation procedure was employed. Vegetation was cleared and shovels were used to find and follow the tops of adobe walls. The fill from each structure (up to 3.0 feet in depth in this area) was removed in several units: (1) fill above the primary wall rubble (removed in arbitrary 0.5 foot levels); (2) fill between the primary wall collapse and the burned roof material; (3) burned roof debris; (4) fill on the floor—no double floors were encountered in this area.

Grid squares and arbitrary levels were used in test excavations in the mission middens and in areas outside the structure walls.

Measured drawings were made of each structure, all associated features, and of the entire quadrangle complex (Fig. 3). The exact brick patterns, both vertical and horizontal, of all walls were recorded. Daily field notes recorded work progress, general excavation observations, and detailed provenience information. Color and black-and-white photographs were taken daily. All artifacts (ceramic, metal, lithic, bone, shell, glass) and faunal and floral remains were collected, and samples of adobe, roof materials, hearth contents, building stones, plaster, and soil types were taken.

After several structures had been partially cleared, an attempt was made to locate all four corners of the mission compound. As a result, structures 7, 8, 10, and 11, which were found to occupy the four corners (Fig. 3), were excavated and as many structures along the four walls were cleared as time and money permitted.

Several tests were made in the mission middens to determine their content, thickness, and extent. Areas adjacent to several structures, both inside the quadrangle and outside the compound walls, were excavated down to the old mission occupation surface. Testing indicated that the central portion of the west wall, including at least three habitation structures, had been bulldozed down to bedrock.

Unexcavated Areas

Several portions of the mission compound need further investigation. These are: (1) the central part of the north wall—which probably includes several large structures; (2) a small area along the east wall just south of Structure 10—possibly the gate area and one small structure; (3) the central part of the south quadrangle wall which includes at least one structure; (4) the central plaza area; (5) the midden areas, containing large quantities of Spanish artifacts; and (6) a probable Lipan Apache village area or areas somewhere in the vicinity which was occupied by the various bands during their visits to the mission.

Fig. 2. Aerial view of the site, taken during excavation, looking toward west. The Nueces River is in the background, and spring-fed tributary is to the right.

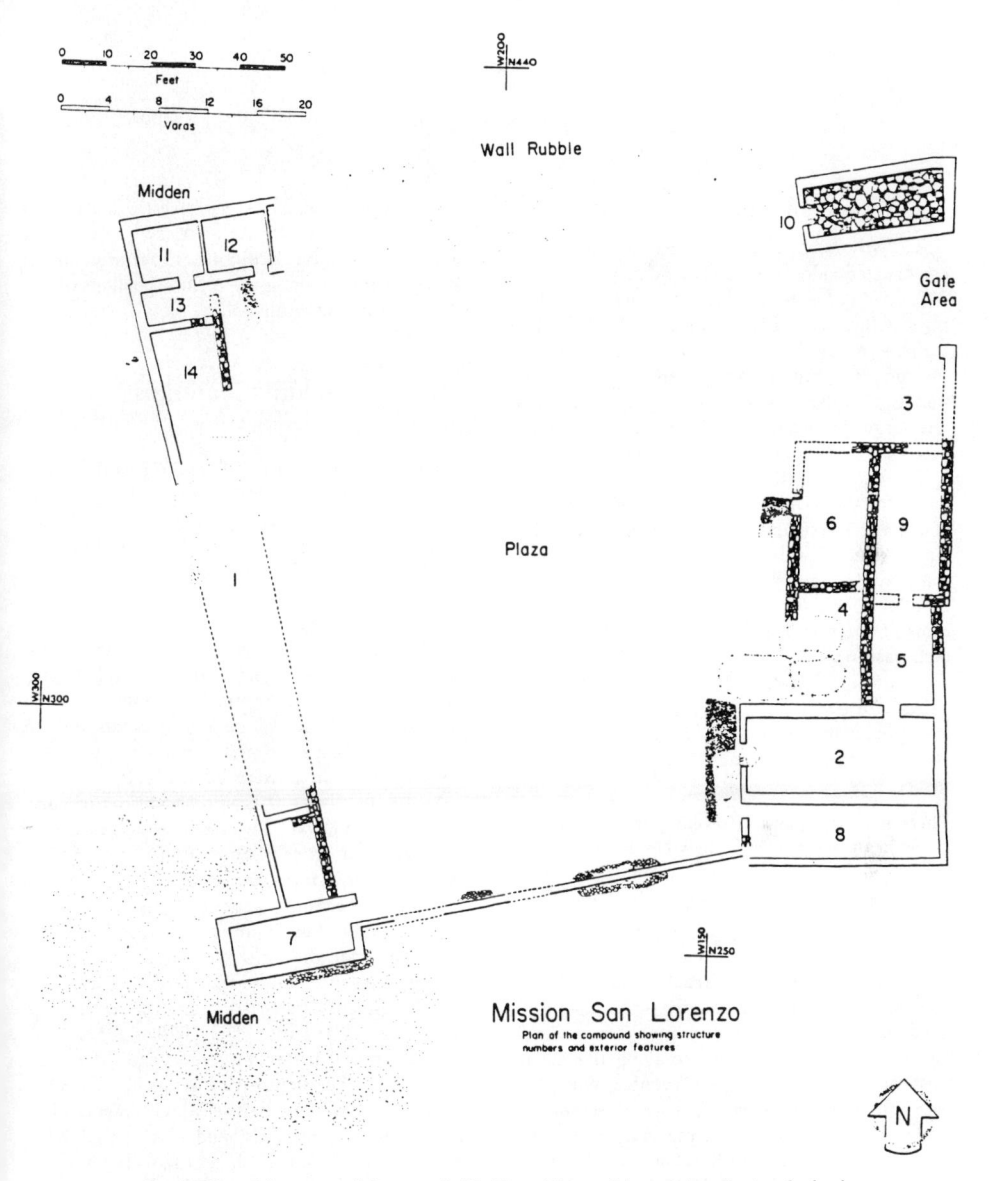

Fig. 3. Plan of the compound. Structures 1, 11, 12, and 14 are living quarters; Structure 2, church; Structure 3, unidentified; Structure 4, storage area; Structure 5, sacristy; Structures 6 and 9, convent; Structure 8, stable; Structure 10, granary; Structure 13, kitchen.

The Structures

Arrangement and Orientation

The structures of Mission San Lorenzo were constructed side by side in a rough quadrangle (Fig. 3). All exterior doorways opened onto a plaza which served for storage of nonperishable supplies, an outdoor work area, and as a stockade for domestic animals at night and when the mission was under attack. The enclosed plaza had one large gateway in the northern end of the east wall leading out toward the spring.

The outside wall of the quadrangle was composed for the most part of the abutted back wall of the various structures. The possible exception was the south wall, which seems to have been free-standing but strengthened along the base by piles of boulders (Fig. 3). The outside dimensions of the quadrangle were: north wall 187.5 feet, east wall 152.5 feet, south wall 163 feet, west wall 166 feet, N-S central axis 157 feet (about 57 *varas*), and E-W central axis 169.5 feet (about 62 *varas*). These figures are somewhat less than an estimate made by a military inspector:

There is in it a plaza of seventy varas square enclosed completely by walls howsoever weak: it has two bulwarks [baluartes] with two stone throwers [pedreros] and only one gate (Arricivita, 1792: 391).

The walls of all the structures in the southeast corner of the plaza (Structures 2, 4, 5, 6, 8, and 9) were oriented exactly with magnetic north and ran along our grid lines. The walls of all the other structures (those along the north, west, and south walls) were oriented about 15° west of magnetic north, giving a somewhat asymmetrical outline to the quadrangle (Fig. 3). The former group of buildings housed the church, sacristy, friary, and a stable. The remainder of the buildings—for housing soldiers, Indians, and supplies—probably represents a later building phase which was laid out on a slightly different orientation for some unknown reason.

Fourteen structures were investigated during the 1962 field season. At least six, and perhaps as many as twelve, additional structures remain to be excavated along the central portions of the north, west, and south walls.

Building Materials

Stone

Limestone slabs from 0.2 to 0.6 feet thick and up to 2.5 feet in length were used in various kinds of construction at the mission site. The larger slabs were probably obtained from the limestone hills within one-half to one mile of the site, while the smaller ones could have been gathered from nearby dry creek beds.

The walls of Structures 6 and 9, parts of the walls of Structures 4 and 5, and the walls facing onto the plaza of all the structures down the west side, were built of limestone slabs. Only one or two courses of these stones remained in the wall foundations. These were carefully leveled and spaced with slivers of limestone and set in dark brown clay mortar. The walls' slabs were laid roughly in an interlocking pattern (Fig. 5, B). Neither interior nor exterior wall plaster was detected on the existing stone foundations.

Large quantities of limestone slabs had been bulldozed from the stone wall bases and stacked in long piles prior to the time of the excavation. Local residents reported that the Barksdale schoolhouse was built largely with slabs carried from the mission site many years ago.

The floor of Structure 10 was paved with carefully fitted limestone slabs (Fig. 17), identical to those used in the walls, and also spaced with limestone slivers and set in a brown clay mortar.

An extra large limestone slab, about 3 feet by 5 feet served as an interior threshold in the west entrance of the church (Structure 2). The upper surface of this stone was worn quite smooth. Smaller limestone slabs were set around the

8

large stone, forming a flagstone pattern (Fig. 8).

Two interior features in Structure 7 (Fig. 14) were constructed of limestone slabs set in adobe plaster. The purpose of these features is unknown. Other structures may have had interior stone platforms prior to the bulldozing operation.

Limestone slivers (snecks) from 7 to 15 cm. in diameter and about 3 cm. thick were chipped from limestone boulders and used in leveling and spacing the stone wall slabs. Each of these stone flakes had a striking platform, bulb of percussion, and thin sharp edges. A stockpile of snecks was found in Structure 4.

Cobbles of various sizes were gathered from the gravel bars of the nearby Nueces River and used at the mission. The large majority of these cobbles were streamworn limestone, but a few were silicified wood, chert, and conglomerate.

Walks made from closely spaced cobbles (up to about 15 cm. in diameter) were found in the plaza at the following locations: outside Structures 12 and 13, along the west wall of Structure 6 and outside the main entrance of the church (Fig. 3). The cobblestone walks are described in detail in the section on structures.

Larger cobbles (up to one foot in diameter) were stacked at the base of the south wall on the inside and outside of the compound and around the outside base of the south wall of Structure 7 (Fig. 14). In these areas there was little or no slope for drainage, and the cobbles probably not only strengthened the lower walls, but kept the water from standing along the wall foundations after rains.

Adobe Bricks

Many thousands of sun-dried building blocks made from local soil were used in the walls of the mission structures. All were mold-made as shown by their uniform size and by striations on the edges made by the mold as it was lifted off the still-moist bricks. The average size of the bricks was 45.6 cm. long, 26.3 cm. wide, and 11.3 cm. thick. The adobes used in the church (Structure 2) were made from a light tan caliche, while the adobes in other structures were made from brown, humus-stained soil identical to the topsoil at the site. A few of the light tan adobes occurred in Structure 10 and the south quadrangle wall, among the dark adobes (Fig. 6, B). These and the light colored adobes in the church seem to be somewhat more durable and were probably made of carefully selected soil, whereas the dark adobes of the other buildings were made from the most readily available topsoil. All of the adobes contained large quantities of river gravel up to 3 cm. in diameter. In some areas the dark adobes contrasted with the topsoil only in their gravel content. No straw or manure could be detected in the adobe bricks at this mission, and it is likely that the readily available river gravels were mixed with the adobe mud to add strength, prevent cracking, and turn aside the rain in lieu of the fibrous materials which are used for the same purposes in modern adobes. An examination of adobe bricks at several other Spanish sites in West Texas reveals that they are consistently of large size and tempered with gravels, as opposed to adobe bricks in more recent structures which are smaller in size and tempered with straw or manure. Many of the adobe bricks at San Lorenzo, especially in the non-bulldozed area, were as hard and solid as modern adobes, although they had lain in the ground for 200 years.

Situated about 100 feet southwest of Structure 7 is a circular depression about four feet deep, which ranges from about 15 feet in diameter at the bottom to about 40 feet in diameter at its maximum extent. Modern trash disposal made it impossible to test, but it is probable that it was a small, natural depression which was developed into a puddle pit for the manufacture of adobe bricks. No other similar depressions were found near the mission. Soil from the surrounding ridge could have been used, and water and gravel were readily available in the Nueces River about 200 feet to the west.

Adobe bricks were used primarily in wall construction, but one was found plastered onto the floor of Structure 10 near the door (Fig. 17), and some others served as an interior threshold in the west entrance of Structure 6.

Four basic brick patterns producing three wall thicknesses were used in the various walls of the mission structure (Fig. 4). Pattern No. 1 (one brick width in thickness) was used for a few interior partition walls such as between Structures 11 and 12. Pattern Nos. 2 and 3 (one brick length in thickness) were used in the east and south walls of Structure 8, the west wall of Structure 2, and in part of the outside wall of the structures along the west side of the quadrangle. Pattern No. 4 (one brick length plus one brick

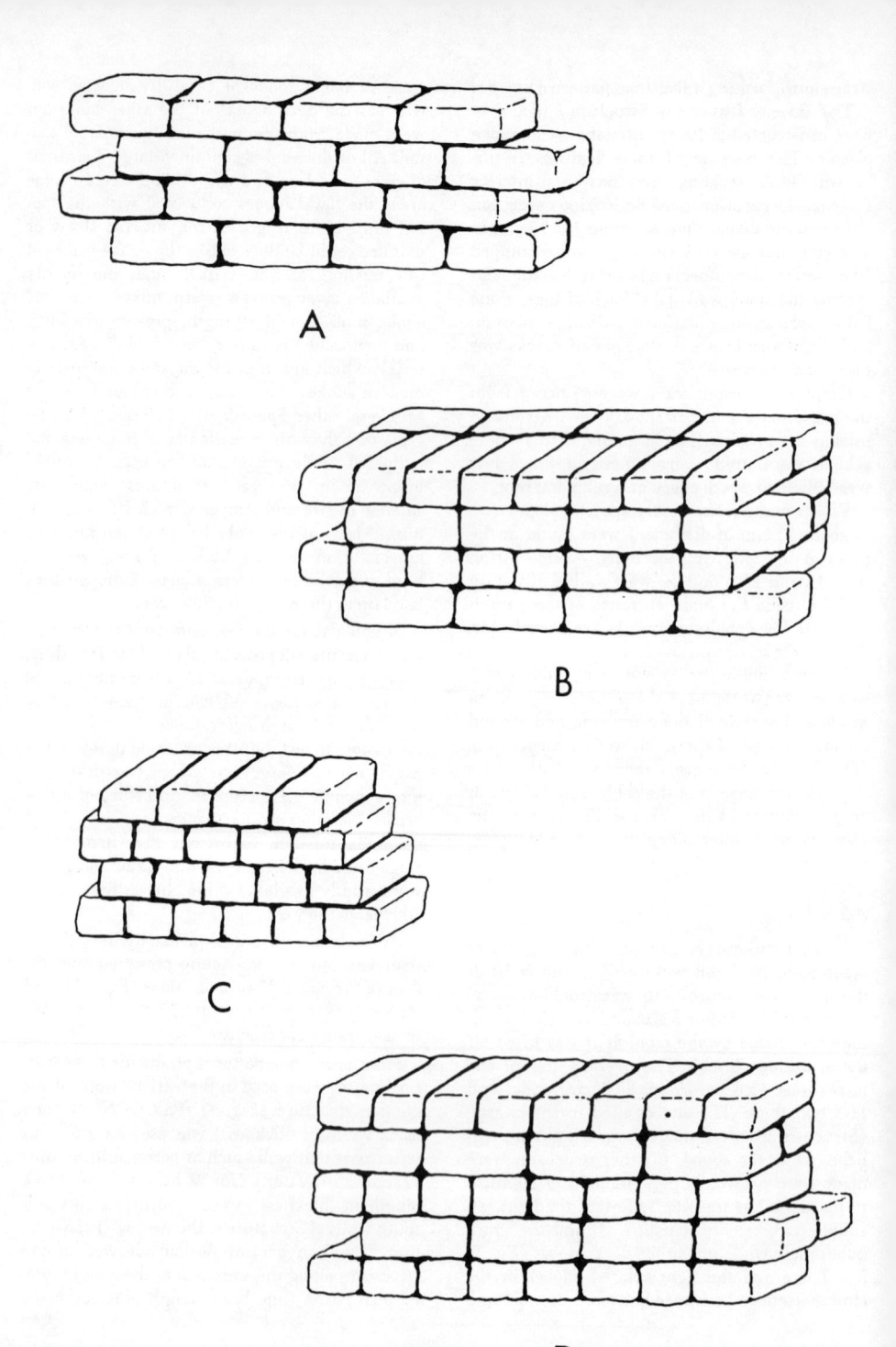

Fig. 4. Details of the four patterns used in adobe brick construction. A, Pattern 1; B, Pattern 4; C, Pattern 2; D, Pattern 3.

width in thickness) was the pattern used in most of the other walls of the mission compound—Structures 2, 7, 10, 11, 12, 13, 14, and the south wall.

Many of the excavated walls had broad cracks up to 12 cm. wide between the bricks (Fig. 8). These cracks were filled with brick fragments and adobe mortar, indicating that these materials were present as the walls were being built. These filled cracks may have resulted partly from the fact that the brick sizes were such that they did not overlap to form perfectly smooth wall faces (especially in Pattern Nos. 3 and 4) without leaving internal crevices. It is also probable that the builders left broad internal cracks (filled with mortar) between the bricks in the lower part of the walls and then gradually narrowed these cracks toward the top, making the walls broader at the bases and thereby somewhat more stable.

Puddled Adobe

This commonly used construction material had the same consistency as the bricks—soil with a high gravel content—and made a very durable surface when dry and hard. The puddled adobe was made with caliche and dark brown soil, as were the bricks, and the light colored puddled abode was used only in the structures built of light colored bricks.

A massive layer of puddled adobe up to 9 cm. in thickness was used to cap the roof of all the structures.

Puddled adobe was used as a floor covering in all structures except Nos. 4, 8, and 10. A layer of mud containing the usual gravels covered the floors to a depth of about 3 cm. When these adobe floors began to get worn and develop low damp spots, a layer of fine brown clay (about 6 cm. thick) was laid over the old floor and a second adobe floor was poured (Fig. 6, C). These double floors were detected in Structures 2 and 5 and may have been present in other structures where the floor was not penetrated. A stockpile of dark brown clay was found in Structure 4 (Fig. 12).

Puddled adobe was used as mortar in setting the bricks in the walls and filling cracks between the bricks. It was also used to form a threshold between Structures 2 and 5 (Fig. 6, D) and as a plaster covering for interior features in Structures 7, 10, and 12.

Plaster

Prepared plaster was used on the interior and exterior surfaces of the adobe walls. The interior plaster of Structures 2 (church) and 10 (granary) was composed of lime and fine-grained river sand. This high quality plaster had been applied in a layer ranging from about 5 to 15 mm. thick, and the surface had been whitewashed. Numerous fragments of such plaster were collected from the floors of these two structures, and some of these lumps showed that the plaster had been applied in two layers with whitewash between. Fragments of this white plaster found at the base of the western end of the north wall of Structure 2 showed patches of red pigment adhering to the surface, and drippings of red pigment were found along the base of the wall in this area. Red religious murals probably adorned this wall of the church.

The plaster used in the other buildings at the site was composed of a fine-grained caliche soil with lime and small pebbles added. This plaster was applied to the walls in coating up to 7 cm. in thickness and was occasionally found preserved in fragments up to 2 feet in diameter (Structure 13). There was no evidence that this coarser plaster was either whitewashed or painted.

Lime for use in the plaster was probably made from locally abundant limestone. A large pile of pure white lime lay on the floor in the southwest corner of Structure 10 (Fig. 17). The present-day landowner of the northern part of the site described a large, circular "oven" in the bank of the spring creek 150–200 feet north of the north quadrangle wall. The oven was several feet in diameter and several feet deep, lined with adobe bricks, and showed signs of intensive burning. Destroyed a few years ago, the oven quite likely was the mission lime kiln.

A stockpile of water-washed sand and gravel, used as a tempering agent in adobe and in preparation of wall plaster, was found in Structure 4 (Fig. 12), and samples of it were collected for comparison with these other materials.

Wood

Although we know from the documents that wood was a common building material at the site, the only surviving evidence of its use is in the charred roof fragments lying on the structure floors and the large charred support post (oak,

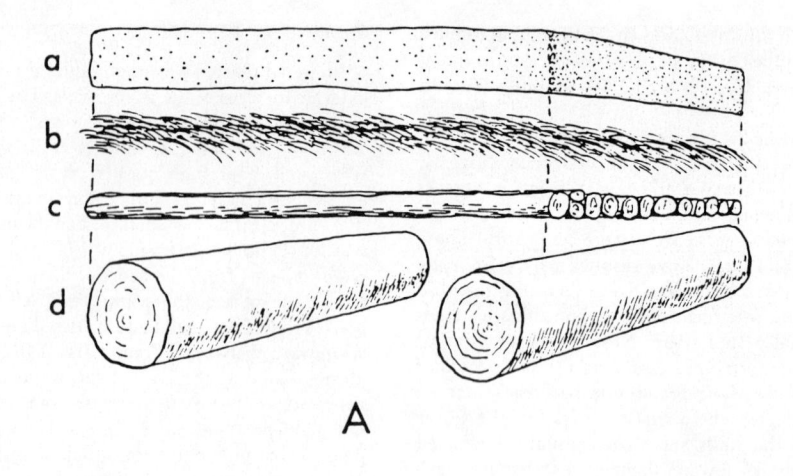

Fig. 5, A. Details of roof construction: a, puddled adobe; b, grass; c, savinas; d, vigas. B. Details of stone wall construction.

about 27 cm. in diameter) in the floor of Structure 14 (Fig. 23, C). Many large charred fragments of roof beams (*vigas*) were made from oak (probably live oak) but several of juniper were found and at least one was made from an unidentified wood.

The small cross pieces (*savinas*) used in the roofs were usually about 3 cm. in diameter, and complete stems, not split fragments, were used (Fig. 5, A). Juniper was the wood most commonly selected for these cross sticks, but a few stems of unidentified shrubs were found. The original length of these *savinas* is not known. Only short broken fragments were recovered.

Wood was probably commonly used for doors, windows, framing, furniture, ladders, tools, and other purposes, but only indirect evidence is furnished by the iron nails found in and around each structure.

Fig. 6. Excavations in the southeast corner of the quadrangle. A, cobblestone walk west of Structure 2; B, light and dark adobe bricks in south quadrangle wall (note reinforcement outside the base of the wall); C, superimposed adobe floors exposed inside a burial pit in floor of Structure 2; D, adobe threshold leading through north wall of Structure 2 into Structure 5.

12

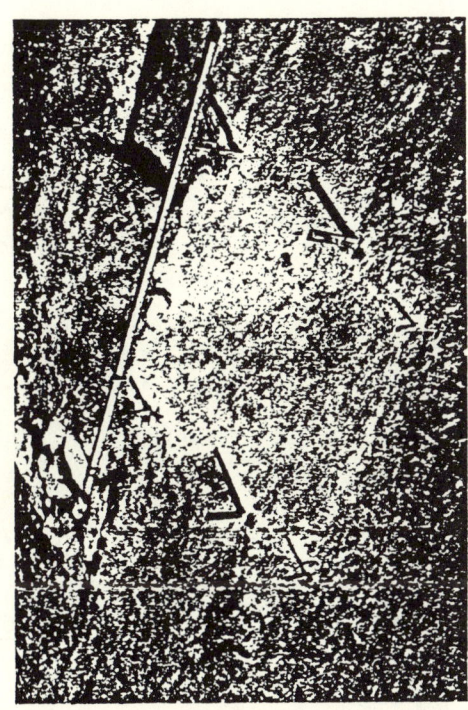

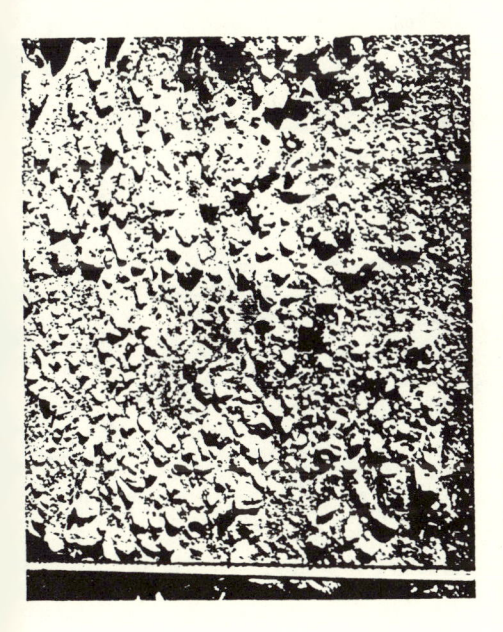

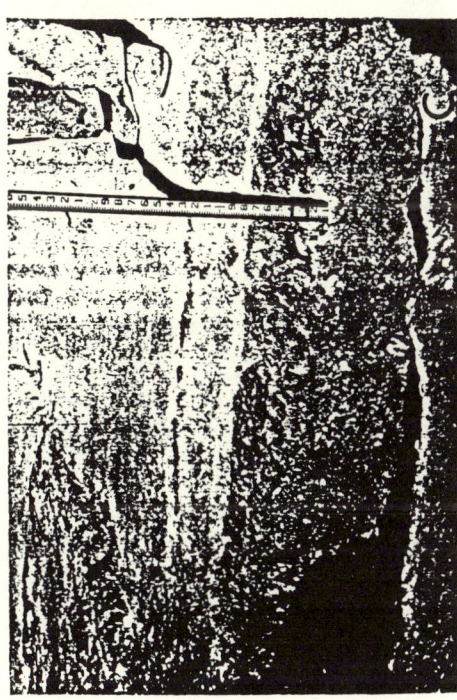

35

Grass

Local grasses were gathered and used between the sticks and the puddled adobe in the roofs (Fig. 5, A). Charred mats of this grass were found preserved in some structures, and impressions of grass stems appear in the undersurface of the puddled adobe roof material. No identifications of the grasses have been obtained.

Clay

Clay-bearing soils were used for the following purposes in the mission buildings: (1) Light tan caliche and brown topsoil were used in the adobe bricks, adobe floors, and adobe roofs. (2) Dark brown clay was used as mortar in the limestone block walls and flagstone floors. (3) Dark brown clay was used between adobe floors in structures which had double floors. These clayey soils were probably acquired locally, but no obvious borrow sources were found in the vicinity. A stockpile of dark brown clay was found in Structure 4 (Fig. 12).

Sand and Gravel

Water-washed sand and gravel from the bed of the nearby Nueces River was used as a tempering agent in the adobe and in the preparation of wall plaster. A stockpile of this sand and gravel was found in Structure 4 (Fig. 12), and samples of it were collected. After each flood, the Nueces River leaves bars of clean, assorted sands and gravels of various diameters near the mission site.

Structure 1 (Fig. 3)

Excavation: The bulldozing operation had partially uncovered the floor of this structure, and some troweling exposed about 60 square feet of floor with a fragment of an adobe wall running along the west edge. The bulldozer had removed the southern portion of the room down to below floor level and the south part of the east wall was completely gone. The north end of this structure extended beyond the property line fence and was not excavated.

Location: This structure lay just inside the central portion of the west quadrangle wall, centered at about N335–W260 on the grid. The area immediately to the north was not excavated and the area to the south of it had been bulldozed down to bedrock.

Dimensions: About 60 square feet (6 feet N–S, 10 feet E–W) of floor was cleared, but the original dimensions could not be determined.

Fill: From 3 to 12 cm. of ashy soil containing burned roof material and cultural debris lay on the floor. This fill, heavily disturbed by the bulldozer, was carefully removed with a trowel but was not screened.

Wall construction: Only a few adobe brick fragments remained in the west wall. The thickness and pattern of this wall and details of the other walls were not determined.

Plaster: No data.

Floors: A single adobe floor lay from 3 to 6 cm. above the limestone bedrock. Dark brown topsoil containing some flint chips and burned rocks lay between the floor and the bedrock. Ranging from 1 to 3 cm. thick, the floor was made of light tan puddled adobe containing some small river gravels. The surface of the floor was smooth and hard though ashy soil and cultural debris lay on it. Overlying the debris were fragments of charred beams and burned clay roof material in several places.

Roof construction: The roof of Structure 1 apparently was constructed in the same manner as Structure 7. Charred beams up to about 9 cm. in diameter, charred sticks, and burned clay with grass impressions were found above the floor along the fence where it was not removed by the bulldozer. This burned roof material reached a thickness of 27 cm. just inside the west wall.

Doors: No data.

Hearths: No data.

Miscellaneous features: No data.

Associated artifacts:
  Copper: 1 perforated overlay.
  Iron: 4 handmade nails; 1 unidentified object.
  Ceramics: 1 dark gray plainware; 18 amber glaze plainware; 5 clear glaze brown painted ware; 6 majolica.
  Stone: 1 Type 5 gunflint; 2 Type 3 flakes; 3 miscellaneous flakes.
  Bone: 6 food bones.

The presence of animal bones and other trash indicates the structure probably was a dwelling, burned perhaps at the time of the mission's abandonment. The northern part of the structure is preserved beneath the property line fence.

Structure 2 (Figs. 3, 7)

Excavation: The bulldozing operation has removed the walls and fill of this structure down to within 3 to 9 cm. of the upper floor on the west end. The upper floor sloped up toward the east and about 18 feet of it had been scraped away, but the lowest course of adobe bricks remained in the walls forming the eastern end. Encountered on the first day of excavation, the structure's entire area eventually was cleared of debris (Fig. 8).

Location: Structure 2 lay just inside the east quadrangle wall near the southeast corner. The east wall formed part of the enclosure and the south wall was shared with Structure 8, which lay parallel to Structure 2 and in the southeast quadrangle corner. Structures 4 and 5 lay just to the north of 2, with a doorway between 2 and 5. Structure 2 was centered about N295-W120 on the grid.

Dimensions: The central dimensions were 16.4 feet N-S by 41.6 feet E-W inside, and 21.8 feet N-S by 45.9 feet E-W outside. The inside dimensions of the structure, in *varas*, were 6 N-S and 15 E-W.

Fill: From 3 to 9 cm. of light brown soil, crumbled adobe, and fine-grained white plaster fragments lay above the upper floor in the west part of Structure 2, and there were large concentrations of burned roof material on the floor in several places. The fill contained few artifacts. All fill, and portions of the floor, had been removed by the bulldozer in the eastern part of the structure.

Wall construction: All of the walls were made of adobe bricks. The north, east, and south walls were one brick-length plus one brick-width thick (Pattern No. 4, Fig. 4, B), and the west wall was one brick-length thick (Pattern No. 3, Fig. 4, D). The north, east, and south walls averaged about 2.75 feet or 1 *vara* in thickness. The north, east, and south walls had adobe-filled cracks up to 15 cm. wide running longitudinally. One of these cracks in the northwest corner had been partially filled with brick fragments which indicated it was present during the construction of the wall rather than having developed later. There was no evidence of special footings beneath the walls. Only a single course of bricks remained in the wall around the east end of the structure, but two or three courses remained around the west end.

Plaster: Traces of white sandy plaster were found along the base of the north wall where it extended about 3 cm. above the upper floor near the west end of the structure. There were drops and streaks of bright red pigment on the surface of the plaster in several places, indicating that there had been red paintings on the wall. Slabs of wall plaster up to 18 cm. in diameter were found on the upper floor in the west end of the structure. It averaged about 2 cm. thick and was composed of fine-grained river sand cemented with lime and coated on the outer surface with whitewash. Patches of red pigment, which once formed designs, were found on several of the larger fragments of fallen plaster. Some of the plaster showed evidence of having been applied in two layers with whitewash between them.

Floors: Structure 2 had two superimposed adobe floors (Fig. 6, C). The western end of the upper floor (No. 1) was cleared of debris except for a few patches of burned roof material. The surface elevation of this floor ranged from 99.49 to 99.73 ft. Toward the eastern end of the structure, the upper floor sloped upward sharply onto what apparently had been a raised area (sanctuary) resting on a hard-packed gravelly soil base. Unfortunately, the bulldozer had removed about 18 feet of the eastern end of the upper floor and the entire sanctuary area. Composed of light tan adobe with small river gravels, the floor averaged about 3 cm. in thickness, and its upper surface was smooth and hard-packed. At least twelve burial outlines (several of which intersected) could be seen in the surface of the upper floor; most of these were later excavated. A lower floor (No. 2) was detected in the edges of the grave pits, and was separated from the upper floor by about 3 to 9 cm. of dark brown, very compact clay which apparently was placed over the lower floor as a base for the upper floor. The lower floor was not cleared; it was studied only in the grave walls. It, too, was composed of light tan adobe with river gravels. Its average thickness was about 3 cm., and its upper surface elevation

Fig. 7. Excavation of southeast corner of quadrangle showing Structure 2 in center with Structure 8 to the right and Structure 5 to the left. Note burial pits through door of Structure 2 and portion of stubby rear wall in front, looking east.

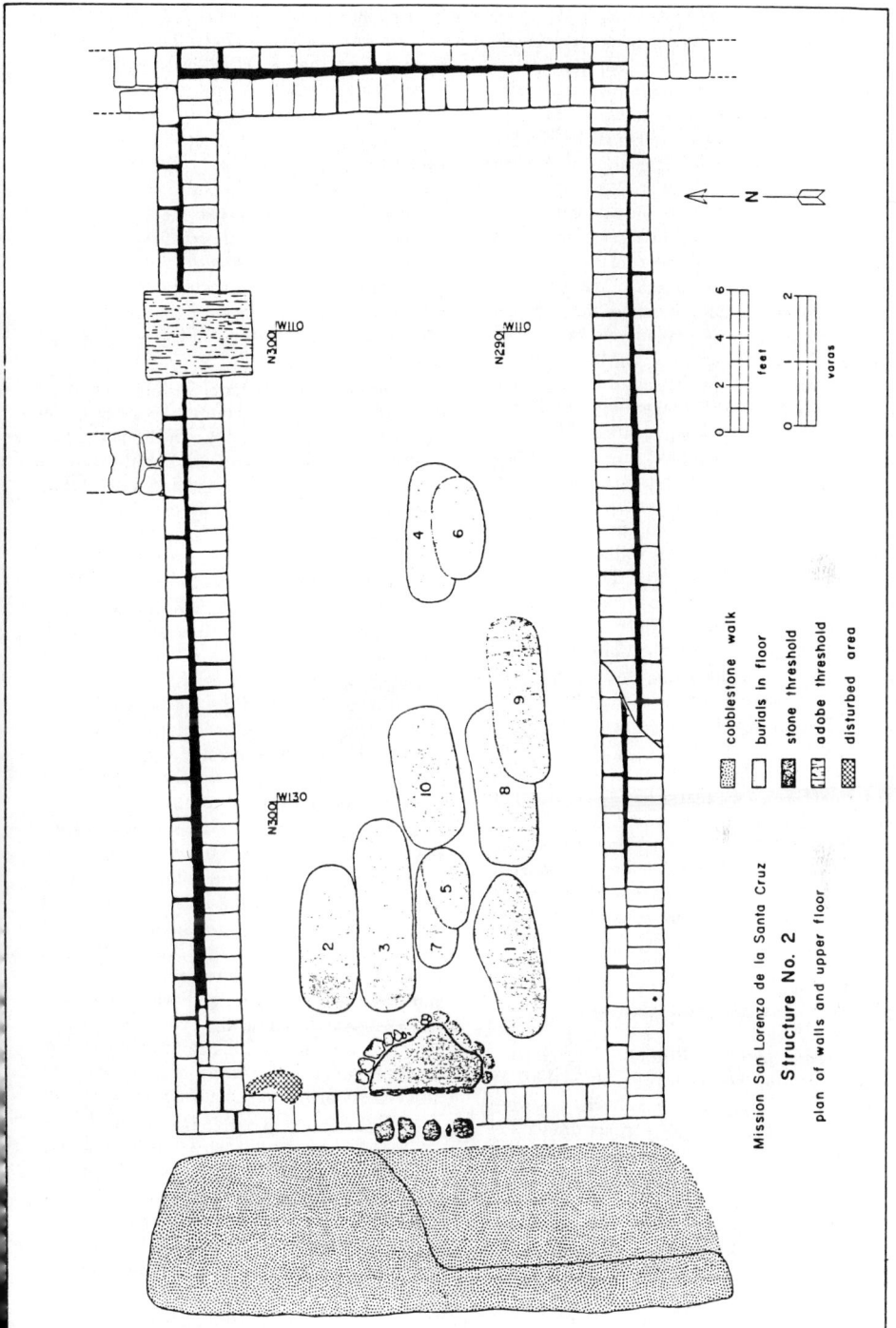

Fig. 8. Structure 2, walls and upper floor.

ranged from 98.99 to 99.37 feet sloping upward toward the east wall. In several instances, burials had been dug while the lower floor was in use (as indicated by the grave profiles) and later burials which originated from the upper floor had encountered and disturbed these older graves. Very few artifacts were found in association with the upper floor.

Roof construction: Several large patches of burned roof materials (up to 4 feet across and 0.3 foot thick) lay on the upper floor in the west end of Structure 2. This material (beams, sticks, and grass-impressed clay) indicates that the roof was constructed in the same manner as that of Structure 7. The majority of the larger beams lay north to south, indicating that they had spanned the structure along the short axis. Burial Pits 2 and 3 contained large quantities of burned roof material in large chunks lying just as it had fallen, indicating that the pits must have been open at the time the roof burned and collapsed.

Doors: Two doorways led into Structure 2 (Fig. 8). One, centered in the west wall, led out onto a cobblestone walk in the plaza. The other door led through the north wall into Structure 5, about 7 feet from the east wall. The north door was 3.5 feet E-W and 4.7 feet N-S. This threshold, made of light tan adobe with small gravels, was smooth, hard-packed, and had a slightly concave surface. The surface elevation ranged from 99.55 to 99.74 feet.

The west doorway was about 5 feet wide with a threshold formed by a large flat stone, irregular in outline and with a very smooth surface. The stone, about 2.5 feet by 5 feet, was surrounded by small flat stones about 0.8 foot in diameter, set at the same elevation. During excavation a cross-mark was cut into the surface of the large stone to serve as a datum point.

Hearths: There is no evidence (ash, burned adobe, etc.) of a hearth in this structure.

Miscellaneous features: Burials (Figs. 9, 10). Burial pit outlines were clearly visible in the floor of the church (Structure 2). Ten burial pits were excavated and several others were left intact due to a lack of time. The pits excavated produced the remains of at least 17 individuals including 9 adults, 3 adolescents, and 4 infants (Appendix A). Most of the skeletons were incomplete because of intersecting pits. The articulated skeletons were extended on the back with the heads toward the west (away from the altar) and hands folded across the lower chest (Fig. 9). Many of the burials contained glass beads and brass religious ornaments.

The burial pits were for the most part arranged in rows in the west half of Structure 2. The pits were filled to floor level and well-packed so that the floor surface remained smooth and flat. The burned roof debris lay above the burial outlines in the south half of the church floor. Burial pits in the north half of the church floor had been opened and the skeletons partially removed prior to the collapse of the burned roof, and the undisturbed burned debris partially filled these pits (Fig. 9).

In many examples, burials from the upper floor level had intersected and disturbed burials which had been placed through the lower floor, and in at least one instance a burial pit on the upper floor clearly intersected and disturbed another upper floor burial. In the restricted nave of this small church, burial plots were apparently at such a premium that disturbance of previous burials was common. A good example of this is found in Burial 8 (Fig. 9), in which a complete adult skeleton associated with a brass crucifix was stacked along one wall of the pit when another adult, also associated with a crucifix, was placed in the bottom of the pit. No bones of the first skeleton remained articulated after it was moved aside, although it could not have been in the ground more than nine years and had been protected beneath the floor of the structure.

Most of the burials were about 2.5 feet below the floor, and the bottom 1.0 to 1.5 feet of the pits extended down into the rotten limestone bedrock (Fig. 10). The fill in the burial pits was composed of limestone fragments, caliche nodules, and a small amount of dirt. Most of the adult burials had a small open cavity above the chest and abdomen (Fig. 10), and when this cavity was encountered, the bones could be seen lying articulated within it. This cavity resulted from the decay and collapse of the torso and there was no evidence of the use of a coffin in any burial.

The bodies were buried in homespun clothing, small fragments of which were preserved through contact with the brass religious medals. Dr. F. E. Petzel of The University of Texas at Austin identified this cloth as plainweave fabric of flax (Burial 8-1) and plainweave fabric of coarse cotton (Burial 4). The bodies were ap-

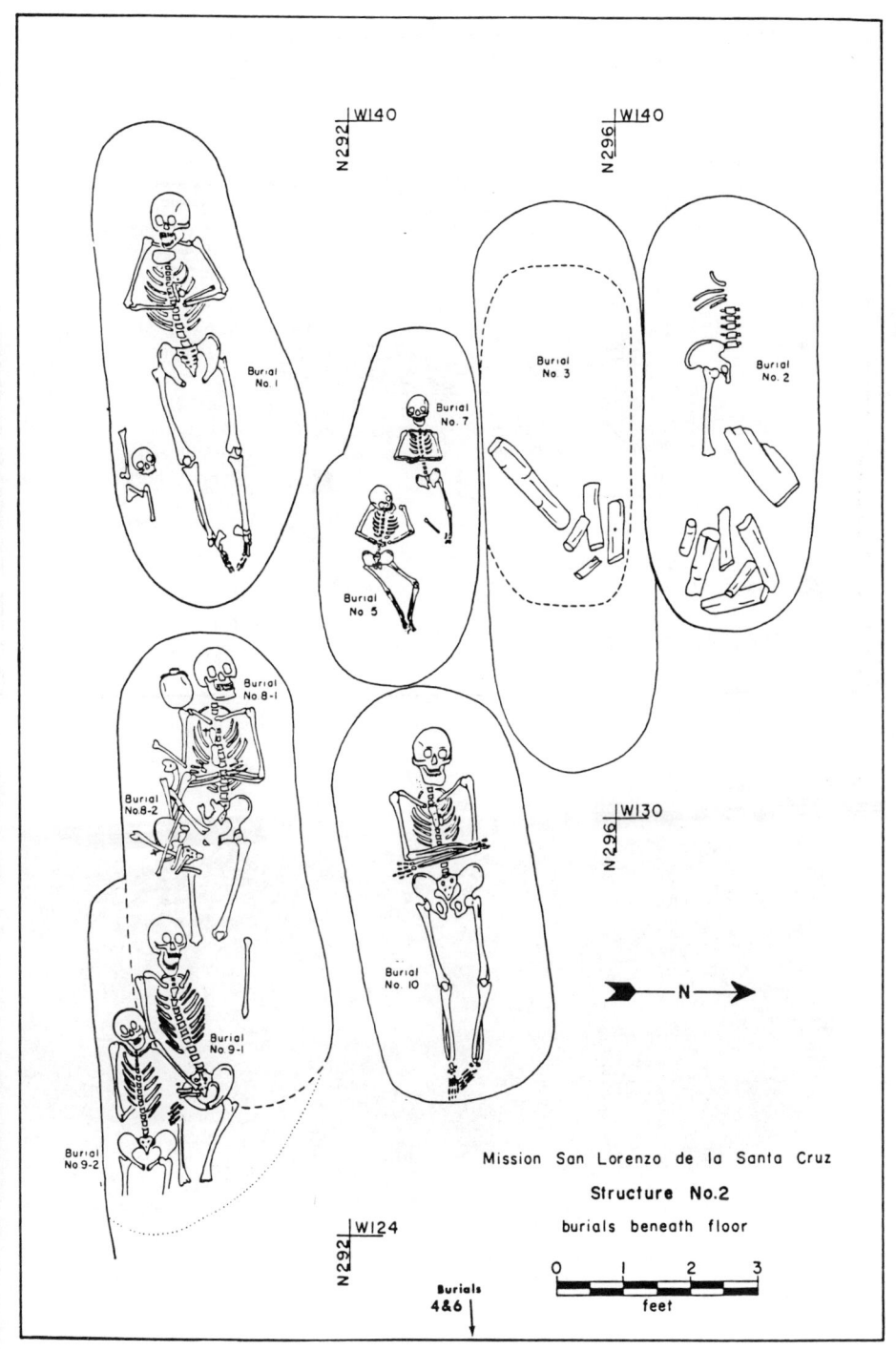

Fig. 9. Structure 2 showing burials beneath floor.

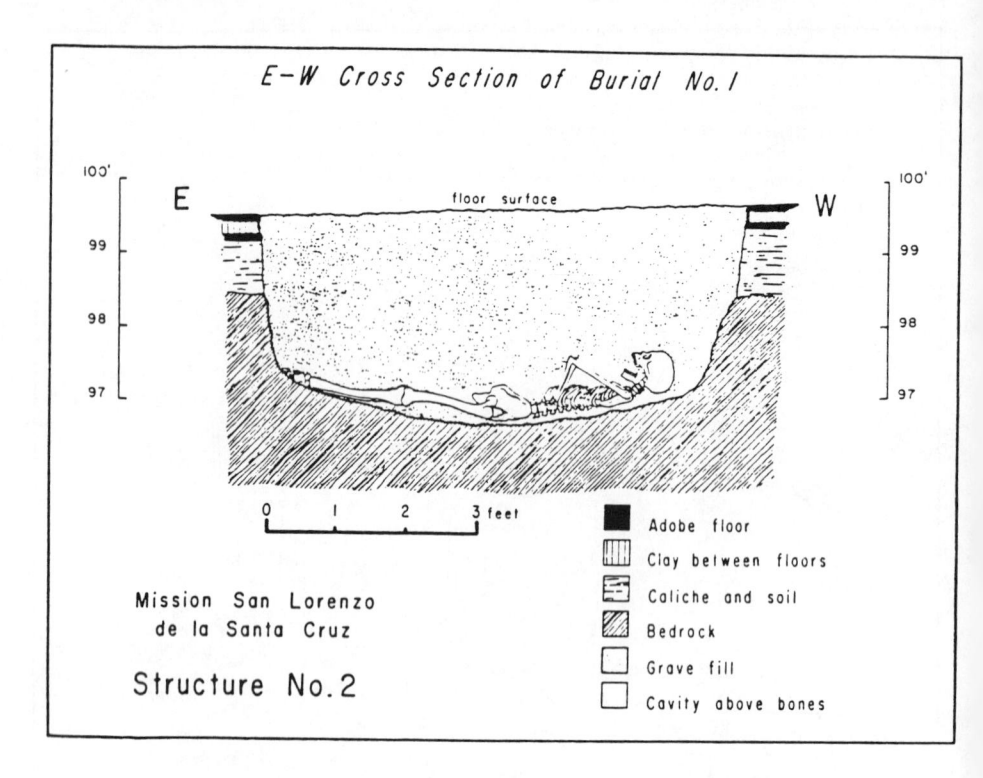

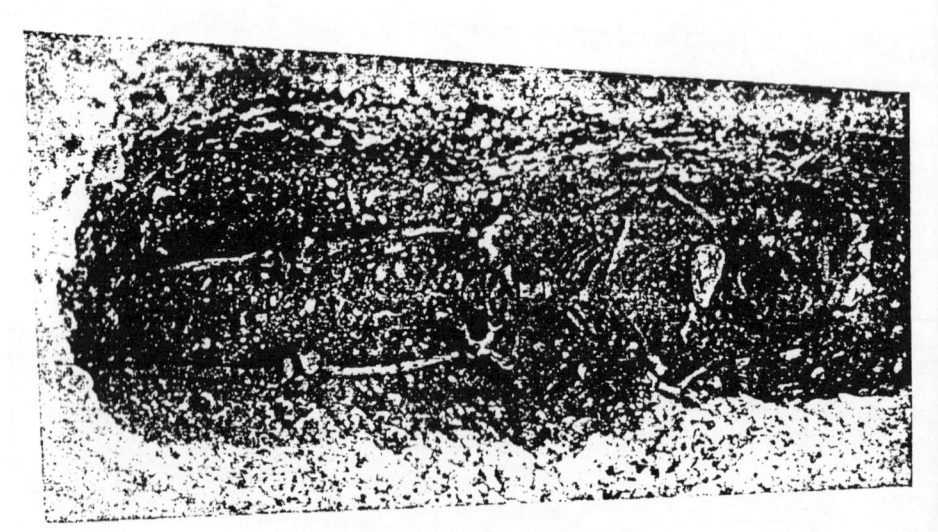

Fig. 10. East-west cross section of Burial 1 (top) and detail of burial.

parently wrapped in sheets before interment and small fragments of this cloth were preserved on some skulls and longbones. Dr. Petzel identified this finely woven fabric as "probably linen." There were no buttons or other clothing fasteners in the graves and no evidence of wood or nails—only glass beads and religious ornaments. The beads, probably presented to the individuals at the time of their conversion, were strung in small numbers, along with the religious medals, around the necks of the individuals.

Burial 1 (Fig. 10) contained one complete, adult female articulated skeleton with fragments of a child's disarticulated skeleton in one corner of the burial pit. The only bones not present with the adult were the end joints of three fingers which apparently were missing at the time of interment. The skeleton was extended on the back with the head toward the west, the hands and forearms folded across the lower chest, right above left. A large brass medallion (No. 1, Fig. 29, B) was strung around the neck (crucifixion scene upward), along with 28 small burgundy red glass beads and one amber bead. In the intestinal area was a concentration of several hundred small seeds. Dr. Hugh Cutler of the Missouri Botanical Garden identified these as "*Opuntia* seeds, from fruits of a pad cactus like *O. engelmanni.*"

Burial 2 (Fig. 9) contained an articulated fragment of an adult postcranial skeleton—right femur, pelvis, lumbar vertebrae, some ribs; oriented head to west in a supine position. This probably was a Spanish burial which was partially disinterred prior to abandonment of the site.

Burial 3 (Fig. 9) contained a few scattered teeth and bone fragments of an adult and apparently was another Spanish burial moved in part to sacred ground elsewhere.

Burial 4 was the upper half of an infant articulated skeleton which was disturbed by Burial 6. The infant was lying extended on the back, head toward the west. A small brass crucifix (No. 2, Fig. 29, E) was strung around the neck (crucifixion scene upward) with 17 small, clear glass beads, 2 alabaster beads, and 1 coral bead.

Burial 5 (Fig. 9) was a child's articulated skeleton, extended on the back, head toward the west; the forearms were folded over the abdomen, right above left. This burial pit, which had no associated artifacts, intersected and disturbed the right leg of Burial 7.

Burial 6 was an articulated fragment of an adult skeleton—left scapula, humerus, radius, ulna, carpals and phalanges, and a few ribs; oriented on back, head to west. This probably was a Spanish burial which was partially moved. The pit disturbed the lower half of Burial 4.

Burial 7 (Fig. 9) was a child's articulated skeleton in a supine position, extended, head to the west. The forearms were folded across the lower chest, right over left. The right leg was removed by Burial 5. There were no associated artifacts.

Burial 8-1 (Fig. 9) was an adult male articulated skeleton lying extended on the back, head toward the west, with forearms folded across the lower chest (right above left). It had been placed in the pit previously occupied by Burial 8-2, which was conveniently stacked to one side. Crucifix No. 3 (Fig. 29, C), with the crucifixion scene upward, was strung around the neck with 29 medium compound red glass beads, 6 small compound red glass beads, 4 medium simple blue-green glass beads, 7 small simple blue glass beads, and 1 coral bead. Some small fragments of finely woven linen adhered to the skull, mandible, and right radius and ulna. Burial 9-1 disturbed the lower legs and feet of Burial 8-1, and some infant bones were scattered in the eastern part of the pit.

Burial 8-2 (Fig. 9) was a complete disarticulated skeleton of a young adult female. The bones were stacked to one side in their approximate relative position (skull to the west) when Burial 8-1 was placed in the same pit. A handmade brass crucifix (No. 1, Fig. 29, D) was found in the pelvic area, and small fragments of finely woven linen were adhering to some of the longbones.

Burial 9-1 (Fig. 9) was the articulated skeleton of an adult male lying fully extended in a supine position with the head toward the west. The entire left arm, including the scapula, was removed by an adjacent burial pit (not explored). The right arm was extended along the right side. Some infant bones were scattered in the grave fill. There were no associated artifacts. Burial 9-2 was lying partially above this skeleton and was possibly buried in the same pit at

the same time. These were the shallowest of all the burials and the pits did not penetrate the bedrock.

Burial 9-2 (Fig. 9) was an articulated skeleton of an adult female, extended on the back, head toward the west. The forearms were crossed on the lower chest. The lower legs were not removed due to a lack of time. Some infant bones, including a complete skull, were scattered in the fill above this individual. Burial 9-2 overlapped Burial 9-1 and may have been buried at the same time.

Burial 10 (Fig. 9) was the complete articulated skeleton of an adult female, buried fully extended on the back, head toward the west. The forearms were crossed over the abdomen, right above left. A complete but disarticulated skeleton of an infant was stacked beside the skull (to the south). A small brass medallion (No. 2, Fig. 29, A) strung with 2 small simple blue glass beads and 5 alabaster beads was around the neck of the adult. The downward face of the medallion depicts "Our Lady of Zaragossa" and the upturned face depicts the "Sacred Heart."

Cobblestone walkway

Extending along the west wall of the church (Structure 2), and forming a walkway in front of the main portal, was a rectangular paved area about 27 feet long and 7 feet wide (Fig. 8). The smooth river cobbles used in this pavement ranged from about 8 to 15 cm. in diameter and were carefully placed to form a smooth, all-weather surface. The surface of this pavement was relatively flat and sloped downward slightly, away from the base of the wall.

Associated Artifacts

There were very few artifacts associated with Structure 2, except for those found in the burials. Three brass vessels (Fig. 27) found during the bulldozing are said to have come from the vicinity of Structure 2, but their provenience is uncertain.

  Copper: 5 religious objects
  Iron: 1 handmade nail
  Glass: 1 pale green bottle glass
  Beads: 93 glass; 1 amber; 7 alabaster; 2 coral
Structure 2 was probably the main church of San Lorenzo de la Santa Cruz because (1) It was the only structure investigated which contained burials under the floor, and burials were frequently placed beneath the nave floor in Spanish missions of this period. (2) The burials all followed Christian tradition. (3) This was the largest structure, and it was built of the best quality adobe. (4) There was very little cultural debris lying on or above the floor. (5) There was evidence that the white plaster walls were decorated with red murals. The sanctuary and high altar probably were in the east end—where the floor sloped up and a side entrance led into the sacristy and friary—but all traces of these features were destroyed by the bulldozer. This structure apparently was burned when it was abandoned. Several burials still remain beneath the nave floor in the areas covered by the burned roof material. The bulldozer operator and other observers said the walls were still standing 2 to 4 feet high before they were bulldozed. The remaining wall bases have been capped with new adobe bricks to help preserve them.

Structure 3 (Fig. 3)

Excavation: The bulldozer removed the walls and fill of this structure down to within about 15 cm. of the floor. The remaining fill was troweled from a section of the floor about 5 feet N-S by 8 feet E-W. The remainder of the structure, including the north end which extends under the property line fence, was not excavated.

Location: Structure 3 was situated against the east quadrangle wall just north of Structure 9 and about 25 feet south of Structure 10 at grid location N370-W110.

Dimensions: About 40 square feet of floor were cleared and the south wall was mapped, but dimensions of the structure were not determined.

Fill: The fill, composed of fine brown soil mixed with crumbled adobe and building stones, was removed by careful troweling and passed through fine-meshed screens. No burned roof material was encountered in the area.

Wall construction: The south wall was constructed of flat, undressed stone slabs ranging from about 9 to 46 cm. in diameter and from 3 to 15 cm. in thickness. The limestone slabs had been laid in horizontal courses, leveled with small stones, and set in place with a dark clay mortar.

Fig. 11. Artist's reconstruction of Structure 2 in southeast corner of quadrangle. Looking southeast.

The other three walls of Structure 3 probably were made of adobe bricks because no stones remained in place to the north, east, or west of the floor area cleared. No details about these other walls were determined.

Plaster: No data.

Floors: A single floor of puddled adobe was partially cleared. Made of light brown adobe, it attained a maximum thickness of about 1 cm, and in some places it was worn through to the dark brown soil beneath. The surface of the floor was fairly smooth, compact, and easy to follow with a trowel.

Roof construction: No data.

Doors: A doorway probably led through the east end of the south wall of this structure into Structure 9. The doorway area was not cleared and no details about its construction are known.

Hearths: The floor showed scattered traces of gray ash, but no hearth was encountered.

Miscellaneous features: None excavated.

Associated artifacts:
   Iron: 2 handmade nails
   Ceramics: 8 amber glaze plainware; 3 majolica
   Glass: 1 pale green bottle glass
   Stone: 1 scraper blade; 1 Type 3 flake

Structure 3 was only partially excavated, and its function in the mission complex is uncertain. It did contain a few sherds and stone artifacts, but far fewer than the obvious habitation structures, 11, 12, and 14. Perhaps this structure served as the living quarters of a priest or other Spanish official and was kept relatively clean. Most of Structure 3 remains to be cleared, and the part beneath the property fence should have at least one foot of fill over the floor and wall bases. In the area excavated, there was no evidence that this structure was burned.

Structure 4 (Fig. 12)

Excavation: This area was heavily bulldozed, but about 1 to 1.5 feet of fill remained above the old ground surface. A small test pit, 2 feet N-S by 4 feet E-W in the center of the area disclosed several layers of material lying on the old sterile surface. The south portion, about 20 feet E-W by 12 feet N-S, was cleared to the old surface, and all of the lenses of construction material were recorded and samples of each were taken.

Location: The area labeled Structure 4 in the field probably was not an actual building, but a partially enclosed area used for storage of building materials. This area was formed by the north wall of Structure 2, the west wall of Structure 5, the south wall of Structure 6, and a short stub of wall extending south from the west wall of Structure 6. This partial enclosure faced the plaza (Fig. 3) at about N315-W125 on the grid.

Dimensions: The area involved was about 24 feet long N-S and extended for about 20 feet along the north wall of Structure 2.

Fill: A layer of brown sandy soil, crushed adobe, plaster fragments, and building stones about 3 to 18 cm. thick covered this area. Between this fill and the old sterile surface were three overlapping lenses (Fig. 12) of building materials: (1) This lens of small river gravels was up to about 0.8 foot thick and 18 feet across; the gravels were all less than about 0.1 foot in diameter, very smooth, and they were not badly contaminated with sand or dirt. The gravel in this lens was the same type and the same size range as the gravels used in the adobe bricks and adobe floors. (2) A lens about 0.3 foot thick and 12 feet across held limestone slivers. These spalls were identical to the leveling snecks or wedges used in constructing the stone walls, and this lens apparently represented a stockpile of them. (3) A third lens, composed of a very fine-grained dark brown clay, was about 0.3 foot thick and 14 feet across. This clay was the same type used as mortar in the stone walls and used, in some instances, as a base for adobe floors.

Wall construction: The three walls enclosing this area are described in the sections on Structures 2, 5, and 6.

Plaster: Fragments of a rather coarse sandy plaster from about 1 to 3 cm. in thickness were found scattered over the bulldozed surface of this area.

Floors: There were no prepared floors in this area, but the old ground surface beneath the lenses of building material was very hard-packed and smooth; it could be trowled easily and swept clean.

Roof construction: There was no evidence that this area was roofed.

Doors: The west side of this area opened out onto the plaza. There were no doorways leading into Structures 2, 5, or 6.

Hearths: There were scattered patches of gray ash on the old ground surface beneath the lenses of construction materials. These seemed to be secondary depositions, however, as there was no evidence of burning on the surface.

Miscellaneous features: Lying on the old ground surface at about N312-W125 were three crushed amber beads and one composite button (brass/wood/glass). A small pit (15 cm. deep and about 37 cm. across) had been dug into the old ground surface about 1 foot from the wall of Structure 2 and 18 feet east of the northwest corner. This pit contained no artifacts and its purpose is unknown.

Associated artifacts:
  Ceramics: 2 majolica
  Glass: 3 amber beads
  Stone: 1 cutting tool; 1 Type 3 flake
  Bone: 5 food bones

This partial enclosure, which opened onto the plaza, was used as a storage area for construction materials. It was heavily bulldozed, but about 1.0 to 1.5 feet of fill remained over the old ground surface. The area was only about one-half excavated.

Structure 5 (Fig. 12)

Excavation: The walls of this structure were largely removed by the bulldozer, but a few inches of fill remained over the floors. A deep test trench, about 6 feet E-W and 2.5 feet N-S was excavated in the south end of the room down to sterile subsoil. Two superimposed floors were visible in the walls of this trench and several square feet of each floor were cleared and examined. The fill on the floors was screened.

Location: This structure lay against the east wall of the quadrangle between Structure 2 (to the south) and Structure 9 (to the north), at about N315-W110 on the grid.

Dimensions: The interior dimensions of this structure were 21 feet N-S and 14 feet E-W, or about 5 by 7.5 *varas*.

Fill: Up to about 6 cm. of fill, composed of adobe brick debris, plaster, and brown sandy soil, remained above the floors of this structure. There were no artifacts or burned roof materials on the floors. The upper floor was separated from the lower by about 9 cm. of dark brown sterile clay which had apparently been placed on the lower floor to serve as a base for the upper one.

Wall construction: The remaining base of the east wall was composed of adobe blocks on the south end and of unshaped limestone blocks on the north end. The adobe portion of this wall seemed to be an extension of the east wall of Structure 2—the adobe was of the same type and the brick pattern was similar. Perhaps adobe bricks left over from the construction of Structure 2 were used to build a part of this wall. The south wall was shared with Structure 2. The west wall, which was abutted against the north wall of Structure 2, was composed of limestone blocks from 0.5 foot to 2.35 feet in diameter and averaging about 0.3 foot in thickness. These building stones were set in place with dark brown clay mortar and leveled with limestone chips. The north wall probably had a doorway which weakened it, making it collapse more completely, and contributed to its being largely removed by the bulldozer.

Plaster: A few small fragments of sandy white plaster about 1 cm. in thickness were scattered across the upper floor. No plaster remained on the lower edges of the walls which were cleared.

Floors: There were two prepared adobe floors, and about 50 square feet of each were exposed along the south wall. The upper floor (No. 1) was composed of light tan adobe with small gravels, had a smooth upper surface, and was about 3 cm. thick. The northern portion was partially removed by the bulldozer. About 6 to 10 cm. of dark brown sterile clay separated floor No. 1 from the lower floor (No. 2). The lower floor showed the same composition and thickness as the upper floor, and it lay on the unprepared old ground surface.

Roof construction: No traces of roof material were found on the upper floor of this structure.

Doors: One doorway in the south end of this room linked it to Structure 2. This doorway and its adobe threshold are described under Structure 2 (Fig. 6, D). A second doorway apparently led through the center of the north wall into Structure 9, but a deep cut by the bulldozer re-

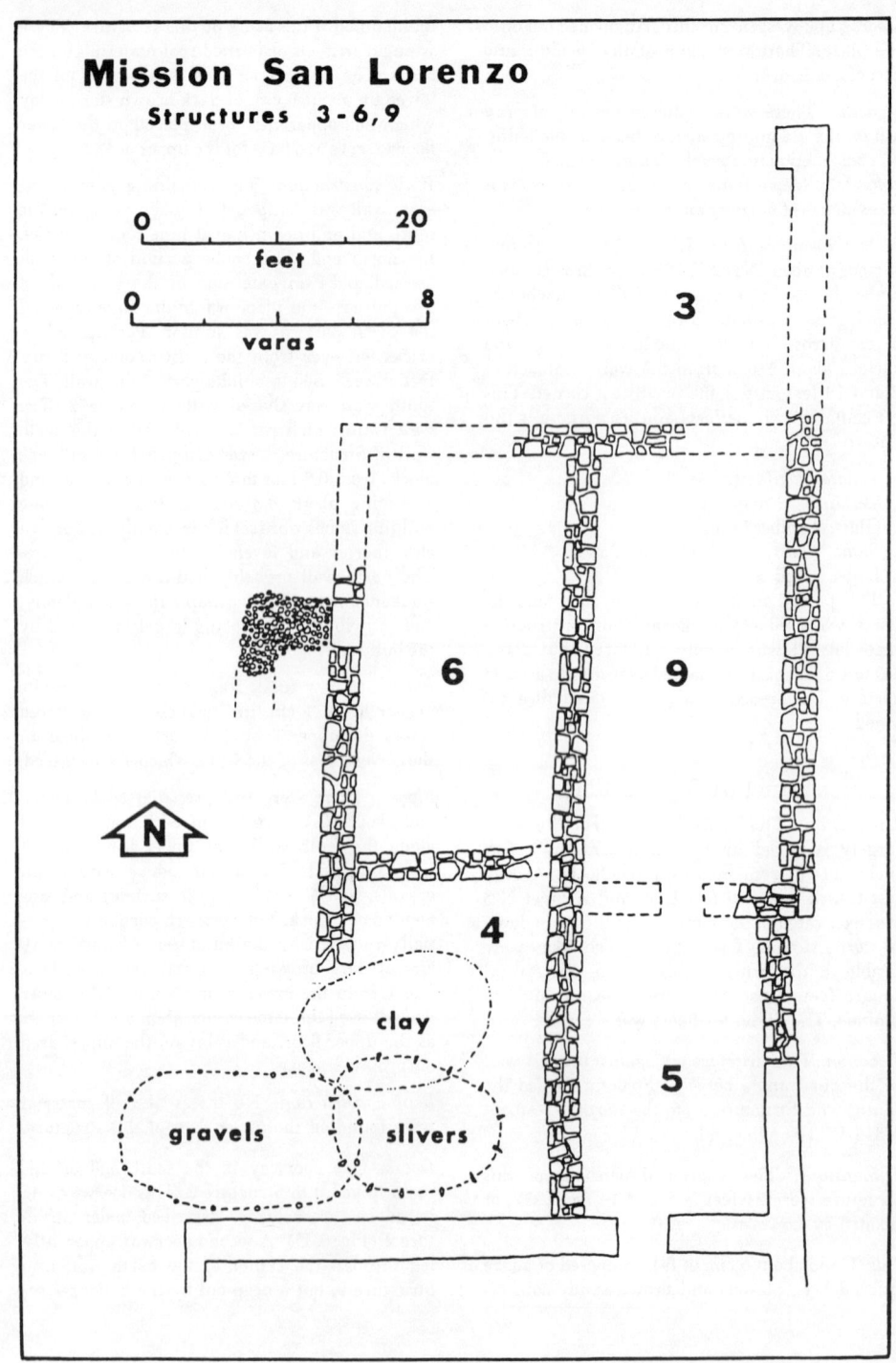

Fig. 12. Structures 3, 4, 5, 6, and 9.

moved the lowest course of stones from the west end of this wall and disturbed the doorway and it was not completely excavated.

Hearths: No traces of hearths were found in the excavated portion of the room.

Miscellaneous features: No data.

Associated artifacts: The floors and fill above the floors were clean and no artifacts were found.

Structure 5 probably served as the sacristy for Mission San Lorenzo. It was linked by a doorway to the sanctuary of the church (Structure 2) toward the south and by a second doorway to the friary (Structure 9) toward the north. The priests would have used this as a dressing room, and as a storage place for the robes, altar furnishings, sacred vessels, and other religious objects. The lack of artifacts on the floor indicates this room was kept clean and there was no evidence that Structure 5 was burned. The northern half remains to be excavated.

Structure 6 (Fig. 12)

Excavation: This structure was in the heavily bulldozed area. The wall foundations were cleared and recorded and a cobblestone walk outside the west wall was exposed, but the interior of the room was not excavated.

Location: West of Structure 9, north of Structure 4, this room faced out onto the plaza. It was centered at about N345-W125 on the grid.

Dimensions: The central dimensions of this structure were 28 feet N-S by 14.5 feet E-W inside and 32.3 feet N-S by 19.5 feet E-W outside. The interior dimensions were about 10.2 *varas* N-S by 5.3 *varas* E-W. The long axis was oriented almost exactly with magnetic north.

Fill: Most of the fill of Structure 6 was removed by the bulldozer. Apparently a few inches of brown sandy soil remained above the floor but this was not excavated because of limited time.

Wall construction: The walls of this structure were all made of unshaped limestone slabs from about 0.5 foot to 2.5 feet in diameter and 0.2 to 0.5 foot thick. Only the lowest one or two courses remained in the walls after the bulldozing, and the northwest corner of the room was completely cut away. The stones in the walls were set in place with a dark brown clay mortar and were spaced with limestone spalls. The walls averaged about 2.7 feet, or one *vara*, in thickness.

Plaster: No data.

Floors: No data.

Roof construction: No data.

Doors: The only doorway detected in this room opened through the center of the west wall out onto the plaza. It was about 3 feet wide and the lowest course of stones in the wall formed the threshold. There was a cobblestone walk leading away from the outside of this doorway and an adobe brick platform extending from the doorway into the room for an undetermined distance.

Hearths: No data.

Miscellaneous features: A walk made of a single layer of smooth river cobbles led away from the west doorway of Structure 6. The cobbles ranged from about 6 to 15 cm. in diameter and were set in the ground in such a way as to produce a rather smooth, level, all-weather surface. This walk, which was from 3 to 5 feet wide, ran westward for about 10 feet, then turned south toward the church (Structure 2). Before the bulldozing, the walk may have extended north toward the granary (Structure 10).

Associated artifacts: While clearing the cobblestone walk outside Structure 6, the following material was collected:
   Cobblestones: 10
   Flint flakes: 11
   Dart point fragment: 1
   Adobe brick fragments: 2

Structure 6 probably formed part of the friary or living quarters for the priests and their assistants. It is one of the sturdy stone structures in close proximity to the church and sacristy, and shows the same orientation as these buildings. The floor of this room was not cleared and consequently many questions, such as the presence or absence of features, artifact content, and whether or not the roof was burned, remain unanswered.

Structure 7 (Fig. 14)

Excavation: Structure 7 was located in the heavily bulldozed portion of the site, but it was partially protected by the primary mission midden

which was mounded around its exterior walls. The interior of the building was cleared down to the floor, the wall bases were completely exposed, and a shallow trench was excavated around the outside of the east and south walls to expose the boulder-covered areas. About one foot of fill on the floor was carefully removed by troweling and most of it was processed through quarter-inch and finer mesh screens.

Location: This structure was situated in the southwest corner of the plaza at approximate grid location N250-W245. Structure 7 extended about 14 feet out beyond the western exterior wall of the enclosure and about 7 feet beyond the south plaza wall (Fig. 3) in the usual manner of a defensive bastion.

Dimensions: The interior dimensions were about 9.5 feet N-S and 27 feet E-W, or about 3.5 by 10 *varas*.

Fill: Lying on the floor was a thick layer of burned roof debris—the largest quantity found in any structure. Above it was about 15 cm. of disturbed fill composed mainly of adobe brick fragments and midden debris from outside the walls. This upper fill produced large quantities of artifacts derived from the mission midden and a few recent artifacts introduced into the upper surface of the fill by the bulldozing operation. The fill was removed in three basic layers: upper fill, roof debris, and fill on floor.

Wall construction: All four walls of this structure were built of dark adobe bricks laid in Pattern No. 4 (Fig. 4, B), one brick length plus one brick width in thickness. From two to four courses of bricks remained in these walls because of the protective mass of midden mounded outside. The walls ranged from about 2 to 3 feet in thickness (average, about one *vara*) depending on the width of the internal cracks between bricks. Against the exterior bases of the south and east walls was a broad band of boulders and cobbles (Fig. 14). It is not known how high these stones may have been stacked against the walls, but they probably were simply low ridges which served to drain rain water away from the bases of the walls which were situated on level ground.

Plaster: No evidence of plaster was found inside or outside the walls of this building or in the fill. The defensive cannons were fired from the top of this bastion.

Floors: The floor of Structure 7, composed of a layer of dark puddled adobe 3 cm. thick, was well preserved beneath the mass of roof debris. The floor was smooth, hard, and relatively level except for a shallow depression about 3 feet wide which ran down the entire length of the north wall base. The floor elevation ranged from 100.46 feet to 100.63 feet and down to 100.24 feet in the depression.

Roof construction: Virtually the entire floor of Structure 7 was covered with a thick layer of well-preserved roof debris. Large quantities of this material were carefully collected to show the exact techniques of roof construction. The roof was constructed in the following manner (Fig. 5, A): (1) Heavy beams (*vigas*) spanned the structure across its short axis. (2) These beams were crossed by a layer of small limbs or sticks (*savinas*). (3) A heavy layer of grass covered the sticks. (4) About 9 cm. of adobe mud tempered with river gravels was poured on the grass. After this layer of mud dried it furnished a strong, waterproof roof. When the structure was burned, large blocks of these roofing materials fell to the floor and were preserved—the beams, sticks, and grass survived as charcoal and the fire-hardened adobe layer retained its smooth upper surface and grass-impressed lower surface.

Doors: One doorway 3 feet wide led out into the plaza through the north end of the east wall. A burned-out post about 15 cm. in diameter on the north interior side of the doorway probably supported the base of a wooden door, and a burned plank on the south interior edge probably was part of the framing for the door (Fig. 14).

Hearths: None was found, although small amounts of wood ash were scattered on the floor. A hearth may have been supported on the stone platform near the southwest corner of the room (see features described below).

Miscellaneous features: Situated near the center and against the base of the east wall (Fig. 14) was a low, triangular platform. The back of this platform, which abutted the wall, was about 3.4 feet wide and was situated just south of the doorway. It extended out into the room about 3 feet at a uniform height above the floor of about 1.0

Fig. 13. Excavation of Structure 7. A, cleared down to floor, looking west; B, feature against south wall and lying on floor.

28

A

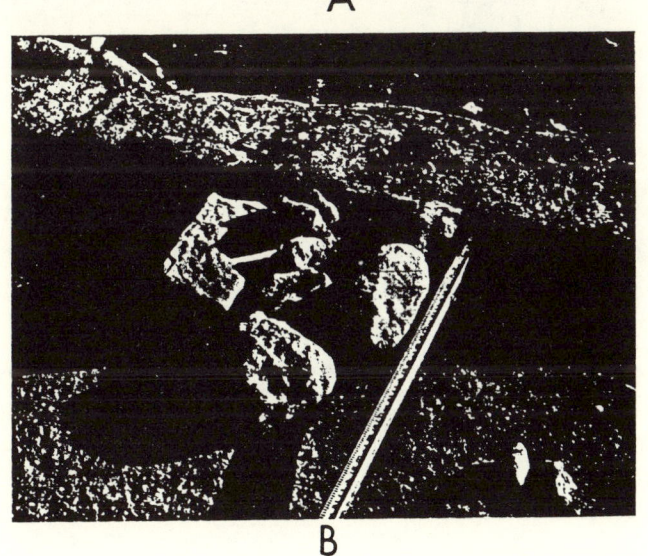

B

Fig. 14. Structure 7, plan of walls and floor.

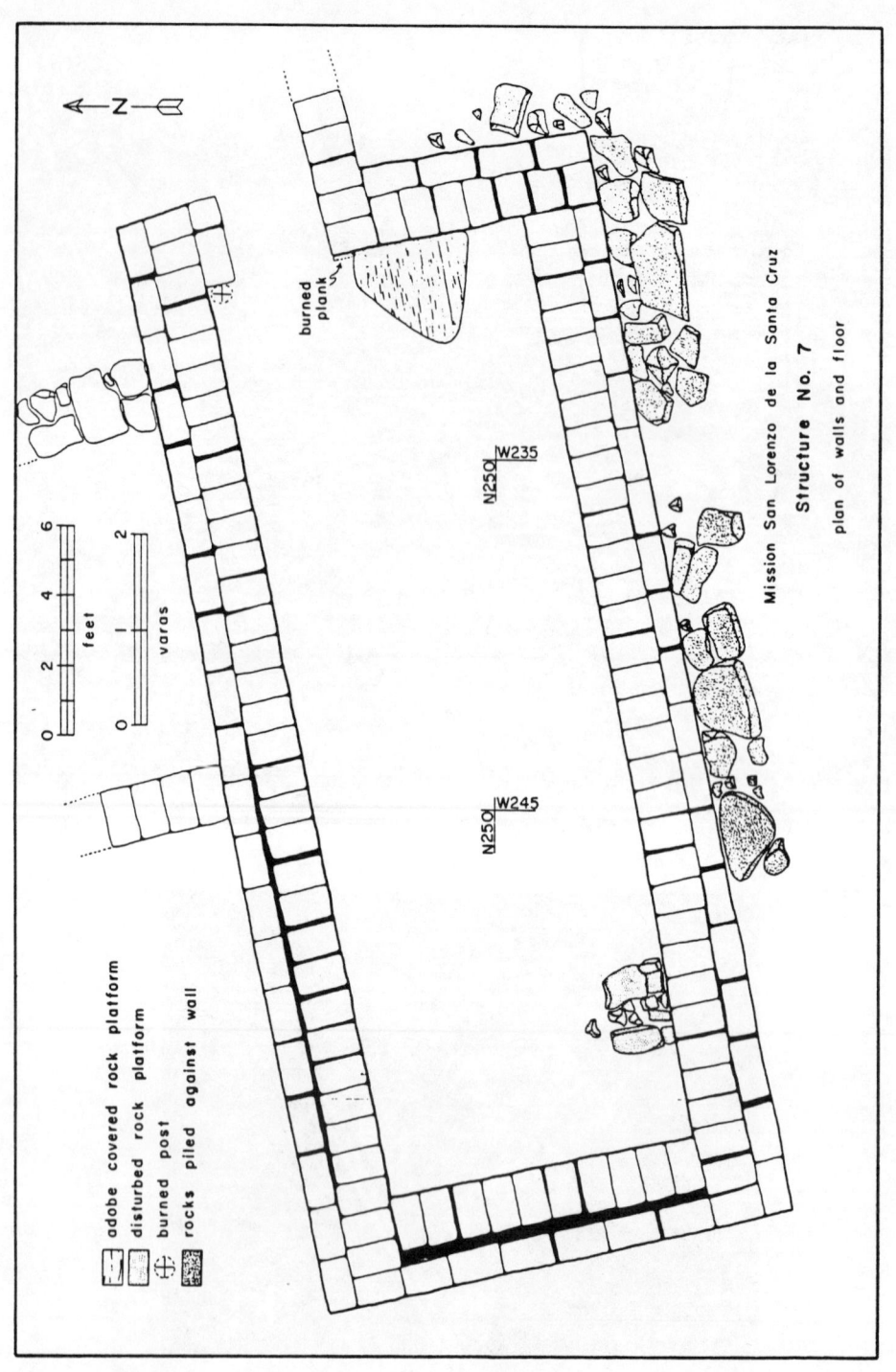

foot. The platform consisted of limestone slabs and cobbles, up to about 15 cm. in thickness and 30 cm. in diameter, carefully fitted together with adobe mortar and plastered with adobe to form vertical sides and a smooth, flat, upper surface. There was no sign of burning on the flat surface of this platform and its function is unknown.

Abutted against the interior of the south wall about 3 feet from the west wall was the base of a small rectangular stone platform. This feature was also formed of limestone slabs and cobbles (Fig. 13, B) set in adobe mortar, but it was not plastered on the edges. This platform was about 2.5 feet wide where it joined the wall and extended out into the room about 2 feet. The top of this feature was removed by the bulldozer, but it may have served as a platform for a hearth because wood ash was scattered on the floor around it.

Associated artifacts:
  Copper: 2 rolls
  Iron: 1 handmade nail
  Ceramics: 2 dark gray plainware; 9 amber glaze plainware; 2 clear glaze brown painted ware; 2 majolica
  Glass: 2 pale green bottle glass
  Stone: 1 Type 2 gunflint; 1 Type 3 gunflint; 3 cutting tools; 1 scraper flake; 2 Type 2 flakes; 6 Type 3 flakes; 9 Type 4 flakes; 16 miscellaneous flakes
  Shell: 2 miscellaneous
  Bone: 170 food bones

Structure 7 was completely excavated and mapped (Fig. 14). It was situated in the southwest corner of the plaza and probably served as the defensive bastion because: (1) It was the only corner structure which extended beyond the exterior wall of the plaza. (2) Defenders on the roof of this building could direct their fire along the outside of the south and west walls of the plaza. (3) Because of the topography, the southwest corner of the south and west walls of the plaza faced the direction from which an attack was most likely to originate. (4) The mass of heavy roof debris on the floor indicates that this building had an especially strong roof. (5) This was the only structure which had all four walls constructed with the thickest brick pattern No. 4, Fig. 4).

The primary mission midden was mounded from 1 to 2 feet deep around the outside walls of Structure 7 in a broad, fan-shaped deposit. The debris extending out from the wall 50 to 100 feet was 1.0 and 1.5 feet in depth. This large mound of trash undoubtedly was thrown from the top of the bastion which offered easy access to a sturdy roof. Considering the predominant southwesterly wind, this seems to have been an unfortunate choice of direction for trash disposal. A smaller concentration of midden debris which surrounded the outside northwest corner of the quadrangle (Structure 11) probably was thrown from the roofs of Structures 11, 12, and 13. The middens contained both Spanish and Indian artifacts plus large quantities of food bones, ashes, stones, and other debris.

Structure 8 (Fig. 15)

Excavation: This long, narrow building was heavily damaged by the bulldozing operation. Only about 10 to 15 cm. of fill and wall foundations remained intact. The entire structure was excavated, most of the fill was screened, and a wide strip outside the east, south, and west walls was cleared down to the old ground surface.

Location: Structure 8 was situated in the southeast corner of the plaza at about N278-W120 on the grid. The church (Structure 2) formed the north wall of this building and the south plaza wall lay to the west (Fig. 3). The west end of the building apparently had two doorways.

Dimensions: This building was longer in relation to its width than any other structure uncovered. Its central interior dimensions were about 11.5 feet N-S and 42.3 feet E-W.

Fill: About 10 to 15 cm. of fill composed of topsoil, disintegrated adobe, and cultural debris lay above and on the floor. In several large areas, especially in the western half of this structure, a thin (about 1 cm.) layer of heavily decomposed, brown, fibrous material lay on the floor surface. Samples of this material examined in the lab seem to be the remains of straw and animal manure.

Separated from the floor by several centimeters of soil and adobe wall debris, two large hearths were found in the western end of the building. These contained large amounts of ash, charcoal, and burned earth. The material from in and around these hearths was collected separately from that which was found on the structure floor or in the fill above the floor. All of the fill was removed and processed.

31

53

Mission San Lorenzo

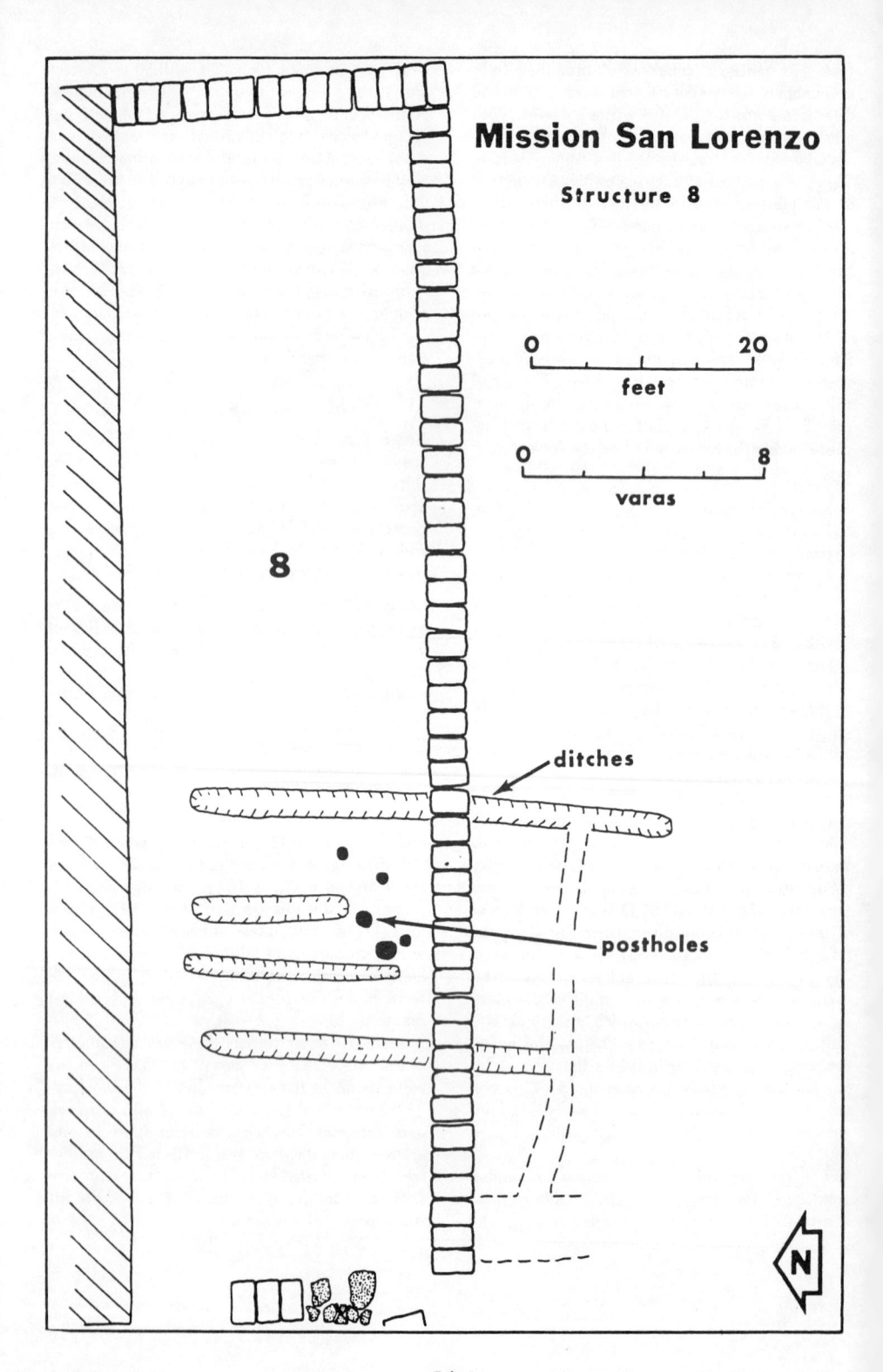

Structure 8

0 — 20 feet

0 — 8 varas

8

ditches

postholes

N

Wall construction: The south wall of the church formed the north wall of Structure 8. The east and south walls were formed by adobe bricks laid one brick length thick in Pattern Nos. 2 and 3 (Figs. 4, C. D). These walls averaged 1.5 feet thick and were built of dark adobe bricks set with dark mortar. There was only about a 5-foot long section of west wall between the two doorways, but it was identical to the south and east walls. The southwest corner of this building was not well aligned with the south plaza wall and a gap of about 2 feet resulted. Exactly how this gap was closed could not be determined, but there were numerous fragments of dark adobe bricks in the vicinity which may have helped plug it up.

Plaster: None was found.

Floors: There was a smooth and hard-packed surface just beneath the decomposed manure layer in this building, but no evidence of a prepared, puddled adobe floor was found. This hard-packed floor was cut by four deep, narrow trenches running along the short axis in the west end of the building, and several scattered postholes were cut through it (Fig. 15). The floor ranged in elevation from 99.47 feet in the northwest corner to 99.05 feet in the southeast corner.

Roof construction: No data.

Doors: Two doorways led through the west wall out onto the plaza—one through the north end of the wall was 4 feet wide and had no threshold or evidence of a door; the one through the south end was about 3 feet wide and had a flagstone threshold made from small limestone slabs (Fig. 15).

Hearths: No data.

Miscellaneous features: Situated in the western end of Structure 8 were four narrow parallel trenches cut through the floor of the building parallel to its short axis (Fig. 15). These trenches ranged from 0.6 to 1.0 foot in width, averaged about 1.0 foot in depth, and were spaced from 1.5 to 3 feet apart. All four trenches originated about 2 feet from the north wall. The east and west ones extended out under the south wall of the building and connected to a cross trench and the other two ended 1 to 3 feet inside the south wall. Small stones, gravel, and soil filled the

Fig. 15. Structure 8 showing ditches and postholes.

trenches up to the floor level. Apparently these served as drainage ditches for the west end of the building.

In a cluster among the trenches were five postholes which penetrated the floor near the south wall. These postholes ranged from 12 to 23 cm. in diameter, were about 30 cm. deep, and were spaced from about 6 to 36 cm. apart.

A cluster of small chunks of limestone lay on the floor about 2 feet from the center of the west wall. There were about 25 stones in this group and they averaged about 10 cm. in diameter.

Associated artifacts:
  Copper: 1 patch; 1 perforated overlay
  Iron: 3 unidentified objects; 1 bit fragment; 1 pronged object
  Lead: 1 sprue; 2 discs
  Ceramics: 2 red-slipped plainware; 1 miscellaneous non-wheel-made earthenware; 12 amber glaze plainware; 8 clear glaze brown painted ware; 4 majolica; 7 wheel-made unglazed red-slipped ware
  Glass: 2 pale green bottle glass; 21 recent bottle glass (1 bottle)
  Stone: 1 Type 5 gunflint; 3 choppers; 1 spokeshave; 1 Type 1 flake; 1 Type 2 flake; 3 Type 3 flakes; 2 Type 4 flakes; 9 miscellaneous flakes
  Shell: 3 scrapers; 3 miscellaneous
  Bone: 1 ulna tool; 98 food bones

It is assumed that Structure 8 served as a stable because: (1) The structure had no prepared adobe floor—only a hard-packed dirt floor. (2) Large patches of decomposed manure and straw lay on the floor in the west end. (3) The trenches probably served to drain away animal waste products and keep the floor relatively dry. (4) The postholes situated among the trenches probably mark the locations of tether posts for animals which were kept in the area.

The eastern half of the building had a clean floor which was devoid of features and, if the building was indeed a stable, may have served for storage of hay for the animals. If these interpretations are correct, the building may have accomodated several choice milk cows and a few fleet horses for use by the missionaries.

In the fill above (and separated from) the floor of this structure were several large hearths filled with ash and food debris and numerous Spanish and Indian artifacts. It is probable that this represents a temporary campsite made in the

33

lee of the church walls after the mission was burned and abandoned. One broken bottle in a disturbed area probably was left during the Camp Wood occupation in the mid-nineteenth century.

Structure 9 (Fig. 12)

Excavation: Structure 9 was in the heavily bulldozed portion of the site. Wall foundations were completely exposed so the exact size, location, and orientation of the building could be recorded, but the fill was not excavated. Several centimeters of fill still remained on the floor.

Location: Structure 9 was situated against the central portion of the east quadrangle wall between Structures 3 to the north, 6 to the west, and 5 to the south. Its grid location was about N345-W107 and the long axis was oriented with magnetic north.

Dimensions: The central interior dimensions were about 30 feet N-S and 14 feet E-W, or about 5 by 11 *varas*.

Fill: Some dark soil and roof debris covered the floor of the building.

Wall construction: All four walls were made of unprepared limestone slabs, up to 2.5 feet in diameter and averaging about 0.3 foot in thickness, set in dark brown clay mortar and leveled and spaced with limestone slivers. From one to two courses of stone remained in the wall foundations except for the east end of the north wall and the west end of the south wall which had been completely removed during the bulldozing of the site. The remaining wall foundations averaged about 2.7 feet or 1 *vara* in thickness.

Plaster: No data.

Floors: A shallow test pit in one corner of the room indicated that the floor was made of puddled adobe.

Roof construction: No data.

Doors: Apparently there had been a doorway in the center of the south wall leading into Structure 5, but it was heavily damaged by the bulldozer. It is possible that there was also a doorway leading through the east end of the north wall into Structure 3.

Hearths: No data.

Miscellaneous features: No data.

Associated artifacts: None.

This large and sturdily built structure probably was part of the friary which was built at the same time as the sacristy (Structure 5 to the south) and the church.

Structure 10 (Fig. 17)

Excavation: This was the first structure excavated in the unbulldozed portion of the site. It was visible on the surface as a large smooth mound covered with vegetation—no walls or outlines were visible. After the vegetation was cleared, the bases of the adobe walls were encountered just beneath the grass roots (Fig. 19. B). About 3 feet of stratified fill was removed from the inside of the building, exposing the entire floor. The fill in the east third of the building was removed in arbitrary levels down to the floor, then the remainder of the fill was excavated by natural strata using the vertical profile (Fig. 18) as a guide. The fill against the outside of the walls was left undisturbed to help protect the walls, and at the end of the field season this structure was backfilled in order to preserve it.

Location: Structure 10 occupied the northeast corner of the quadrangle at about N412-W115 on the grid. The main gate leading into the plaza from outside was just south of this building, and the area to the west was not excavated.

Dimensions: The outside wall dimensions were 36.2 feet north, 16.2 feet east, 33.6 feet south, and 15.8 feet west. The central interior dimensions were 11.2 feet N-S and 30.6 feet E-W, or about 4 by 11 *varas*.

Fill: About 3 feet of well-stratified fill in this structure showed clearly how the buildings of San Lorenzo had filled and become low mounds (Fig. 18). (1) Lying on the flagstone floor was from 12 to 35 cm. of loose, grayish soil which contained large quantities of burned roof material and wall plaster which probably was deposited as the building was burned and abandoned. (2) Above this material was a layer of dark brown sandy soil from 15 to 40 cm. thick which probably drifted into the ruined structure before the walls began to collapse. It contained

Fig. 16. Excavation of northeast corner of quadrangle showing Structure 10 with its cobblestone floor. Looking east.

an occasional stone but was otherwise sterile. (3) Next was a layer composed almost entirely of melted adobe and fragments of adobe bricks, and it must have represented the material deposited by the walls as they collapsed down to where they were protected by the growing mound of debris. (4) The top layer, lying on the collapsed wall material and covering the remaining wall bases, was a dark brown sandy soil from about 15 to 40 cm. in thickness.

Wall construction: All four walls were built with adobe bricks—the north, east, and south walls were one brick length plus one brick width in thickness and generally were in Pattern No. 4 (Fig. 4, B), and the west wall was one brick length in thickness in Pattern No. 3 (Fig. 4, D). At several places in the walls there were anomalies in the brick patterns (Fig. 19, C, D) such as several courses of bricks laid identically (one brick directly superimposed on the one below) without breaking the joints. These anomalies were usually not more than three courses in height and four bricks in length.

The east wall and about 3 feet of the east end of the north wall were oriented exactly with magnetic north (and the grid) but the remaining walls were oriented about 15 degrees off magnetic north. This gave the building an unusual outline (Fig. 17). The masons may have begun Structure 10 by laying the base of the east wall oriented with the previously finished buildings, but when they turned the corner and began laying the north wall they found that a rather steep slope made it necessary to orient the remaining walls of the structure about 15 degrees off magnetic north. As construction progressed around the quadrangle (probably along the north wall, then the west wall, and finally the south wall, back to the original buildings) the new structures were all oriented off-north like No. 10.

The walls of Structure 10 were preserved beneath the mound of rubble to a height of about 3 feet. The north, east, and south walls averaged about 2.7 feet or 1 *vara* in thickness.

Plaster: Large quantities of wall plaster were found in the debris on the floor. This plaster, made of fine river sand and lime, was very similar to that found on the interior of the church. It averaged from 1 to 3 cm. in thickness and some fragments showed evidence of having been applied in two layers with whitewash between. Some plaster was still in place along the base of the east and south walls.

Floors: This was the only building excavated which had a flagstone floor. Since this was the storehouse and granary, a good dry, durable stone floor was probably considered to be a necessity.

The flagstones were all limestone slabs up to about 3.5 feet in diameter, but averaging about 2 feet in diameter and 0.5 foot in thickness. Spaces between the larger stones were filled with small limestone fragments (Fig. 19, A) and a dark brown clay mortar filled the cracks and kept the stones tightly in position. The floor was quite smooth but sloped slightly from east to west with a maximum elevation of 98.75 feet along the east wall and a minimum of 98.03 feet along the west wall.

Four flagstones, all about 1 foot in diameter, had been removed from the floor. Three of these were situated along the south wall in the west end of the room and the other was centrally located about 5 feet from the center of the west wall (Fig. 17).

Roof construction: The roof was constructed like that described for Structure 7. Large quantities of burned roof debris lay on the floor and various samples of it were collected.

Doors: One doorway led from the building, through the south-central part of the west wall, into the plaza. This doorway was 3.7 feet wide and the walls abutting it were faced with vertical adobe slabs about 0.3 foot in thickness. There was no evidence of how the door had been attached to this opening. A layer of sandy plaster about 0.1 foot thick served as a threshold and extended out into the room for about 1.5 foot.

Hearths: Apparently there was none.

Miscellaneous features: As previously mentioned, four small flagstones had been removed from the floor—three adjacent to the south wall and one centrally situated near the doorway. This latter hole was cleaned out and contained a post mold about 15 cm. in diameter extending about 30 cm. below floor level. Each of these four features probably represents where posts were inserted in the floor and served to brace sagging *vigas* in the roof.

36

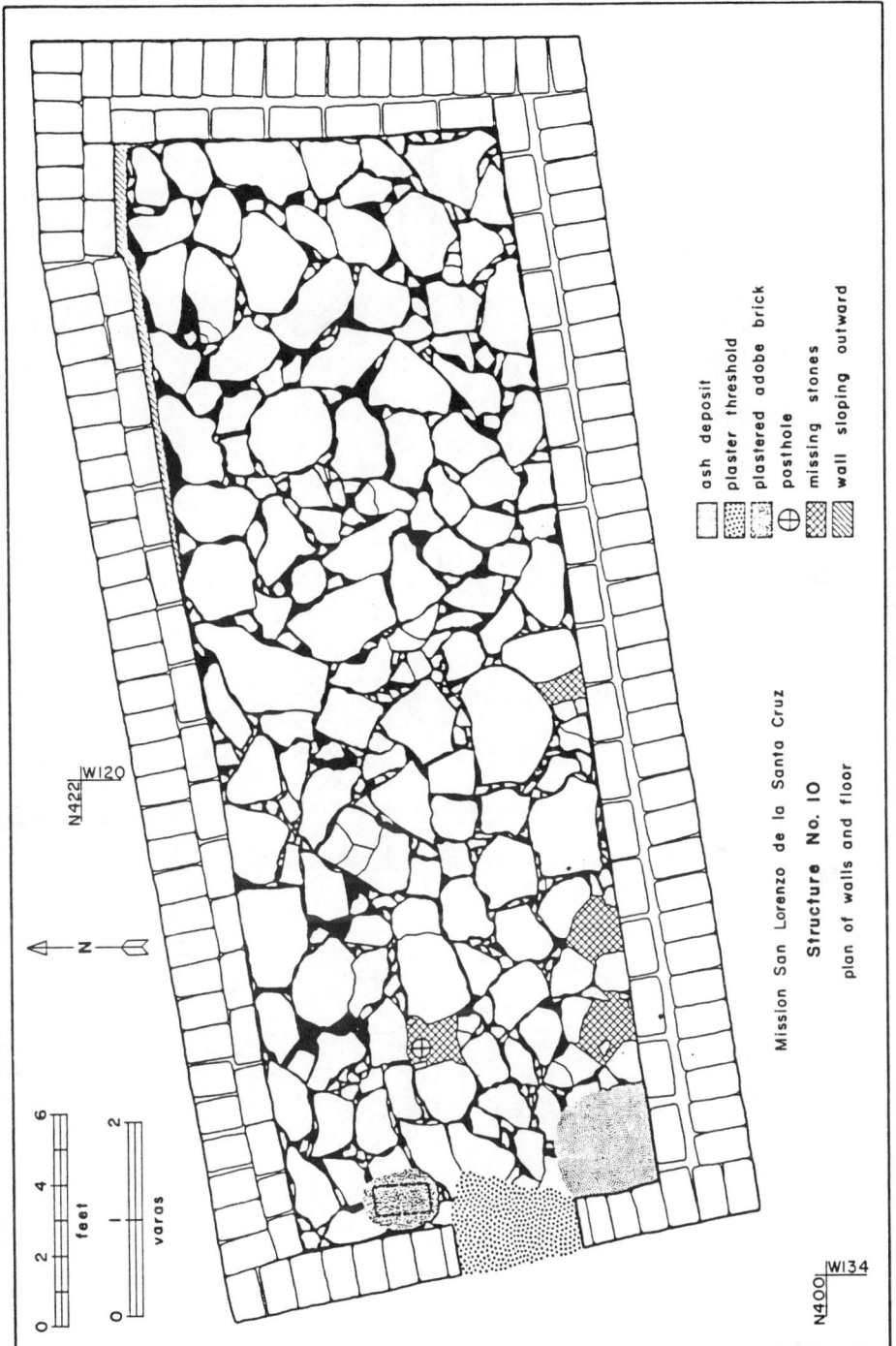

Fig. 17. Structure 10, plan of walls and floor.

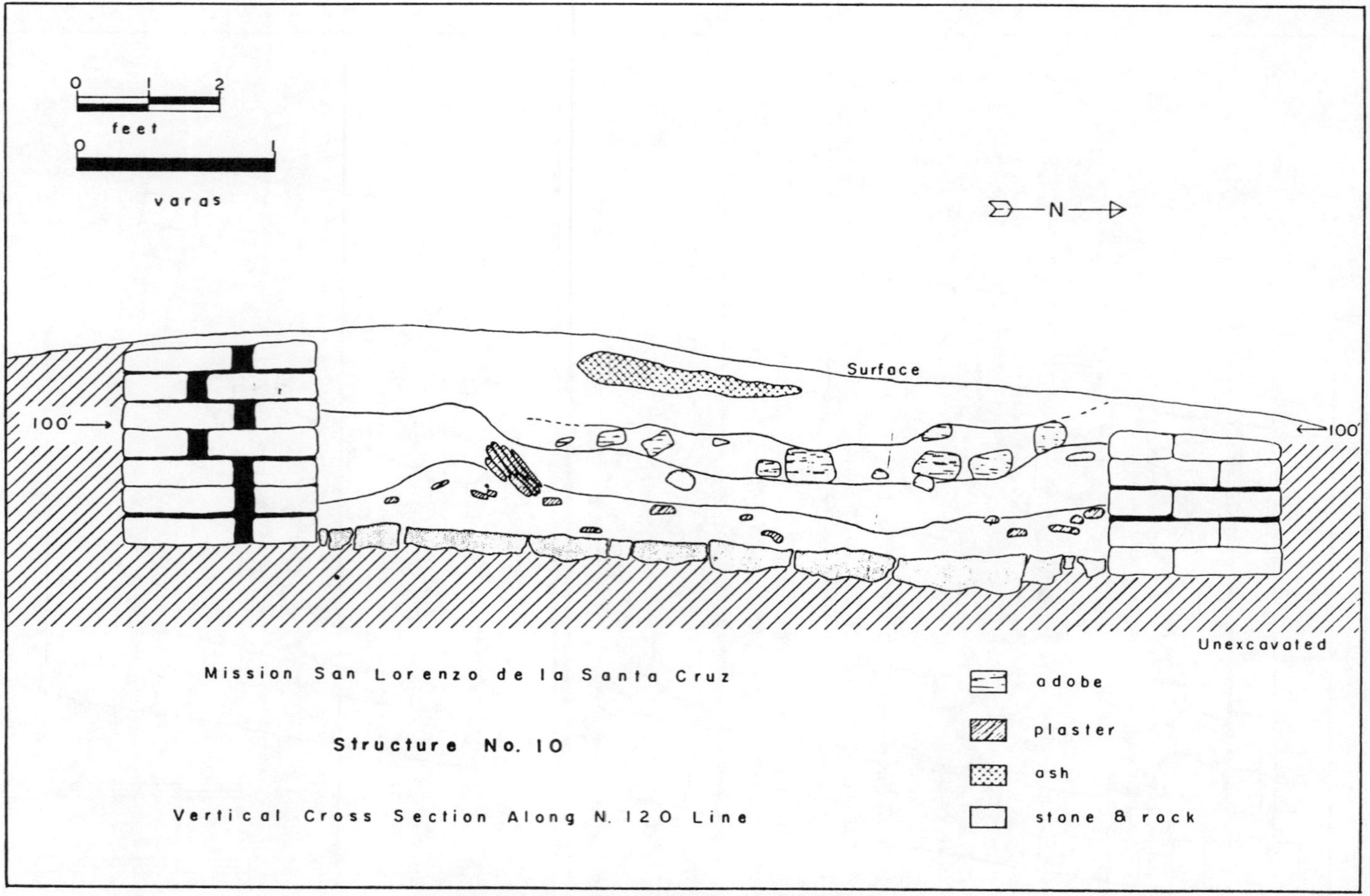

Fig. 18. Structure 10, vertical cross section along N. 120 line.

Along the base of the south wall, about 10 feet from the west wall, there was a crack about 0.1 foot wide, 2 feet long, and 0.5 foot deep between the plaster and the brick wall. This cavity was completely filled with grains of shelled corn, (Fig. 60) which had apparently fallen through cracks in the plaster and were charred when the building burned. Dr. Hugh Cutler of the Missouri Botanical Gardens furnished the following comments on the charred corn grains found in Structure 10:

... carbonized kernels, mainly from 14–16–18-rowed long-grained dents, similar to recent Southern and some Mexican dents. There are a few kernels from 8 or 10-rowed ears, usually shorter and broader in proportion and apparently also dent corn. The long-grain dents are 4–5 mm. thick, 8–9 mm. wide, 10–11 mm. long. A few have a burned area in the center of the top of the grain and the surrounding hard shoulders are puffed out. All kernels were carbonized when loose, not on cobs.
... These dent corns are similar to some Southern dents which were grown in the delta region and perhaps along part of the east Texas coast in early historic times and may have been grown there in prehistoric times. I suspect that your [the San Lorenzo] dents came from Mexico where a number of races of corn, with kernels almost identical to yours, may still be found today and has been grown since at least 1300 A.D. In other words, your [San Lorenzo] corn is probably introduced from Mexico and does not represent the native kinds of corn.

Situated in the southwest corner was a stockpile of fine quality lime about 3 feet in diameter and a maximum of 0.83 foot in height. This probably was produced in the mission limekiln and used to make fine plaster for the buildings and as a whitewash.

Just north of the doorway and about 10 cm. from the wall, a single adobe brick lying on its side was plastered to the floor. It possibly served as a kneeling block beneath an icon.

Associated artifacts:
 Ceramics: 2 amber glaze plainware
 Bone: 10 food bones

Structure 10 was the best preserved of all the excavated buildings. This undoubtedly was the storehouse and granary mentioned in the documents as being built after the church, sacristy, and friary. The following data support this identification: (1) It was a sturdily constructed building, situated near the main gate, and the only structure with a durable, dry, flagstone floor. (2) Shelled corn was found between the plaster and the wall (the only occurrence at the site). (3) Pure white lime was stored in one corner. (4) There was no hearth for either cooking or heating.

Structure 10 was backfilled at the end of the field season to protect it from weathering and vandals.

Structure 11 (Fig. 21)

Excavation: Structure 11 was situated in the northwest corner of the quadrangle. This area was not bulldozed and was covered with low mounds of rubble supporting cactus and shrubs (Fig. 23, A). The fill of the room was removed by natural strata and screened.

Location: This room was in the extreme northwest corner with Structure 12 to the east and Structure 13 to the south. It was at about N397-W274 on the grid.

Dimensions: The interior dimensions of this room were 11.3 feet N-S and 14.2 feet E-W, or about 4 by 5 *varas*.

Fill: The fill was very similar to that of Structure 10, but it was only about 1.5 feet deep. A relatively large quantity of food bones, artifacts, and other debris lay on the floor beneath the roof and wall rubble.

Wall construction: All four walls were built of adobe bricks. The north, west, and south walls were one brick length plus one brick width in thickness (Pattern No. 4, Fig. 4, B) and averaged about 2.5 feet thick. The east wall was a partition one brick width in thickness (Pattern No. 1, Fig. 4, A) which was interlocked into the more massive side walls (Fig. 21). The remaining wall bases were from 1 to 1.5 feet high.

Plaster: Fragments of coarse, thick, dull brown plaster were found in the fill and around the bases of the walls in a few places. These fragments were up to 3 cm. thick and some had been applied in 2 or 3 layers.

Floors: The floor consisted of the smooth surface of limestone bedrock which had been leveled by filling the low spots with puddled adobe—about

39

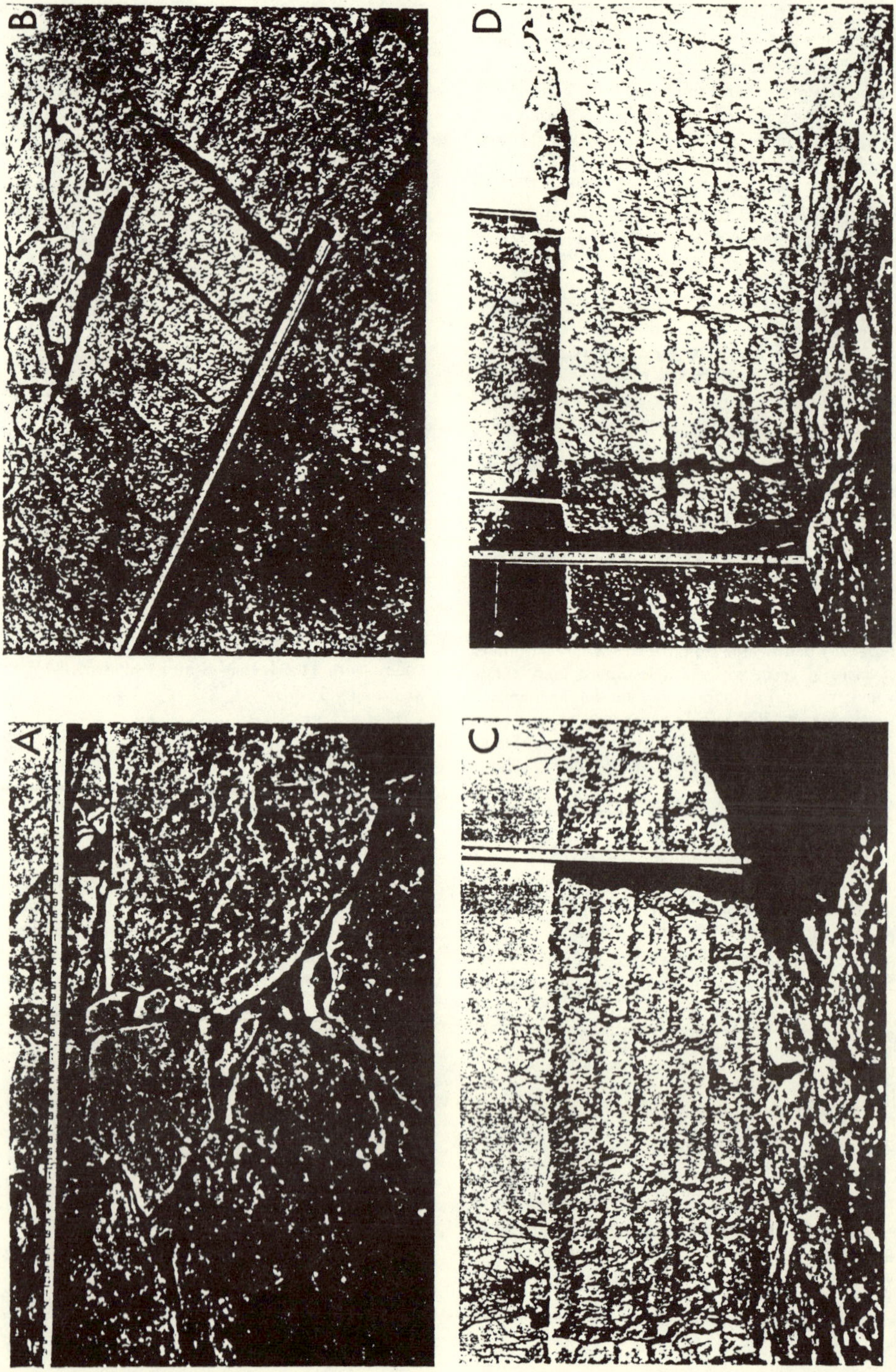
A
B
C
D

50 per cent of the floor area was covered with the patches of adobe (Fig. 21). The floor ranged from 98.63 to 99.51 feet in elevation.

Roof construction: The roof construction was the same as described for Structure 7. Small quantities of burned roof debris lay on the floor fill.

Doors: One doorway led from this room through the eastern end of the south wall, into Structure 13. This doorway was 2.9 feet in width, and had a threshold composed of two layers of adobe bricks (about 0.66 foot in height) capped with a layer of puddled adobe about 0.2 foot thick. The exterior edge of this threshold ended in an abrupt step, but on the inside of the room a fan-shaped, puddled adobe ramp sloped gently from the threshold down to the floor (Fig. 21). There was no evidence to indicate how a door was attached to close this doorway.

Hearths: There were several lenses of wood ash on the floor, but no intensively burned area was found.

Miscellaneous features: From 20 to about 40 cm. of midden debris was mounded against the exterior north wall of this room (Fig. 3) and probably was thrown from its roof.

Associated artifacts:
Iron: 1 unidentified lump
Lead: 1 disc
Ceramics: 1 non-wheel-made red-slipped plainware; 8 amber glaze plainware; 1 majolica; 1 stoneware, white, salt-glazed
Glass: 1 pale green flat glass
Stone: 1 Type 5 gunflint; 1 spokeshave; 1 Type 1 flake; 4 Type 2 flakes; 3 Type 3 flakes; 1 Type 4 flake; 10 miscellaneous flakes; 1 metate fragment; 1 chert core, No. 2
Bone: 182 food bones.

The occurrence of a metate fragment, numerous chert flakes, a large chert core, cactus fruit seeds, and many food bones suggests that a family of mission Indians may have used this structure. The mission soldiers may have lived in rooms nearer the bastion (Structure 7). Structure 11 was backfilled for preservation.

Fig. 19. Excavation of Structure 10. A, flagstone floor; B, horizontal adobe brick patterns in wall at southeast corner; C, vertical adobe brick patterns in east wall; D, vertical adobe brick patterns, north wall.

Structure 12 (Fig. 21)

Excavation: This room, located in the unbulldozed part of the site, was completely excavated. About 1 to 1.5 feet of fill was removed by natural strata and screened, but the room was backfilled before the end of the field season.

Location: This room was situated against the north wall just east of Structure 11 in the northwest corner and adjacent to Structure 15. The approximate grid location of Structure 12 was N400-W258. It was one of a row of small rooms separated by narrow partition walls.

Dimensions: The central interior dimensions of Structure 12 were 11.3 feet N-S and 14 feet E-W, or about 4 by 5 *varas*.

Fill: About 1.5 feet of fill, stratified in the usual manner, lay above the floor, and living debris littered the floor surface.

Wall construction: The north and south walls were made of adobe bricks, one brick length plus one brick width in thickness (Pattern No. 4, Fig. 4, B), and the east and west walls were adobe brick partitions only one brick width in thickness (Pattern No. 1, Fig. 4, A). The wall bases were from 1.5 to 2.0 feet in height after excavation.

Plaster: Fragments of coarse brown plaster up to about 3 cm. thick were found in the fill and adhering to the bases of the walls in several places.

Floors: A single puddled adobe floor had been poured over the uneven surface of limestone bedrock. The exposed bedrock surface formed the floor in the northwest corner of the room (Fig. 21). The adobe floor ranged up to about 4 cm. in thickness and had a smooth, hard, upper surface. The floor ranged from 99.30 to 99.57 feet in elevation.

Roof construction: Small fragments of burned roof debris from the fill indicated that the roof was constructed in the same manner as described for Structure 7.

Doors: One doorway, leading through the east end of the south wall (Fig. 21) into the plaza, was 3.2 feet wide. It showed no evidence of facing, or of a prepared threshold, or how the door was hung.

Hearths: A hearth was situated in the adobe floor about 2.5 feet from the center of the south

41

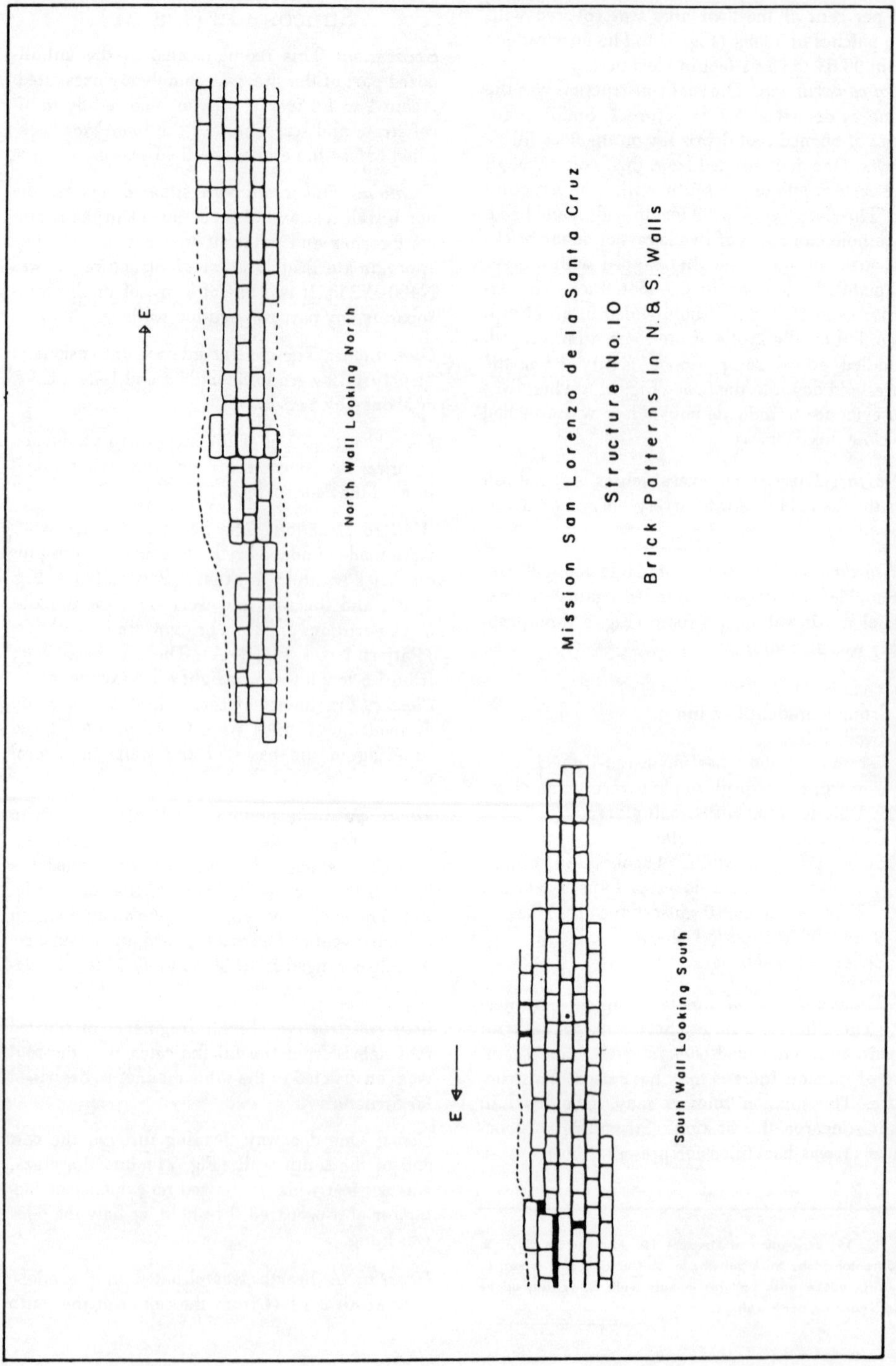

Fig. 20. Structure 10, brick patterns in north and south walls.

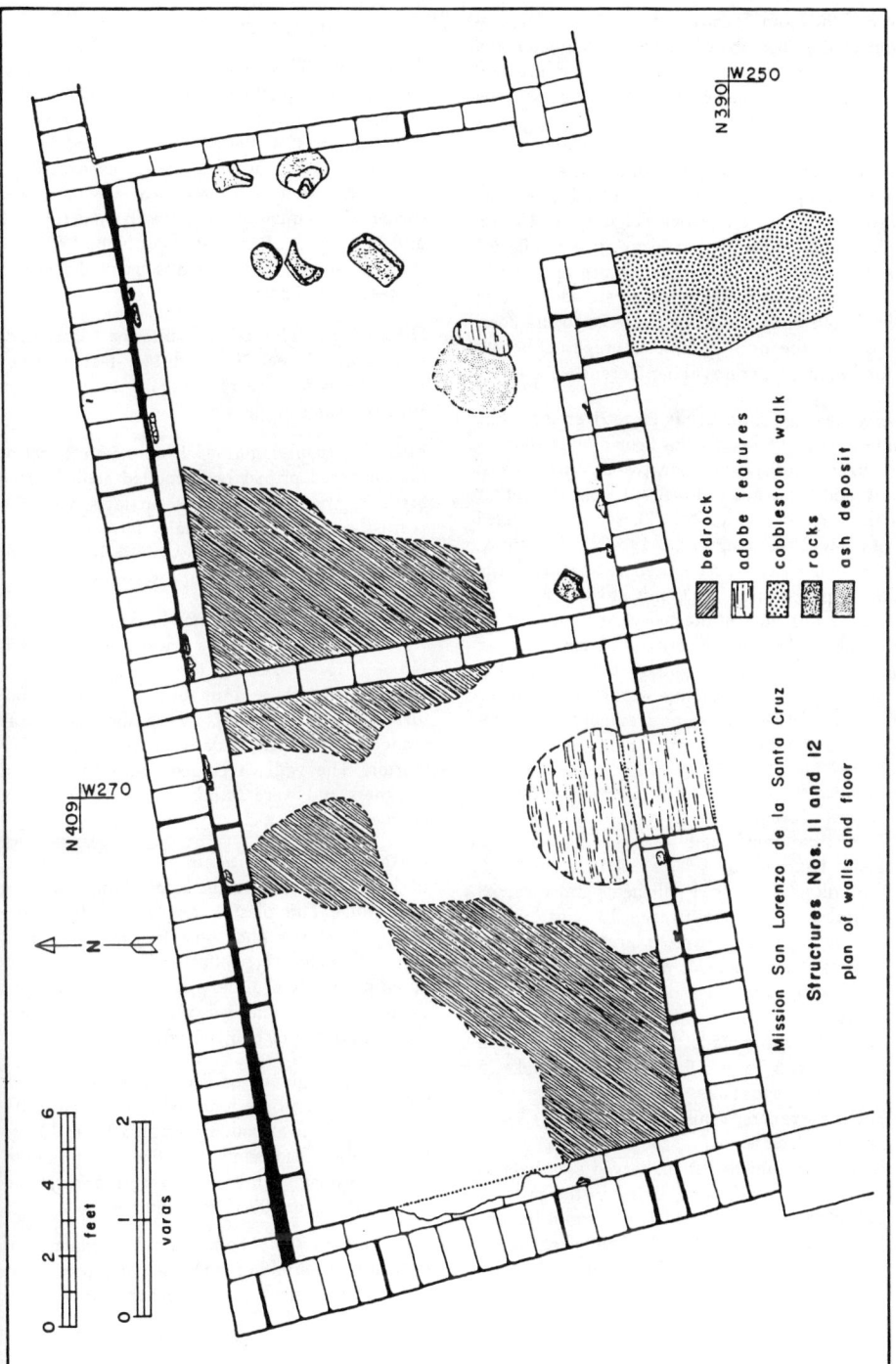

Fig. 21. Structures 11 and 12, plan of walls and floor.

wall of the room. It consisted of a circular depression in the floor about 2.5 feet in diameter and 0.13 foot in maximum depth. This depression was baked hard and contained light gray wood ash which produced evidence of burned eggshells and bone slivers when examined microscopically in the laboratory. Along the southeast edge of the depression—between the hearth and the doorway—was a smooth adobe ridge about 15 cm. high which probably served as an air deflector for the fire (Fig. 21). This feature apparently was formed by a fragment of an adobe brick which had been smoothly plastered to the floor. This was the only complete, prepared hearth found in the structures at San Lorenzo.

Miscellaneous features: Six large river-smoothed limestone rocks lay on the floor of this room—one in the southwest corner, two against the east wall, and three about 3 feet out from the center of the east wall (Fig. 22). These stones ranged from 1 to 2 feet long and 0.3 to 0.66 foot thick. They do not seem to have been incorporated into platforms and their function is unknown.

At the west edge of the doorway, a cobblestone walk about 2.7 feet (1 *vara*) wide led from the exterior surface of the wall southward into the plaza (Fig. 3). It was composed of a single layer of closely spaced limestone fragments and cobbles from about 6 to 15 cm. in diameter.

Associated artifacts:
  Copper: 2 strips
  Iron: 1 handmade nail
  Lead: 1 sprue
  Ceramics: 2 dark red polished plainware; 28 amber glaze plainware; 13 clear glaze brown painted ware; 3 green glaze olive jars; 2 majolica; 1 wheel-made unglazed red-slipped ware; 1 dark brown appliquéd ware
  Stone: 1 scraper blade; 1 scraper flake; 4 Type 2 flakes; 5 Type 3 flakes; 1 Type 4 flake; 6 miscellaneous flakes
  Shell: 3 scrapers; 2 miscellaneous
  Bone: 46 food bones

It is likely that this room served as a habitation, probably for Indians living in the mission establishment, because: (1) It was small in size. (2) It contained a hearth. (3) The floor was littered with potsherds, food bones, and other debris. (4) Chert tools and flakes and red ochre were found on the floor.

44

Structure 13 (Fig. 24)

Excavation: This small room, like the two preceding ones, was situated in the unbulldozed area of the site and was relatively well preserved beneath mounds of melted adobe covered by native vegetation. It was completely excavated.

Location: Structure 13 was near the northwest corner of the quadrangle between Structures 11 and 14 (Fig. 3). It was at about N387-W270 on the grid. and its short axis was oriented about 15 degrees west of north.

Dimensions: The central interior dimensions were about 7 feet N-S and 14.4 feet E-W, or about 2.5 by 5 *varas*. This was the smallest structure excavated at the site.

Fill: The room contained from 1.5 to 2 feet of fill composed primarily of melted adobe, adobe brick fragments, roof debris, artifacts, wind-deposited sand, and an especially large amount of wall plaster (described below). The fill was carefully excavated by hand and screened.

Wall construction: The north, west, and south walls were made of adobe bricks laid in Pattern No. 4 (Fig. 4, B). The north wall was shared with Structure 11 and the south wall with Structure 14. The east wall, facing the plaza, was made of flat limestone slabs set with brown clay mortar. The walls averaged about 2.2 feet in thickness and were standing about 2 feet high after excavation.

Plaster: Large quantities of plaster were present in the room fill and on the bases of the south and west walls. This plaster ranged from 0.2 to 0.3 foot in thickness and some fragments up to 2 feet in diameter were collected. The plaster, composed primarily of lime, ash, and soil, was light in weight. It contained very little sand and showed no sign of paint or whitewash.

Floors: A single adobe floor about 3 cm. thick lay partially on limestone bedrock and partially on dark brown topsoil. Penetrated by the large hearth (described below), the floor had a smooth surface, sloped slightly east to west, and ranged in elevation from 99.19 to 99.60 feet.

Roof construction: Some small fragments of burned roof found in the fill indicated that it was constructed in the same manner as that of Structure 7.

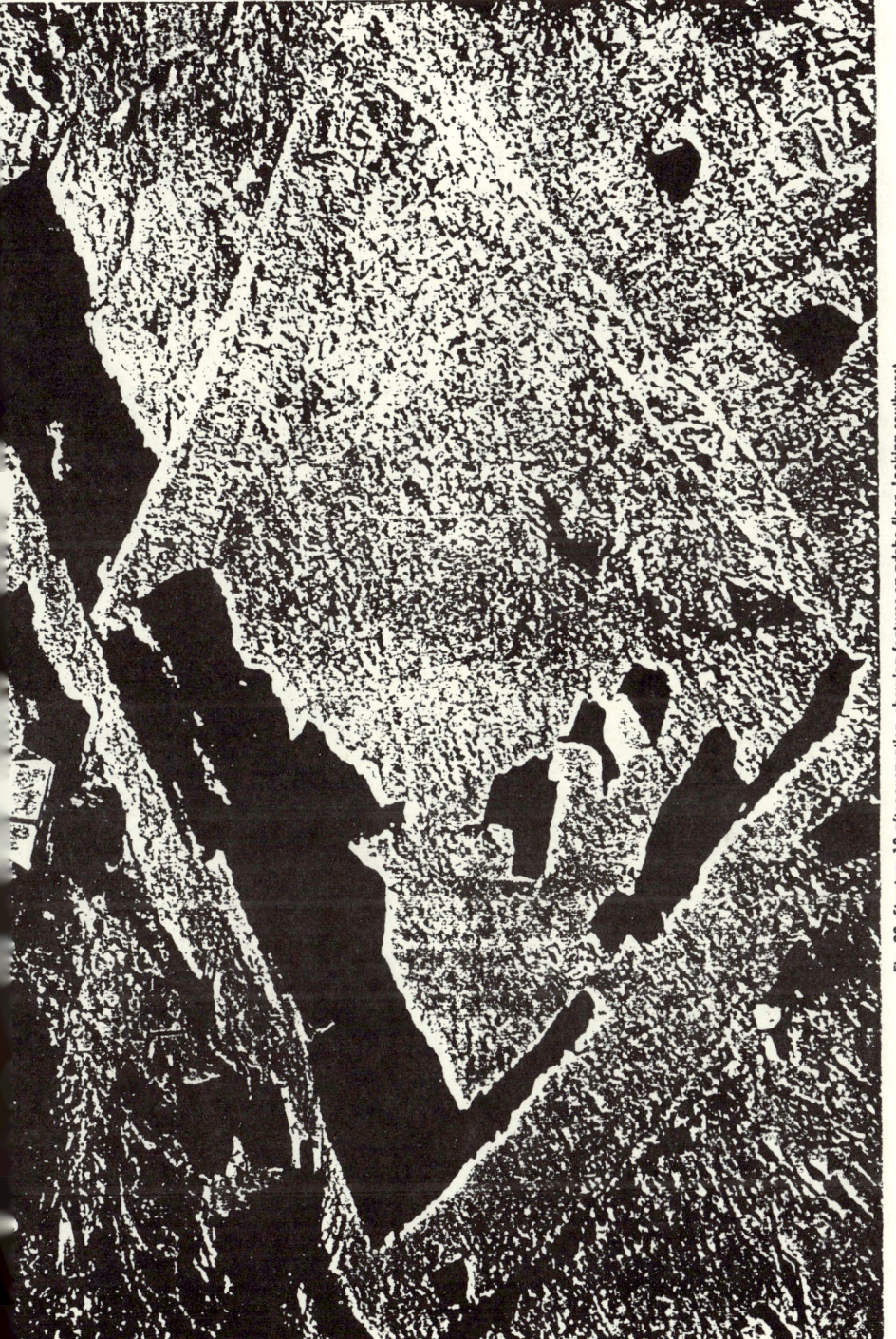

Fig. 22. Structure 12 after excavation, showing features on adobe floor. Looking southwest.

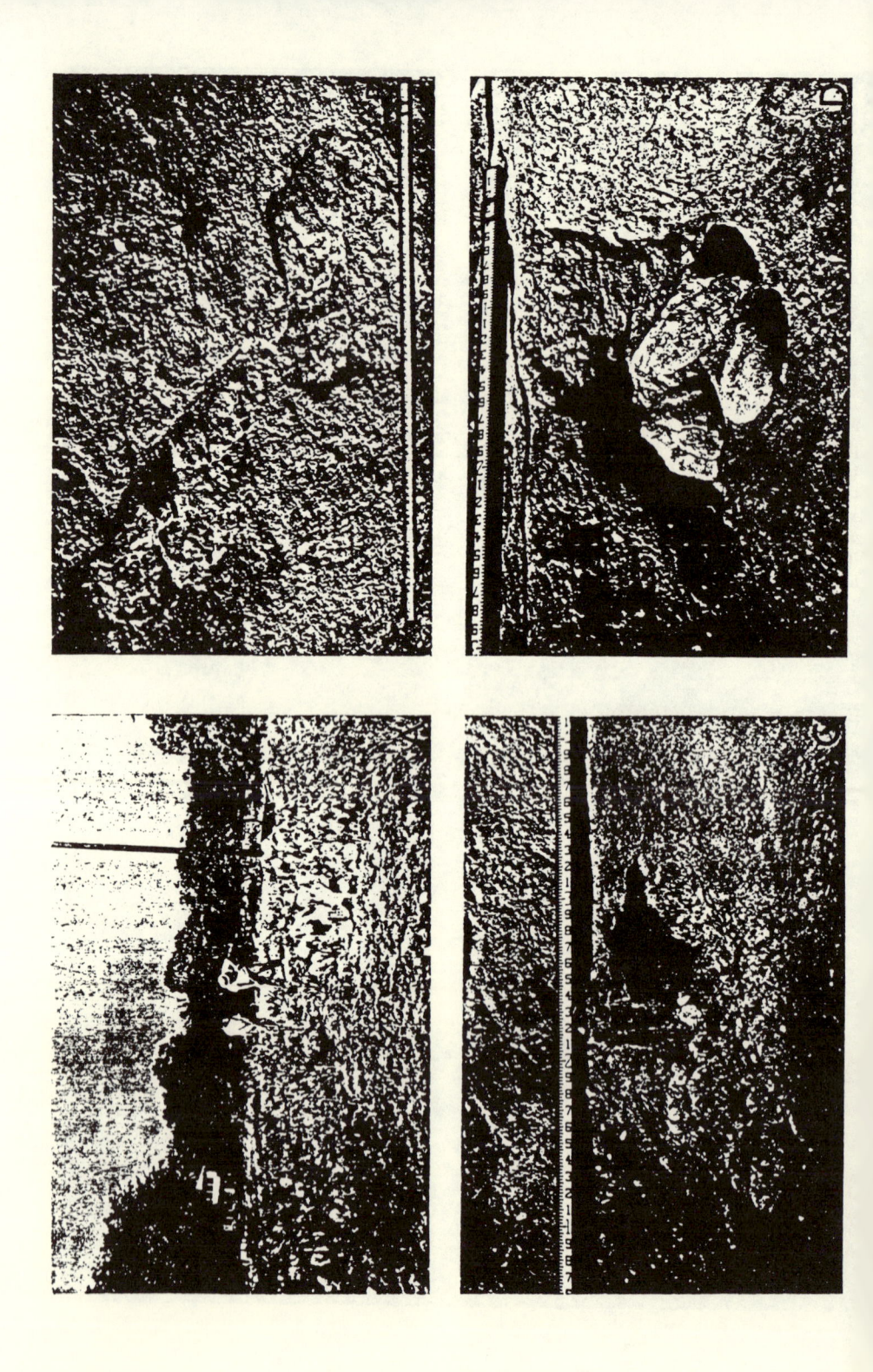

68

Doors: One doorway led through the east end of the north wall (see Structure 11 for description). Another doorway, about 2.6 feet or 1 *vara* in width, opened through the north end of the east wall into the plaza. It showed no evidence of a threshold nor how the door had been attached. A disturbed area near the east end of the south wall (Fig. 24) appeared to be a doorway which had been plugged with adobe brick fragments and stones. Its original characteristics could not be determined.

Hearths: One large oval hearth occupied the southwest corner of this small room (Fig. 24). It was about 5 feet long NE-SW, and about 4 feet wide, and penetrated the floor to a depth of about 0.66 foot. It consisted of a large, unlined pit which showed some evidence of burning on the bottom and around the edges. The pit contained about 20 cm. of concentrated, light gray wood ash, a few potsherds, some rust fragments which had probably been nails, and microscopic fragments of burned eggshell, bone and other debris.

Miscellaneous features: In the northwest corner of the room, a hole about 2 feet wide and 1 foot high penetrated the exterior quadrangle wall at floor level. Three large smooth limestone cobbles were wedged into the hole to plug it (Fig. 23, D). This feature may have served as a ventilator to create a draft for the large hearth described above.

Associated artifacts:
 Copper: 1 roll; 1 rivet; 1 perforated overlay; 1 buckle
 Iron: 5 unidentified lumps; 5 unidentified objects; 1 ladle
 Ceramics: 2 polychrome polished; 4 red polished decorated ware; 4 red-slipped plainware; 1 non-wheel-made miscellaneous; 48 amber glaze plainware; 20 clear brown painted ware; 1 green glaze olive jar; 3 miscellaneous lead glazed; 14 majolica; 7 wheel-made unglazed red-slipped ware; 1 dark brown appliquéd ware; 3 hard paste blue featheredge

Fig. 23. Excavation in northwest corner of quadrangle. A, initial clearing; B, adobe floor on bedrock in Structure 11; C, burned roof support post in floor of Structure 14; D, boulder-plugged hole in west wall of Structure 13.

 Glass: 1 pale green flat glass
 Beads: 1 coral; 3 glass
 Stone: 1 type 5 gunflint; 1 cutting tool, 1 scraper flake; 1 spokeshave; 3 Type 2 flakes; 5 Type 3 flakes; 4 Type 4 flakes; 13 miscellaneous flakes
 Shell: 1 miscellaneous
 Bone: 6 cut ribs; 475 food bones

This small structure probably served as a food preparation room for the following reasons: (1) There was a very large ash basin in the floor and a probable vent hole in the wall. (2) The floor was littered with potsherds and food bones. (3) A common kitchen would have made it unnecessary to have large cooking hearths in other quarters—and most structures did not contain hearths. (4) From a kitchen in this corner, food rations could have been conveniently distributed to soldiers and Indians in the rows of living quarters along the west and north walls. (5) A copper pot rivet and an iron ladle were found on the floor.

Structure 14 (Fig. 24)

Excavation: Structure 14, undisturbed by the bulldozer, was one of the last rooms excavated and could not be completely cleared before the end of the field season.

Location: This room was situated along the northern end of the west side of the quadrangle between Structures 1 and 13 at about N370-W268 on the grid.

Dimensions: The interior width near the north end was 14.1 feet or about 5 *varas*. Other dimensions were not determined.

Fill: About 2 feet of the usual fill lay above the floor of this building. There was an especially thick layer (up to about 8 cm.) of refuse between the floor and the fallen roof and wall debris which seemed to have accumulated while the structure was in use. In order to accelerate excavation, the upper fill was removed rapidly with shovels, but the material on the floor was troweled up and processed on the screens.

Wall construction: The north and west walls were about 2.3 feet thick and made of adobe bricks laid in Pattern No. 4 (Fig. 4, B), the west wall forming part of the exterior quadrangle

47

wall. The east wall, facing the plaza, was built of unshaped limestone slabs up to about 2 feet across and 0.4 foot thick set in dark brown clay mortar. This wall was about 2 feet thick and was not as carefully constructed as were the stone walls of Structures 5, 6, and 9. When the fill was cleared, the wall bases stood about 2 feet high.

Plaster: There were traces of thick wall plaster in the north part of this room. The plaster was composed of soil with a small amount of lime and sand and it decomposes easily through weathering.

Floors: This structure had a prepared floor composed of dark dirt adobe. The upper floor surface was smooth but somewhat undulating and sloped upward slightly toward the north. The floor elevation ranged from 99.17 to 99.61 feet.

Roof construction: Small quantities of burned roof material in the fill of this room indicated that the roof was constructed like that of Structure 7. A few large fragments of charred *vigas* were oriented east-west and had apparently spanned the room across its short axis.

Doors: One doorway about 2.7 feet wide led through the east end of the north wall into Structure 13 at one time. This doorway had been thoroughly plugged with adobe bricks sometime during the mission occupation and its original characteristics could not be determined. Perhaps smoke from the large hearth in Structure 13 led to the plugging of this doorway. In the part of Structure 14 excavated, no other entrances were found.

Hearths: No prepared hearths were found in Structure 14, but there was a concentration of fine gray ash about 1.5 feet in diameter and 0.1 foot thick situated about 18 feet from the north wall and 3 feet from the west wall. Here, as in other structures, a small fire was apparently maintained directly on the floor.

Miscellaneous features: (1) Centered about 6 feet from the north wall and 4 feet from the east wall was a circular concentration of limestone slabs. This group of rocks, lying on the floor, was about 4 feet in diameter and the individual stones ranged from about 0.3 to 2.0 feet across. There were at least 25 stones in this concentration. Its function is unknown. (2) Seven large smooth chunks of limestone were laying on the floor (Fig. 24). These stones ranged in size from 1.0 foot in diameter and 0.3 foot thick, up to 2.0 feet in diameter and 1.0 foot thick, and like the ones in Structure 12, probably constituted part of the furnishings of the room. (3) The basal portion of the two burned-off posts were found near the west wall. These posts had been inserted in holes through the adobe floor. One post base, 0.5 foot in diameter, was centered 1.5 feet from the north wall and 1.2 feet from the west wall. These posts were probably installed to support the ends of sagging *vigas* and were destroyed when the structure was burned.

Associated artifacts:
Copper: 2 strips; 1 perforated overlay
Iron: 1 disc lunate
Lead: 1 ring
Ceramics: 1 polychrome polished; 4 dark red polished plainware; 28 amber glaze plainware; 13 clear glaze brown painted ware; 1 green glaze olive jar; 5 majolica
Glass: 1 pale green flat glass
Stone: 1 Type 1 gunflint; 1 Type 3 gunflint; 2 Type 2 flakes; 2 Type 3 flakes; 1 Type 4 flake; 9 miscellaneous flakes
Shell: 1 miscellaneous
Bone: 1 ulna tool; 1 cut rib; 118 food bones

The large amount of debris, apparently accumulated while the room was in use, would indicate that it served as living quarters. Spanish and Indian artifacts found on the floor along with a large quantity of food bones included such things as a complete bison scapula.

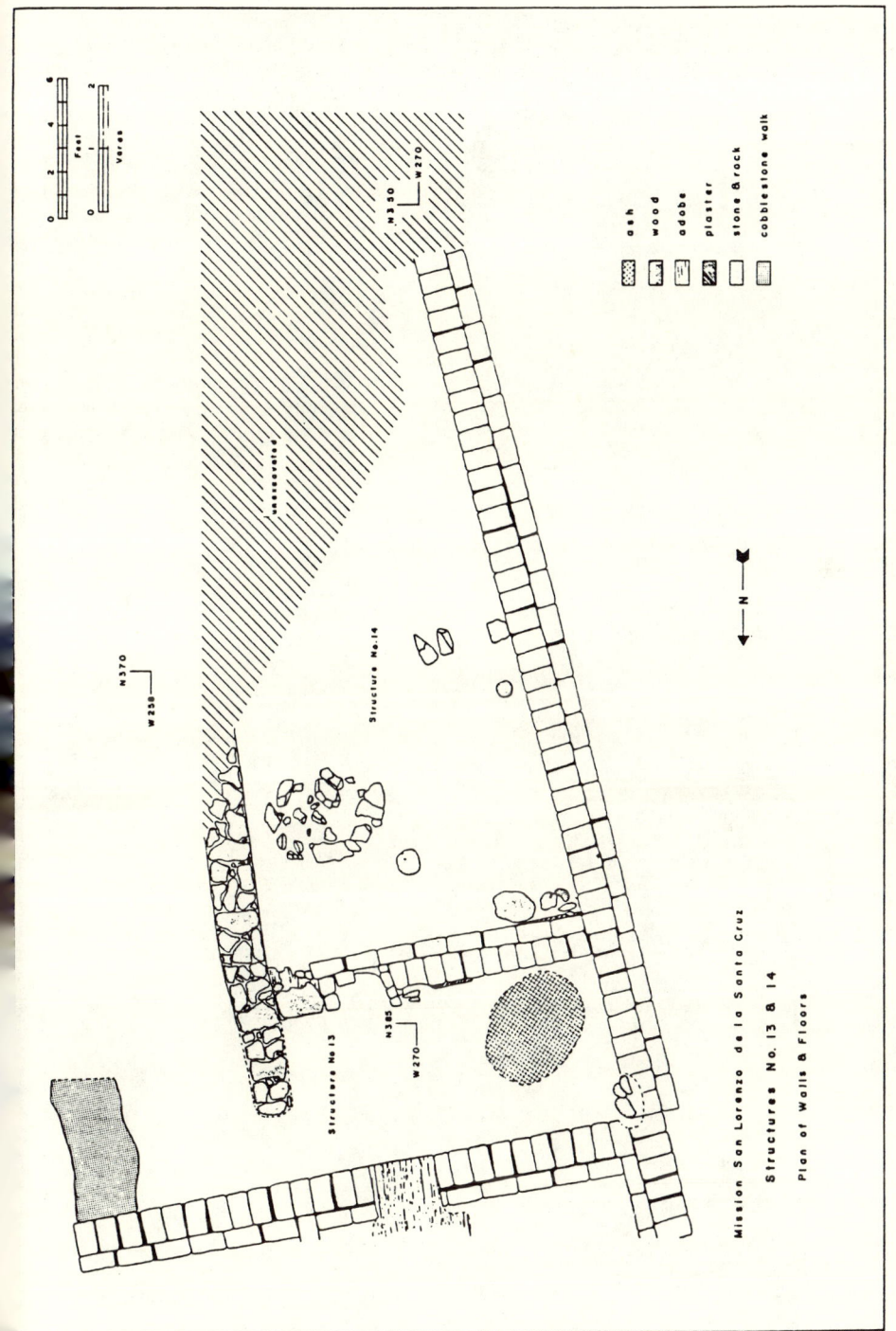

Fig. 24. Structures 13 and 14, plan of walls and floor.

Fig. 25. Excavation of northwest corner of quadrangle showing Structures 11–14, looking west. Nueces River is visible through trees in background.

Fig. 26. Artist's reconstruction of northwest corner of quadrangle showing doorways (l. to r.) into Structures 13, 11, and 12. Looking northwest.

REFERENCES

Arricivita, Juan Domingo
    1792   Crónica y apostólica del Colegio de propaganda fide de la Santa Cruz de Querétaro en la Nueva España, segunda parte, F. de Zuñiga y Ontiveros, México.

Webb, Walter Prescott (editor)
    1952   **Handbook of Texas.** Texas State Historical Association, 2 vols., Austin.

DOCUMENTARY SERIES NO. 1

GUIDELINES FOR A TEXAS MISSION

Instructions for the Missionary of Mission Concepcion
in San Antonio, Texas

Transcript of the Spanish Original
with English Translation and Notes

by

Father Benedict Leutenegger, O.F.M.

Completely revised by

Sister Carmelita Casso, I.W.B.S.

and

Sister Margaret Rose Warburton, C.D.P.

Old Spanish Missions Historical Research Library at

Our Lady of the Lake University

San Antonio, Texas

INTRODUCTION

The document presented here under the title of _Guidelines for a Texas Mission_ was found in the archives of the Missionary College of Our Lady of Guadalupe of Zacatecas. The manuscript was chosen by Father Marion Habig, O.F.M., and Father Benedict Leutenegger, O.F.M., to be the first publication in the "Documentary Series" of the Old Spanish Missions Historical Research Library. This series, which now has seven volumes, fulfills one of the goals of OSMHRL; namely, to acquire, transcribe, translate, and publish documents relating to the Spanish influence in the United States. The text is printed in two columns, with the transcription of the original on the left and the translation on the right to enable researchers to accept or reject the translation.

The first printing of the "Instruccion para el Ministro de la Mision de la Purissima Concepcion de la Provincia de Texas" appeared in 1976. The authorship of the document was unknown and it was believed to have been written around 1760. The document is undated and unsigned, and it was only after Fray José Rafael Oliva's _Management of the Missions in Texas_ was published as the second volume of the Documentary Series that the probable authorship and approximate date of the _Instruccion_ could be established with greater certainty.

Fray José Oliva was appointed President of the Texas missions in the year 1786. Accompanied by several other Friars, among whom was Fray Joseph M. García, who was to go to Mission Concepcion, he arrived in San Antonio in October of 1786. On January 23, 1787, Fray Oliva wrote a letter to all the missionaries in Texas with instructions as to how the missions in their care were to be managed. In his effort to establish something "firm, stable, and uniform" he asks each missionary to put in writing the practices followed in the mission under his care. This, he says, will help newcomers in the administration of the missions.

The _Guidelines_ were probably written in 1787 or 1788 by Fray Joseph García in response to this directive of the Father President. In a note at the end of his _Methodo_, Fray García states that the guidelines "are meant for a missionary who has never been in charge of a mission, who finding himself all alone, does not know where to turn for advice in order not to make mistakes." In his conclusion he expresses the hope that his _Instruccion_ will be of assistance to one who follows him. Fray Joseph García returned to Zacatecas in April of 1788 because of ill health. His successor, Fray Joseph Camarena, the last missionary in residence at Concepcion, remained there until 1794.

This revised transcription of the _Guidelines_, made from the microfilm copy in the Old Spanish Missions Historical Research Library, attempts to present an accurate text of the original document. It is hoped that it will serve as a faithful account of "the way it was" in Mission Concepcion and the other Texas missions in the late 18th century.

Sister Margaret Rose Warburton, C.D.P.
    Curator, Old Spanish Missions Historical Research Library
            September 20, 1990

v

ACKNOWLEDGMENTS

A special debt of gratitude is due to Father Benedict Leutenegger, O.F.M. (1904-1985), for his indefatigable zeal in locating and microfilming documents in the Franciscan archives of Querétaro and Zacatecas. He not only discovered the <u>Guidelines</u> but transcribed, translated, and annotated the original document. The revised edition is offered as a tribute to "Father Ben" and all who participated in the preparation of the first printing.

Sincere thanks are due to Adán Benavides, Jr., for his constant encouragement and his skillful deciphering of many difficult passages.

Dr. Malcolm D. McLean must be given credit for putting the bull back in the mission plaza by means of his correct reading of the manuscript text. (See No. 67)

To Sister Carmelita Casso, I.W.B.S., who is outstanding among the "corps of faithful volunteers" of the Old Spanish Missions Historical Research Library, I am deeply indebted for her careful editing, proofreading, and typing of the final manuscript.

I thank these and all who have helped in any way, and I assume responsibility for any errors found in the work.

MRW

Methodo de Govierno que se observa en esta Mision de la Purissima Concepcion
espiritual, como en lo temporal.

N.º 1 Todos los dias de fiesta, se dan de dos Cruces, que obligan a los Yndios: y sean de una
Vease el Cruz se dice Misa: y deben concurrir todos à oyrla; con la diferencia, que la Vi-
Suplemento pera del dia de dos Cruces se repica al medio dia, à la noche, y antes de la
à fox. 12 Misa; pero el dia de una Cruz no se repica al medio dia, sino solam.te à la
noche, y antes de la Misa.

n.º 2 Todos los Sabados del año se acostumbra tambien decir Misa, à la qual se repica
antes de ella, y si ay comodidad de que sea cantada, quando haiga quien la
ofiçie, siete son de Concepcion los dias no impedidos.

n.º 3 El dia de Ceniza tambien se les dice Misa, despues de bendecirla, y de haver-
les puesto la Ceniza à todos; para lo qual el Ministro previene al Fiscal la vispera
para que queme la Palma, y la tenga dispuesta à su tiempo.

         El hacer los Oficios la Semana Santa esta al arbitrio de los Ministros, y siempre
         es conveniente por aumentar la devocion al Pueblo, y evitar pleytos. Y quando se
         hace la Semana Santa, se previene al Mayordomo para que tenga la de-
         ze, que han de servir de Apostoles en el Sanctuario. El Jueves Santo en la tar-
         de Procession sacando en andas por dentro de la Plaza à Jesus Nazareno con
         la Cruz acuestas, y à la Virgen de los Dolores, cargando los Yndios las Cruces en
         los ombros, q.e para este fin estan guardadas: à la noche predica el Ministro
         los Misterios del dia, ó de Passion; y entre tanto anda la Procession van rezando
         el Rosario haciendo Coro el Ministro. El Viernes Santo sale otra Procession sa-
         cando à Jesus desnudo, y atado à la Columna, à otros centurios, y la Virgen
         vestida de negro, rezando entre tanto el Via Crucis: y luego que entra se con-
         cluye con Sermon de Pasion, sino es que quieran hacer Descendimiento. Mien-
         tras esta el Santissimo Sacramento en el Tabernaculo deben estar dos hombres
         con Armas puesto al Presbiterio en Centinela, y otros dos en la Puerta de la Ygle-
         sia, teniendo cuidado el Fiscal de andarlos mudando de dia, y de noche, has-
         ta que se concluyen los Oficios el Viernes Santo.

n.º 4 Los Domingos despues del Evangelio avisa el Ministro al Pueblo
         fiesta, que huviere entre Semana esperandose obligan à to-

ERRATA

This document has been photographically reproduced from the typed manuscript. The following are corrections for typographical errors in the text.

P. 1, No. 2, column 1, line 8: "impedido" should read "impedidos"

P. 18, No. 29, column 2, line 7: "the" should read "they"

P. 30, No. 53, column 1, line 4: "pudiera" should read "pudiere"

P. 34, No. 62, column 2, line 5: "seeklings" should read "seedlings"

18.

La elección de Juezes, que se componen de un Governador, y un Alcalde se hace cada año el día de la Circuncisión del Señor. Acabada la Misa se mandan juntar todos los hombres en el Corredor, o Portal de la Celda del Ministro, y luego que están todos juntos, el Ministro tomando papel, y tintero, irá llamando uno por uno comensando

18.

The election of the official judges, which comprise a governor and a mayor, is held each year on the feast of the Circumcision of Our Lord. When Mass is over, all the men are told to assemble in the corridor or the entrance to the missionary's cell. As soon as they are gathered, the missionary takes paper and ink. He

por el **Mayordomo**, y les preguntará a quien quiere para Governador y **respondiendo** a Fulano lo pondrá en el papel con su Rayita: y la misma diligencia hará para el Alcalde. Luego entra otro, y acabado con esto otro hasta q^e todos hayan dado su voto. Pero debe advertir el Ministro que se ha acostumbrado la alternativa entre las dos Naciones Pajalaches, y Tacames, y a aquella pertenecen los de las otras Naciones: de manera que un año es Governador Pajalache, Alcalde Tacame; y otro año es Governador Tacame, y Alcalde Pajalache, por lo qual en vezes es menester advertir a algunos de los vocales, que suelen votar por un Tacame para Governador acabando de serlo, o por un Pajalache para Alcalde, acabando tambien de serlo, <u>vel e contra</u>. Asi que todos han dado sus votos sale el Ministro a la Puerta de la Celda y publica la Elección avisando al Pueblo quantos votos han sacado cada uno, y al que tuviera mas votos para Governador lo llama ante sí, le hace hincar de rodillas, y le entrega el baston (que ya le ha entregado el Governador viejo al Ministro quando salió de Misa) exortandole al cumplimiento de su obligación, que zele no haiga en el Pueblo ofensas de Dios, &^{a} y que aquel baston se lo da en nombre del Rey, &^{a}. Luego llama al que sacó mas votos para Alcalde, y hace las mismas ceremonias. Hecho esto, el Ministro haviendo pensado antes a quien quiera para Fiscal de aquel año, si quiere mudar el antiguo (que esto está a su arbitrio porque al Fiscal assí como lo elige el Ministro sin Elección del Pueblo, assí tambien lo quita quando quiere

calls each one, beginning with the superintendent, and asks him whom he wants for governor. As each replies, the missionary will place the name on the paper with his appropriate mark. The same will be done for the mayor. Then another enters and, when he is finished, another enters until all have voted. But the missionary must keep in mind that it is the custom to alternate between the two nations: the Pajalaches and the Tacames. The former also include members of other tribes. Thus, one year the governor is a Pajalache, and the mayor is a Tacame. The next year, the governor is a Tacame, and the mayor a Pajalache. For this reason, it is necessary at times to remind some of the voters, who usually vote for a Tacame for governor to alternate after his term is up, or who are accustomed to vote for a Pajalache as mayor after his term is up. When all have voted, the missionary comes to the door of his cell and makes known the results of the election, telling the people how many votes each one received. He calls before him the one who got the most votes for governor, has him kneel down, and gives him the staff (which the outgoing governor has turned over to the missionary after Mass). He exhorts him to carry out his duties to see that no offense against God takes place in the pueblo, etc. In the name of the King, he presents him with the staff, etc. Then he calls the one who got the most votes for mayor and performs the same ceremonies for him. This done, the missionary having previously decided upon the one he

aunque regularmente es acabado el año) lo llama y hace hincar ante sí y le entrega la Cuarta, que es la insignia de Fiscal, haciendole tambien una exortación sobre sus obligaciones. Acabadas las Elecciones van todos a la Yglesia y cantan el Alabado y mientras previene el Ministro si quiere el Refresco en su Celda, que regularmente es un Frasco de Vino, y quando vuelven de la Yglesia se los reparte. Despues escrive al Sr Governador una Carta presentando a los nuevos Juezes para que los confirme, y los despacha con ella al Presidio.

wants for fiscal for that year, should he want to change the old one (for this is left up to the missionary, since the fiscal is chosen by the missionary without the people's vote, and can be changed, when advisable, though generally this occurs at the end of the year). He calls the fiscal before him to kneel and receive the quirt, which is the sign of the fiscal, and exhorts him about his duties. When the elections are over, all go to the church and sing the "Alabado". Meanwhile, if he so wishes, the missionary prepares a refreshment in his cell, which generally consists of a bottle of wine. When they come from church, he divides it among them. Later, he writes a letter to the governor, introducing the new judges to be confirmed by him, and sends them to the presidio with it.

Note:

The feast of the Circumcision of Our Lord was January 1. Today the feast is called the Solemnity of the Mother of God.

19.

El Mayordomo es perpetuo, y solo por causas graves se podrá deponer al que lo fuere: mas en caso de deposición, o muerte puede el Ministro poner al que fuere mas a proposito para ello; atendiendo siempre a que el Yndio que se huviere de poner sea de los mas racionales, ladinos, y que sepan mandar y hacer lo que mandan; y no será fuera de camino, que privadam^{te} consulte el Ministro con los mismos Yndios, que desinteresadam^{te} puedan aconsejar. El Caporal sirve para traher semanariamente la Racion

19.

The superintendent's office is permanent and only for grave reasons may he be deposed, should this be necessary. But in case of removal or death, the missionary may appoint one better suited to the task, always careful that the Indian whom he appoints be one of the more intelligent, bilingual, and who knows how to command and how to follow orders. It would not be out of order for the missionary to consult privately with the other Indians who can in a disinterested way give him good

de **Carne,** y cuidar de la **Caballada,** que para este fin se mantiene **en** le Misión. Tambien es perpetuo <u>ad nutum</u> del Ministro, aunque no **se** requiere tanta causa para quitarlo como al Mayordomo. El Caballerizo no siempre lo hay porque este sirve para cuidar la Caballada de la Misión quando se mantiene separada del Situado del Rey, y es tambien perpetuo y amovible a voluntad del Ministro.

advice. The head of the cowboys sees to it that each week the meat supply is brought, and the horses, which are kept at the mission for this purpose, are cared for. He is also permanently in office at the wish of the missionary, though not so grave a reason is required to remove him as it is to remove the superintendent. Not always is there a head groom who takes care of the mission horses because he takes care of the mission herd of horses when it is kept apart from the area under the King's control. He is also perpetually in office and can be removed by the missionary when necessary.

20.

Los Musicos que sirven para tocar en la Yglesia lo son frequentem^{te} los que se aplican a este exercicio, y es preciso que el Ministro les avie de los instrumentos cada ves que necesitaren renovarse, y que de quando en quando haga que aprenda un muchacho, para que nunca falte quien sepa tocar.

20.

The musicians who perform in church usually are those who specialize in this. The missionary must supply them with musical instruments and repair the latter when necessary. From time to time, he sees to it that a boy learns how to play, so that there is always one who can do so.

Note:

Music played an important part in the lives of the mission Indians. They sang in Church during Mass and played their violins and guitars.

21.

El Cosinero puede mudarlo el Ministro quando quisiere, o alternarlo por semanas, o meses con los que saben, atendiendo a que siempre sea hombre, respecto a que con las mugeres puede haver su desorden con la concurrencia de los Solteros en la Cosina.

21.

The missionary can change the cook when he wants to or alternate cooks by weeks or months, always selecting a man for the job. The employment of women could lead to disorder with single men in the kitchen.

Note:

What attracted the Indians in the beginning was food, as well as glass beads and trinkets.

22.

El Obrajero es uno que entienda de todo lo que pertenece a su Oficio, y tambien debe ser hombre de juicio y de madura edad por el continuo trato con las mugeres y para que le tengan respeto los muchachos que govierna.

23.

Todas las semanas tiene cuidado el Ministro de mandar traher Ración de Reses p^a el abasto de los Yndios para esto, debe prevenir el Caporal que con tiempo trahiga los Caballos que fuesen menester, para que el con los Baqueros, que deben ser cuatro o seis se vayan el Jueves, y estén aqui con el Ganado el Sabado. Pero se advierte que algunas vezes es conveniente que no se trahigan Caballos de la Caballada cada semana, por el estropeo que en este caso tendrán; sino cada mes trahera los precisos, y estos podrán servir todas las semanas, cui- dando el Caporal de ponerlos donde coman, y encerrarlos de noche si fuere menester. Todo esto se deja a la prudencia del Ministro segun la ocurrencia de los tiempos.
Traida pues la ración el Sabado, se matan el Domingo por la mañana las Reses, que sean necesarias para proveer a todos los Yndios, que por lo comun son cuatro, o seis quando no hay mucha Gente, y una se mata para el Convento, teniendo obligación el Fiscal de meter la carne, y cocinarla en el

22.

The overseer is one who understands all that pertains to his work and must be a man of judgment and maturity, since he deals with women constantly, and the boys whom he directs must find him worthy of respect.

23.

Every week the missionary must see to it that the supply of beef cattle is brought to be rationed for the sustenance of the Indians. To do this, he must advise the foreman to bring the horses that are needed in due time, so that he with the cowboys, four or six in number, may go on Thursday and be back with the cattle on Saturday. But one must recognize that at times it is not good to bring the horses each week from the herd because of fatigue. Instead, the ones needed are brought each month, and they can be of service every week. The foreman is to take care that the horses have something to eat and corral them at night, if necessary. All this is left to the judgment of the missionary, according to the season of the year. The cattle are brought on Saturday and slaughtered on Sunday morning as needed to supply all the Indians. Generally, four or six are slaughtered when the natives are few, and one beef is butchered for the friary. The fiscal has the duty to bring the meat and to

Verano para que no se hieda, y de recojer el Cebo y manteca de todas las Reses, que se mataren, freir esta, y guardarlo todo en su lugar.	cook it so that will not spoil in the summer time. The tallow and fat from all the slaughtered cattle are to be collected, fried and put away in a proper place.
24.	24.
El Sabado despues de Misa todas las semanas tienen obligación las mugeres de barrer los Patios del Convento, y el Fiscal señala dos que barran la Yglesia y Sacristia. Acabada de barrer ocurren todas las mugeres por la ración de jabon, que reparte el Fiscal dando a cada una segun la familia, y ropa que huviere que lavar.	Every Saturday after Mass, the women have the duty to sweep the patios of the friary, and the fiscal appoints two women to sweep the church and sacristy. When that is finished, all the women come for a portion of soap, which the fiscal distributes according to the size of the family and the clothing that is to be washed.
25.	25.
Todos los Domingos, despues que salen de Missa da el Ministro al Fiscal dos manojos de Tabaco para que les de ración a todos los grandes, hombres y mugeres y esto debe hacerlo en el Portal, u otro lugar donde lo puede veer el Ministro a quien se le devuelve en la Batea lo que sobra, para que les provea entre semana a los que vienen a pedirle, observando no darles hasta el miercoles en adelante, por que si se les da antes del miercoles con la satisfacción de que lo tienen q^{do} lo piden, desperdician el que se les da el Domingo, quitandoseles los del Presidio por qualquier vagatela: y quando se les da entre semana es solo dos o tres ojas para que les alcanse hasta el Domingo.	Every Sunday after Mass, as the people leave the church, the missionary gives the fiscal two bundles of tobacco to be distributed to the adults, men and women. This is to be done in the doorway or some other place where the missionary can oversee it. What is left is returned to the missionary. He gives to those who request tobacco during the week, observing the rule, however, not to give until Wednesday. If he gives before Wednesday when they know they still have some, they squander what is given them on Sunday, bartering with the people at the presidio for any trifle. Only two or three leaves of tobacco should be given them during the week to last until Sunday.
26.	26.
Los Lunes de todas las semanas acuden todas las mugeres por la	Every Monday, all the women come for their ration of corn

ración de mays, que les da el Fiscal, sacando de la Celda del Ministro la Llave de la Troje, que siempre esta alli colgada. La cantidad de mays que a cada una se le da es diferente en los tiempos: porque cuando se alsa mucho mays, de manera que se considere sobrante se les dan quatro almudes en masorca a las Casadas, y dos y medio, o tres a las Viudas; pero cuando ay poco mays sólo se les dan tres almudes a las Casadas, y dos a las Viudas: y quando pueda darseles desgranado se les darán dos almudes.

Para que el Ministro pueda regular si el Mays que se alsó es mucho, o poco, debe estar advertido que regularmente son menester quatrocientas fan^s al año poco mas, o menos para el abasto de la Gente atendiendo siempre al numero de Personas que huviere en el Pueblo, y a las fanegas, que el Ministro pueda expender o en pago de Salarios, o por venta &^{a}.

which is given them by the fiscal. He gets the key for the granary from its usual place in the missionary's cell. The amount of corn given to each woman varies with the seasons. When an abundance of corn is harvested, the married women are given four almudes of unshucked corn, and two and a half or three almudes to the widows. When there is little corn, only three almudes are given to the married women and two to the widows. When shelled corn is available, two almudes are given.

In order that the missionary may regulate the corn and decide whether the supply is large or small, he must keep in mind that regularly about 400 fanegas are needed each year to maintain the Indians, taking into account the number of persons in the pueblo and the fanegas the missionary can give out either as payment of salaries or for selling purposes.

Note:

A fanega was about 1½ bushels; an almud was about half a bushel.
(Haggard cites on pp. 71-77:
   a fanega in Mexico: 2.577 bu.
   an almud, U.S. equiv.: 1.2885 bu.)

28.

En algunas Missiones acostumbran los Ministros dar ración de Sal semanariamente; en esta no se acostumbra, sino que el Ministro la da cada vez, que se la piden, acomodándose a la necesidad de la que pide, y a la frequencia con que algunas piden. Para proveerse de Sal el Ministro debe estar cuidadoso de encargarla a los que suelen ir por ella del Presidio, conchabandose con el Arriero por mays, dinero, u otros

28.

At some missions, the missionaries have the custom of distributing salt each week, but that is not the practice at Mission Concepción. Here the missionary gives it out whenever the Indians ask for it. He appraises the need of the one asking and the frequency of the request. To get the salt, the missionary is to make arrangements with those who usually go for it to the presidio and bargain with the muleteer with

efectos segun le huviere mas quenta.

29.

Las peticiones de las Yndias son frequentes importunando al Ministro por dulce, manteca, frijoles, chile, y otra mil cosas: y si el Ministro es blando para darles todo lo que piden, no havrá con la Casa de la Moneda; por lo qual debe acomodarse a lo que huviere, segun las ocurrencias de los tiempos, y demas circunstancias, que acaecieren.

30.

Todos los Viernes de Quaresma manda el Ministro poner un perol de frijoles, q^e el Fiscal tiene cuidado de guisar para dar de comer a la Gente al medio dia para evitarles que pongan Carne en sus Casas, y si huviere Calabasas tambien se les da. Pero quando haiga proporción de darles frijoles toda la Quaresma, no se debe omitir, aunque rara vez se alsará tanto frijol q^e alcanse a abastecer una Quaresma entera si se gasta todos los dias, y el Ministro debe atender a que él lo gasta todo el año en los dias de abstinencia. La Vigilia de Navidad se les pone tambien un perol de frijoles, otra de Calabasa cocida, y otro de Camotes, los que si no los sembrara en la Misión tendrá cuidado de comprarlos en el Presidio: y regularmente se

corn, money or other goods, according to what he has most.

29.

The Indian women frequently ask for things, importuning the missionary for sweets, lard, beans, chili and a thousand other items. If the missionary is so lenient as to give them what the all ask for, he will have nothing left in the treasury. Therefore, he must act according to what he has on hand, the season of the year and other prevailing conditions.

Note:

That the Indian women should ask for "a thousand other things" was another reason why the missionary had to be a patient man.

30.

On all Fridays of Lent, the missionary orders a big pot of beans to be prepared. The fiscal sees to it that they are cooked so that the natives have something to eat at noon and do not eat meat at home. In addition, if squash is available, it is to be prepared for them also. When possible, beans should be given them every day during Lent. But seldom is the bean crop so plentiful as to permit this every single day of Lent. Yet the missionary should bear this in mind on days of abstinence during the whole year. On Christmas Eve, there are prepared a kettle of beans, one of squash and another of sweet potatoes, which, if they are not planted at the mission, can be bought at the presidio. Regularly, buñuelos are made, together with sweets

les mandan hacer sus buñuelos con dulce, y se les da tambien ración.

Note:

Friday was a day of abstinence for all Catholics who were seven years of age or older. A buñuelo is a fried, sweetened bread.

which are then distributed.

31.

En el tiempo del cumplimiento de Yglesia, el dia que comulgan, es uso antiguo el darle a cada uno una tablilla de Chocolate para que se desayune: y si el Ministro no tuviere providencia de este genero, ya quedarán unos contentos con un pilonsillo, o medio para suplirse. Item: el dia que llega el Avio ya están impuestos a que se les destripe un tercio de Dulce, y se les dé a cada uno su Pilonsillo, y a los muchachos a medio.

31.

During the time of Easter duty, the Indians receive a bar of chocolate for breakfast on the day they receive Holy Communion. If the missionary should be unable to provide this, the Indians are content with a sugar cone or half of one. Also, on the day when the supplies arrive at the mission, they generally get a portion of sweets, and each one is given a sugar cone, and the children get a half.

32.

En tiempo de fruto es indispensable darles ración de Sandias, y melones segun lo piscaren cada vez que se huviere fruta de sason en la huerta para lo qual tendrá cuidado el Ministro de mandar recoger la Semilla, y de que se siembre a su tiempo todo lo mas que pudiere, p^a que no le falte el gusto de que sus hijos coman, y no lo busquen en otra parte.

32.

At harvest time, one must ration the watermelons and other melons according to the quota of work, whenever fruit is available. For this purpose, the missionary is careful to order the seed to be collected and planted in due season. This is done so that food is not wanting to the members of the mission, and thus they do not search for food in other regions.

33.

Y para que las dos principales fiestas de la Misión, que son la del Corpus, y la de la Purissima Concepción lleguen a ser mas plausibles para los Yndios en ambos dias se les mata

33.

So that the two principal feasts of this mission, namely Corpus Christi and the Immaculate Conception, are the most appealing to the Indians, a cow is butchered on both days

dios en ambos dias se les mata una Res, y se pone a cocer en el Perol para repartirles a medio dia; y si huviere Pilonsillo se les dará ración de el, o quando no haiga para tanto se les pone un caso de atole de Pinole; que mandará hacer el Ministro, y mesclado con dulce, se les distribuye, como la carne.

and prepared in a kettle to give the Indians at noon. If sugar cones are on hand, they are given also, or when there is not enough for so many, porridge is prepared. This the missionary will have made and mixed with sugar and distributed like the meat.

Note:

On December 8, 1854, Pope Pius IX solemnly declared and defined: "The doctrine which holds that the most Blessed Virgin Mary, at the first instance of her conception, by a singular privilege granted her by God, was preserved from any stain of original sin, is a doctrine taught and revealed by God, and is therefore to be believed with firmness and constancy by all the faithful."

This occurred more than 100 years after the founding of the Mission of the Immaculate Conception under this title in San Antonio in 1731.

34.

Para el vestido de los hombres debe tener la providencia el Ministro de mandar tejer con tiempo las mantas, que fueren necessarias segun abajo se dirá. De estas mantas criollas, o hechas en la Misión, en estando para entrar los frios se les da ración de camisas, y calsones blancos, distribuyendolo de este modo. Un dia que quiere destinar el Ministro para este exercicio manda llamar a los hombres, y de uno en uno les toma medida del largo de la camisa, y de las mangas, y cortandole lo que entrare, se lo da con lo que entrare para los calsones (con advertencia, que si fuere grueso o corpulento le dará un pedaso de manta angosta para fundillo) para que lleve a

34.

For men's clothing, the missionary must provide in due time for the necessary weaving of cloth, as will be described below. From this native cloth made at the mission, shirts and white pants are distributed when the cold weather arrives. On the day appointed by the missionary for this distribution, he calls the men and, one by one, takes their measurements for the length of shirts and sleeves. Cutting the material thus, he gives them what is needed for pants (paying attention that, if the Indian is fat or corpulent, he is given a piece of narrow cloth for piecing), so that he may take it to his wife to sew for him. As regards the single

su mujer que se lo cuesa; y lo de los Solteros lo apartará el Ministro para que el lo mande coser a una o mas mugeres de las que saben y acabando con los grandes hará lo mismo con los muchachos, cortandoles de la pieza angosta, que para esto se tejerá, y lo dará a sus Madres, si las tienen o a las que los cuiden. Si las mantas no alcansaren para vestirlos a todos de camisa, y calsones, en lugar de camisa podrá cortarles coton a algunos segun le pareciere y la necesidad lo pidiere.

35.

Aunque a los hombres siempre se les provee de ropa blanca, de la que se hace, y fabrica en la Misión, como queda dicho; pero no es generalmente a todos, por que se hace distinción entre ellos como entre toda la Gente. Al Mayordomo, Ayudante de Mayordomo, Governador, Alcalde, y Fiscal se les da para camisa, y calsones blancos de la manta de Puebla, que cada año se encarga en la Memoria, y si el Ministro quiere hacer esta gracia a otro, u otros, que lo merescan, es libre para ello, como para darles a estos, dos mudas, si gusta, una de manta delgada, y otra de gruessa, y assi mismo tal qual vez que haiga proporción para darles de lienzo puede hacerlo.

men, the missionary divides the material so that one or more women who know how, may do the sewing. When the missionary has taken care of the men, he does the same for the boys, cutting from a narrow piece of cloth, woven for this purpose. This will be given to their mothers or, if they have none, to those women who take care of them. Should the cloth not suffice to provide them with shirts and pants, then, in place of a shirt, a pull-over garment will be cut, as seems expedient.

35.

Although white cloth, made and woven at the mission, is always provided for the men, as described above, still this does not hold good for all, since distinctions are made among all people. The superintendent, his assistant, the governor, the alcalde and fiscal are given cloth from Puebla with which to make their white shirts and pants. This is ordered each year in the list of supplies. If the missionary wishes to favor some others with this material, he is free to do so. He may give them two changes, if he wishes, one of thin and the other of thick cloth. He may do this whenever there is enough material on hand.

Note:

Making their own clothing was one of the activities of the Indians at the mission, and the author here gives us many interesting details.

Puebla is a city in east central Mexico. Both flax and cotton are produced in the surrounding area.

36.

De las mugeres unas ay que necesariam^te se deben vestir de esta manta hechisa, otras, que voluntariam^te quieren ponersela porque les es mas comodidad; y assi, por este mismo tiempo, que a los hombres, se les van dando a las mugeres sus camisas conforme las van pidiendo: porque las que prefieren de manta gruesa, ellas la piden, y entonces se les dará lo que fuere menester para camisa, porque Naguas blancas no se les da de esta manta, sino de las que trahen hechas en el Avio. Y a estas a quien se les huviera dado de esta manta, se apuntan para no darles de la de Puebla quando se da ración de ropa, salvo que el Ministro quiera duplicarles a algunas. Otras hay a quienes todos los años se les da camisa de lienzo, aunque estas son tan pocas que regularmente solo son dos, porque si a otras se les da alguna vez, no es anualmente; y tambien suele de manta poblana, para que tengan que mudarse. Para esto, y para todo lo demas, el Ministro cobrará experiencia con lo que fuere mirando.

37.

Para este tiempo ya debe haver puestas en el Telar telas de fresada para que el Ministro vaya repartiendo conforme corta el Texedor; sino es que quiera esperar que se acaben de texer todas las fresadas para distribuirlas por junto; pero esto suele servir de confusión: y debe hecharse una Tela angosta para las fresaditas de los muchachos: y para que el Mini-

36.

There are some women who of necessity must be clothed with this homespun material. Others prefer it because of its greater comfort. Therefore, at the same time that distribution is made to the men, the shifts are given to the women who ask for them. Those who prefer thick material ask for it and get whatever they need to make a shift, because white underskirts are not given them from this cloth. Instead, they receive ready-made ones which come with the supplies. A note is made on those who receive this material, so as not to give them cloth from Puebla during the distribution unless the missionary wishes to do so. There are others to whom linen shifts are given every year, though these are so few that there are usually only two. These are not given annually. They also get these same shifts made of Puebla cloth, so that they have a change of clothing. For this matter and for all the rest, the missionary will gain experience as matters develop.

37.

By this time, the looms should be in operation, making blankets which the missionary will distribute according as the weaver binds off the material, unless he prefers waiting until all are woven, so that they may be given out at the same time. However, this causes confusion. There should be a narrow cloth for small blankets for the children. The missionary draws

stro se acuerde a los que les va dando fresada hace su lista de todos los hombres, mugeres, y muchachos, y segun les fuere dando los señala; y esta misma lista sirve para las demas raciones de ropa, y vestuario.

38.

En llegando el Avio, a tiempo que el Ministro le paresca conveniente va distribuyendo las cosas por su orden: el dia que destinare para las Mugeres, antes de llamarlas ha de tener prevenido en su Celda todo lo que les ha de dar por junto, haciendole a cada una su ración. Ya tiene contadas quantas son las mugeres y muchachas, y a cada una les pone su Xicara o Chacual y dentro de el pone tres o quatro hilos de quentas (conforme fuera la cantidad, que huviera) una Gargantilla, si las ay, vara y media o vara y quarto de liston, dos varas, y media, o dos varas, y tres quartas de cinta de reata, el Rosario, y la escoveta si huviere. Tiene tambien prevenidas las Naguas blancas, o Faldillas, que llaman aqui, y ya debe tener cortadas las Camisas de la manta poblana, para las que llevan de ella (sabiendo que en cada Camisa entran dos varas, y quarta de la manta ancha para el cuerpo, y vara, y tercia de la angosta para las mangas) y poniendo las faldillas juntas con las camisas, tiene cuidado de veer a quien le ha de dar solo faldillas, o porque ya llevó camisa de manta criolla, o porque se le ha de dar de lienso, aunque a estas por lo comun, tambien se les da de manta, como ya dije. Con este se junta tambien el pedazo de

up a list of all men, women and children and checks their names as they receive their items. This list serves as a guide for the other rationing of material and clothing.

38.

When the supplies arrive, at a time when the missionary thinks fitting, he begins to distribute the goods according to his list. Before he calls the women, he prepares in his cell all that is to be rationed out to them at the same time. He has now calculated how many women and children there are, and for each one he designates a basket. In each, he puts three or four strings of beads (according to how many he has); a necklace, if there are any; one and half, or one and three-fourths varas of ribbon; two and one half or two and three-fourths varas of straps; a rosary and a small brush, if there are any. Also, he has ready white underskirts or petticoats, as they call them here, and now he should have the camisoles cut from Puebla cloth for those who use that, (knowing that for each camisole two and one-fourth varas of the wide cloth are needed for the body and one and one-third of the narrow cloth for the sleeves). He puts the petticoats together with the camisoles, taking care to see to whom he gives them. Some will get only a petticoat because they have received a camisole made of native cloth or because they are given a linen one, though generally they get both, as I have said. A corresponding piece of lining is added

mitan para forro de las Naguas, acomodandose al ancho de la balleta y tamaño de las Naguas.+

+ (Nota marginal) Los paños de rebozo puede el Ministro no darlos cada año, si quiere, porque a vexes bien los aguardan dos años.

Tiene prevenida tambien las dos piezas de balleta para cortarles alli mismo las naguas: y estando todo dispuesto llamando a las mugeres va tomando medida a cada una de las naguas (o hace que otra muger lo haga en su presencia) y le da a cada una dos lienzos, haciendo cargo de lo que encoge para que siempre se mida mas largo para alforsa, pero a las gruesas de cuerpo, y a algunas otras aunque no sean gruesas se les dan dos liensos, y medio para q^e tengan algun buelo. A las Viejas no se les da forro, porque no lo ponen. Acabado de medir a una, se le da su balleta, sus faldillas con lo que tienen dentro (que como dije es la Camisa, y el mitan. Tambien con cada camisa se ponen seis u ocho madejitas de hilo) y el chacual con todo su recaudo, y se despacha, y siguiendo otra, se surte del mismo modo hasta acabar con los grandes.

Note:

A <u>vara</u> is a linear measure of about .84 meters or about one yard.

39.

Entran luego las muchachas y tomandoles medida de naguas y fundillas se les cortan de balleta, de cinta segun lo que huviere menester cada una: y si quiere el Ministro les da

for lining the underskirts.

Marginal note: The missionary does not have to give material for rebozos every year, if he so wishes, because at times they last two years.

Also, he has ready two pieces of flannel from which to cut the skirts. When all this is arranged, he calls the women and measures their skirts (or has another woman do this in his presence), and gives each one two linen cloths, making allowances for what has to be taken in. For the stouter women and some others who are not corpulent, two and one-half linen cloths are allowed, so that they have sufficient material. To the old women, no lining is given because they do not use it. When the measurements are over, one by one, the older women receive their flannel, petticoats, or camisoles and other material (with each camisole are placed six or eight skeins of thread) and the basket with all its contents. As another woman follows, she is given the same amount until the supply runs out.

39.

Now the girls come and, when their measurements for underskirts and petticoats are taken, flannel is cut for them, and tape is also given to those who need it. If the missionary

sus quentas, un pedasito de liston, chagual, &ᵃ y se despachan.

40.

De las faldillas suele darse a algunas mugeres otro lienso para que ensanchen, y no queden angostas. A las que se les huviere de dar camisa de lienso se llaman aparte, y con su hilo, o seda blanca se les da, para que las cuesan, o mandar coser. La pita para las naguas, aunque regularmente se les dan junto con todo lo demas, pero lo mas acertado es darle a cada una quando la vengan a pedir, porque communmente no hacen sus naguas luego luego, y mientras las hacen se les pierde, y ocurren otra vez por ella: lo que entra de pita en cada par de naguas son seis o siete madejitas.

41.

A algunas mugeres se les dan Sapatos, una, o dos vezes al año, y regularmente para el dia de la Virgen de la Concepción tienen buen cuidado de pedirlos para que se los ponen: y por lo qual debe tener providencia el Ministro de encargarlos a Saltillo, sino los trajere el Conductor. Medias de seda a tal qual se les da quando conozca el Ministro que se les han acabado las que tenian. Y si a una u otra muger quiere el Ministro vestirla mas decente, porque ella se lo merezca por su juicio, o por otro motivo honesto, puede hacerlo; que lo mismo se acostumbra en las otras Missiones: y lo mismo que digo de estas mugeres, digo tambien de algunos hombres, y muchachos.

wishes, he gives them beads, a little piece of ribbon, a basket, etc., and they leave.

40.

An extra piece of goods is given to some women to add to their skirts so that they are not too tight. Those to whom he is to give a linen shift are called apart and given thread of white silk, so that they can sew it or have it sewn. The thread for the skirts is regularly given with all the rest. However, the best way is to give it to the one who asks for it, because they do not make their skirts immediately, and, if the thread gets lost, the women ask for more. The amount of thread for each skirt is six or seven spools.

41.

Some women are given shoes once or twice a year. Ordinarily, by the feast of the Immaculate Conception, they have made their request. The missionary must take care to order them from Saltillo, if the conductor of supplies did not bring them. Silk hose are given them when the missionary knows they need them. Should he wish to have one or the other dressed better than the others, either because she deserves it or for some other good reason, he may do so. The same thing is done at the other missions. This also refers to the men and children.

42.

El dia que destinare el Ministro para la ración de los hombres, teniendo ya contado los que son, y prevenido en la Celda lo que les ha de dar, los manda llamar, y a cada uno le da Sombrero, belduque, y Sapatos. De los Sombreros puede dar a los principales de los de uno en tarea, si huviere, reservando siempre para aviar a los sirvientes no Yndios, que regularmente ay en la Misión.

43.

Las Espuelas, los frenos, los aderezos de silla, fustes, herrajes, &^{a} , ya se deja entender, que no se da por ración: sino que lo distribuye el Ministro segun la necessidad de cada uno, y atendiendo al exercicio que tiene. Regularmente vienen en el Avio medias de lana y calsetas de algodon: y de este genero tampoco se da a todos, sino a los que el Ministro quisiere: como tambien para las mugeres los Comales, casos, cobres para agua, &^{a} , que solo dará el Ministro quando lo hayan menester, procurando siempre que le piden, assi los hombres como las mugeres averiguar si es verdadera la necessidad, o no: porque suelen algunos pedir la cosa, aunque la tengan, o no la hayan menester, para venderla, o jugarla.

44.

Desocupado ya el Ministro de todo este trafique, manda llamar al Sastre, que regularmente está ya igualado con la Misión,

42.

On the day assigned by the missionary for rationing among the men who are listed and after making preparations in his cell of what is to be given them, he orders them to be summoned, and, to each one, he gives a hat, a large knife and shoes. He gives hats to those who are doing heavy work outdoors, if there is a supply of them, reserving some always for non-Indian servants who regularly are in the mission.

43.

Spurs, bridles, saddles and other trappings, metal fittings, etc., are not rationed because the missionary gives them out as needed to each one according to the work he is doing. Regularly, the supplies include woolen stockings and cotton socks. These items are not given to all, but to those whom the missionary selects, as is done for the women with griddles, kettles, copper water pots, etc. The missionary takes care to determine the need, so as to avoid unnecessary selling and gambling to which some Indians are so prone.

44.

When the missionary is free of all these duties, he calls for the tailor, who regularly is well acquainted with the mis-

y les irá cortando la ropa de encima a los hombres. Algunas veces lleva la obra a hacerla a su casa, cortando de un tiro lo que puede acabar en una semana; y otras vezes la trabaja en la Misión. Capote no se le hace mas que al Governador cada año, porque cada año se muda. Al Mayordomo solo quando lo ha menester. A estos dos, al Alcalde y al Fiscal se les hace Chupa, o Chulo con bueltas, como se usa; y a todos estos, y al Ayudante de Mayordomo, al Caporal, y a otros, que quiera el Ministro se les dan calsones forrados, y ojalados: y a toda la demas Gente calson sin forro, o desolladoa como aqui llaman.

45.

Y para que el Ministro sepa lo que debe encargar anualm^te en la Memoria para el Culto de la Yglesia, para proveer el Convento, para vestir el Pueblo, y para aviar a los Sirvientes, vea las Memorias de los años pasados, mientras la experiencia le va enseñando todo lo que es necesario para un completo abastecimiento de la Misión.

46.

Los Sirvientes españoles, o no Yndios, son comunmente muy necessarios en la Misión, porque ay algunos empleos, que no saben, o no pueden exercer los Yndios con la fidelidad, y exigencia, que se debe. El oficio de Basiero en todas las Misiones siempre lo obtiene Español (quando digo Español se entiende no Yndio, que assi es corriente en este pais) y este está acomodado por un tanto

sion and cuts the outer clothing for the men. Sometimes he takes the work to his house after cutting what he can finish in a week. At other times, he works at the mission. Only for the governor is a coat made annually, because he is changed every year. A coat is made for the superintendent only when it is needed. For the alcalde and the fiscal, he makes an attractive coverall that goes to the knees, as they wear them today. To all these and to the assistant of the superintendent, to the foreman and to others chosen by the missionary are given lined trousers, trimmed with buttonholes, and to all the others are given breeches without lining or plain, as they say here.

45.

In order that the missionary may know what he is to include in the annual report for what is needed in church for divine worship, and to provide for the friary, for the natives' clothing and to keep the servants supplied, he scans the reports of past years. Experience teaches him what is needed to provide for the mission.

46.

Spanish servants or non-Indians are generally very necessary in the mission because some tasks the Indians cannot perform or are not able to perform with fidelity and with the necessary requirements. The work of making saddles in all the missions is always done by a Spaniard (when I say Spaniard, I mean a non-Indian; this is the usage here.) He is given a certain amount of corn and meat each

cada mes, dandole mays, y carne, como puede veer el Ministro el libro de quentas. Los Pastores tambien conviene que haiga uno o dos Españoles, pero suelen escasearse de modo, que se vee obligado el Ministro a poner Yndios, y quando estos estan de Pastores se mudan cada mes, o cada dos meses, conforme pareciere mejor, hablando con el Mayordomo para que señala los que deben ir.

47.

El Mayordomo tambien señala los Baqueros, que han de ir cada semana con el Caporal a traher la Ración, avisandole al Ministro los que ha señalado, y siempre debe preguntarle quantos deben ir para que disponga segun las ocurrencias de los tiempos. El Bueyero es el que cuida de recoger todas las tardes los Bueyes, y Bacas que se mantienen en la Misión, meterlas en el Corral, y sacarlas por la mañana a comer. Este no es perpetuo, ni tampoco se alterna con otro fixamente; sino que el Mayordomo pone al que fuere a proposito, y lo muda quando es necessario.

48.

Tambien señala el Mayordomo uno que trahiga leña para la Cosina del Convento los dias que debe traherse. Para traher sacate al Cavallo del Ministro debe haver uno, o dos Sacateros, que no tengan otro exercisio, y estos regularm^{te} son aquellos que o por vejés, o inutilidad no sirven para otra cosa. Estos los pone el Ministro, o el Mayordomo conforme les pareciere.

month as the missionary judges best from the book of accounts. One or two of the shepherds are Spaniards, but generally there are few Spaniards available, and this forces the missionary to appoint Indians. These are changed every month or every two months as seems best to him after talking things over with the superintendent about the assignments.

47.

The superintendent also appoints the cowboys who are to go each week with the foreman to bring the supplies. He reports to the missionary those appointed and asks how many cowboys should go to arrange matters according to the demands of the season. The man in charge of the oxen must see to it that all the oxen as well as the cows that are kept at the mission are herded together every evening into the corral and led out in the morning to pasture. This job is not permanent, nor does it alternate on a fixed schedule. The superintendent appoints the one best qualified and changes him when necessary.

48.

Also, the superintendent appoints the one who brings in the wood for the kitchen of the friary on the days when wood is to be brought in. To bring in hay for the missionary's horse, one or two men are needed. They have no other work and generally are advanced in years and incapable of doing any other work. The missionary or the superintendent hires them.

49.

En tiempo de huertas, quando ya comienza a crecer la fruta se ponen dos o tres Huerteros que para que no se la hurten, y estos con el Fiscal son los que hacen las piscas para las raciones, y deben traher el Ministro todos los dias la fruta, que se va madurando. Assimismo quando el Mays ya está en elote, debe haver uno q^e cuide de el rodeando todos los dias, y todo el dia la Labor a caballo, y en tiempo que ya comienzan a venir las Grullas se ponen tres o cuatro Grulleros para que las espanten, y cuiden de que no se coman el mays.

50.

Debe haver siempre en la Misión uno, o dos Carpinteros de los mismos Yndios para que a sus tiempos fabriquen los Arados, y Yugos, que han de servir en las Siembras, y renovesen y compongan los que huviesen menester. Deben hacer tambien las Carretas necessarias para el servicio de la Misión, y estos tienen obligación de cortar las maderas que fueren utiles para esto; y quando necessitan de Compañeros p^a este fin avisarán al Ministro p^a que los señale. En poder de ellos esta toda la erramienta de Carpinteria, y el Ministro tendrá cuidado no la pierdan, o presten a alguno sin su consentimiento.

51.

Quando en la Misión no ay algun Yndio que entienda de herreria, debe el Ministro tener un

49.

When the fruit trees are ready, two or three gardeners are appointed to take care of the orchard so that the fruit is not stolen. These gardeners with the Fiscal gather the fruit for rationing and bring ripe fruit to the missionary every day. Likewise, when the corn is ripening, one man is in charge of guarding the area every day. When the crows begin to arrive, three or four men are placed to scare them away and to see to it that they do not eat the corn.

50.

There must always be in the mission one or two carpenters from the Indians themselves who can make the plows and yokes used in planting and repair these when needed. Also, they are to make the carts that are needed in the mission. They also have the job of cutting the planks required for these implements. When they need help for this work, they inform the missionary who appoints the helpers. The carpenters are in charge of the implements in the carpenter shop, and the missionary shall see to it that they are not lost or lent to anyone without his consent.

51.

When among the Indians of the mission there is no blacksmith, the missionary is to get a

Español en el Presidio, que componga los hierros, que sirven en la Misión, calce las rejas de arar quando lo necessiten, &^{a}, y el herrero estará asalariado con iguala por cada año o le pagará el Ministro cada obra de por sí, segun mas acomodare.

52.

El Barbero que resura al Ministro está acomodado por iguala, pagandosele cada año su trabajo o en generos, o en dinero, y tiene obligación de venir a la resura un dia cada semana que regularm^{te} es el Sabado. Y tambien suele ajustarse con iguala para las sangrías y otras incisiones, que se ofrescan en la Misión o se le paga cada una de estas operaciones de por sí, segun fuere voluntad del Ministro.

53.

Cada año por el mes de Octubre o de Noviembre tiene cuidado el Ministro de embiar toda la Gente, que pudiera a juntar el Ganado en los agostaderos de la Misión, y herrar el Orejano, avisando con tiempo a las demas Misiones, y vezinos del Presidio para que aparten lo que cayere suyo, haciendo lo mismo, quando les avisan de las Misiones, y del Presidio, que dan apartadero en la junta de sus ganados.

54.

Por el mes de Marzo, o Abril es la trasquila del Ganado menor y para esto debe embiar el Ministro los trasquiladores, que fueren necessarios, si la trasquila se haya de hacer en

Spaniard from the presidio to work on the irons needed in the mission, sharpen the plowshares when necessary, etc. The blacksmith will be paid justly each year, or the missionary will pay him as each job is done, according to their agreement.

52.

The barber who shaves the missionary is paid as agreed upon. He is paid each year in kind or in money and must come to shave on one day of the week which is usually Saturday. An agreement on payment is made for any bleedings or incisions he is called upon to perform at the mission. He may be paid for each job, if the missionary so wishes.

53.

Each year during the month of October or November, the missionary sees to it that all who can go are sent to herd the cattle in the mission pasture and brand the unbranded cattle. He informs the other missions and the dwellers of the presidio in due time, so that they may separate their cattle from the rest. He cooperates with them in like manner when it is their turn to brand.

54.

During March or April, the sheep are sheared. The missionary sends the shearers who are needed if the shearing is to be done on the ranch where they pasture or in another

el Rancho donde pasteà, o en otro paraje, que le paresca a proposito o si le parece conveniente puede mandar traher el Ganado a la Misión, y trasquilar en ella; aunque esto tiene el peligro de menoscabo por la cercanía del Poblado. El Baciero tiene obligación de dar quenta al Ministro del número de Ovejas, Carneros y Corderitos que tiene a su cargo, y de castrar los Carneros que están de tiempo, avisando los que fueran, para que el Ministro los mande entregar en la remesa, que cada año se hace al Río Grande.

55.

Por el tiempo en que ya está de sason el Quelite silvestre, o simarron tendrá cuidado el Ministro de que los muchachos con el Fiscal, y otros si le pareciere, corten todo los dias de que hay en el Patio de la Misión, y en los contornos de ella, y antes de secarse lo queme el Fiscal, y redusga a Cenisa, y hecho esto lo guarde en el Chapil, que para este fin ay en la Oficina: y si esto no bastare para todo el Javon, que se ha de hacer entre año, dará providencia el Ministro de que se alejen mas a buscarlo. Cada vez que al Ministro le pareciere, y se hallare abastecido de cebo mandará hacer una o dos Peroladas de Javon, poniendo uno, que lo esté meneando, y que sepa hecharle la Lexia correspondiente, y darle el punto que ha menester; y no haviendo otro que lo haga, cuidará de esto el Fiscal, industriandole el Ministro de como lo ha de hacer, &[a].

place which seems fitting. If preferable, he can order the sheep to be brought to the Mission and sheared there, though this carries the risk of losing some because of the nearby settlements. The shepherd has the obligation to inform the missionary about the number of sheep, ewes and lambs under his care, of castrating the sheep when the time comes and making known those which were castrated so that the missionary may send them in the shipment that takes place each year to the Rio Grande.

55.

When the wild or <u>cimarron quelite</u> is ready for <u>cutting</u>, the missionary will see to it that the boys together with the fiscal and others, if it seems necessary, daily cut all that is in the patio of the mission and in the neighboring area. Before it dries, the fiscal burns it and reduces it to ashes. This done, he will put it in a pile which is kept in the workshop for this purpose. If this amount is not sufficient for all the soap that is to be made for the year, the missionary will send them to more distant places to gather more. Whenever it seems good to the missionary, and there is a supply of grease, he orders one or two kettles of soap to be made. He assigns one man to do the stirring who knows how much lye to add and how long to boil it. If no one knows how to do this job, the missionary will direct the fiscal in doing it, etc.

56.

Quando quiera el Ministro mandar hacer Velas, que regularmente es en invierno, hará llamar al Velero del Presidio, y entregandole el Cebo, y Pabilo, le dará un muchacho que le ayude si fuere necessario en lo que huviere menester: y caso de no tener la Misión Velero igualado, deberá ajustarse por Años, o como le pareciere.

57.

En el quarto de la Cal debe procurar el Ministro que siempre haiga providencia para el gasto de las Yndias, y para las obras que se ofrecieren; y quando vea que ya se va acabando mandará al Mayordomo, que haga traher piedras de cal y hechen una ornada, haciendo que trahigan tambien las Carretadas de leña que fueren menester para el horno.

58.

En la Misión por lo comun ay alguna o algunas Españolas mugeres de los Sirvientes las quales pueden amasar la Arina para el Viscocho, con que el Ministro se desayuna, y hacer Pan quando quiera: y si aconteciere no haver ninguna que pueda hacerlo, ni Yndia que sepa, el Ministro se dará maña para que no le falte lo necesario para su sustento, atendiendo tambien que a algunos enfermos no es posible negarles a tabilla, y el viscocho quando lo piden.

56.

When the missionary gives orders for candle-making, which generally is in the wintertime, he will have the candle-maker called from the presidio. Besides the tallow and the wicks, he is given a boy to assist him if necessary. In case the mission does not have a hired candle-maker, compensation will be made annually or as agreed upon.

57.

In the room where the lime is kept, the missionary will see to it that there is always a sufficient supply for the needs of the Indian women and for all the work that comes up. When he sees the supply dwindling, he has the superintendent arrange to have limestone brought in, a batch prepared and the cartloads of wood ready for the oven.

58.

In the mission, there are generally one or more Spanish women, wives of the servants, who can knead the flour for the biscuits and have them ready for the missionary's breakfast, and also homemade bread, when he wants it. Should there be no one present who can do this, nor any Indian woman who knows how, the missionary will manage to get what he needs for his sustenance. He bears in mind also the needs of the sick and provides chocolate bars and biscuits for them when they request them.

59.

Debe ser el Ministro provido, procurando tener siempre en la Misión medicamentos para los enfermos, yerba para los animales, azote para los discolos. En el trato con los Yndios debe ser afable con todos, prudente, economico, y conservador de sus bienes. No debe consentir alsados ni sobervios: debe castigar los viciosos, y zelar la honra de Dios. Con los enfermos debe ser caritativo, sufrido, y paciente: visitarlos segun lo necessitaren, y hacer que les apliquen los remedios que pudiere; y por ultimo Padre y todo de los Yndios, haciendose todo al todos para ganarlos a todos.

60.

Quando va acercandose el tiempo de la Siembra, todos los años se limpia la assequia, quitando para esto el agua en donde entra del Rio, teniendo tambien cuidado el Ministro de mandar componer las Puentes y la Presa, cuando lo necessiten.

61.

Acaba la limpia de la assequia se acomoda la Gente a tapar los portillos q^e huviere en la cerca de la Labor, y remendar lo que huviere malo: y si el tiempo urge, pueden destinarse algunos a esto, y otros a comensar a romper la tierra, si ya estuviere dispuesto, o a quemar la caña, que quedó de la Cosecha pasada: de manera que el Ministro ha de procurar labrar la tierra de modo que por Mayo se pueda ya sembrar el

59.

The missionary must have on hand medicines for the infirm, hay for the animals, a whip for the intractable. In his dealings with the Indians, he must be pleasant towards all, prudent, and protector of their possessions. He must not give in to the rebellious nor to the arrogant. He must punish the wicked and be always zealous for the honor of God. Toward the sick, he must be charitable, long-suffering and patient, visiting them when they need it and see to it that the use the remedies he can obtain. Finally, he is Padre and everything to the Indians, being all to all in order to win them all.

60.

When the time for planting nears, the irrigation ditches are cleaned, removing the water that comes from the river. The missionary will also see to it that the bridges and the dam are repaired when needed.

61.

When the irrigation ditches are cleared, the natives will mend the gaps in the fence around the field and repair what is in poor condition. If the weather requires urgency, some can be appointed for this work, while others begin to plow the land, if opportune, or burn the cane which remained from the past harvest. Thus, the missionary sees to it that the field is tilled, so that in May, which is the best time of year, corn

mays, que es el tiempo mas a proposito y si no alcansare, estenderse hasta Junio.

62.

Mientras unos anden en la compostura de la Cerca, otros pueden ocuparse en disponer la tierra en que se ha de sembrar el algodon, la fruta, el chile, teniendo ya de antemano puestos los almasigos. El frijol se siembra por el mes de Junio y assi debe darse lugar en la Labor, o en otra parte que disponga el Ministro, quien tambien tiene cuidado de que a todo se le acuda a su tiempo con el riego, con las escardas, limpias, &^{a}. Y si huviere seca, o reseca de algodon, que se le dé el beneficio que necessita para que fructifique aquel año.

63.

Si el Ministro hechare de veer, que el mays que se alsó en la Cosecha pasada no es suficiente para el gasto de la Misión, sembrará mays temprano por el mes de Febrero o Marzo para que supla necessidad y escasés del otro.

64.

En tiempo de limpia se acostumbraba antiguamente el que las mugeres fueran a ayudar a los hombres, haciendo su tarea como qualquier gañán; pero esto se quitó con justa razon por el desorden que havia, que prescindiendo de otras cosas, se seguia, que los hombres no trabajaban bien lo suyo por atender a lo de las mugeres, y tambien, que mejor es que las mugeres estén en sus casas moliendo, y haciendo de comer a

can be planted. If the work cannot be finished, then extend it into June.

62.

While some do repair work on the wall, others are busy preparing the soil for the planting of cotton, fruit, chile; the seeklings having already been prepared. The beans are planted in June, and there is a designated area for them in the field or wherever the missionary directs. He must also provide for irrigation in due time and for the hoeing and weeding. If the cotton has to be replanted, every effort should be made to have a good crop that year.

63.

If the missionary sees that the corn from the past harvest is not enough for the Indians at the mission, he will have it sown early in February or March to have on hand a sufficient supply.

64.

Formerly, during the time of preparing the soil, it was customary for the women to help the men, working like any farm-hand. However, this was stopped for a good reason, due to the disorder that resulted, which, prescinding from other matters, the men did not do their own work fully because they were helping the women with theirs. Also, and this is more important, the women should be at home grinding

sus maridos que no el que anden en el campo haciendo el oficio de los hombres. Para la Pisca se permite (solam^{te} quando la necessidad lo pide por escasearse los hombres) el que vayan las mugeres, que no estuvieren enfermas, criando, o en cinta, despues que han hecho de almorsar, y llevarse el almuerso a sus maridos, y ayudan a piscar no siguiendose entonces el inconveniente de que larguen los hombres lo suyo por atender a lo ageno, porque no ay tareas, sino que se procura meter y encerrar todo lo que se pueda en el dia; y las mugeres, y muchachos que quedan en la Misión acarrean el mays de la Carreta a la Troje, cuidando de esto el Fiscal.

65.

El dia que se acaba la Pisca, acostumbran los Yndios traher la ultima Carretada engalanda con banderas y listones y trahen amarrados con bandas, o ceñidores al Mayordomo, Governador y Alcalde, y con musica vienen cantando el Alabado, que rematan dentro de la Yglesia, y luego van a la Celda del Ministro a tomar su refresco, que suele ser un frasco de Vino. Pero toda esta fiesta se puede hacer quando la cosecha es abundante; que quando es corta mal pueden festejarla.

66.

La noche de la Vigilia de Navidad, o Nochebuena sacan los Yndios su danza de Matachines, y se están baylando en el Portal del Convento todo el

grain and preparing the meals for their husbands and not going through the fields doing men's work. During harvest time, it is permitted (only when necessity demands it because of the scarcity of men) for women who are not infirm, rearing children or expecting a child, to go and 'help after they have prepared a meal and taken it to their husbands. They may help gather the crop, and care must be taken so that the men do not slow down in their work to take care of other matters. Every effort is to be made that as much as possible is gathered in and put away each day. The women and children who are in the mission take the corn from the carts to the granary with the Fiscal directing operations.

65.

When the harvest is all gathered in, the Indians are accustomed to draw the last cart decorated with banners and ribbons, and go to the superintendent, governor, and alcalde and sing the "Alabado" with accompanying music. This ends in church. Then they go to the missionary's cell to enjoy a refreshment which usually is a bottle of wine. But all this rejoicing takes place when the harvest is abundant; when it is meager, one can hardly celebrate.

66.

On Christmas Eve, the Indians do the dance of the Matachines and go on dancing at the entrance of the friary as long as the missionary allows it. He

tiempo que el Ministro les permite, quien suele darles su refresco acostumbrado, si la Frasquera lo permite, y el primer dia de la Pascua se van a baylar al Presidio a casa del Governador, y otras particulares. En algunas Misiones tiene sus vestidos a proposito para estas fiestas; en esta, y en donde no lo hay, se acomodan con los paños de rebozo, y camisas de sus mugeres. Tambien es regular salga esta danza en la Procession del Corpus por suplemento de los Gigantes.

generally gives them a drink of wine if there is enough on hand. On Christmas Day, they go and dance at the presidio, at the governor's house and other places. In some missions, they wear outfits in keeping with the spirit of the feast. When these are not available, they use the women's scarves and shifts. This dance is regularly performed also in the procession of Corpus Christi instead of using the giant figures.

Note:

The earliest Corpus Christi procession in Spain took place in Barcelona in 1320, and the custom continues to this day. Besides religious and civic officials and musicians, the procession traditionally includes <u>gigantes</u> (giant figures), <u>comparsas</u> (costumed figures) and <u>cabezudos</u> (figures with very large heads). Many famous Spanish poets, such as Calderon, composed <u>autos sacramentales</u> (allegorical one-act dramas in honor of the Eucharist) which were performed outdoors during the festivities.

<u>Matachin</u> is a term of Arabic origin for dancers who wore masks and long multicolored robes. In the New World, their costumes generally included a crown of flowers or bark, and they carried a rattle and a pronged stick or wand. They evolved into societies called "soldiers of the Virgin". The simple steps and figures of their dances were accompanied by violins and sometimes also guitars.

67.

La tarde de la festividad principal de la Misión suele permitírseles metan un Toro en la Plaza de la Misión, y se diviertan con él, yendose todo en carreras y gritos.

67.

On the afternoon of the principal festivity of the Mission, it is customary to permit them to put a bull in the Mission Plaza, and they amuse themselves with him, and it all goes off with a lot of running and shouting. (Translation by Dr. Malcolm McLean, May 11, 1990.)

68.

Los hombres tienen sus diversiones en los juegos al Patolo, y Chueca y aunque a vezes se les permite; pero debe zelar el Ministro no vengan del Presidio ni de otra Misión a jugar con los Yndios, porque son tan dados a el juego, que pierden sus fresadas, su ropa y quanto tienen y esto es muy general, y comun en la Misión, y por esto procuren esconderse del Ministro para estar jugando. Las mugeres es distinto, porque no apuestan tan frecuentemen^te su ropa sino sus cuentas, y a estas se les permite el juego que llaman del Palillo, aún con las de otra Misión; no con las del Presidio, ni menos a la Chueca aún entre ellas mismas, porque este es un juego casi como el de la Pelota, y no es decente que anden dando carreras, y exercitándose con aquella fatiga, que pide el juego, particularm^te las enfermas a quienes es indispensable se les aumente su enfermedad con este genero de diversión: por lo qual se ha procurado ya desterrar de esta Misión semejante abuso a solicitud del Ministro.

69.

Sobre la licitud del bayle que usan los Yndios llamado Mitote quidquid sit de illo, lo cierto es, que ellos lo tienen por malo y por esto lo hacen a escusas del Ministro; que regularmente tienen sus supersticiones, y que con la concurrencia de hombres, y mugeres equivale a lo mismo que los fandangos y Saraos: por lo qual debe zelar el Ministro no

68.

The men find their diversion in games such as patolo y chueca, and, though sometimes these games are permitted, the missionary must not permit residents of the presidio or of another mission to play these games with the Indians, because they are so taken up with the game that they would forfeit their blankets, their clothing, and whatever they may have. This is quite common in the mission, and the Indians try to hide from the missionary while playing them. The women are different, because they do not gamble away their clothing very readily, but they do their beads. The game called palillo is permitted them even with the women of other missions but not with the women from the presidio. They are not permitted to play chueca even with their own group, because this game is like that of pelota. It is not becoming for them to run and exercise in the manner the game demands, especially the infirm, for this kind of diversion intensifies their infirmity. For this reason, the missionary is solicitous to banish such abuse from the mission.

69.

Regarding the lawfulness of the dance called the mitote, performed by the Indians, whatever one can say about it, this much is certain, that they consider it evil, and therefore they hide it from the missionary. The Indians have their superstitious practices, and for them this dance is like the fandangos and soirées among the Spaniards. Therefore, the mis-

haiga de esto en la Misión. Tambien es verdad, que no haviendo superstición, no siendo por motivo de muerte de enemigo, u otro semejante y no haviendo peligro de pecado aliunde, yo no tengo por ilícito el Mitote quando lo hacen por mera diversión, porque es entre los Yndios lo mismo, que entre los Españoles los fandangos.

70.

Quando es tiempo de piscar el Algodon, que regularm^te es por el mes de Septiembre, los dias, que ya estuviere avierto en la mata, es incumbencia del Fiscal con los muchachos, y si no ay de estos, las mugeres, el piscarlo, y traherlo con Capuyos al patio de la Misión, donde tendidos unos Cueros se está asoleando hasta que está bien seco, y estando assí, las muchachitas con una muger, que las cuide vienen al Portal del Convento a descapuyarlo, y ponerlo segunda vez al Sol para que acabe de secar, teniendo cuidado el Fiscal de meterlo, y sacarlo todos los dias, y subirlo al Tapanco donde se guarda quando esté ya bien seco.

71.

Trahida la lana del paraje donde fue la trasquila, como se dijo arriba, ya quando haya de comensar a beneficiar para tejer las fresadas, teniendo el Ministro provisión de Chiquihuites, los muchachos con el obrajero van lavando en la assequia, quanta pueden en el dia, dejando a remojar de un dia para otro en uno, o dos peroles la que se ha de lavar para que dé menos trabajo, y

sionary must be alert to prevent wrongdoing in the mission. Still, it is my conviction that when no superstition, no question of celebrating an enemy's death, or any sinful motive is present, then the mitote is not unlawful when done for mere diversion, because among the Indians it is the same as the fandango among the Spaniards.

70.

At cotton-picking time, usually in September when the bolls are completely opened, the fiscal must see to it that the children, and if they are not available, the women pick the cotton and bring it with the bolls to the patio of the mission, where it is placed on hides to dry in the sun. The girls with the woman who is directing them come to the friary to clean the cotton. They put it in the sun to dry some more. Every day the fiscal must take care that it is put away in the loft and taken out to dry. This occurs until it is completely dry.

71.

When the wool is taken from the place where the sheep were sheared, as has been said, preparations are made for weaving blankets, and the missionary has the supply of baskets ready. The boys with the foreman go to the acequia and wash the wool, as much as they can in a day, leaving it to soak from day to day in one or two kettles. This makes the washing easier and more effec-

quede mejor lavada. Antes se observaba que las mugeres la iban a lavar al Rio; pero se ha observado, que esto no tiene cuenta por el mucho desperdicio, que ay con la que se lleva el agua: y haciéndolo los muchachos en la assequia (y tambien algunas mugeres si aquellos no bastan) a vista del Ministro se pierde menos o nada y queda mejor lavada: y a la tarde luego que acaban la llevan a asolear al Patio.

tive. Formerly, this was done by the women who went to the river to wash the wool, but so much was lost in this way, carried away by the water, that it is better to have the boys wash it in the acequia (women can help, too, if there are not enough boys). When the work is done in this way, less is lost, and the results are better. In the afternoon as soon as the washing is finished, it is brought to the patio to dry in the sun.

Note:

In 1745, Mission Concepción had 300 sheep; in 1756, 1,800; in 1772, 3,840.

72.

Haviendo ya porción de lana lavada, y seca manda traher el Ministro al obraje quatro o seis cardadores, que con su cosulta [sic] señalará el Mayordomo, y de esto cardado, el Obrajero dará todos los dias a los muchachos la tarea q^e han de hilar en torno para trama; y a las mugeres les da sin cardar lo q^e han de hilar en malacate para pie, teniendo obligación estas de traher su madeja todos los dias, y entregarla al Obrajero, quien la debe pesar para ver si la trahen cabal, o han desperdiciado alguna: y para dar las tareas a los Cardadores, muchachos, y mugeres está present el Fiscal, para hacer que entreguen las que no la trajeren con tiempo.

72.

When there is a quantity of washed and dried wool, the missionary has four or six carders come to the workshop. They are appointed by the superintendent after consultation. When a certain amount is carded, the overseer each day will give the children the task of making thread for the material. To the women, he gives uncarded wool to be spun on the spinning wheel. They are obliged to turn in their skeins every day to the overseer who is to weigh them to find out if they are doing it right or have wasted some. The fiscal is there to give work to the carders, the women and the children, to see that they hand in what they have not done on time.

73.

Assí que el Ministro vea que ya ay porción de lana hilada para hechar una, o dos telas de

73.

When the missionary sees that a sufficient amount of spun wool to make one or two cloth

fresada, manda venir al Texedor, que él señalara de los que saben tejer, y comienza a hacer las fresadas, haciendo quantas se necessitaren para el Pueblo, debiendo tejer una tela angosta para los muchachitos; y otra demas para algunos pobres, que quiera hacerles caridad el Ministro: y acabada una tela, o conforme corta el Tejedor todos los dias las reparte el Ministro, como se dijo arriba. Con el Tejedor se pone uno, o dos muchachos para que estén haciendo Canillas, y le ayuden a añadir los hilos que se cortaren, y desenredar los que se enrredaren.

74.

Las madejas de lana, que entregan las mujeres todos los dias las debe meter el Obrajero a la Celda del Ministro, y guardarlas en la Oficina, de donde se saca cada vez, que se han de hacer cañones para la tela, y las que fueren necessarias: y no conviene, que el Obrajero guarde las madejas en su poder, porque suele haver sus drogas con las hiladoras. Acabadas las fresadas, si sobre bastante lana hilada, puede el Ministro si quiere mandar tejer una Pieza de Sayal, para hacer Cotones, que algunos apetecen en el Ivierno [sic].

75.

Pasados algunos diaz de haver concluido la fábrica de fresadas, comienza la de las mantas, y para esto se ocupan en el Obraje los muchachos, que huviere, unos escarmenando algodon, y otros hilando en los tornos la trama, y el Obrajero cardando, quien da todos los

blankets is ready, he calls for the weaver who designates those who know how to weave. Blanket material is made according to how much is needed by the natives. A narrow cloth is woven for the children and also for the poor, if the missionary wishes to practice charity. When a piece of cloth is finished, the weaver binds it off, and the missionary distributes the blankets every day, as was said above. With the weaver are stationed one or two boys, who make spools and aid him in adding the thread which was cut and disentangle the knotted thread.

74.

The overseer should deposit the skeins of wool brought daily by the women to the missionary's cell and then kept in the workshop. Only the estimated amount needed to prepare the spindles for the loom is taken out each time. The overseer is not to keep the skeins in his possession, because he may yield to some stratagem with the spinners. When the blankets are finished, if threaded wool is left over, the missionary may, if he wishes, order the weaver to make a piece of coarse woolen material in order to make pull-overs which some prefer in winter.

75.

A few days after the blanket-making is finished, the process of making cotton cloth is begun. The available children are employed in the workshop. Some make thread for the woof on the spinning wheels, and the overseer is carding. Every day, he gives each child three

diaz a cada muchacho tres onsas de algodon cardado, y a la tarde le entregan al Ministro las madejas, que debe ir guardando para su tiempo. La tarea que se da a las mugeres para que hilen para pie es regularmente onsa, y media, o dos onsas con pepitas, para que todos los dias por la mañana entreguen su madeja de onsa; y quando va faltando algodon escamenado [sic] para las tareas de los muchachos se les da a las mugeres solo para que escarmenen, teniendo cuidado de que trahigan las pepitas para semilla: y todos los diaz acabado de entregar las tareas, las lleva el obrajero al Ministro para que las guarde, asistiendo tambien el Fiscal a dar las tareas, como se dijo de la lana.

76.

Haviendo ya suficiente algodon hilado assi de pie, como de trama se comienzan a tejer las mantas por el mismo Tejedor, que hizo las fresadas, u otro si el Ministro quiere; y para que las mantas salgan iguales en cuanto se pueda, da el Ministro al Tejedor todo el algodon pesado; de manera que con lo que sobra en cada Cañon de hilo se ajustan veinte onsas en cada una; y haviendo pesado los doze Cañones que entran en el Urdidor, se le da uno por uno con sus madejas correspondientes para que con un muchacho que se le pone, lo vaya enbolviendo, y acabados de hacer todos los Cañones, se urde la Tela poniendo las Estacas donde ya tienen medidas las diez varas que deben entrar para urdir la Tela. Puesta ya en el Julio [sic] (i.e., puesta ya el enjulio) y para comenzar a

ounces of carded cotton. In the evening, they must turn in their skeins to the missionary, which he sets aside until they are needed. The quota given to the women for spinning is generally one and a half ounces per foot or two ounces with seeds. Every day in the morning, they hand in their one-ounce skeins. When more carded cotton is needed for the children's work, the women are given some only for carding, taking care to bring the pips for seed: and every day when the work is over, the overseer turns in the finished amounts to the missionary to take care of. The fiscal is to assist in assigning the jobs as was said with regard to the wool.

76.

With enough thread woven for the warp as well as for the woof, the cloths are now woven by the same weaver who made the blankets, or by someone else if the missionary so wishes. To have the cloths come out as evenly as possible, the missionary gives the weaver all the weighed cotton. Twenty ounces of thread are allowed for each piece and are wound on the cylinders. After the twelve cylinders used on the warping frame have been weighed, they are fed into it, one by one, by means of their corresponding skeins so that with one boy to put them in, they are wound, and when all the cylinders have been put into the loom, the cloth is woven, with the pegs placed where the ten-vara lengths have been measured. With the warp rod already in place, the

tejer da el Ministro al muchacho una madeja de las de trama para que haga Canillas, y acabada una da otra, y acabada esta, otra hasta que se concluye la manta, que entonces la enrolla el Tejedor y la entrega al Ministro para que la guarde. La pieza de manta urdida es de este modo, esto es, con veinte onzas en cada Cañón, que por todo hacen quince libras con sinco estacas y diez varas de largo, saca por lo comun sincuenta varas o sincuenta y una, que debe saber el Ministro para su govierno. El ancho de la manta es de tres cuartas poco mas, de manera que no llega a vara: y ya en el Peine tienen cogida la medida del ancho que han de llevar. Otra pieza se hace de manta mas angosta para los muchachos, y para fundillos de los calsones blancos, a los que se les ha de hechar, como se dijo en su lugar.

77.

Despues que se ha concluido todo la manifactura del Obraje, se ocupan los muchachos en cortar quelite para Cenisa del javon, en limpiar el patio, la Cavalleriza y en lo que quiera el Ministro, mientras llega el tiempo de lavar la lana, y volver a los Exercicios de Obraje.

78.

Han observado los Ministros mantener muchachos en la Celda, recogiéndolos desde que ya son grandecitos, no solo para emplearlos en los ministerios, que van dichos, ni tampoco precisamente para servirse de ellos, sino tambien para edu-

missionary gives the boy a skein of the woof in order to prepare bobbins. He continues to do this until the cloth is finished. The weaver then rolls it up and gives it to the missionary to put away. The cloth woven in this way, that is, with twenty ounces in each cylinder, which in all equals fifteen pounds with five pegs and ten varas in length, generally yields fifty or fifty-one varas of material. The missionary ought to keep this in mind.

The width of the cloth is a little more than three-fourths of a vara, not quite one vara. The frame can be prepared according to the width desired. Another narrower piece is made for the children and for the lining of the white trousers for those who are to get them, as was said above.

77.

After all the fabrics have been made in the workshop, the boys are busy cutting the quelite for ashes to make the soap, cleaning the patio, the stable and in whatever the missionary wants them to do until it is time to wash the wool and return to the duties in the workshop.

78.

In the past, the missionaries have kept the boys in the cell, inviting them when they have grown up a little, not only to have them work, as has been said, nor employ them personally, but to educate them, civilize them and make them

carlos, civilisarlos, hacerlos Gente; y para esto viven siempre en el Convento, comen de la Cosina del Ministro, y duermen en su Celda, no teniendo, que ir a sus casas mas que a almorzar, a que los laven y expulguen. Y es una costumbre muy laudable, porque criándose fuera del Convento, por lo comun salen simarrones, vosales y viciosos, pues les falta la enseñansa de los Ministros y la comunicación y trato con él, que es lo que les aprovecha. Y el Ministro tiene cuidado de que sepan la Doctrina, de enseñarles el ayudar a Missa, de apajarles [sic] sus malas inclinaciones, de corregirles lo malo en enseñarles lo bueno. Y assi que ya son capaces de trabajar en el Campo los despacha al trabajo, volviendo a comer y dormir en la Celda hasta que se casen o han crecido de modo q^e dejan de ser muchachos, que entonces se les da libertad para que se vayan a sus Casas, contándose en el numero de los Solteros.

79.

Tambien debe cuidar el Ministro de que los muchachos chiquitos hablen el idioma español: para acomodarse a lo mandado por varias Cédulas y por la utilidad que resulta, assí al Ministro de entender lo que dicen, como a los mismos Yndios. Y ha sido tanto el empeño del Ministro en esta Misión sobre este assunto, que da gusto oyr a todos los Ynditos, Ynditas, y aun muchachitos pequeñitos, que apenas comiensan a hablar, ya pronuncia el Castellano y generalmente hombres, y mugeres lo hablan, excepto algunos, que se han que-

genuinely human. Therefore, they always live in the friary, eat from the missionary's kitchen and sleep in his cell, not having to go to their homes except for breakfast, to be washed and deloused. Growing up within the friary is a very laudable custom, because otherwise they generally end up wild, rebellious and vicious, since they lack instruction by the missionaries and the communication and dealing with them, which is to their benefit. The missionary takes care that they learn the catechism, are taught to serve Mass, to subdue their bad inclinations, correcting what is bad and showing them what is good. As soon as they are able to work in the field, he sends them there. They return to eat and sleep in the cell of the missionary until they marry or have grown and are no longer children. They then may go home and are counted as bachelors.

79.

The missionary should see to it also that the small children speak Spanish in order to meet the demands of various decrees and because of the facility it promotes both for the missionary to understand what they are saying and for the Indians to understand him. At this mission, the missionary has worked so hard on this that it is a pleasure to listen to the Indian children, even the tiniest ones, speaking Spanish. In general, the men and women speak it now, except some who have remained untamed, for the missionary spares no effort in

dado vosales, no sufragando
diligencia alguna para hacerles
entra la lengua castellana.

helping them understand the
language.

Note:

A royal decree issued on April 16, 1770, for
example, ordered that in all the provinces of the
Indies the use of different Indian dialects was
to cease, and only Spanish was to be spoken. The
Archbishop of Mexico was instructed to implement
the decree. (See the letter of Fray Juan Joseph
de Aguina in the Archivo de Indias, Sevilla,
España, Section Guadalajara, legajo 337.)

80.

De tiempo en tiempo debe el Ministro hacer viaje a la Costa, y traher los fugitivos, que regularmente ay, haciendo diligencia de traher tambien si puede, algunos Gentiles, para q^e siempre se verifiquen vivas conversiones, y la Misión no se acabe por falta de Gente: y entretanto va el Ministro a esta diligencia queda el Supernumerario supliendo en la Misión, como está determinado por el Sr Comandante General y nuestros Prelados.

80.

From time to time, the missionary should journey to the coast and bring back the fugitives, who regularly leave the mission, trying at the same time to gain some pagans, if possible, so that more conversions are realized and the mission does not come to an end because of a lack of natives. While the missionary is away on this errand, the supernumerary takes his place at the mission, as has been decided by the commandant general and our superiors.

Note:

The supernumerary was an extra friar on hand who
took the place of a sick or absent missionary.

Runaway Indians were always a problem, but, once
the missionary caught up with them, they were
willing most of the time to return to mission
life.

81.

El trato y comunicación de los Yndios con los Españoles no solo es permitido sino mandado por el Sr Comand^{te} Gral. que no

81.

Dealings and communication between the Indians and the Spaniards are not only allowed but are ordered by the com-

se les impida; mas con todo esso debe el Ministro desterrar de la Misión algunos de estos Españoles q^e no viene a otra cosa mas que a quitarles a los Yndios lo que pueden, a jugar con ellos, a vender vagatelas por la ropa, y trastes de ellos, y a otras maldades, que no se pueden tolerar: a estos tales no debe consentir el Ministro en la Misión, y si exhortados que no vengan, persisten en bolver, mándelos atar al Palo, y dar una tunda de azotes, que assi escarmentarán.

mandant general. Nonetheless, the missionary must expel from the mission those Spaniards who come only to take from the Indians all that they can, gambling with them and exchanging trifles for their clothing and utensils, and other perversities which cannot be tolerated: the missionary should not allow such people in the mission. If he asks them not to come and they persist in returning, he will have them tied to the stake and given a whipping with a lash, so that they may take warning.

82.

La sujeción de los inferiores al Superior y de los Subditos al Prelado es tan necessaria en las Comunidades, y en los Pueblos que sin ella, nada havrá bien governado, y todo seria un monstruo. Debe el Ministro portarse con los Yndios, de modo que todos le estén sujetos, le tengan respeto, y le obedescan castigando a los inobedientes, rebeldes, y díscolos, sin apartarse de la mansedumbre, afabilidad, y prudencia para governar.

82.

The submission of inferiors to the superior and subjects to the prelate is indispensable in communities and in pueblos. Without it, nothing could be well managed, but all would end up in confusion and disorder. The missionary must so conduct himself toward the Indians so that all will show him respect, submission and obedience. He must punish the disobedient, the rebellious and the intractable without losing his usual gentleness, affability and prudence in governing.

83.

Acostumbran algunas mugeres salir sobre tarde de la Misión a comer tunas, sarsamoras, cuacomites, agritos, nueces, camotitos, y otras frutitas, y raises del campo y el Ministro les permite todos estos paseos acomodándose a su genio, si no halla algun inconveniente o peligro de Enemigos. Suelen tambien irse a pasear a otras Misiones o al Presidio, y para

83.

Some women are in the habit of leaving the mission toward evening to eat tunas, blackberries, yucca, agaritas, nuts, sweet potatoes and other fruits and roots from the field. The missionary allows these excursions if there is no inconvenience or danger from any enemies. Also, they are accustomed to go to other missions or to the presidio, but, for

esto deben pedir licencia al Ministro quien la da o niega segun conviene.

Advertencia

Para todas las demas menudencias que aqui faltaren, e irá mirando el Ministro en el govierno de la Misión, la misma practica, y exercicio le enseñarán lo que debe hacer, pues para muchas cosas no se puede dar regla general, y otras suele ser necessario mudar segun la ocurrencia y variación de los tiempos: y estas instrucciones solamente se han puesto para un Ministro, que no haviendo governado Misión, se halla solo, y sin saber a quien consultar el methodo que debe observar, para no exponerse a errar mientras cobra experiencia de las cosas.

Y porque en los números antecedentes faltaron algunos puntos dignos de advertirse, que despues se han reflexionado, acordamos ponerlos en este lugar con relación al numero, que pertenecen, y pueden saberse por este.

SUPLEMENTO

Nos 1 y 2

Assi como en la variación de las horas de repicar para las Misas que se dicen al Pueblo, conoce la Gente, si es dia de fiesta para los Yndios, o solo para los no Yndios, assi tambien se varia el Reso, que tiene en la Yglesia al tiempo de la Misa: porque los Domingos todos del año, y los dias de dos Cruces, acabado de alzar

this, they must first ask permission from the missionary who grants or denies it as he judges best.

Notice

For other details that are lacking here and as the missionary is constantly solicitous about the best way to manage the mission, the very practice and activity in the mission will teach him what should be done. No general rule can be given for everything, and changes are necessary according to events and seasons. These instructions are meant for a missionary who has never been in charge of a mission, is all alone and does not know whom to consult for advice in order to avoid making mistakes, as he gains wisdom through experience.

Some worthwhile points were omitted above and are now being added to the corresponding numbers.

SUPPLEMENT

Nos. 1 and 2

Since the hours for ringing the bell varies for the Mass said for the pueblo, the people know when it is a feast-day for the Indians or only for the non-Indians. Likewise, the prayers said in church during the Mass vary. Every Sunday of the year and on first-class feast-days, after the priest has elevated the Sacred Host, they all pray

la Sagrada Hostia el Sacerdote, resan todos la Estación del Santíssimo Sacramento, y luego cantan el Alabado; pero los dias de una Cruz y los Sabados no se resan al tiempo de la Misa cosa alguna, sino que acabado el ultimo Evangelio cantan la Salve en verso, que acostumbran despues de la Doctrina, que comienza Salve Virgen Pura; y lo mismo se hace quando la Misa es cantada aunque la fiesta sea de dos Cruces.

N°s. 1, y 2 y 7

Todos los dias que se dice Misa al Pueblo havrá sea dia de fiesta, havrá no sea, al tiempo de la Misa están los Musicos tocando sus instrumentos en el Coro: y los Sabados en la tarde el Rosario tambien acostumbran para los Misterios tocar el Violin y la Guitarra.

Para las ocasiones que sirven en la Yglesia la Cruz y los Ciriales, los muchachos sirven de Acólitos, vistiendose las Sobrepelises [sic] que para este fin ay en la Sacristia, como tambien para ayudar las Misas que el Ministro celebra: y aunque hasta haora no hay hechas Opas [sic] para los Acólitos, puede el Ministro mandar hacer dos, o tres para la mayor decencia, como usan algunas Misiones.

N°. 14

El doble de Campanas el dia de finados se observa en esta Misión como en las demas Yglesias, comensando desde la Víspera en la tarde hasta la hora del Responso, que dice el Ministro todas las noches: y al otro dia comienza desde la Alva

the special prayer to the Most Blessed Sacrament and then sing the Alabado. On second-class feasts and on Saturdays, they do not say those prayers during the Mass, but, at the end of the Last Gospel, they sing the Salve which begins Salve Virgen Pura, and is usually sung after the catechism. They do the same thing whenever it is a sung Mass, although it is a first-class feast.

Nos. 1, 2 and 7

Every day when Mass is said for the people, whether it is a feast-day or not, the musicians are in the choir, playing their instruments. On Saturday evenings when the Rosary is said, they usually play the violin and the guitar for the mysteries.

On those occasions when the cross and the candlesticks are used in the church, the boys serve as acolytes vested in surplices (sobrepellices) which are kept in the sacristy, and also when they serve the Masses the missionary says: and although up to now no cassocks (hopas) have been made for the acolytes, the missionary can have them make two or three to add greater dignity, as is done in some missions.

No. 14

On All-Souls Day, the bell is tolled at this mission as in the other churches, beginning in the evening at Vespers up to the hour of the prayer for the dead, which the missionary says every evening. The next day, the bell is tolled at dawn and

hasta concluidos los Sufragios en la **Yglesia**.

Aunque en todas las Parroquias, o Capillas donde ay Pila baptismal, regularmente no se consagra agua mas que una vez al año, por el peligro que ay de que se corrompa con las excesivas calores que acen en el Verano en todo este payz: bien que si el Ministro viere que no se ha corrompido y está util para baptizar, consagrará quando quisiere.

Quando se acaba el agua bendita en la Pila de la Yglesia, el Fiscal tiene cuidado de llenarla, y avisarle al Ministro para que la bendiga y todos los Domingos se acostumbra el Asperges al Pueblo antes de la Misa.

En la Celda del Ministro se guardan los Libros, donde se asientan las Partidas de Baptismos, Casamientos y Entierros: y para que el Ministro halle con facilidad alguna Partida que quiere buscar, se ha hecho un Yndice, que se guarda junto con los Libros, encargandole que **cada vez,** q̀ assentase alguna **Partida** de Baptismo ponga **tambien en el** Yndice el **nombre del baptisado** con el numero, que **le corresponde:** y si es de Casamiento no tendrá que poner mas que el numero correspondiente a los nombres de los Contrayentes, que ya deberán constar en su propio Yndice.

continues until the prayers are finished in church.

In all parishes and chapels where there is a baptismal font, ordinarily water is blessed only once a year. But at this mission, water is blessed generally twice a year, because of the danger that it will deteriorate on account of the excessive heat that prevails during the summer in all of this country. Whenever the missionary sees that the water is still good and can be used for baptizing, he will bless the water when he chooses to do so.

When the blessed water in the baptismal font in church is all used up, the fiscal is to refill it and advise the missionary to bless the water. On Sundays, the "Asperges" is usually given before Mass for the people.

In the missionary's cell are kept the books where the entries are made for baptisms, marriages and burials. So that the missionary may easily find an entry, an index has been prepared which is kept with the books. He is urged to record the number and name in the index whenever he makes an entry in the baptismal record. If it is a marriage, he will place only the corresponding number of the names of the contracting parties which are already properly recorded.

Note:

The "Asperges" is the blessing with holy water given by the celebrant before Mass.

N° 19.

Entre los cargos que el Ministro da en la Misión, uno es el de Ayudante del Mayordomo, el cual sirve de lo que suena su oficio y de suplir las ausencias, y enfermedades del Mayordomo, y hacer en todas las cosas lo mismo que él puede hacer, y tambien toma las Ordenes del Ministro para señalar Baqueros, Pastores, para sembrar, y todo lo demas. Este no es tan necessario, que faltando no se puede hacer nada, como es el Mayordomo; pero regularmente lo ay por la mayor utilidad, y comodidad de la Misión.

19.

Ay tambien un Pescador, que sirve para traher en el Adviento, Quaresma, y demas dias de abstinencia el Pescado para la mesa del Ministro: y ya saben todos que semejantes dias no se ocupa al Pescador en otra cosa, y assimismo lo señala el Ministro, o el Mayordomo, quando se haya de mudar, o sea necessario poner otro.

40.

Regular**mente** se encarga en la memoria **Revesillo** (i.e., Ribecillo) que sirve para rivelear [sic] (i.e., ribetear) las Naguas, de algunas mugeres, a quien el Ministro quiera darles.

No. 19.

Among the responsibilities that the missionary delegates is that of the assistant to the superintendent. This person substitutes for the superintendent when the latter is absent or sick. He also takes orders from the Missionary for appointing the vaqueros and shepherds; for the planting and everything else. He is not so indispensable that if he is absent, nothing can be done, as would be the case if the superintendent were gone. But, in general, it is for the greater usefulness and profit of the Mission.

19.

Also, there is a fisherman who is to bring the fish in Advent, Lent and other days of abstinence, for the missionary's table. Everyone knows that on such days the fisherman is occupied with nothing else. Whenever a replacement is necessary, it is made by the missionary or the superintendent.

40.

Generally, the supply list includes trimming for the petticoats of certain women selected by the missionary.

83.

En tiempo de las fiestas del Presidio es inescusable dar licencia un dia a las mugeres, y muchachos, para que vayan a veer los Toros, y este dia se le da a cada uno de estos su mediecito [sic], para que compren lo que quieren, y lo mismo a las mugeres.

24. y 25.

Aunque en los numeros 24 y 25 se dijo que el Fiscal da las raciones de Javon, y Tabaco; lo mas conveniente es que el Ministro lo haga personalmente, pues por haverse experimentado poca fidelidad en el manejo de estas cosas, se ha mudado la costumbre de que el Fiscal lo repartiera. No dejará de estrañar el Ministro el que no se haya tenido curia en plantar arboles frutales, viendo que en otras Misiones los ay; pero la satisfacción le sacará de la duda, y es, que no se puede conseguir con estos Yndios tener arbol frutal ninguno, porque todo lo hurtan antes de que se aprovecha; siendo tanta su propensión a el hurto de estas cosas, que sin embargo de la vigilancia que el Ministro tiene en cuidar los Arboles de Nísperos, el tiempo que están con fruta, no le vale para que dejen de cojerlos aun cuando comiensan a sasonarse, de manera, que nunca se verifica lograrse todo el fruto, aun advirtiendoles a los Yndios, que se les dará de ellos assi que estén maduros. Y por la misma causa muchas vezes no se cultiva al Tachacual, manteniendo hortalizas, que pudieran

83.

During the fiestas at the presidio, it is a matter of course to give the women and children permission to go to watch the bulls. On this day, they are given a small sum of money to buy whatever they want.

24 and 25

Although numbers 24 and 25 advocate that the Fiscal distribute the rations of soap and tobacco, it is better for the missionary to do this personally. Since experience has shown that discrepancies have arisen in conducting these affairs, the custom of having the fiscal distribute things has been changed. The missionary who has not had experience in raising fruit trees will no doubt find it strange since the other missions have them, but the doubt will be removed when he has the satisfaction of knowing that it is impossible with these Indians to have any kind of fruit tree, because they rob them before they are ready. Their propensity for taking the fruit is such that, in spite of the vigilance of the missionary to care for the loquat trees when they are bearing fruit, it does not matter, for they do not stop picking it even when it begins to ripen. Thus, a full crop is not possible, even though the Indians have been assured that the fruit will be given to them as soon as it is fully ripe. For the same reason, the tachacual is not cultivated so

darse, como lo experimentará el Ministro si quiere dedicarse al cultivo de todas estas Plantas. Y porque no deja de venirse a los ojos la replica, que puede hacer objetando el exemplo de las otras Misiones, que mantienen Arboles frutales y hortalisas, y se le satisface con la verdad diciendole: que las otras Misiones tienen la ventaja de que sus Yndios son mas dociles que estos: pues es fama comun la que tienen los Pajalaches de perversos, duros de condición, y poco dociles: y aunque el que escrive esto, es cierto, que quiere a sus Yndios porque los ha tratado, y manejado; no por esso le ciega la passión para dejar de conocer la verdad, y declarar lo que siente; y por la misma razon dice, que aunque son los Pajalaches como se ha dicho; no son como muchos dicen, que ciegos de la passión, o faltos de conocimiento les atribuyen mas de los que tienen. Todo lo experimentará el Ministro con la comunicación, y trato de los Yndios, de que en todas partes ay bueno, y ay malo, como en todo el mundo.

Tambien conviene advertirle, que mientras va conociendo las propriedades de cada uno, no dejarán de venirle algunos o algunas, con cuentos, y embustes, procurando desdorar al Ministro antecesor, trayendole ejemplo de que le daba o no le daba, que hacia esto o aquello, y otras mil cosas: mas la prudencia del Ministro se guardará de creer semejantes cosas, y obrará en todo como le conviene a su Estado, y Religion, dispensando los defectos, que no-

as to yield vegetables, as the missionary would discover should he wish to undertake to grow all of these plants. When he has to refute the charge that the other missions have fruit trees and vegetables, he can truthfully say that the other missions have more docile Indians. It is common knowledge that the Pajalaches are perverse, set in their ways and not at all docile. However, the author of these lines certainly loves his Indians because he has dealt with them and guided them. But his feelings do not prevent his recognizing the truth and saying how he feels. Therefore, he states that, although the Pajalaches are as he has described them above, they are not like what some people (blinded by passion or who do not know the truth) say, who charge them with faults they do not have. The missionary will find out through his communication and his relationships with the Indians, that it is true that there are some good and some bad, just as in the rest of the world.

Furthermore, while he is becoming acquainted with the gifts of each one, there will be those who come to him with stories and lies, trying to tarnish the reputation of the previous missionary by giving examples of what he gave or did not give, that he did this or that, and a thousand other things. But the missionary's prudence will keep him from believing such tales. He will always conduct himself according to the demands of his state

tare en esta Instrucción que solo es hecha por la utilidad, y comodidad del Ministro, y con la sana intención de que le aproveche, y se sirva de ella en las cosas, que dudare: y todo sea para la mayor honra, y gloria de Dios nuestro Señor y ceda en alabansa de su Santissima Madre la Virgen María.

of life and Religion. May he excuse all the shortcomings he sees in these Guidelines which have been written for the sole purpose of benefitting him, and may he make use of them on those occasions when he is doubtful. May all be for the greater honor and glory of Our Lord God, and may it redound to the praise of his Most Holy Mother, the Virgin Mary.

THE SAN JOSÉ PAPERS

THE PRIMARY SOURCES

FOR THE HISTORY OF

MISSION SAN JOSÉ Y SAN MIGUEL DE AGUAYO

FROM ITS FOUNDING IN 1720 TO THE PRESENT

PART II: AUGUST 1791 - JUNE 1809

OLD SPANISH MISSIONS HISTORICAL

RESEARCH LIBRARY AT SAN JOSÉ MISSION

SAN ANTONIO, TEXAS

1983

792.9.3 - 818.68

COLEGIO AP^CO DE N. S. DE GUADALUPE SEPT^E 3 DE 1792	APOSTOLIC COLLEGE OF OUR LADY OF GUADALUPE SEPTEMBER 3, 1792
MEMORIA QUE REMITE EL R. P. G. FR. YGN^O MARIA LAVA AL P. P. FR. JOSÉ MAN^L PEDRAJO MTRO DE LA MISS^ON DE S^OR S. JOSÉ	REPORT SUBMITTED BY REV. FATHER GENERAL, FRAY YGNACIO MARIA LAVA TO THE FATHER PRESIDENT, FRAY JOSÉ MANUEL PEDRAJO, MINISTER AT MISSION SAN JOSÉ

1 p̃za de Balleta con 97 v^s â 4 3/4 r^s	057 . 4 3/4	1 length of thick flannel, 97 varas long at 4 3/4 reals
1 Dozena de Rebozos quatrados finos en	22 . 0	1 dozen fine quality shawls
2 dhas de ydem jaspeados â 19 p^s	038 . 0	2 dozen variegated shawls at 19 pesos
1 dha de ydem trezados ordinarios en	010 . 0	1 dozen poncho-styled ordinary shawls
58 varas de Liston de ojuela â 1 r^l	007 . 0	58 varas of eyelet ribbon at
6 P̃zas de Liston N° 40 â 20 r^s	015 . 0	6 spools of Number 40 ribbon at 20 reals
1 Libra de seda az^l y blanca, en	013 . 0	1 pound of blue and white silk
1 Ydem de Pita de china en	001 . 0	1 pound of India cord
42 v^s de liston de terciopelo â 1 r^l	005 . 2	42 varas velvet ribbon at 1 real
1 par de zaraz^s finas de Yndian^a en	006 . 6	1 pair of fine calico breeches at
4 pares de Naguas de Duroy y Estam^a â 4 p^s 5 r^s	018 . 4	4 felt and wool underskirts at 4 pesos 4 reals
3 yd. de yd. de Yndianilla az^l â 5 p^s	015 . 0	3 blue calico underskirts at 5 pesos

12

6 ydem de ydem de Castor â 4 p^s 6 r^s	019 . 0	4 felt underskirts at 4 pesos 6 reals
2 Frezad^s â 8½ r^s Petat^s y arpill^s en	003 . 0¼	2 blankets at 8½ reals, mats and sacks at
½ Paño con 39 v^s a 11¼ r^s	056 . 0½	½ length of fabric: 39 varas long at 11½ reals
4 Rebozos Chimistlan^s de seda a 5 p^s	020 . 0	4 silk Chimistlan scarves at 5 pesos
4 Dozen^s de Mascadas de Marca â 11 p^s 4 r^s	046 . 0	4 dozen excellent quality silk kerchiefs at 11 pesos 4 reals
2 d$\widetilde{ha}$s de Mascadas de 7/8 â 9 p^s	018 . 0	2 dozen silk kerchiefs size 7/8 at 9 pesos
1 Petaquilla de hilo muñequilla en 3 p^s 4 r^s	003 . 4	1 small carpet bag at 3 pesos 4 reals
4 rebozos Chimistlan^s de Algodon â 18 r^s	009 . 0	4 cotton Chimistlan scarves at 18 reals
12 Gruezas de Botones de Metal â 5 r^s	007 . 4	12 gross metal buttons at 5 reals
200 v^s de sinta Criolla a 60 v^s p^r 1 p^o	003 . 2½	200 varas of fishing net at 60 varas for 1 peso
300 v^s de sinta de reata â 8 v^s p^r 1 p^o	004 . 0	300 varas of lasso at 8 varas for 1 peso
10 v^s sinta blanca en 3 r^s	000 . 3	10 varas white tape at 3 reals
4 Rebozos en papelados Mex^{nos} a 2 p^s 6 r^s	011 . 0	4 gift-wrapped Mexican shawls at 2 pesos 6 reals
Passa a la B$\widetilde{ta}$	410 . 1	Balance forward

13

Por la de la B̂ta	410 . 1	Balance forward
2 Libr^S de Pita az^l á 9 r^S	002 . 2	2 pounds of blue agave thread at 9 reals
2 P$\widehat{za}$s de Manta de 7/8 â 8 p^S 5 r^S	017 . 2	2 rolls of heavy cotton cloth 7/8 at 8 pesos 5 reals
2 Ydem de Manta angosta â 6 p^S 1 r^l	012 . 2	2 rolls of narrow heavy cotton cloth at 6 pesos 1 real
3 Frezadas â 8½ r^S Petates y Arp^S en 7 1/4 r^S	004 . 0 3/4	3 blankets at 8½ reals, mats and sacks at 7 1/4
½ Paño con 39 v^S a 11½ r^S	056 . 0½	½ length of woolen material; 39 varas at 11½ reals
2 Mazos de Avalorios â 8½ rr	002 . 1	2 bundles of beads at 8½ reals
4 Doz$^{\widehat{as}}$ de Gargant^S y Cruz^S â 2½ rr	001 . 2	4 dozen necklaces and crosses at 2½ reals
10 Doz$^{\widehat{nas}}$ de Anillos lizos y con piedras en 12½ r^S	001 . 4½	10 dozen plain rings and some with stones at 12½ reals
6 doz$^{\widehat{nas}}$ de Rosarios de Frutilla â 2½ r^S	001 . 7	6 dozen rosaries made of nuts at 2½ reals
3 Doz$^{\widehat{nas}}$ de Sarcillos de Piedras â 2½ r^S digo 2 doz^S	000 . 5	3 dozen earrings with stones at 2½ reals, I mean 2 dozen
3 hilos de Perlas del Mambrú à 4 r^S	001 . 4	3 strings of Marlborough pearls at 4 reals
1 Dozena de Tixeras entrefin^S en 8 r^S	001 . 0	1 dozen medium quality scissors at 8 reals
3 Gruezas Botones de hilo à 2 r^S	000 . 6	3 gross of thread-covered buttons at 2 reals
3 Pares de Chiguead^S y un liston bordado en 4 r^S	000 . 4	3 pair turtle shell disks an 1 embroidered ribbon at 4 reals
1 Bejuquillo de hilo de oro en 2 p^S	002 . 0	1 Chinese gold necklace at 2 pesos
42 Medallas Romanas en 12 rr^S	001 . 4	42 Roman medals at 12 reals

14

10 Dozenas de Belduquez â 2 p^s	020 . 0	10 dozen large pointed knives at 2 pesos
3 Dozenas de Zapatos de Muger â 6 p^s	021 . 0	3 dozen women's shoes at 6 pesos
3 P̂zas de Manta de 7/8 â 8 p^s 5 r^s	025 . 7	3 rolls of 7/8 cotton material at 8 pesos 5 reals
4 Ydem de Manta Ang̑ta â 6 p^s 1 r^l	024 . 4	4 rolls of narrow cotton cloth at 6 pesos 1 real
3 Frezad^s a 8½ r^s Petat^s y Arpiller^s en 7¼ r^s	004 . 0 3/	3 blankets at 8½ reals, mats and sacks at 7¼ reals
50 Mantas de la Villa alta â 12 r^s	075 . 0	50 mantles at 12 reals
28½ v^s de Manfort de varios color^s â 5 r^s	017 . 6½	28½ varas of different colors of Manfort material
0 v^s de Tripe azul â 12 rr^s	030 . 0	20 varas of blue shag cloth at 12 reals
3 P̂zas de Ralladillo â 8 p^s 4 r^s	025 . 4	3 rolls of striped cotton ducking at 8 pesos 4 reals
3 Ydem de Manta de 7/8 â 8 p^s 5 r^s	025 . 7	6 rolls of heavy cotton material at 8 pesos 5 reals
8 Ydem de Manta angosta â 6 p^s 1 r^l	018 . 3	8 rolls of narrow heavy cotton cloth at 6 pesos 1 real
3 Dozenas de Calcetas de hilo â 18 r^s	006 . 6	3 dozen stockings at 18 reals
1 P̂za Cambaya angosta en 5 p^s 6 r^s	005 . 6	1 roll of narrow Chambray material at 5 pesos 6 reals
2 Frezad^s a 8½ r^s en Petates y Arpill^s	003 . 0	2 blankets at 8½ reals and mats and sacks
Passa al Frente	820 . 2	Balance forward
(Page 284) Por la de Enfrente	820 . 2	Balance forward

15

Por la de enfrente	820 . 2	Balance forward
6 P$\widehat{za}$s de Cambaya ancha á 10 p^s	060 . 0	6 rolls of wide Chambray material at 10 pesos
48 v^s de Yndian^a azul â 6½ r^s	039 . 0	48 varas of blue calico at 6½ reals
18 v^s de Yndianilla fina â 8 r^s	018 . 0	18 varas of fine calico at 8 reals
1 P$\widehat{za}$: de Roan corriente con 55 v^s á 5 r^s	034 . 3	1 roll of ordinary Roanne linen at 55 varas for 5 reals
2 P$\widehat{za}$s de Pontivi corrte. â 16 p^{os}	032 . 0	2 rolls of ordinary Pontivi cloth at 16 pesos
2 Ydem de Manta angosta â 6 p^s 1 r^l	012 . 2	2 rolls of narrow cotton cloth at 6 pesos 1 real
1 Ydem de Manta Languina de Puebla en	008 . 2	1 roll of Languina cotton cloth from Puebla
1 Ydem de Cambaya angosta en	005 . 6	1 roll of narrow Chambray material
1 Pza de Pontivi Superfino en	021 . 0	1 roll of super-fine Pontivi cloth
3 Frezadas a 8½ r^s petates y Arpiller^s en	004 . 0½	3 blankets at 8½ reals, mats and sacks
3 P$\widehat{za}$s de Manta de 7/8 a 8 p^s 5 r^s	025 . 7	3 rolls of 7/8 cotton cloth at 8 pesos 5 reals
2 Ydem de Cambaya angosta â 5 p^s 6 r^s	011 . 4	2 rolls of narrow Chambray material at 5 pesos 6 reals (cambric)
1 Ydem de Manta angosta en	006 . 1	1 roll of narrow cotton material
1 Ydem de Manta pintada en	006 . 7	1 roll of colored cotton material
5 Pañitos de Polvos de España a 6 r^s	003 . 6	5 small bags of powders from Spain at 6 reals
2 Ydem de Ydem de Puebla â 5 r^s	001 . 2	2 small bags of powders from Puebla at 5 reals
2 Pares Paños menores de Languin â 20 r^s	005 . 0	2 pair of Languin underwear at 20 reals

16

7 Pares de Escarapelas â 4 r^s par	003 . 4	7 pair of at 4 reals a pair
1 Pieza de Yndian^a de Barcelona, con 20 v^s â 7 r^s	17 . 4	1 length of Barcelona calico at 20 varas for 7 reals
1 Frezada con Especias y un bote de Azafran en	008 . 4	1 container of spices and 1 can of saffron
1 Pza Roan â Bramantado con 75 1/3 v^s â 5 r^s	047 . 0½	1 roll of brabant linen material at 75 1/3 varas for 5 reals
2 Pares de Andalias y zapatos â 8 rs	002 . 0	2 pair of sandals and shoes at 8 reals
2 Avitos con Capillas de Sayalete â 9 p^s	018 . 0	2 Habits with cowls, of light woolen cloth at 9 pesos
3 Frezadas â 8½ r^s petates y Arpilleras	004 . 0½	3 blankets at 8½ reals, mats and sacks
3 Tercios de Tavaco con 481 tt met^s â 3 r^s y 8 r^s de Arpill^s	180 . 3	3 tercios of tabacco and 481 tomines metates at 3 reals and 8 reals of sacks
1 Caxon con 5@ de chocolate fino â 9 p^s y 1 p^s del cax^n	046 . 0	1 crate with 5 arrobas of fine chocolate at 9 pesos and 1 peso for the crate
2 Caxon^s con 10 @ de Ydem ordin^o â 6 p^s 6 r^s y 2 p^s de cax^s	069 . 4	2 crates with 10 arrobas of ordinary chocolate at 6 pesos 6 reals and 2 pesos for the crates
2 Tom^s en 8º Compendio de la Religión en	004 . 0	2 volumes in octavo: Compendium of Religion at
1 Ydem en 8º Eloquencia Española en	002 . 0	1 volume in octavo: Spanish Eloquence at
Passa a la Bta	1 . 517 . 6½	Balance forward

17

Por la de la Bta	1 . 517 . 6½	Balance forward
3 Ydem en 4° Actas de los Martirez en	006 . 0	3 volumes in quarto: Acts of the Martyrs
1 Dozena de Pañitos ordin^os Poblan^s en	002 . 2	1 dozen ordinary Puebla neckerchiefs
Cargo p^r el costo de Mex^co al Colegio de 12 terc^s a 3 p^s 3 r^s	040 . 4	Freight cost from Mexico to the College for 12 tercios at 3 pesos 3 reals
Ymporta	1 . 566 . 4½	Amount
Cargo Trecientos diez p^s 2 r^s que resta en la cta de Fr. José Antonio Garcia	310 . 2	Due: Three hundred ten pesos 2 reals to the account of Fr. José Antonio Garcia
Cargo 117 p^s de 6 Partid^s que p^r menos constan en el Libro de Caxa viejo, $10	117 . 0	Due: 117 pesos for 6 shipments recorded in the old Account book, $10
Cargo 1.528 p^s 2½ r^s que importó la Memoria que cogió de los Rezagos y consta en la cta sig^te		Due: 1.528 pesos 2½ reals registered in the Account book from the sale of cattle and figures in the following charge
	1 . 598 . 2	
Suma	3 . 592 . 1	Total

18

Related Structures

ARCHAEOLOGICAL MONITORING OF THE
SAN JOSE ACEQUIA (41 BX 267),
WASTEWATER FACILITIES IMPROVEMENTS PROGRAM,
SAN ANTONIO, TEXAS

I. Waynne Cox

Center for Archaeological Research
The University of Texas at San Antonio
Archaeological Survey Report, No. 175

1988

INTRODUCTION

On January 3, 1986, the Center for Archaeological Research of The University of Texas at San Antonio entered into a contract with the City of San Antonio, through the PD VA Group, to provide monitoring of construction for a planned sewer line for the San Antonio Wastewater Improvements Program, Category No. 4, Package F. Based upon the information available before work began, it was expected that the San José Acequia would be encountered at three locations along the intended route of the excavations (at Hart Avenue, between Akers Street and East Southcross Street, and south of East Southcross Street near Kelly Street).

After the project was initiated, further research in the Bexar County Archives revealed that the original assessment was essentially correct, but that the extent of impact between East Southcross Street and Hart Avenue would be more extensive than had been anticipated. The monitoring was done by I. Waynne Cox, Center research associate, under the general supervision of Thomas R. Hester and Jack D. Eaton, Center director and associate director, respectively, and Anne A. Fox, project director. Monitoring operations began on October 24, 1986, and ended on January 2, 1987, a total of 71 days.

PREVIOUS ARCHAEOLOGICAL RESEARCH

Several limited archaeological investigations of the San Antonio acequias have been conducted during the past several years, but they have been primarily in the downtown area of San Antonio (Schuetz 1970; Sorrow 1972; Adams and Hester 1973; Katz 1978; Fox 1978a, 1978b; Valdez and Eaton 1979; Frkuska 1981; Cox 1985, 1986; Ellis 1986). There has been very limited professional investigation of the San José Acequia. Harvey P. Smith, an architect, cleared a section of the acequia near Mission San José in the 1930s (Henderson and Clark 1984). In 1974, the Texas Historical Commission conducted an excellent archival search and surface survey in conjunction with their investigations for the Mission Parkway (Scurlock et al. 1976:27, 145-147). In 1981, the State Department of Highways and Public Transportation excavated a section of the acequia south of the mission (Henderson and Clark 1984).

HISTORY OF THE SAN JOSE ACEQUIA

The San José Acequia, one of seven major Spanish irrigation systems in the San Antonio area, was probably constructed around 1730 (Arneson 1921:125; Holmes 1962:12). The acequia irrigated some 600 acres of land in the vicinity of Mission San José. Its diversion point was a short distance below the mouth of San Pedro Creek, approximately two miles above the present mission and one-half mile above Mission Road Bridge (Harston 1935). The acequia, of necessity, followed the contours of the terrain along a convoluted course in the direction of Mission Road to the south and southeast to beyond Mission San José.

The location of the acequia was probably dictated by the relocation of Mission San José to its third, and present, site in approximately 1729 (Habig 1968:88). The mission had previously been located on the west bank of the San Antonio River, prior to 1727 (*ibid.*:86). Traces of three ruin structures were reported by Harston (1935) "where a continuation of Harlan Avenue crosses the Mission Road and about 300 feet from the Mission Road." Father Hoermann (1932:27), a priest at the mission from 1859 to 1864, also reported ruins in this vicinity. It is possible that the ruins described by Harston and Hoermann could have been structures constructed by Antonio Huizar, who obtained the land from the sale of the mission labors in 1824 (Smith 1874) and may have not been related to the mission. However, this location for the mission is strengthened by evidence of an "*acequia medio*" farther to the east, between the "*Madre*" and the river, rising from an old bow of the San Antonio River (*BCDR* Vol. 22:242).

In 1768, Fray Solis described the acequia: "They take a copious and abundant amount of water such that it seems a small river and it contains many fish" (Henderson and Clark 1984:6). In 1777, the acequia was described in a portion of an inspection report (Morfi 1978:211).

The farm occupies an area about a league /2½ miles/ square [4428.4 acres] and is all fenced, the fence being in good condition. For its benefit, water is taken from the San Antonio River and distributed by means of a beautiful irrigation ditch to all parts of the field where corn, beans, lentils, cotton, sugar cane, watermelons, melons, and sweet potatoes are raised.

The acequia functioned as an irrigation system for the needs of the mission and its Indian residents. After the mission lands were secularized, the new landowners were responsible for the upkeep of the acequia.

The dam experienced several episodes of destruction by the flooding of the San Antonio River, it was replaced once by wood, and later by mortared stone (Harston 1935). A final flood, in 1860, led to its abandonment (Arneson 1921:125). Although the acequia ceased to flow after the destruction of its dam, the abandoned channel remained a landmark and was used as a boundary marker in deed records. However, without its flow it became less of a visible barrier, and property owners in the area began to encroach upon the road that followed its channel.

In January 1869, the County Commissioners Court found it necessary to form a committee to investigate the road and the river crossing to determine if repairs were needed "as public safety may require" (*MCC* 1869 Journal 3a:26). In 1877, Leonardo Garza found it necessary to petition the court to have the road reopened (*MCC* 1877 Journal B1:233). This resulted in a series of petitions, committees, claims, and counterclaims that were not resolved until 1884, when the road was finally reopened and a bridge was approved for the river crossing (*MCC* 1883 Journal C:303, 1884 Journal C:534, 573). In 1885, a contract for the construction of an iron bridge across the river was awarded to W. R. Freeman at a cost of $2600 (*MCC* 1885 Journal D:54). By 1889, this bridge proved inadequate to withstand the frequent river floods, and a resolution was passed to remove the bridge to "a point near Berg's Mill" and erect a new bridge (*MCC* 1889 Journal F:153). A contract was awarded to the King Bridge Company, at a cost of $10,808, and the bridge was accepted as "complete and ready for travel" in October 1890 (*MCC* 1890 Journal F:465).

In 1894, the acequia was reopened under the Texas Water Act of 1889 by landowners along its course. However, the dam was relocated farther south on the San Antonio River, near the present Mission Road bridge, and the channel rejoined the old acequia to the south (Brook 1904; Fig. 1). At that time it was described as being "four feet deep and 12 feet wide and the carrying capacity thereof shall be 100 cubic feet per second" (*Water Board Records* Vol. 1 August 10, 1894:4).

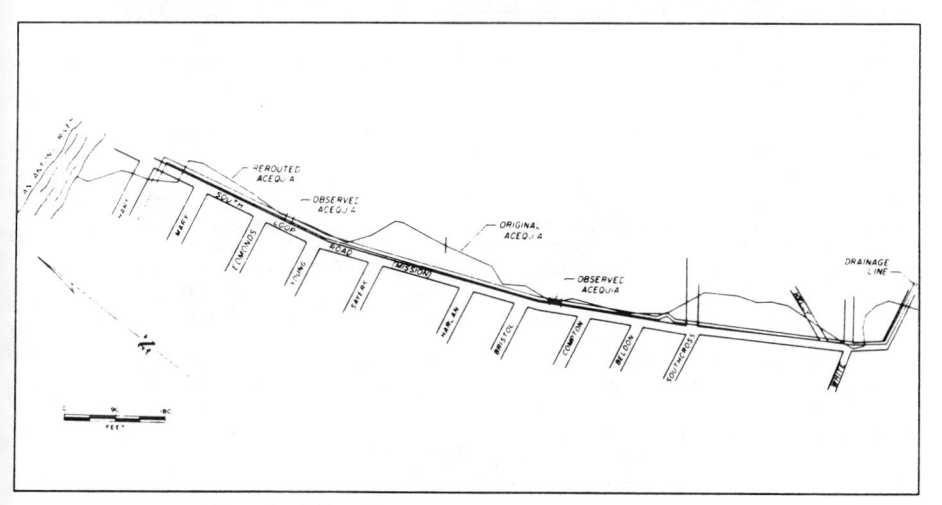

Figure 1. *Original, Rerouted, and Observed San José Acequia.*

J. E. Harston (1935), an engineer, described the old dam as seen in 1935,

> A wing dam was made at the present intersection of Loraine [sic] Street and the river by rolling tufa stone into place along the north bank of the river which was much lower than the south side which has a 25-foot embankment where no wall was necessary. This dam was almost 100 feet wide at the lower end and with with [sic] walls about five feet thick at the base across the river.

The acequia remained in use until the 1950s (Scurlock et al. 1976:145).

MONITORING OPERATIONS

The Center was contacted the first week of October 1986 by the contractor, Martin K. Eby Construction Company, Inc., that they were beginning excavations at the corner of Mission Road and Roosevelt Avenue. A meeting was scheduled for October 7, 1986.

Waynne Cox, Center research associate, met with Dwayne Opella, Phil Handley, and Larry Rein, representatives from the PD VA Group. The areas of sensitivity were reviewed, and a copy of the Center's working map was made for field use. The PD VA Group personnel agreed to notify the Center representative when a sensitive area would be reached (estimated within two weeks), and they understood that the Center archaeologist would remain on call prior to that time. Active field monitoring began as construction approached the area of Mission Road and White Street and continued to Hart Avenue when the route turned westward away from the sensitive area (Fig. 1).

The contractor notified the Center on October 23, 1986, that a feature had been revealed in a trench on Mission Road just to the east of the intersection of East Huff Avenue. A large, deep cut at roughly a right angle to the roadway had been revealed, but it was a recent excavation, not the acequia (Fig. 2,a). The cut was approximately 10 feet wide and eight feet deep. The sides were extremely sharp and cut into the underlying caliche base approximately two feet. The trench showed no sign of weathering and had marks of modern machine excavation techniques across an extremely flat bottom. Richard Garay (personal communication) has documented evidence that a western branch of the acequia was constructed in this area, but the trench revealed none of the classic characteristics of an acequia.

On October 27, 1986, the contractor again notified the Center that they would be working to the north of White Avenue, another sensitive area. Richard Garay contacted Anne Fox at Mission Concepción, where the Center was engaged in excavations, requesting that she examine what he thought might be the acequia. She found no evidence that the acequia was exposed. The excavations continued to Mission Road between White Avenue and Kelly Street (Fig. 1). In the western profile of a trench a 12-inch sewer main was revealed that had been placed to a depth of five feet and rested on a base of caliche. The eastern profile showed a mottled layer of dark clay loam that overlay an irregular layer of caliche approximately eight feet thick that rested on a thick layer of water-bearing gravels. No sign of the acequia was present. After Garay and Cox consulted archival material on the route of the acequia, it was verified that the acequia was to the east of the present excavations by about one-half block. It was also agreed that the acequia would probably be encountered to the north of Southcross Avenue where Mission Road intersects with Sayer Drive and Compton Street. Cox continued to monitor the progress of the excavations at random through October 31.

Since the sewer line construction did not excavate across White Street, the sharp bend in the acequia at that point was not exposed. However, a city crew was excavating a gas main across the intersection, and the north profile of a trench revealed an unlined ditch six feet wide and four feet deep of what might have been the acequia. The trench had a black brown clay base and was filled with mixed black loamy soil laced with traces of caliche. There were no artifacts. The south profile revealed that all traces of the acequia had been destroyed by several large recent excavations in association with the gas main. A sketch map was produced and is on file with the Center.

3

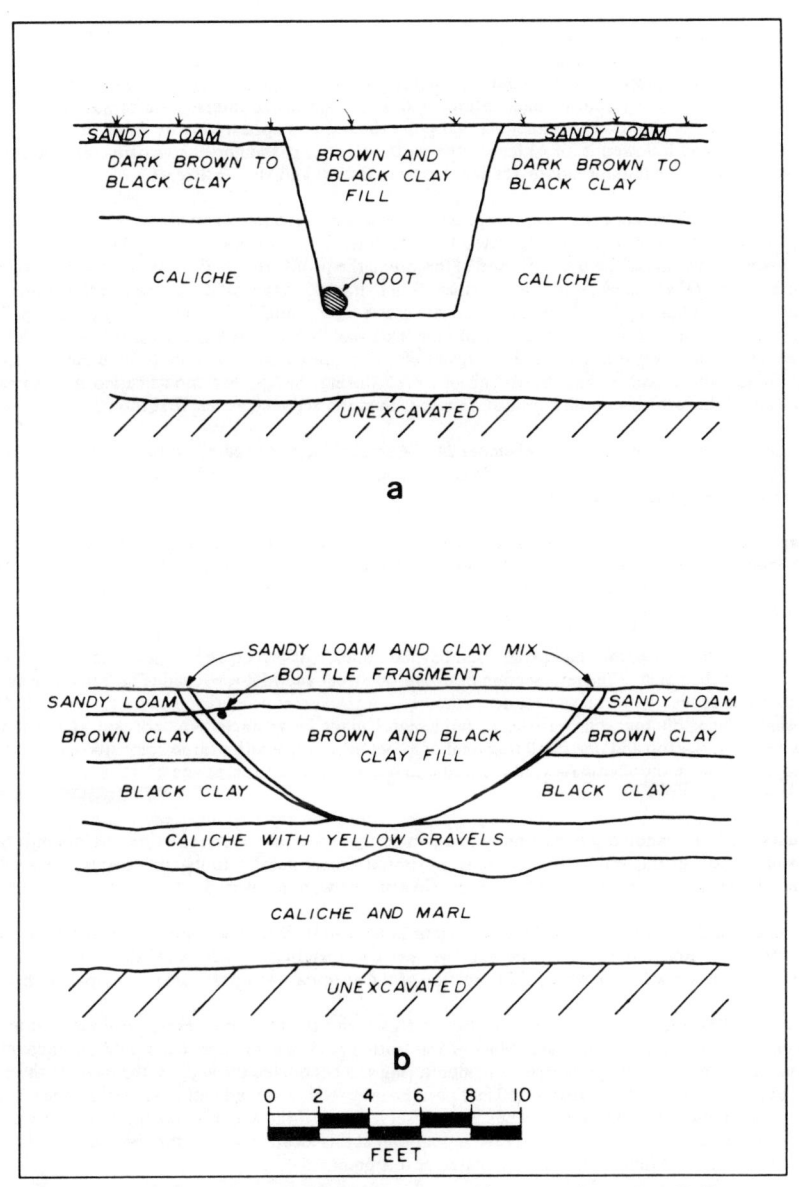

Figure 2. *Profiles Observed During Field Work.* a, machine excavation at East Huff Avenue; b, acequia profile at Compton Street.

A deed record was obtained that indicated the path of the acequia as it existed in 1927 (*BCDR* Vol. 944:211-214). Upon replotting the metes and bounds as indicated in the deed, it was found that two measurements were omitted in the deed but were noted partially on the plat map. A replot of the plat map indicated that the acequia would be encountered 700 feet north of the intersection of Southcross Street, along the north line of Compton Avenue. At that point the acequia appeared to be along the eastern edge of Mission Road, and followed it for 43 feet to the north. Farther to the north, approximately 420 feet, the acequia was shown to be in the road for 150 feet between Bristol and Harlan Streets.

The second week of November the Center representative was notified that excavations were anticipated for White Street on November 10, but rain delayed the schedule. The excavation actually began on November 11. During the excavation of the south portion of the street, the profile revealed a totally disturbed condition due to several natural gas, sewer, and water mains. Work stopped in the middle of the street at a main line, and because it was a holiday (Veterans' Day), no city crews were available for contingency purposes. Work on the north side resumed on November 12, and the area was found to be equally disturbed by additional pipe trenches. At least eight trenches, as the result of utility construction, had obliterated any trace of the acequia. It is quite possible that the trench observed during the gas line modification was, in fact, a manifestation of this extensive utility excavation rather than the acequia, as was first thought.

Operations were again monitored on November 24. The trenching had progressed to a point about 100 feet north of Southcross Street. The acequia ditch can still be followed across the Harlandale School grounds, since there has been no fill in this area.

Upon departing the area it was noted that a City Water Board crew was conducting excavations on the east side of Southcross Street, approximately 200 feet south of Sayers Street. Their purpose was to relocate a check valve that was within the path of the sewer excavation. Their excavations were well to the west of the path of the acequia at that point, and no signs of it were visible in their trench.

On December 1, the excavations had progressed beyond Southcross Street, and the acequia was exposed at a point 50 feet to the north of the intersection of Compton Street and Mission Road (Fig. 2,b). The acequia at that point was 18 feet wide and six feet deep, the width was so great primarily because the ditch had been cut on a slight angle. Photographs were taken and a search made for artifacts. An unbroken glass gallon jug with handle and screw top and one small fragment of a root beer bottle with a three color silk-screened label were recovered. Since the acequia was in use well into this century, the recent age of the artifacts was to be expected.

On December 22, the acequia was encountered again 50 feet south of the intersection of Edmonds Street and Mission Road. At this point the acequia was exposed almost parallel to its course and appeared as a broad unlined ditch, approximately six feet deep. No artifacts were recovered.

On December 30, the acequia was encountered again 50 feet south of Hart Avenue. As expected, it was an unlined ditch approximately six feet wide and five feet deep, and crossed Mission Road in an east-west direction. No artifacts were recovered. This portion of the acequia was a part that was reopened in 1894.

On January 2, 1987, the excavation crossed Mission Road, and the trenches were placed parallel to Hart Avenue on the south side of the road. Since it was anticipated that the acequia would be encountered approximately 25 feet west of the intersection, monitoring was conducted throughout the day. At the end of the work day, the trench had progressed 150 feet past the intersection; no indication of the acequia was seen. However, several old pipelines and trenches were observed, and if the acequia was shallow, and a portion of the 1894 construction, and also very near the input point at this location, then it may have been obliterated by these disturbances. Monitoring was terminated at this point.

CONCLUSIONS AND RECOMMENDATIONS

Since the construction of the San José Acequia in the early years of the 18th century, both major and minor alterations of the channel have taken place. There is no evidence that any of the route was lined or riprapped, but reinforcement of the main channel could well have been a practice at lateral points where irrigation ditches tapped the main flow for individual fields. The very nature of such an excavated watercourse, subject to the existing gradation of the terrain, would dictate almost constant minor deviation from its intended channel, and this was observed in the width of the channel as exposed in two encounters during the monitoring. With the abandonment of the San José Acequia in 1860, the normal yearly cleaning and frequent repair cycles would have ceased, and the channel was relegated to a fossil trace of importance as a demarcation of property boundaries. With the reopening of the public road in the 1880s and the relocation of the dam in the 1890s, the channel again experienced major revisions. The section exposed December 1, near Compton Street, appears to be a part of the original acequia, while the section exposed between the intersection of Young Street and Edmonds Street was a part of the post-1894 ditch. Past experience has shown that the artifacts recovered during excavations of the acequias in the San Antonio area will date to the period after the channel was abandoned, due to the flow of the water and annual maintenance during its use. Therefore, to date the sections of the acequia from physical evidence is almost impossible.

The monitoring of the acequia has indicated that reliable maps and records of the route of the acequia do exist and can provide positive predictions as to where the acequia will be encountered, but it has also revealed that within the right-of-way, construction has all but obliterated most traces of the past channel. Therefore, no further work is recommended at this time in the immediate vicinity of Mission Road, but should other construction be considered in this area on-site monitoring is recommended in the event that surviving traces of the acequia should be encountered. The area to the east of the intersection of Mission Road and Harlan Avenue is especially sensitive as the possible second location of Mission San José y San Miguel de Aguayo. Any excavation to the east of Mission Road, on either private or public lands, that penetrates below a depth of three feet could intrude upon the ancient or more modern path of the waterway. Therefore, consideration should be given for archaeological monitoring and possibly excavation throughout the area. We recommend that the San José Acequia merits consideration for National Register eligibility at the state level.

REFERENCES CITED

Adams, R. E. W. and T. R. Hester

    1973   Letter to Dr. Fred Wendorf, Texas Antiquities Committee, concerning completion of excavations at Mission San Antonio de Valero, November 26. On file at the Center for Archaeological Research, The University of Texas at San Antonio.

Arneson, E. P.

    1921   Early Irrigation in Texas. *Southwestern Historical Quarterly* 25(2):121-130. Texas Historical Association, Austin, Texas

Bexar County, Texas

    Bexar County Deed Records (BCDR)

        Originals and microfilm located at Bexar County Courthouse, San Antonio, Texas.

    Minutes of County Commissioners Court (MCC)

        Located in the Bexar County Courthouse, San Antonio, Texas.

Bexar County, Texas (continued)

Water Board Records

Located in the Bexar County Courthouse, San Antonio, Texas.

Brook, J. F.

1904 Survey of Creamery Dairy Company's Irrigation Ditch, Bexar County, Texas. Survey Map, Bexar County Archives. Copy on file at the Center for Archaeological Research, The University of Texas at San Antonio.

Cox, I. W.

1985 10th Street Substation Excavation of the Acequia Madre (41 BX 8), San Antonio, Bexar County, Texas. *Center for Archaeological Research, The University of Texas at San Antonio, Archaeological Survey Report* 153.

1986 Excavations of Portions of the San Pedro Acequia (41 BX 337) and a Search for the Arocha Acequia, San Antonio, Texas. *Center for Archaeological Research, The University of Texas at San Antonio, Archaeological Survey Report* 161.

Ellis, W. B.

1986 Preliminary Archaeological Assessment of the Northeast Parking Lot Area (Phase III) Site of the New Bexar County Justice Center, San Antonio. Manuscript on file at the Center for Archaeological Research, The University of Texas at San Antonio.

Fox, A. A.

1978a Preliminary Archaeological Assessment of South Parking Lot Area (Phase I) Site of Courthouse Annex, San Antonio, Texas. Letter report to Bexar County Commissioners Court. On file at the Center for Archaeological Research, The University of Texas at San Antonio.

1978b Archaeological Investigations of Portions of the San Pedro and Alazan Acequias in San Antonio, Texas. *Center for Archaeological Research, The University of Texas at San Antonio, Archaeological Survey Report* 49.

Frkuska, A. J., Jr.

1981 Archaeological Investigations at the San Pedro Acequia, San Antonio, Texas. *Center for Archaeological Research, The University of Texas at San Antonio, Archaeological Survey Report* 103.

Habig, M. A.

1968 *The Alamo Chain of Missions, A History of San Antonio's Five Old Missions.* Franciscan Herald Press, Chicago, Illinois.

Harston, J. E.

1935 Almost Forgotten Mission Waterway Which Determined San José Location Bared by Geologist During Surveys. *San Antonio Express*, September 1.

REFERENCES CITED

Henderson, J. and J. W. Clark, Jr.

    1984   The Acequia and Other Features at Mission San José, Bexar County, Texas. *State Department of Highways and Public Transportation, Highway Design Division, Publications in Archaeology, Report* 25, Austin, Texas.

Hoermann, P. A. S.

    1932   *The Daughter of Tehuan, or Texas of the Past Century*. Standard Printing Company, San Antonio, Texas.

Holmes, W. H.

    1962   The Acequias of San Antonio. M.A. thesis, St. Mary's University, San Antonio, Texas.

Katz, P. R.

    1978   Archaeological and Historical Investigations in the Arciniega Street Area, Downtown San Antonio, Texas. *Center for Archaeological Research, The University of Texas at San Antonio, Archaeological Survey Report* 61.

Morfi, Fr. J. A. de

    1978   *The San José Papers: The Primary Sources for the History of San José y San Miguel de Aquayo from its Founding in 1720 to the Present*. Part I: 1719-1791. Translated by Fr. B. Leutenegger. Compiled and annotated by Fr. M. A. Habig. Old Spanish Missions Historical Research Library at San José Mission, Our Lady of the Lake University, San Antonio, Texas.

Schuetz, M. K.

    1970   Excavation of a Section of the Acequia Madre in Bexar County, Texas, and Archeological Investigations at Mission San José in April, 1968. *Texas Historical Survey Committee Archeological Report* 19.

Scurlock, D., A. Benavides, Jr., D. Isham, and J. W. Clark, Jr.

    1976   *An Archeological and Historical Survey of the Proposed Mission Parkway, San Antonio, Texas*. Office of the State Archeologist, Texas Historical Commission, Austin, Texas.

Smith, S. S.

    1874   *Map Showing the Names of the Original Claimants to the Irrigable Lands Comprised of the Missions of Concepción, San José and La Espada*. Copy on file at the Center for Archaeological Research, The University of Texas at San Antonio and the Daughters of the Republic of Texas Research Library, The Alamo.

Sorrow, W. M.

    1972   Archeological Salvage Excavations at the Alamo (Mission San Antonio de Valero), 1970. *Texas Archeological Salvage Project, The University of Texas at Austin, Research Report* 4.

Valdez, F., Jr. and J. D. Eaton

    1979   Preliminary Archaeological Investigations of Part of the San Pedro Acequia, San Antonio, Texas. *Center for Archaeological Research, The University of Texas at San Antonio, Archaeological Survey Report* 85.

ARCHAEOLOGICAL INVESTIGATION OF THE SAN JUAN DAM, 41 BX 266, BEXAR COUNTY, TEXAS

David B. Hafernik, I. Waynne Cox, and Anne A. Fox

Center for Archaeological Research
The University of Texas at San Antonio
Archaeological Survey Report, No. 179

1989

INTRODUCTION

In April 1988, personnel from the Center for Archaeological Research at The University of Texas at San Antonio conducted test excavations in an attempt to locate and document the dam associated with Mission San Juan Capistrano under contract with the San Antonio River Authority (SARA). The dam, constructed in the early 1730s, diverted water from the San Antonio River into an acequia (ditch) to provide water for the irrigation of the mission fields.

The dam had not had water flowing over it since 1957, and had become covered with dirt and overgrown with vegetation. Prior to testing it was unsure if the dam was still intact, and if so, in what condition it might be found. Through testing we hoped to determine the exact location of the dam and the beginning point of the acequia with its corresponding headgate.

The project was conducted under the supervision of Jack Eaton, acting Center director. Anne A. Fox was the project director and field director. The work was done under Texas Antiquities Committee Permit No. 686.

ENVIRONMENTAL BACKGROUND

The San Juan dam is situated on an old channel of the San Antonio River above the eastern bank of the present channel opposite Mission San José (Fig. 1). The river was rechannelized, and much of the spoil was placed on the area west of the site to a depth of several feet. The area was at one time utilized as a city park but is currently abandoned.

Vegetation at the site consists of grasses, herbaceous plants, and shrubs. The old river channel is lined with large pecan, mesquite, and hackberry trees. Many of the pecan trees are large enough to have served as witness trees for deed record information.

HISTORY OF THE SAN JUAN DAM

Mission San Juan Capistrano was first established in 1716 in east Texas as Mission San José de las Nazonis. The mission was abandoned in 1719 because of French incursions into the area, but reestablished in 1721 (Webb 1952 Vol. II:556). In

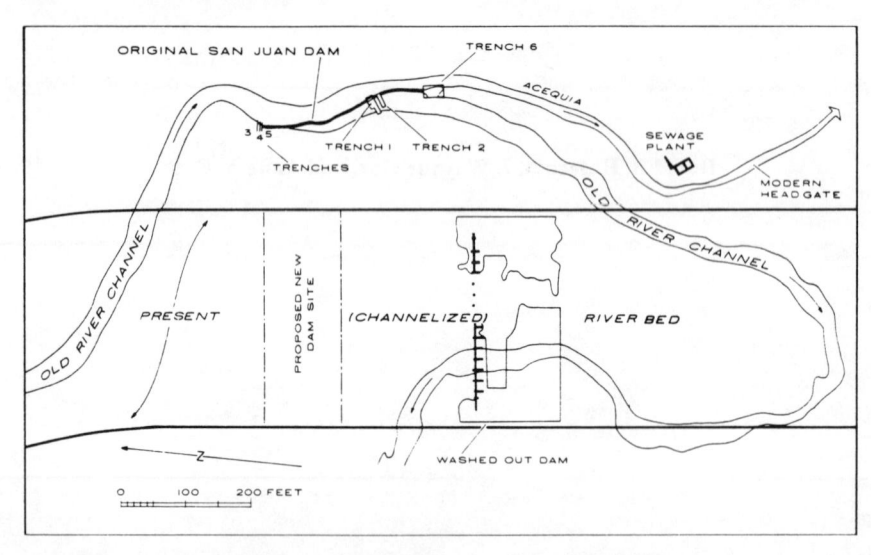

Figure 1. *Location of the San Juan Dam and Trenches 1-6.*

1730, it was moved to the Colorado River near present-day Austin, and the following year was re-established on the San Antonio River about seven miles south of downtown San Antonio. Because of its proximity to Mission San José y San Miguel de Aguayo, the mission was renamed San Juan Capistrano. By May 4, 1731, the first temporary structures had been completed (Habig 1968:169). It is highly likely that the acequia, or irrigation ditch, was also begun at that time, as this was the normal procedure of the Spanish. The ability to develop an irrigation system was a primary factor in selecting a site for any mission.

Despite the importance of the acequias, there is little recorded detail on the construction of these vital waterways. One exception is the report of Fray Mariano on the establishment of the missions on the San Xavier River (now the San Gabriel River) as evidenced by the following account:

> He proceeded to order the ministers to be prepared to assist in the work on the fifteenth (October, 1750), each mission provided as many yokes of oxen as it might have, seven bars, fifteen picks, four axes, and one cauldron. In excess of the regular rations, which would be continued, each mission was asked to provide each week during the continuance of the work, a tierce [(sic) this should read tercio, one third] or half a mule load of salt, six bulls for slaughter, two handfuls of tobacco, and whatever else was possible. Fray Mariano promised to provide for distribution each day a fanega [generally accepted to be a hundred weight or 1.60 bushels], or two hundred pounds of hominy (Bolton 1915:235).

Even with the encouragement of these extra rations to coax the Indians to work, Fray Mariano also instructed the military to send "enough soldiers to cause respect" (*ibid.*:236).

Progress on the construction of Mission San Juan Capistrano, and probably its acequia, was slow during the first ten years due to frequent Apache raids, the obstructionist tactics of Governor Franquis de Lugo, and an epidemic in 1739 (Habig 1968:162). However, the acequia was in operation by at least 1740, for the fields are reported as newly planted in the spring of that year (*ibid.*:167). In 1745, the report of Fray Francisco Xavier Ortiz stated:

> The mission farm was watered by a very good irrigation ditch. As a rule 6 2/5 bushels of seed corn were planted each year, and in good years they yield 1,280. About 2 2/5 bushels of beans produced about 64 bushels ... (Habig 1968:167).

The dam that serviced the San Juan acequia was not a water barrier as in the conventional manner, but rather a diverting device to direct the water into the acequia toward the headgate some distance from the channel. The lengthy structure was constructed along the west bank of the river jutting out into the stream to direct the flow toward the ditch. At normal water levels the proper amount of water filled the acequia, but at higher levels the flow was allowed to spill over the dam and return to its original channel (Fig. 1).

In April 1749, San Juan Capistrano was partially secularized. Portions of the mission lands were set aside as communal farms, and small plots were distributed to the 12 heads of families of the mission Indians. San Juan Capistrano then came under the jurisdiction of the priest of Mission San Francisco de la Espada. The mission operation continued on a small scale until full secularization occurred in 1824 (Habig 1968:180).

The acequia continued to be used to irrigate the 486 acres of mission lands that were then owned by individuals. In 1889, the State of Texas enacted legislation to "encourage irrigation and provide for the construction and maintenance of canals, ditches, flumes, reservoirs and wells for irrigation, and for mining, milling, and stock raising in the arid districts of Texas" (*BCA* Water Rights Book of Records 1880-1900:5). At the time of the legislation the San Juan ditch had been abandoned but was still in a good state of preservation (Everett 1975:13).

In 1900, a corporation, the San Juan Ditch Company, was established to maintain and administer the system. The persons entitled to use water from the ditch transferred their water rights to the company in return for shares. The first president of the company was Celestine Villemain (SACS 1977:11). He had 300 acres in cultivation, five acres of which were in grapes from which he produced wine (Everett 1975:17). In April 1914,

the company was rechartered with Milton Meier as president and P. J. Pfeiffer as secretary and treasurer. Their charter stated that the dam diverted 21 cubic feet of water per second into the ditch to water the "San Juan Mission Fields." The fields are described as "Beginning at the intake or head-gate of the San Juan Ditch on the San Antonio River . . . thence in a southerly direction along said San Juan Ditch to the San Antonio River thence up said river to the place of beginning" (*BCA* Water Rights Book of Records 1880-1900:196-203).

In the 1950s, the Corps of Engineers and SARA, the local sponsor, in their efforts to maintain flood control, straightened and widened the river channel diverting the flow away from the San Juan dam and its headgate, thus terminating irrigation. This resulted in lawsuits and countersuits between the SARA and the landowners. After several court decisions, the case was settled in favor of the landowners. The SARA agreed to restore the operation of the dam and provided gravity diversion of water to the ditch (SACS 1977:6). The dam was destroyed by a flood in September 1977. The SARA installed a pumping system to divert water into the acequia, but because the acequia had been filled in places or washed out, the pumps are temporarily off until repairs are made by the owners or the National Park Service.

ARCHAEOLOGICAL BACKGROUND

No archaeological excavations have been done in the area of the San Juan dam, and limited archaeological research has been done concerning the location and construction of the San Juan dam. In 1978, Fred Valdez of the Center staff conducted test excavations just north of the current investigations (Valdez 1978). Before 1976, archaeologists from the Texas Historical Commission conducted research on the location and history of the dam for the Mission Parkway project, but no archaeological excavations were done at that time (Scurlock *et al.* 1976).

ARCHAEOLOGICAL INVESTIGATIONS

The archaeological investigations of the San Juan dam site had three objectives: (1) to determine the location and physical boundaries of the dam; (2) to investigate the construction methods used in building the dam; and (3) to determine the location of the original San Juan acequia and its headgate. All field notes, photographs, and drawings pertaining to this project are on file at the CAR-UTSA.

First, the exact location of the dam needed to be determined. With the help of SARA personnel, who had previously located parts of the dam, the top of the dam was quickly exposed with a backhoe. The structure has a north-south orientation, extending approximately 300 feet along the west side of a section of the old river channel (Fig. 1). This section of the old channel is situated to the east of the existing rechanneled river. The dam appears to be about three feet thick and three feet high at the center. This translates into approximately one vara by one vara in Spanish measurements. These measurements seem to be rather consistent along the length of the dam except for the southern or trailing end, which flares out to a greater dimension.

With the location and extent of the dam structure confirmed, six test trenches were excavated to investigate the subsurface construction methods and original materials. Three areas of the dam were exposed by trenching: the northern (leading) end, the midsection, and the southern (trailing) end. The soil color evaluations are rated according to the *Munsell Soil Color Charts* (1975).

The first area exposed was the midsection of the dam. Trench 1 was located perpendicular to the dam structure and extended across the dam, exposing both sides of the structure. The upstream (eastern) face appears to be composed of river gravel and a caliche and lime mortar forming an early type of concrete. The top of the dam in this area has been capped with a modern cement (Fig. 2,a). Below (underneath) the modern cement cap the original dam can be seen. The western portion of this trench exposed the downstream (western) surface of the dam. With this portion cleared, it is possible to see that the modern concrete cap extends only six to eight inches below the top of the dam.

The top of the dam currently lies two to four inches below the ground surface in Trench 1 (Fig. 3). At this point, below the ground surface, there is a distinct soil change. Above this point is a very dark gray brown clay (2.5Y 3/2) with large gravel. This soil deposit (A) is associated with the

3

146

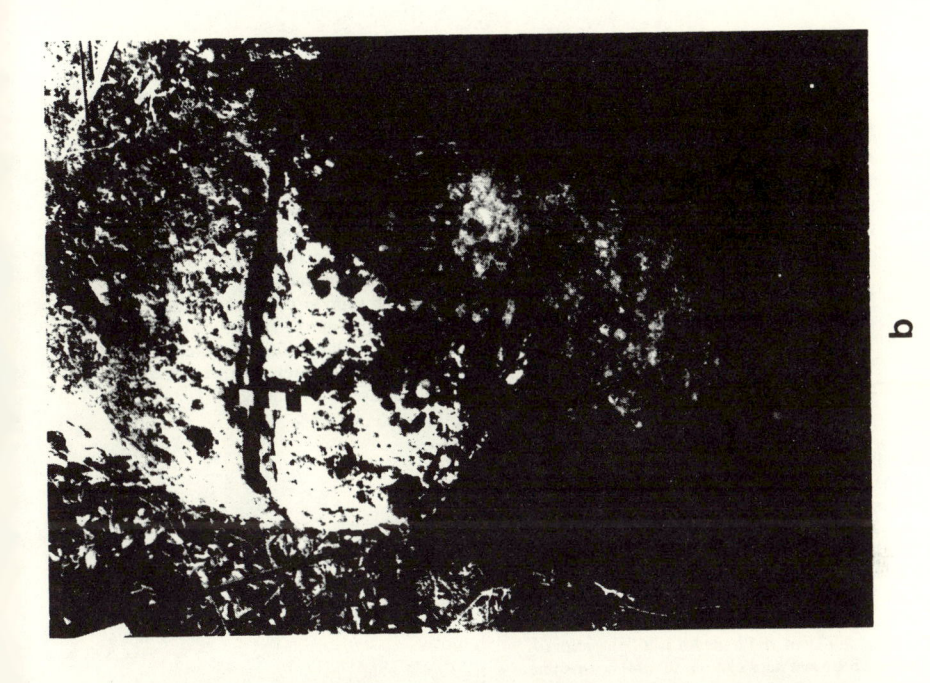

Figure 2. *Views of Excavations.* a, cement cap on dam looking south; b, end view of dam (Trench 5) showing construction.

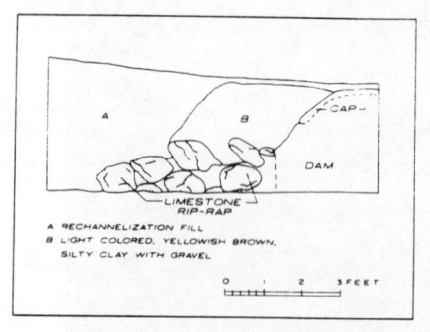

Figure 3. *Trench 1, South Wall Profile.*

rechanneling of the river that took place in the late 1950s. When the river was rechanneled and widened, the dirt that was removed was used to fill and raise this area. This deposit contained debris such as a plastic cigarette lighter, clear glass, screw top bottle fragments, shoe leather, and bricks. These are all artifacts that could have been deposited during the dredging of the river.

The soil layer (B) beneath is a light colored, yellowish brown silty clay (2.5Y 6/4) with some gravel. This layer appears to be associated with the overrun of the dam. Soil was carried downstream by the river and deposited in front of the dam. This soil continued to be deposited year after year causing this layer to be built up. Some of the artifacts found in this layer were ceramic sewer tile, fragments of a composition battery case, and clear glass.

A small lens (C) of a very compact, dark gray clay (10YR 3/1) was encountered next. Since there were no artifacts recovered from this deposit, and it did not appear to continue either north or south along the dam, it is difficult to be certain of the exact origin of this lens; however, it did appear to be sedimentary. It is possible that this lens is also associated with an earlier period of overrun of the dam. The lens is above a layer of large limestone boulders. The stones do not seem to be shaped and appear to be random in their placement, and also appear to be associated with the original construction of the dam. They form a foundation and rear rip-rap formation. These stones would have helped support the dam structure against the rushing water.

The second trench was located approximately 1 m south of the first. This trench exposed only the downstream (western) face of the dam (Fig.4). The dam structure and soil deposition here appear to be very similar to that in the first trench. The first two soil layers (A and B) are still present in this trench in very much the same configuration as in Trench 1. The third soil layer (C) in the first trench, however, does not seem to have continued this far south along the dam. Trench 2 does, however, provide a much better view of the limestone rip-rap support than does Trench 1. The modern concrete cap can also be clearly noted in this trench. Similar artifacts as noted in the first two layers of Trench 1 were also present in the corresponding layers of Trench 2.

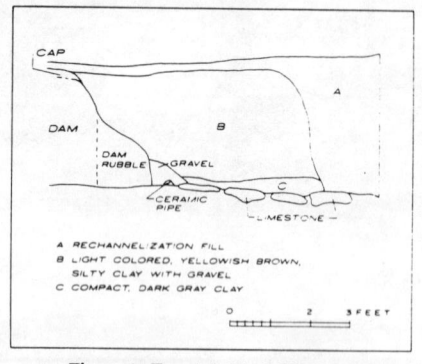

Figure 4. *Trench 2, North Wall Profile.*

The third and fourth trenches were positioned to test for the northern end of the original dam structure. These trenches were placed in the approximate location of the northern end of the dam, about 1.5 m apart. The trenches extended approximately 4 m in an east-west orientation and were about 1 m wide by 1.5 m deep. No evidence of the dam or any other subsurface disturbance indicating previous construction was noted in either of these trenches. Once observations of these trenches were made, they were backfilled.

Trench 5 was located about 1 m to the south of Trench 4 and exposed the northern end of the original dam structure in its southern profile (Fig. 2,b). The soil deposits in this trench seem to differ somewhat from those of the first two trenches (Fig. 5). The first layer (A) in Trench 5 seems to be a continuation of the fill associated with the rechannelization of the river.

5

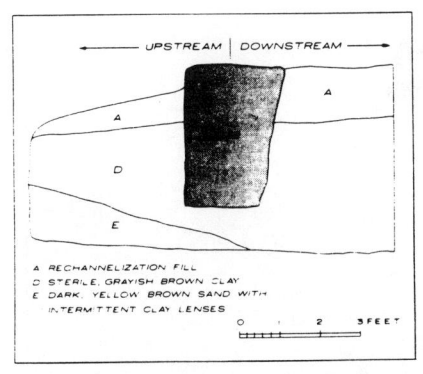

Figure 5. *Trench 5, South Wall Profile.*

Below this fill layer, however, is a thick layer (D) of sterile, grayish brown clay (10YR5/2). Since this clay is present on both sides of the dam and appears to be *in situ*, it is possible that when the dam was originally constructed it was cut down into this clay to provide additional support to the leading end of the dam. Below this thick layer (D) is dark, yellow brown sand (10YR 4/6) with several intermittent lenses of clay (E). This layer (E) is thought to represent the original riverbed in the channel. The intermittent lenses of sand and clay in this layer represent the periods of meandering and silting common to this part of the river. No artifacts were recovered from any of the layers in this trench, giving further support to the idea that layers D and E are intact soil deposits.

The original construction of the dam can be seen clearly from this trench. The front (upstream) side of the dam appears to have been straight, while the back (downstream) side seems to have sloped back from top to bottom. The material used in construction seems to have been the same as previously noted – a caliche and lime mortar with gravel forming an early type of concrete. The modern concrete cap visible in the first two trenches is not present in this profile.

Trench 6 was located approximately 20 m to the south of Trench 2 and exposed the southern end of the dam. This end of the dam varies a great deal more in its construction than the other areas previously exposed (Fig. 6). This section flared out to a much wider dimension than the rest of the dam. Partially exposed, it appeared that the end of the dam branched off in a westerly direction.

Modern support and reinforcement are obvious in this section of the dam. Along the eastern edge, a concrete boulder rip-rap is visible. Several of the concrete boulders still have imprints of the burlap bags in which they were formed. On the southern edge is a portion of a concrete slab with metal strapping and wire mesh reinforcement. The modern concrete cap that was noted in the first two trenches can be followed along the ground surface to the northern end of this area. All of the soil that overlies this end of the dam seems to resemble the fill associated with the rechannelization of the river.

An archival search of the San Juan Ditch Company records revealed a probable location of the headgate as it existed during the late 1800s (*BCA* Water Rights Book of Records 1880-1900:196). The area was located, and an intensive search and limited shovel testing were conducted both in the channel and the upper terrace, but no evidence of the headgate could be detected.

DISCUSSION AND CONCLUSIONS

It is difficult to trace the exact route of the old river channel from where the acequia branched off. The topography of the area has been drastically modified by the rechanneling of the river in the late 1950s and the landscaping that was undertaken in 1966 for the construction of a park.

As it turns out, the area first thought to be part of the old river channel is actually the original route of the acequia. Heading southwest, from the dam structure, the river took a route to the south of the dam. The existing ditch to the southeast of the dam is actually the acequia. The dam structure was used to divert water from the San Antonio River into the acequia. Only when the water in the river was over the height of the dam was water put back into the river channel (Fig. 7,a). All of the water that was lower than the top of the dam was directed into the acequia (Fig. 7,b).

There are reports that the headgate to the acequia was a large, stone structure located 150 feet south of the dam (*BCA* Water Rights Book of Records 1880-1900:196-203). However, no visible evidence remains that might help substantiate these reports. It is possible that the original headgate was destroyed by one of two large floods that occurred along the San Antonio River during

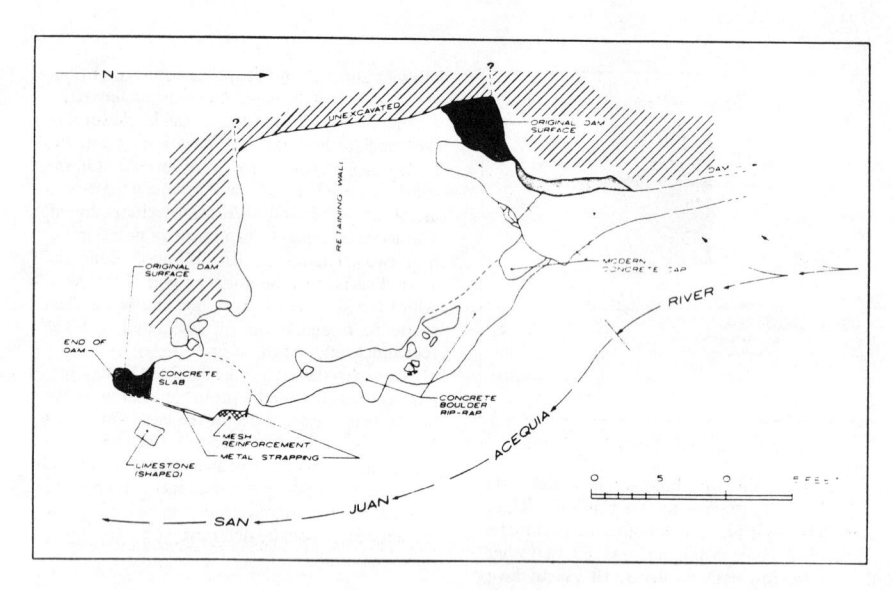

Figure 6. *Plan of Trench 6.*

the 1920s. Located some 400 feet downstream from the dam in the acequia is a modern concrete, stone, and metal gate. It was first thought that this modern gate (constructed when the river was rechannelized [Walter Stewart, personal communication]) might have been placed in the same location as the original, but no evidence supports the original headgate being located this far downstream from the dam.

The modern concrete cap that is present in Trenches 1, 2, and 6 appears to have been put on in an effort to preserve the original dam structure and prevent any additional deterioration. This modern work may have been done in conjunction with the improvements made in 1966 when the area became part of a park.

The large formation partially exposed by Trench 6 appears to have been used as a retaining wall. This part of the structure was designed to make sure that all of the water coming over the dam was forced back into the river channel. It prevented the area between the acequia and the river channel from becoming a swamp. This also prevented the water from running around the south end and undercutting the dam, and kept the acequia and river from joining together below the dam.

All of the previous work done in this area states that the structure that we investigated is a dam. The term "dam" is not only misleading, but technically incorrect. The word dam is defined as:

> A bank or barrier of earth, masonry, etc., constructed across a stream to obstruct its flow and raise its level, so as to make it available for turning a mill-wheel or for other purposes; a similar work constructed to confine water so as to form a pond or reservoir, or to protect the land from being flooded (*Oxford English Dictionary* 1981).

The structure constructed at the beginning of the San Juan acequia was never intended to obstruct the flow of the river, or cause a pond and reservoir to be formed. More correctly, this structure was intended only to divert or direct the flow of the river into the acequia. Therefore, the word dam is not correct. Since the structure does not span the width of the river and it is not constructed to pool water, a weir is the more accurate description of the structure's form and function. The term "weir" is defined as:

7

Figure 7. *Views of the San Juan Dam in 1940.* a, water flowing over the San Juan dam in 1940, looking north; b, looking south into the acequia from the same location, 1940. Photographs taken from the Schuchard collection at the Daughters of the Republic of Texas Research Library, The Alamo.

A fence or embankment to prevent the encroachment of a river or sea-sand, or to turn the course of a stream (*Oxford English Dictionary* 1981).

RECOMMENDATIONS

As a result of the excavations, we now have a better understanding of the construction and purpose of the San Juan dam. In order to obtain any additional information, we recommend that a qualified archaeologist monitor any work in or around the area of the dam.

Although not specifically listed as a property on the National Register, the San Juan dam is protected as a portion of the National Register Mission Parkway Historical/Archaeological District. It is recommended that the San Juan dam be nominated for State Archeological Landmark status.

REFERENCES CITED

Bexar County, Texas
 Bexar County Archives (BCA)
  1880- Water Rights Book of Records, Bexar
  1890 County Courthouse, San Antonio, Texas.

Bolton, H.
 1915 *Texas in the Middle Eighteenth Century*. University of Texas Press, Austin.

Everett, D. E.
 1975 *San Antonio, The Flavor of its Past, 1845-1898*. Trinity University Press, San Antonio.

Habig, Fr. M. A.
 1968 *The Alamo Chain of Missions, A History of San Antonio's Five Old Missions*. Franciscan Herald Press, Chicago, Illinois.

Munsell Soil Color Charts
 1975 Macbeth Division of Kollmorgen Corporation, Baltimore, Maryland.

Oxford English Dictionary
 1981 Oxford University Press, London.

San Antonio Conservation Society (SACS)
 1977 *Newsletter*. September-October. San Antonio.

Scurlock, D., A. Benavides, Jr., D. Isham, and J. W. Clark, Jr.
 1976 An Archeological and Historical Survey of the Proposed Mission Parkway, San Antonio, Texas. *Office of the State Archeologist, Texas Historical Commission, Archeological Survey Report* 17, Austin.

Valdez, F., Jr.
 1978 Archaeological Investigations at the San Juan Damsite (41 BX 266). Letter report on file at the Center for Archaeological Research, The University of Texas at San Antonio.

Webb, W. P., editor
 1952 *Handbook of Texas*. Two volumes. The Texas State Historical Association, Austin.

ARCHAEOLOGICAL SURVEY AND TESTING

AT RANCHO DE LAS CABRAS,

WILSON COUNTY, TEXAS

James E. Ivey

and

Anne A. Fox

Center for Archaeological Research
The University of Texas at San Antonio
Archaeological Survey Report, No. 104

1981

INTRODUCTION

In July 1980, the Center for Archaeological Research, The University of Texas at San Antonio, carried out preliminary survey and test excavations at the site of Rancho de las Cabras on the San Antonio River just south of Floresville, Texas (Fig. 1). The contract called for the following activities:

(1) an intensive survey of the proposed entrance road, 100 feet wide (see Fig. 1);

(2) an intensive survey of the "Southern" tract, with shovel testing where necessary to delimit the historic site deposits;

(3) archaeological testing north-northwest of the rancho compound to delineate the archaeologically sensitive zone and to determine the location of culturally sterile areas which could be used for support facilities. This will include patterned shovel testing and 1-m^2 excavation units where necessary;

(4) archaeological testing in and immediately around the rancho compound to determine the nature and extent of cultural deposits;

(5) cooperation with a professional surveyor provided by the Texas Parks and Wildlife Department in establishing permanent grid markers and making a topographic map of the rancho compound and related features;

(6) production of a scientific report of the results of the investigations.

The materials recovered and all maps, notes, and records will be stored at the Center for Archaeological Research Laboratory, The University of Texas at San Antonio.

THE SITE

Rancho de las Cabras is the site of the livestock ranching operations which reputedly was begun in connection with the mission San Francisco de la Espada in the mid-18th century. The mission was founded on the San Antonio River south of the town of San Antonio de Bexar in 1731. Comparatively little research has been done on Mission Espada, and hardly any information on the ranch thus far has been found. This project was intended to make some basic determinations about the nature of the site itself, to be used in planning further excavations, and to assist in planning future development of the park to be located there. Additional excavations will be done to answer specific questions formulated during this preliminary investigation.

The site is located on a high point of land which overlooks the San Antonio River valley to the east, and for some distance along the river to the north and south. Sandstone block walls up to five and six feet high still remain along the north edge of what was apparently an irregularly-shaped walled compound. The rolling countryside around the site is shaped by arroyos which drain into the river about

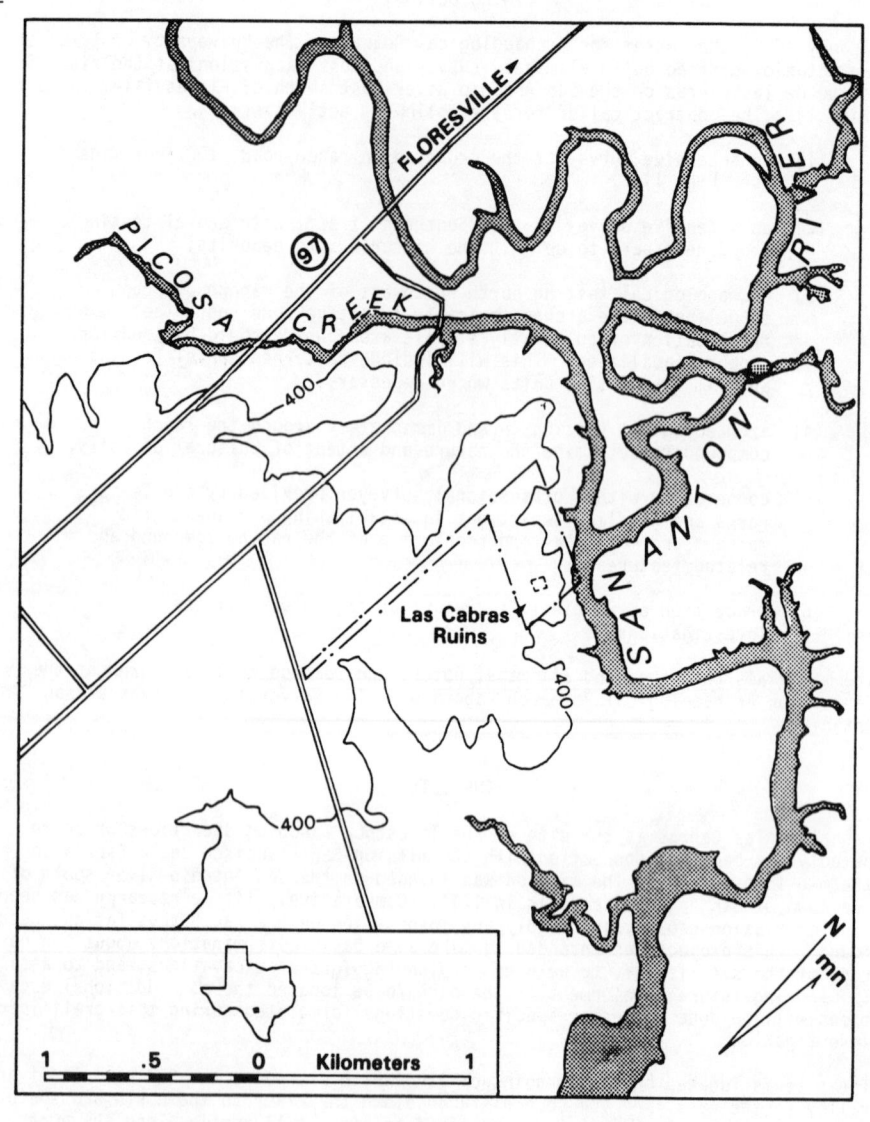

Figure 1. *Locational Map of Rancho de las Cabras.*

two kilometers to the east of the ruins and Picosa Creek to the northeast. The Southern tract portion of the land acquired by the Parks and Wildlife Department from Winston Southern consists of ca. 55.5 acres of upland which contain the ruins at the southern end, and an area to the north which is apparently free of historical remains and could be used for development of visitor facilities.

The soil is a gray brown sandy clay loam over a yellow brown clay loam subsoil. Upland areas, where they have not been cleared for pasture, are overgrown with mesquite and thorny brush. Live oak, post oak, and pecan are present in the arroyos and river bottom areas. The fields around the ruins have, in recent years, been completely cleared of brush and used for pasture by the former owner, who carefully left the ruins and an area immediately around them untouched.

The existence and location of Las Cabras have been known to the local people and to a few historians and archaeologists for many years, and a body of local stories has accumulated about the site and its former occupants. The spot has been visited numerous times by hunters and fishermen traveling the river valley, and by local Floresville citizens who liked to visit the spot in the late 19th and early 20th centuries. A number of deep disturbances along the north wall reflect the insatiable turn-of-the-century gold hunting fever which also left the San Antonio missions pockmarked and crumbling by 1930. Stone blocks from the walls were, for many years, carried away to build walls and other architectural features in and around the town of Floresville. Stone monuments which once marked the limits of the town, built of Las Cabras stones, have been carried back to the site and dumped with the walls (Jack Bruce, personal communication). The sight of stones set in contemporary cement mortar which match those in the 18th century structures are a bit startling to the archaeologist, until their origin is explained.

Despite the above described intrusions, the site of Rancho de las Cabras is remarkably well preserved and, as can be seen from this report, contains tremendous potential for years of historical, archaeological, and ethnographic research.

METHODOLOGY

The field work was carried out from late June 1980 to the end of July 1980. Anne Fox was Project Director. The crew consisted of James Ivey (Field Director), Lois Flynn, Augustine Frkuska, and Roberta McGregor. Principal Investigators for the project were Thomas R. Hester, Director, and Jack D. Eaton, Associate Director, of the Center for Archaeological Research.

The scope of the contract was designed to answer a specific set of questions. Since virtually nothing was known about the archaeology of the site or its environs, no effective planning of future archaeological work could be done. At the same time, very little was known about the history of the site, a difficulty for which archaeology could offer some help.

The primary emphasis, however, was on the determination of the nature and extent of the cultural deposits. Work was done to determine the amount of overburden, (if any); the thickness and depth of cultural deposits throughout the site; and what sort of architectural features could be expected in terms of wall and floor material. It was important to find the location of the refuse from day-to-day life at the site, and whether the actual zone of occupation extended outside the

wall lines of the structures. Equally important, Texas Parks and Wildlife wanted to know if certain areas of the property were without cultural deposits, either historic or prehistoric, so that such areas could be used for the access road and visitors' center with minimum disturbance to the cultural resources of the area.

In practice, while excavating within the structural ruins, several basic rules were followed. The first and most important was to minimize disturbance. Small units in the range of 1-m^2 to 2-m^2, used as isolated tests, are insufficient in size to deal effectively with the remains of a large structure, especially one which might have several periods of occupation and contain several types of construction. The urge to put in another unit to find out where a wall is going or to locate the other edge of a pit is frequently tempting, but consumes time. Units of a specific size were opened and, regardless of what was found, were not enlarged. Units were so placed as to answer the questions defined by the contract as their first purpose, and to supply some answers to more specific questions about the distribution of structures within the site secondarily.

The second rule was to answer the questions proposed by the contract. New questions about the site would be noted, but no attempt was made to find the answers outside the test units. When a feature such as an unsuspected wall, trash pit, gateway, or floor was located, its position was plotted and a note made to include it in recommended future work.

Areas of major structural debris were avoided where possible. Problems such as the clearing and excavation of probable bastion locations were left for more specific contracts. The moving of a large volume of debris would not be an effective use of our limited field time, and would be an attempt to find an answer rather than to define the problem.

With these considerations in mind, a coordinate grid was established and a series of units selected. The grid was set up as indicated in Figure 1, with an arbitrary grid north at right angles to the longest face of the compound wall, on the true northwest side. The south face of the (grid) north wall was designated as the line determining the orientation of the coordinate system, and was defined as being 105 meters south of the zero-point of the coordinates.

The reasoning behind the selection of the position of each unit will be presented in the next section, along with the other pertinent information about the unit.

Units were excavated by natural strata. Control was maintained by measurements of selected thicknesses of strata as the excavation proceeded. Section drawings were then made, and the stratum as an excavation unit was indicated on the section.

All excavated material was screened through 1/4-inch hardware cloth. Recovered artifacts were collected in sacks on which were recorded the name and number of the site, the unit and stratum, the date, the names of the excavators, and any remark, sketch, or other information considered necessary to insure that the point of origin of the enclosed artifacts could be determined.

Notes were kept on all aspects of the excavation. The individuals excavating a structure recorded their impressions of the stratum on a standardized form, and a general narrative and impressions were recorded in a daily journal by the field supervisor. This journal was narrated to a person assigned the job of journal recorder in addition to other duties (Lois Flynn on this excavation). It has been found that the act of describing the impressions to another person defines and clarifies the observations, and the oral evaluation keeps the crew up-to-date on the current views of the field director. An informed crew digs more intelligently, and can supply ideas, interpretations, and insights which may not occur to the field director.

The photographic recording of the excavation was assigned to Augustine Frkuska who, in addition, maintained the log, and recorded the technical details of the photograph along with a brief description of the subject.

Transit measurements of depth or other explicit information were recorded by the crew member who made the measurement. Profiles were drawn by Augustine Frkuska after a detailed discussion of what was being observed, and were then checked by the field director.

Artifacts from specific strata and features were assigned a unique lot number. These lot assignments were done each night in the field, and a log was maintained recording the precise origins of the material in each lot. A second log was maintained indicating which lot numbers were assigned to specific units, strata, and/or features. All contained, in addition to the point of origin, such information as the name(s) of the excavator(s), the date of excavation, and necessary remarks. Lot numbers were cross-indexed onto unit/strata sheets.

When laboratory processing began, however, the artifacts received labels which gave their locations, rather than an abstract lot number. This was done to reduce the amount of back reference to lists of lot numbers and their locations. Such back-referencing greatly increases the chance of error and confusion.

All units were plotted on a field map which is reproduced here (Fig. 2).

THE INVESTIGATIONS

Surface Surveys

As part of this initial investigation of Las Cabras, an intensive surface inspection of the route to be followed by the access road to the future visitors' center and of the general location of the visitors' center itself was carried out. Several other areas indicated by local informants as having produced some artifacts or considered to be potential occupation areas associated with the Las Cabras structures were also intensively surveyed. The remainder of the future park area was walked over randomly, but not intensively.

Neither the access road nor the proposed visitors' center site showed any significant artifact concentrations. Twenty or 30 chert fragments were examined but were largely judged to be plow-broken cobbles. A very few are considered to be the project of a chert-knapping activity. These chert fragments were found almost exclusively along the northern quarter of the northeastern fence line of the Southern tract, and are probably from an aboriginal site across the fence line to the northeast (Fig. 1).

RANCHO DE LAS CABRAS

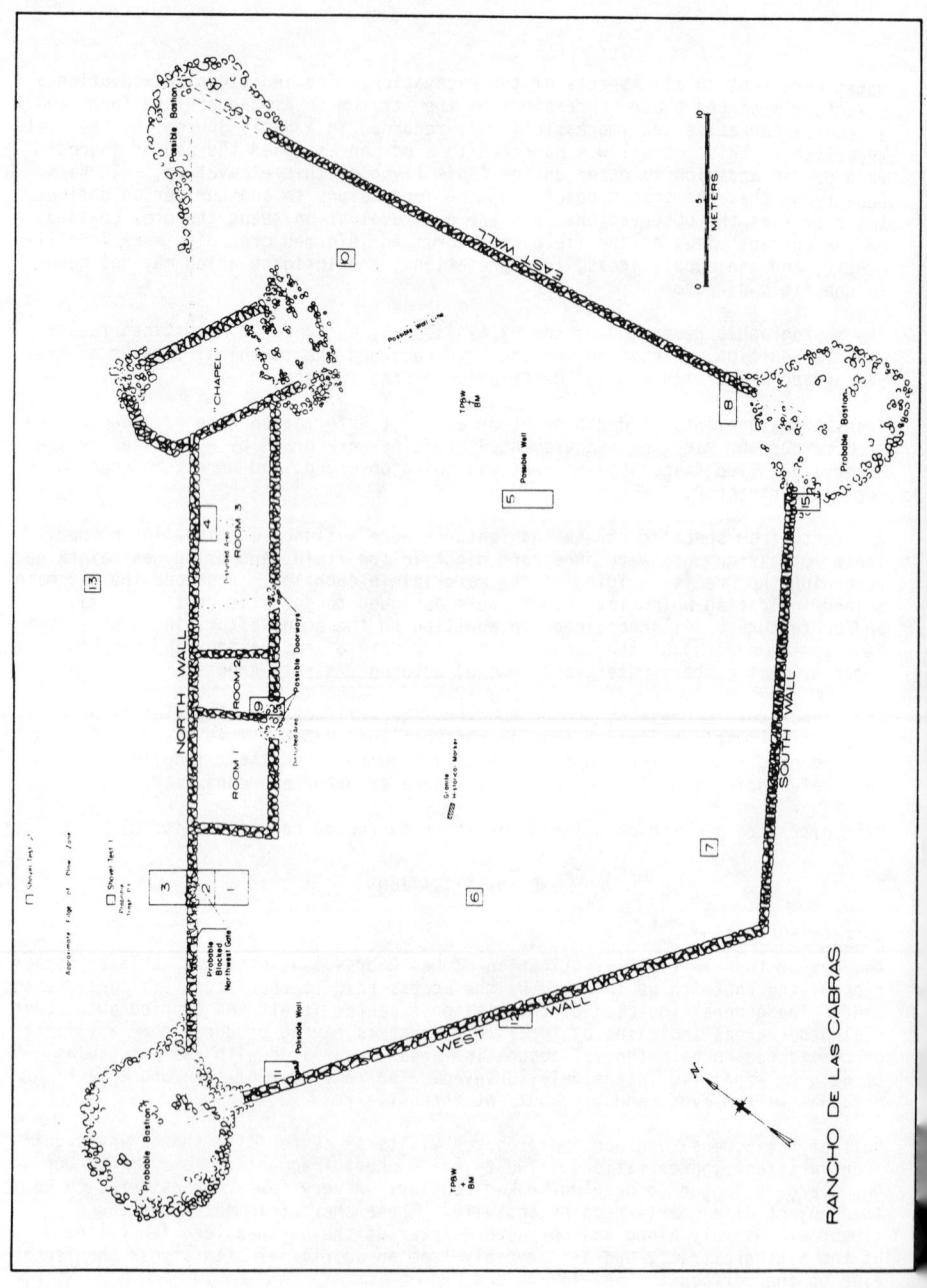

Two Anglo stoneware sherds were picked up in a field just west of the future park property line, in an area where a local informant said he had seen some potsherds while plowing. No other artifacts were found, making it likely that these sherds were a random occurrence.

An intensive survey was done around the ruins of Las Cabras and over most of the south half of the Southern tract. No artifacts of any kind (other than a few beer cans and shotgun shells) were found, except in the areas immediately adjacent to the northwest and southeast angles of the compound wall.

Surface Collection

Artifacts found outside the southeast corner were of sufficient number to warrant collection, since it was thought that they would contribute some information about the history and culture of the site. These artifacts are listed in Table 1.

Shovel Tests

A series of 50-cm^2 shovel tests was carried out along north-south coordinate line 118 at five-meter intervals, beginning at five meters from the wall. They were intended to test the extent to which debris in the area of the northwest gateway was scattered away from the compound, and to locate the general edge of the plow zone surrounding the compound. Units which extended outside the wall on the south and west indicated that virtually no artifacts had been deposited in these areas.

Shovel test 1 showed a marked increase in artifact density with depth, and several strata high in ash and charcoal content were seen. The strata resembled those in Unit 3 (see below). At a depth of ca. 20 cm, sterile yellow tan clay was encountered in the northern half of the test, but the artifacts and debris continued into the ground in the southern portion, and the bone and pottery fragments became much larger. The restrictions imposed by the site of the test stopped excavation at this point.

Observations

The feature encountered at the bottom of the test would appear to be an intentionally dug, vertical-walled pit filled with trash and garbage. The depth and limits of the pit are not known. The pit seemed to originate at a slightly higher level than the earliest occupation surface in this area.

Test Excavation Units

Each test unit excavated was placed in such a manner as to answer a specific set of questions, and each produced a distinctive set of data. We will discuss each unit separately in this section. The discussion will include the reasons for selecting the position of the unit, stratigraphy and features observed while the unit was being excavated, and the artifacts found in association with these components. Some interpretive discussion of selected features within each unit will be included.

TABLE 1. PROVENIENCE OF ARTIFACTS FROM 1980 EXCAVATIONS.

		SPANISH OCCUPATION Ceramics	locally made	unidentified sandy paste	red-painted	Valero	red burnished	Tonalá burnished	galera	sandy paste lead glaze	Guadalajara	black luster	olive jar	plain white majolica	blue on white majolica	blue on white w/black	polychrome majolica	faience	oriental porcelain	Glass	trade beads	faceted set	containers
Surface																							
Southeast			30			1				3							1	1					
Southwest																							
Shovel Tests																							
1			139	2						7	1				1	1							
2			18							4						2							
3			7		1					1				1									
Unit 1																							
Strat. 1			2							1													
Unit 2																							
Strat. 1			15	1						9	1			1	3	1				1			
2			5							2				1									
3			6							2				2									
4			8							3				2									
Features 1-4			5																				
Unit 3																							
Strat. 1			164	2		2	2	1	65		1	2	6	12	3								
2			66	1	1		1	1	11				3		2					1	1		
3			84						19				1							1			
4 E 1/2			87					8	3								1	1					
W 1/2			74	1				3	2				2	1									
Feature 11			11					5					2		1								
Unit 4																							
Strat. 1 E 1/2																							
W 1/2																							
2 E 1/2																							
3 E 1/2																							
4 E 1/2			1																				
5 E 1/2																							
6 E 1/2																							
Feature 6																							
Unit 5																							
Strat. 1			2											1									
Unit 6																							
Strat. 1			2		1					6				1									
2			1										1										
3			2		1										1								
Unit 7																							
Strat. 1																							
2																							
3																							
4			1							3													
5			3							7													
Feature 7																							

TABLE 1. continued

Metal						Stone				Subtotal 18th Century	Ceramics	Glass	Rusted Metal	Nails, Screws, Wire	Misc.	Subtotal 19th Century	Grand Total of Artifacts	Food Remains		Building Materials		
rusted fragments	buckles	hinges	hand-wrought nails	copper/brass	musket balls	mano	gun flints	projectile points	biface fragments	debitage								mussel shell (grams)	bone (grams)	plaster (grams)	daub (grams)	

											4	40			1		1	41	3	26		
													2				2	2				
										1	33	185		2			2	187	33	2673		
											9	33						33	13	349		
											7	17						17		16		
												3	1	10			11	14	2	258		
					1				2	50	85	1		1	2	4	89	22	1366		
					1					3	12						12	8	1363		5
										20	30						30		262		58
										17	30						30	2	217		
											5						5		12		
	1	2		1				1	1	1	189	456		3			3	459	135	6964		30
1			1								44	134						134	32	548		
		1	1								14	121						121	28	369	6	
1											31	132						132	11	1122	95	
											33	116						116	26	634	7	
1									1		29	50						50	9	761		
																			1	1		
											1	1						1		4		
											2	2						2	12	1		
																				7		
												1						1	1	82		
											1	1						1		11		
				1								1						1		69		
																				11		
											7	10	85	26	4	2	117	127		73	21	29
											6	16			1	1	2	18		56		
											12	14						14	1	313		
											4	8						8		26		
														2			2	2				
																				14		
											1	1						1		17		
											5	9						9		43		
											18	28						28		820		
											12	12						12		462		

TABLE 1. continued

SPANISH OCCUPATION	Ceramics	locally made	unidentified sandy paste	red-painted	Valero	red burnished	Tonalá burnished	galera	sandy paste lead glaze	Guadalajara	black luster	olive jar	plain white majolica	blue on white majolica	blue on white w/black	polychrome majolica	faience	oriental porcelain	Glass	trade beads	faceted set	containers

Unit 8
 Strat. 1
  2   2   1 1   1
  3   5   1   3 1   1 3

Unit 9
 Strat. 1
  2
  3
  4
  5   1 2
 Feature 8 1   2
 Feature 9 1

Unit 10
 Strat. 1   1   1   1
  2
  3
  4   3   1
  5   2   1
  6
  7
  8   33   1

Unit 11
 Surface   6   1   5 2
 Strat. 1 65   4   22   7 4   1
  2   2   3   1 1
  3   16   1   7   4 1
  4   27   1   4   2 3 5   1
  5   4   1   2   1 1   1
 Feature 10 3

Unit 12
 Strat. 1   7   6
  2   4   1

Unit 13
 Strat. 1
  2   6   1   1 4   1
  3   10   1   1   1

Unit 14   No Artifacts

Unit 15
 Strat. 1
  2
  3   2
  4   3

Totals   936 7 10 1 7 3 3 215 9 3 4 43 31 20 10 1 1   4 1 3

TABLE 1. continued

Metal						Stone					Subtotal 18th Century	Ceramics	Glass	Rusted Metal	Nails, Screws, Wire	Misc.	Subtotal 19th Century	Grand Total of Artifacts	Food Remains	mussel shell (grams)	bone (grams)	Building Materials	plaster (grams)	daub (grams)
rusted fragments	buckles	hinges	hand-wrought nails	copper/brass	musket balls	mano	gun flints	projectile points	biface fragments	debitage														
											3	15		1		16	19			69			
											9	1				1	10			195			
										3	13						13		1	31			
																				12			
											1	1					1						
											5	8					8		2	131			
																				41			
											12	15					15			84			
											1	2					2		3	4			
											5	8			1	1	9			26			
																				53			
																				29			
												4					4			136			
												3					3			41	5		
																			1	5	47		
																			5	19			
											3	37					37			666			
								1			2	17		2	2	4	21		1	1			
								1			34	138					138		52	459			
					1						20	28					28		3	730			
											23	53					53		28	4248	4		
											18	61					61		5	482			
											9	18					18		3	27			
												3					3		1	16			
							1				23	38		2	2	40		2	317				
											32	36					36		29	58			
												2					2		7	7			
											11	23					23		3	1815			
											7	20					20		16	3295			
											4	4					4			10			
												2					2		3	96			
											12	15					15		2	43			
											1	1					1						
3	1	1	3	5	2	1	3	2	3	779	2115	89	46	13	8	10	168	2283	506	32633	185	122

165

Units 1, 2, and 3 were established as a block on a portion of the north wall line where the wall structure was not visible above ground. They were intended as an initial look at the soil, stratigraphy, and the depth of original occupation below the present surface in this area. Other general information expected from these units was to determine if a wall was indeed present across the block of units and, if so, what problems, if any, might be encountered with its excavation.

Unit 1 was a 2-m^2 unit. Unit 2 was a 1 x 2-m unit against the south face of the wall, and Unit 3 was a 2 x 3-m unit against the north face of the wall, and extending across it.

The surfaces of these units were cleared of brush and weeds, and the loose surface dirt was swept up and screened. It was decided that Unit 1 would be excavated only if necessary to define features extending into it from Unit 2.

UNIT 2 (see Fig. 3)

Stratigraphy

Stratum 1 was dominated by fallen wall stones, in a matrix of tan, sandy soil. This stratum was 20-cm thick at the south edge of the unit, and lensed out as it sloped upward to the top of the surviving wall stub.

Stratum 2 was a similar tan, sandy soil, but with a high percentage of ash stains and lenses, and a few large stones. It was 19-cm thick at the south edge of the unit, and its upper surface sloped up to the face of the extant wall. The lower surface bottomed onto a generally level, hard-packed gray surface of clay, ash, and charcoal. This surface had a slight slope downward toward the southeast corner of the unit. A large rodent disturbance about 30 cm in diameter penetrated this hard-packed surface in the northeast corner against the north wall. The hard surface occupied most of the east half of the unit. The east half was badly disturbed by roots and rodent burrowing extending downward from the present surface. The area of rodent disturbance increased with depth.

Two post holes were recognized at the surface of stratum 2 near the center of the south wall of the unit. Upon the completion of the stratum, the post holes were seen to be associated with a disturbed area on the south profile, extending up into stratum 1.

The hard-packed ash and clay were removed as stratum 3, and found to be multiple layers of ash, dirt, and burned clay ranging from 2 to 4 cm in thickness.

Stratum 3 rested on a hard yellow-tan clay surface, which was designated stratum 4. When the surface of stratum 4 was cleaned, an oval pit was found to have been dug into this surface. This pit was about 61 cm long and 35 cm wide, and extended some 20 cm below the surface of stratum 4. The entire interior of the pit was heavily fire-reddened, and this fire-reddening extended out onto the surface of stratum 4 about 5 cm. The two post holes extending downwards from stratum 1 penetrated the south end of this fire pit.

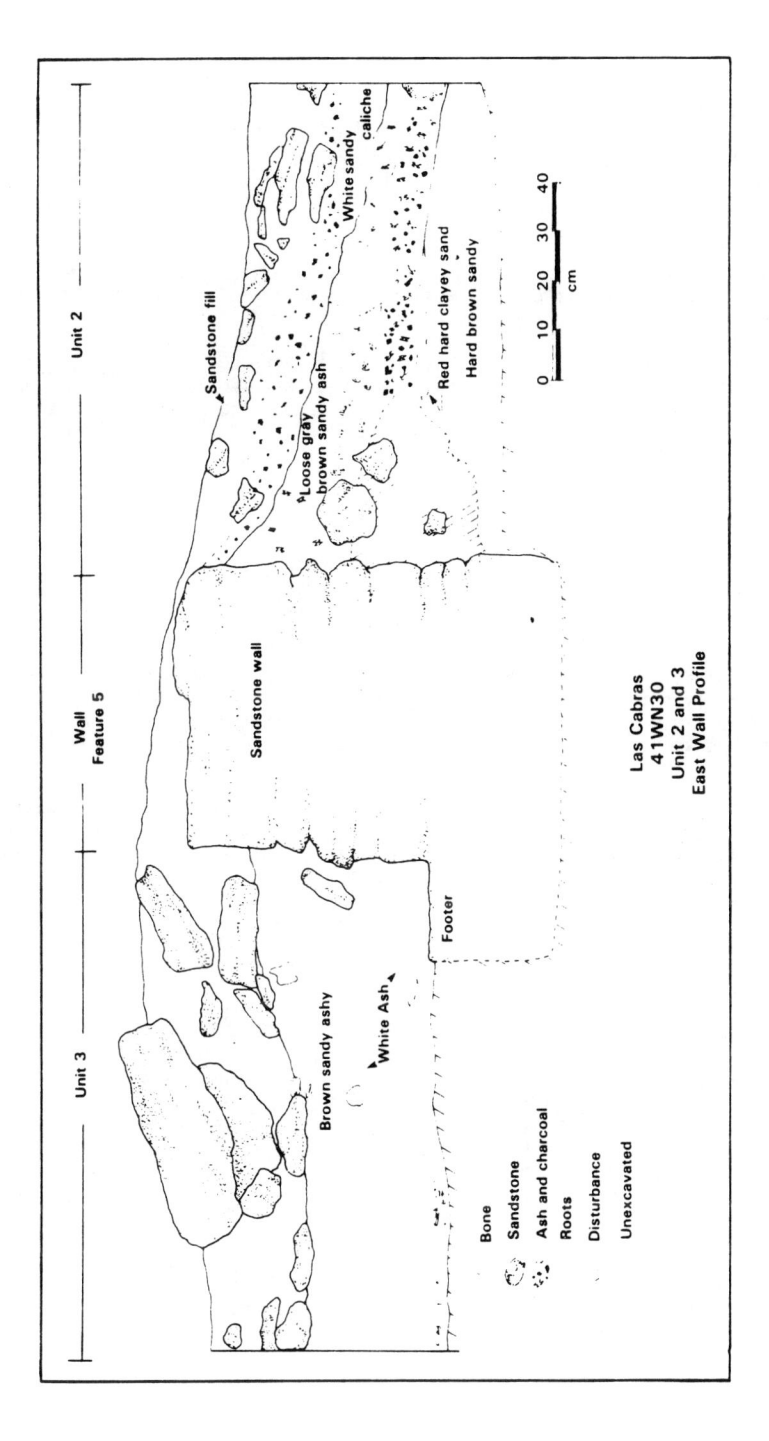

Figure 3. Profile of Units 2 and 3.

The pit was full of ash, charcoal, and sandy earth. The lowest 5 cm were packed with ash and large chunks of charcoal. The eastern half was a 4 to 5 cm thick lens of flat sandstone chunks and what appeared to be a sandy lime mortar. This lens had the appearance of spill rather than part of a sandstone floor. The western edge of the lens was broken by the rodent disturbance. The fire pit was apparently dug through the eastern edge of this lens of mortar.

Stratum 4 was excavated to a depth of about 18 cm. It was found to be sterile except for the top 3 cm and a few artifacts found in rodent-disturbed areas. Very soon after beginning the excavation of stratum 4, traces of the footing trench for the north wall were located. Along most of the wall, the stones were flush with the inner face of the footing trench, but in some areas gaps of up to 4 cm were found. This footing trench was observed across only the eastern 70 cm of the wall face. The rest of the wall across the north side of this unit was irregular and had a larger footing trench, badly disturbed in Unit 2 by rodent activity.

Observations

The surface of stratum 4 appears to be the original occupation surface in this unit. Most artifacts in stratum 4 are apparently packed into its surface. During the time of this original occupation, a gate or doorway apparently existed in the wall at this point.

The area of spilled mortar and flat sandstone chunks in the west half of stratum 3 is probably from the filling of the gateway. After this opening was blocked, the fire pit was dug through the spilled mortar into the underlying occupation surface and the sterile clay beneath. Much of the ash in stratum 3 is probably a product of this fire pit.

Stratum 2 is apparently a buildup of soil during a period of very low-level use, perhaps no more than an occasional overnight camp in the area. In fact, most of the artifact material in stratum 2 could be from root and rodent disturbance of lower strata. Stratum 1 is dominated by wall rubble. Most of the actual volume of the wall in this area is gone, probably through stone robbing, so stratum 1 contains mostly scrap stone and perhaps windblown dirt.

UNIT 3 (see Fig. 3)

Stratigraphy

The stratigraphy of Unit 3 is quite similar to that of Unit 2. Stratum 1, 23 cm thick against the wall and thinning out to 2-3 cm at 4 m from the face of the wall is dominated by wall fall, with a hard tan, sandy clay fill. Portions of stratum 1 extend across the top of the wall, especially in the western half of the unit. A large quantity of bone was found in this stratum, more than in any other single stratum in these excavations.

Stratum 2 was a brown sandy clay with a large admixture of ash, somewhat more compacted than was stratum 2 inside the wall. The upper surface of this stratum sloped downward away from the wall, with a thickness at the wall of 22 cm, and approximately 2 cm thick at 2.4 m from the wall. Stratum 2 overlaid a level surface with a patchy layer of ash and some charcoal, up to 1 cm thick in some areas.

At this level, it was decided to reduce Unit 3 in size. The length along the wall was kept at 2 m, but the width outward from the north face was reduced to 1 m. The wall itself was designated as Feature 5. Stratum 3 was then begun.

Stratum 3 was almost level, 8 cm thick at the wall and 6 cm thick, 1 m from the north face of the wall. It was a gray sandy clay with some charcoal and ash, and had another thin layer of white ash and some charcoal at its base, similar to the one on its upper surface. No burned earth or fire-reddening was seen anywhere in the stratum.

Stratum 4 appeared to be a multiple-lensed, hard-packed scatter of bone, charcoal, ceramics, and other material. Since the appearance of the stone construction of the north wall differed so noticeably in the east and west halves of the unit, the unit was divided into an east and a west half to test for artifact differences.

As the last of stratum 3 was removed from the surface of stratum 4, a footing trench was found, dug from the surface of 4. The irregular western portion of the north wall had been built in this trench. After most of stratum 4 had been removed, the surface of a footing was found along the eastern, well-built portion of the wall, extending 20 cm out from its northern face. The footing was 70 cm long, and had a fairly distinct squared end. The footing trench for the western portion of the wall was irregular in shape and 20 cm wide at the western edge of the unit. Most of the stone was virtually dumped into the trench, and much of it was in relatively massive chunks, 30-40 cm across. Soft brown sandy clay filled the spaces between these stones, and this earth was full of artifacts and bone. On the south side of the wall this trench faded into the rodent and root disturbance which occupied most of the west half of Unit 2.

Stratum 4 became sterile at about the level of the surface of the footing. This is at about the same level as was the last occupation surface in Unit 2 (the top of stratum 4; see Fig. 3).

Observations

Stratum 4 is apparently debris from the first occupation in this area. This occupation began at the time the stone wall of the compound was built, and continued to collect to a depth of 6 cm against the base of the wall, and 13 cm at the north edge of Unit 3 (south section). During this period the wall ended 70 cm into the eastern edge of the unit, probably in a squared face, forming one edge of a gateway, either arched or open-topped.

At the end of this period the decision was made to seal this gateway, either completely or leaving only a small doorway somewhere west of Unit 3. This sealing was done by digging a trench along the alignment of the wall in the gateway and building a roughly laid stone wall into this trench, filling the gateway. The persons building this plug had little or none of the expertise for stonework possessed by those who did the original construction.

After the gate was filled, the fire pit hearth was dug in Unit 2, and the heavy ash buildup occurred which formed stratum 3 in that unit. This is reflected in the generally gray color of the deposits of stratum 3 outside the wall in Unit 3. Then the site was effectively abandoned and stratum 2 built up from washout from the wall structure, blown in dirt, animal activity, and other random events. Stratum 1 is a product of the series of wall robbings and destruction beginning early this century.

UNIT 4 (see Fig. 4 profile drawing)

Unit 4 was a 1 m by 1 m unit placed inside room 3 to examine the wall and any surviving floor surface, and to survey the extent of damage done to the room's living surfaces by a large treasure-hunter's pit about 15 feet wide along the wall and extending about 10 feet south from the wall face.

Stratigraphy

Stratum 1 is a layer of wall fall and natural soil buildup, sloping upward toward the wall. Against the wall at the north side of the unit, this stratum was 54 cm thick; at the south edge of the unit it was 19 cm thick. This stratum sloped steeply downward toward the west into the large disturbed area, which penetrated the lower strata.

At the east end of the unit, stratum 1 bottomed onto a relatively level dark gray brown layer of earth. The lower half of stratum 1 was fairly free of stones, indicating that the wall deterioration was not occurring at any speed. In stratum 2, a noticeable increase in fist-sized or somewhat larger stone was seen. Stratum 2 was 10 cm thick, and overlaid a grayish brown, fine ashy sand with a few rocks. This sand was interrupted at a depth of about 10 cm by a lens of charcoal and ash, with some brown clay along the south side of the unit. This appeared to be the remains of a short-term event during the deposition of the sand, because beneath this lens, stratum 4 is virtually identical, being a gray-brown fine sand with some ash. The sand grain size seemed to be coarser in the lowest parts of the stratum.

Stratum 5 was a hard-packed, light gray clay, with an irregular surface. It overlaid a loose tan clay, stratum 6. At the bottom of stratum 6 was found a hard, light gray-tan sandy lime surface, apparently a floor. On this floor was a fragment of copper sheet, 11 x 12 cm, with irregular edges and one rivet still in place near one edge. The hard sandy lime surface was only along the south side of the unit, ending in an irregular line with a 2 cm drop-off to a hard-packed earthen surface. The treasure-hunter's pit continued through this floor and on into hard, yellow-tan sterile clay. This disturbed area was removed to a depth of ca. 5 cm, sufficient to show that the hard sandy-lime floor was about 3 cm thick.

Observations

As Table 1 shows, there were very few artifacts found in this unit. Those that were found, other than the copper sheet lying on the sandy lime floor, are apparently randomly scattered objects, not representative of an occupational deposit.

It would appear from the stratigraphy that there was no major destruction event at the end of the primary occupation-no burned roof debris or collapsed wall on the floor, for example. The simplest explanation of the stratigraphy is that the building was abandoned and the roof rotted away with no effects of fire and no subsequent occupation, except a brief interval represented by the thin lens of ash and charcoal at the top of stratum 4. If the roof was of clay and caliche supported by large log roof-beams, then this roof structure decayed and dissolved slowly over a long period of time, slowly depositing the roof material into the room. The approximately level deposits of sand, clay, and caliche are about 40

Las Cabras
41WN 30
Unit 4
East Wall Profile

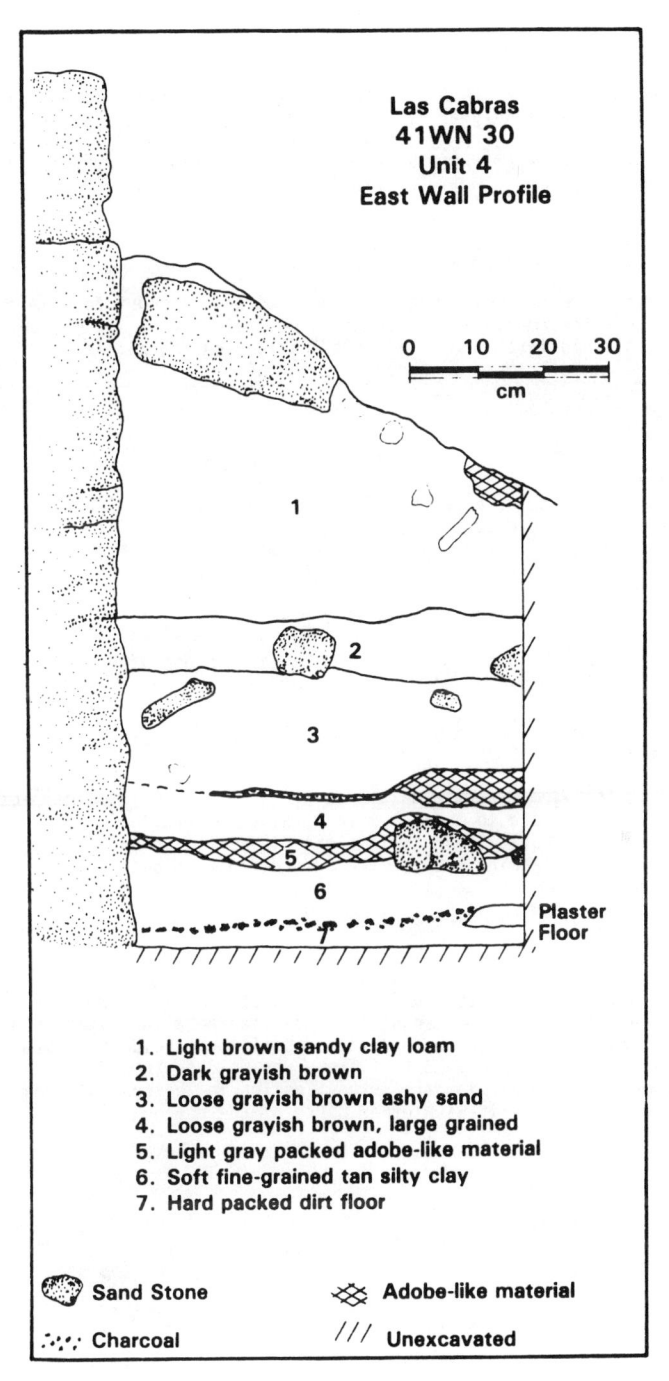

1. Light brown sandy clay loam
2. Dark grayish brown
3. Loose grayish brown ashy sand
4. Loose grayish brown, large grained
5. Light gray packed adobe-like material
6. Soft fine-grained tan silty clay
7. Hard packed dirt floor

Sand Stone   Adobe-like material
Charcoal   /// Unexcavated

Figure 4. Profile of Unit 4.

cm thick, which is on the order of thickness to be expected from the decay of an
adobe roof (Santleben 1862:23). It is considered a reasonable assumption, based
on these observations, that room 3 had a flat adobe and caliche roof, supported
by beams (vigas), and that through long-term decay the majority of the roof is
now the fill of the room.

UNIT 5

Unit 5 was placed in the west center of the compound in order to examine a depression which local informants indicated might be the well. A 1 x 3 m unit was established, divided into three 1 m^2 sections labeled 5A, 5B, and 5C. The long axis of the rectangular unit extended grid north.

Stratigraphy

Although an attempt was made to excavate this unit by natural strata, the attempt was unsuccessful, since no apparent stratification appeared. The soil was a hard, gray clay which changed gradually to a softer, gray clay. This ended on a hard flat surface of gray clay which seemed to resemble the hard-packed surface of the patio encountered elsewhere. The excavation stopped on this surface.

The depression capped a circular area of darker clay with circular cracks within and around it. Anglo artifacts were found to the base of the excavation, but only in this area. When the digging was halted, a large piece of barbed wire was visible in the circular stain.

Observations

It is apparent that some feature exists in the ground at this point. Exactly what sort of feature will have to await a more detailed excavation. The lack of any masonry construction could indicate that this is merely an Anglo trash pit, but the masonry could be lacking because the unit did not go deep enough to reveal any such structure.

UNIT 6

Unit 6 was placed a short distance inside the supposed gate through the west wall. It was intended to examine the amount of deposition near the interior of the gateway, in order to compare with the expected deposition outside the gateway. (Unit 12, discussed below, later showed that there was no gate through the west wall). A second purpose was to examine the stratification in the central area of the compound in order to compare it with other parts of the compound.

Stratigraphy

Stratum 1 was 4 to 6 cm thick and was a hard-packed gray clay with some artifacts. This graded into stratum 2, a less hard-packed stratum with fewer artifacts. It ended on a hard, flat earth surface of gray clay. Only the top centimeter of this stratum contained artifacts.

Observations

Very little deposition occurred in this area of the site. It is probable that much of the central area of the compound will have a similar depositional history.

UNIT 7

Unit 7 was established in the southwestern angle of the compound to sample the stratigraphy in this area and to check for traces of structures which might have been built in the angle.

Stratigraphy

Stratum 1 was a loose, tan dirt containing a few fragments of a modern beer bottle. The stratum was 1 cm thick.

Stratum 2 was a more firmly packed tan clay, relatively flat and 5 cm thick. It contained only a few fragments of bone.

In stratum 3, several components were found. These consisted of two layers of animal manure with a layer of tan silty clay between. The upper component of manure, 10 cm thick, was fragmented into small pieces, while the lower was in large chunks, and was 13 cm thick.

Stratum 4 was a dark gray-brown, ashy-looking sand 6 cm thick, and contained two ceramic sherds and some bone fragments. It appeared to be dust or dirt which had collected onto the underlying hard-packed gray clay surface, stratum 5.

Stratum 5 contained several sherds in its top 2 to 3 cm. Below this occupation surface the hard clay was sterile.

In the southwestern quadrant of the surface of stratum 5 was a post hole ca. 15 cm in diameter. This post hole had rocks packed into it around its edges, apparently to wedge the post into place. The post hole extended 45 cm below the surface of stratum 5.

Observations

The hard-packed earthen surface of stratum 5 resembled that found in Unit 6, but the overlying dark ashy sand is not seen in that unit. No explanation for this odd stratum can be offered.

After the unknown episode which produced this dark, sandy layer (stratum 4), the same manure deposition occurred here as occurred in Units 8 and 10 below. The thickness of the manure layer and its restriction to the southern and eastern portions of the compound may indicate that the animals producing the deposition were penned here, separated from the rest of the compound by a fence.

UNIT 8 (see Fig. 5)

Unit 8 was established to test for possible structures within the southeastern angle of the compound, and to examine the strata in this area. It was a 1 x 2 m unit with its long axis east and west.

Stratigraphy

Stratum 1 was a hard-packed, light brown clay and sand layer with a considerable amount of stone debris. It ranged in thickness from 10 cm near the wall to 4 cm at the west end of the unit.

Stratum 2 was a thick layer of manure ca. 31 cm deep. It was divided into two horizontal components as were the manure strata in Units 7 and 10. The upper component was 12 cm thick and consisted of fragmented manure in a matrix of brown sandy silt, while the lower was 18 cm thick and was much more solidly bedded, with fine multiple strata visible in the fragments as they were removed. A 1 cm thick lens of sandy silt with no manure separated the two components at the east end of the unit against the wall. This lens thickened to 8 cm at the west end of the unit, and the overlying manure component thinned to 8 cm at the same point. Most of the artifacts from stratum 2 came from this lens of manure-free sand.

Stratum 3 was fairly dark, dusty tan sand 2 to 4 cm thick, with patches of brown clay. It was packed onto a hard, tan sandy plaster floor. The sand and dirt stratum contained most of the artifacts, but several potsherds were embedded in the surface of the floor plaster.

The decision was made to leave the plaster floor undamaged at this stage of the excavations.

Observations

It is assumed that the plaster floor was inside a structure in this southeastern corner. If so, the structure left no hint on the present ground surface of walls separating the floor from the rest of the compound, so far as could be seen while examining the present surface in the area. In addition, the lack of a thick deposit of clay and adobe on the floor indicates that there were no substantial wall supporting a flat caliche roof over the floor, as room 3 appears to have had. This probably indicates that the structure had wooden walls and a thatched roof.

The manure layers resemble those found in Units 7 and 10, both in general thickness and the structure of the two components. They undoubtedly all represent the same two phases of a usage of the compound as a cattle or sheep pen. Because of the great similarity in deposition between the various areas where the manure was seen, it is likely that the building surrounding the floor found in Unit 8 had fallen, and did not separate it from the other areas containing animals.

UNIT 9

Unit 4 supplied only a very limited look at the stone structures along the north wall. Peculiarities in the wall lines of the south side of these structures

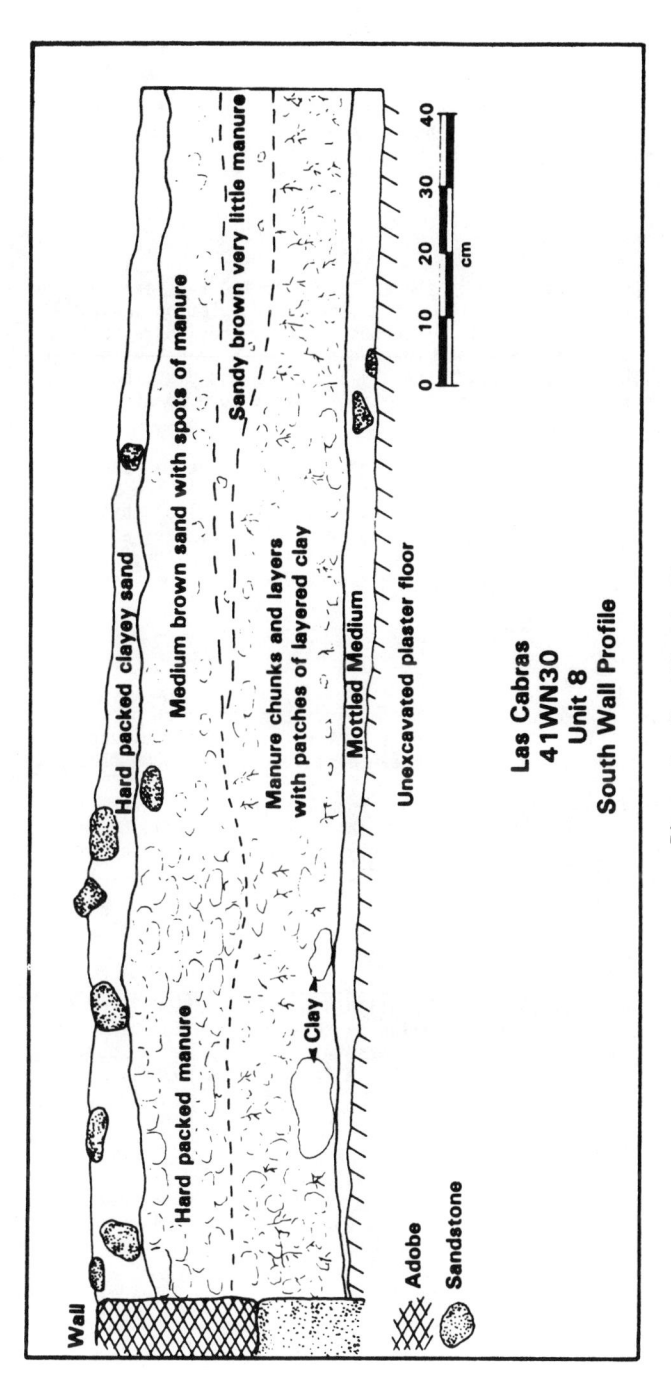

Figure 5. *Profile of Unit 8.*

indicated the possibility that a doorway existed at the southwest corner of room 2, in conjunction with a treasure-hunter's pit. Unit 9 was established to examine the interior of a portion of room 2, and at the same time check for the presence of a doorway in the southwestern corner of the room.

Stratigraphy

Although a stratigraphic excavation of the unit was carried out, examination of the stratigraphy in the walls of the unit after its completion indicated that the room fill had been seriously disturbed, both by previous excavation and by rodent holes. A floor level was reached at a depth of below the top of the wall. This floor surface was extremely broken up and disturbed, but retained enough of its characteristics to make us fairly sure of its identification.

This floor appears to have been of a dark, hard-packed, orange-tan sandy clay, which may or may not have had a plastered surface. The area of the possible doorway was excavated to within a few centimeters of the level of this surface, but when the very disturbed condition of the original surface was recognized, the excavation was halted. If a doorway is in this area, then the excavation of it should be done in a much more exacting manner than could be managed in a 1 m² unit.

Observations

The multiple, disturbed strata found in room 2 indicate that much of the present fill of room 2 is probably treasure-hunter's back dirt, and it would appear that most of the southwestern corner has also been disturbed by the same process.

It is very likely that the doorway into this room was in this corner. The only other possible place for it is the center of the room's west wall, connected with room 1. Careful excavation could possibly record the remains or imprint of woodwork in this doorway, if it survived the disturbing effects of the treasure-hunter's pit.

UNIT 10 (see Fig. 6)

Unit 10 was a 1 x 1 m² unit placed on the alignment of the east wall of the chapel. One of the reasons for the location of this unit was to check for any extension of the wall of the chapel across this area. A second purpose was to examine the stratigraphy at the probable front of the chapel.

Stratigraphy

Stratum 1 ranged from 14 to 20 cm in thickness, and was hard-packed clay with some sandstone debris, without any patterning. This stratum ended with a 2-3 cm thick zone of red-brown sandy clay and ash in thin level lenses, forming the division between stratum 1 and stratum 2.

1. Light gray clayey loam with spots of caliche
2. Reddish brown sand
3. Light gray sandy ash
4. Loose medium gray brown sandy loam
5. Fine pieces of manure with sand
6. Manure in layered chunks
7. Reddish tan soil
8. Dark brown charcoal stain
9. Medium brown fine sandy loam
10. Hard packed brown sand with ash
11. Layered white plaster
12. Reddish brown hard packed sand with clayey loam
13. Hard, light tan sandy clay

● Sandstone
/ / / Unexcavated

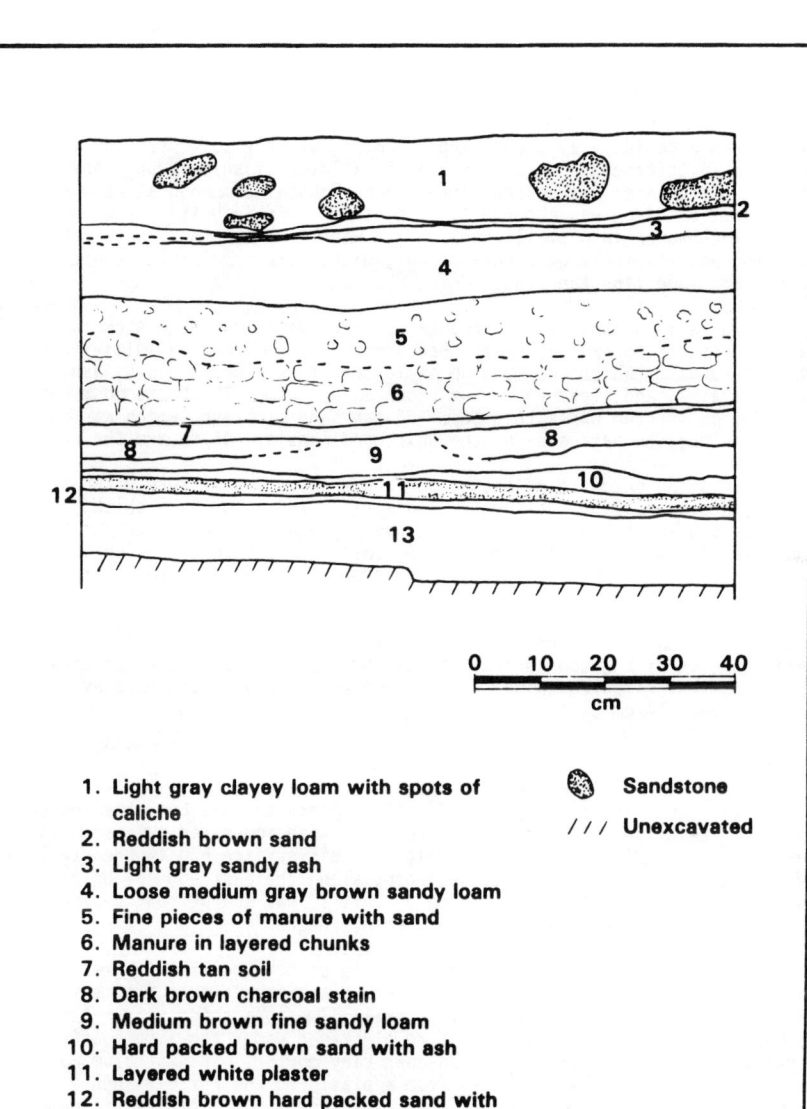

**Las Cabras
41WN30
Unit 10
East Wall Profile**

Figure 6. *Profile of Unit 10.*

177

Stratum 2 was a medium gray-brown sandy loam, relatively soft, ranging from 17 to 20 cm in thickness. It overlaid a thick layer of animal dung, forming stratum 3. This layer was divided into two horizontal components, as was found in Unit 8. Each was about 8 to 10 cm thick. As in Unit 8, the upper component was broken into small chunks mixed with fine tan sand, while the lower component was in large pieces of dung with a clear multiple-layered structure and some fine tan sand.

Stratum 4 was a thin zone of fine red-tan sand ranging from 0 to 4 cm in thickness, thicker toward the west. Beneath this was a complex multi-lensed stratum, stratum 5, which was made up of lenses of dark brown clays, ash, charcoal, stains, and light to medium brown sandy loam. The bottommost component of this stratum was a thin layer of tan sand with ash, which was ca. 1 cm thick along the east side of the unit, and lensing out toward the west.

This was deposited onto a hard-packed surface which was a mixture of white lime and tan clay forming stratum 6. The stratum was about 5 cm thick, and fairly flat and level. At its base it graded into a very sandy stratum (7), with chunks of lime and some charcoal. On the eastern side of the unit there was some indication of fire-reddening of the tan clay surface beneath this stratum.

Stratum 8 was a tan, sandy clay, with artifacts only in the top 2-4 cm. Along the eastern edge of the top surface of this stratum were darker brown areas and some apparent fire-reddening. Excavation was stopped when the clay became sterile at about 64 cm below the surface.

Observations

The original occupation surface in this unit appears to have been the top of stratum 8. The pattern of hard-packed tan clay with impressed artifacts is seen also in Units 2, 3, and 11. In Unit 11, this surface had two hearth features similar to that seen as just beginning along the east edge of Unit 10. The artifact collection for the surface of Unit 10 was sparse, but typical of the collections from the primary occupation elsewhere.

Strata 6 and 7 are anomalous and unique to this unit. The lime fragments found in these two strata were not a plaster floor, but rather broken fragments of white plaster, white lime, sandy mortar, small limestone chips with white lime or mortar adhering to them (some are fire blackened under the lime coating), and tan, sandy clay, which could be broken-down clay mortar. This stratum would appear to be broken debris, possibly from a plastered and white-washed finishing layer on the wall of a structure, or from a plaster floor. After this deposition of plaster chunks, there was a midden-like deposition again resembling that in Unit 11, but far less productive in bone and artifacts, and much thinner. This occupies the position of the dark gray brown ashy sand in Unit 7. Above this was deposited the massive slabs of multiple-layered animal dung with intermixed sandy clay, the same sequence seen in Units 7 and 8, but not in 11 or 6.

UNIT 11 (see Fig. 7)

The presence of a gateway on the northwestern portion of the compound wall led us to surmise that there might have been a gatehouse structure in the northwestern

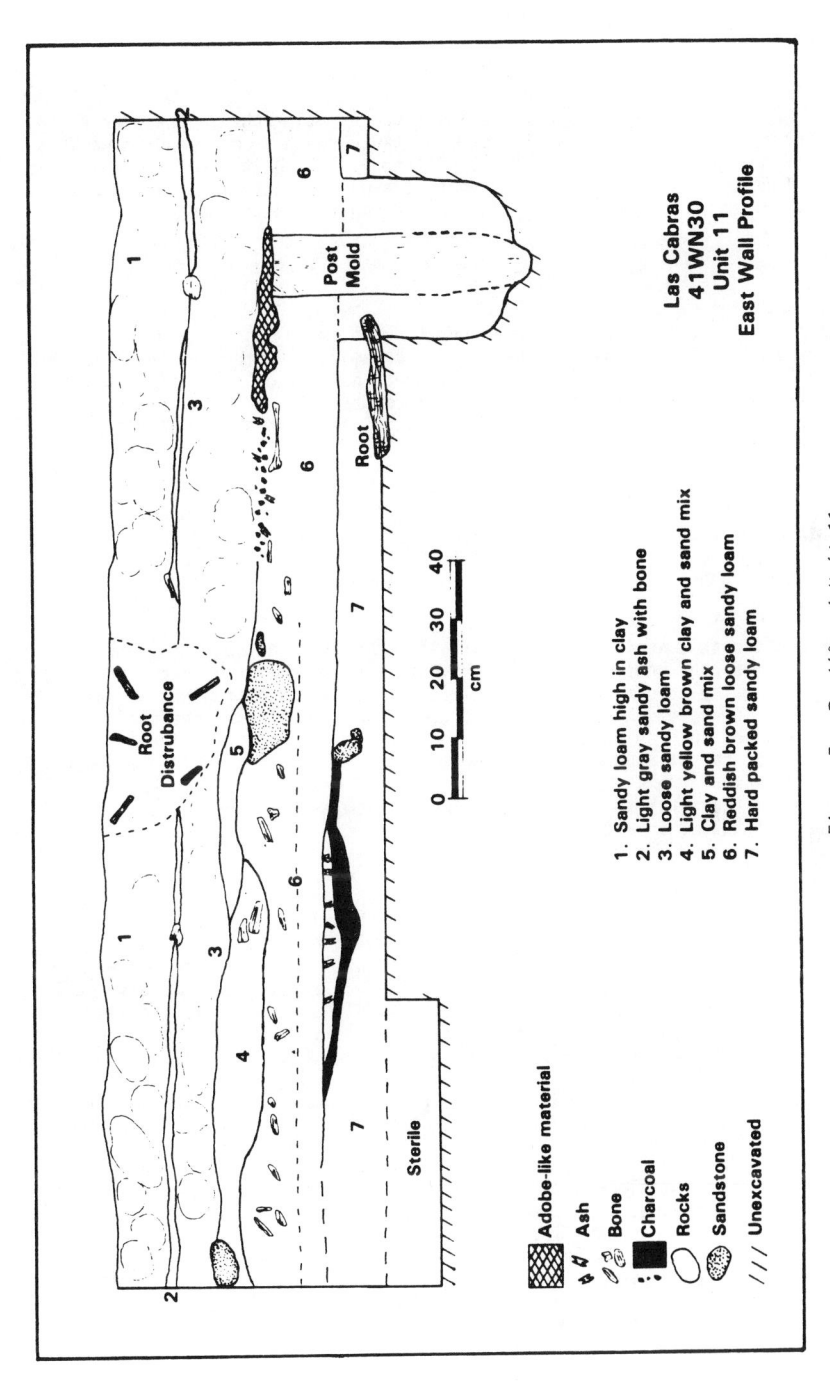

Figure 7. *Profile of Unit 11.*

corner. Unit 11 was placed so as to examine the stratigraphy in the area of this corner and to test for a wall at the same distance south from the north wall as are the standing stone walls of rooms 1, 2, and 3. The unit was 1 x 2 m in size, with its long axis to grid north; the west side of the unit was extended beyond the one meter point up to the wall line, which ran toward the northwest in this area.

Stratigraphy

Stratum 1 was characterized by a large quantity of small stones, probably associated with wall fall. A surprising amount of ceramics and other cultural material was found on the surface and in stratum 1, more than was usual in other units. The stratum was a gray-brown sandy clay of a constant 10-12 cm in thickness, and rested on a 1-2 cm thick zone of light gray sand, ash, and scattered bone fragments, the top components of stratum 2.

Stratum 2 was ash-stained in its upper several centimeters across most of the unit, but was basically a brown, sandy clay. A number of rocks were found together in the south quarter of the stratum, and scattered bone and ceramics in the remainder. The deposit showed few of the characteristics of a buildup on an occupation surface. This stratum ranged in thickness from 8 cm in the northern end of the unit to 14 cm in the south.

Stratum 3 began as a series of lenses of ash, charcoal, and some clay and caliche scattered across the unit. These ranged in thickness from 2 to 12 cm, and a large quantity of articulated bone was intermixed. Large areas of red-brown clay were intermixed. Toward the base of this stratum, the areas of ash, charcoal, and caliche disappeared, and the bone concentration rapidly dropped off. The last several centimeters of the stratum were a red-brown sandy clay virtually free of bone. The total thickness of the stratum, including the ash lenses and other debris, ranged from 18 cm in the north to 13 cm in the south, with a maximum thickness of about 20 cm in the central area of the unit.

Stratum 3 bottomed onto a hard-packed, flat surface. A number of artifacts were packed into this flat surface, and two fire hearth features were located in the north end of the unit. One, near the center of the north wall, was a series of thin layers of ash and charcoal overlying a circular bed of small gravel placed in a shallow bowl-like depression, with considerable fire-reddening of the clay in and around the depression. The second hearth was bisected by the east wall of the unit, and was similar in plan and structure, being multiple ash and charcoal layers in a shallow bowl-shaped depression. This hearth had no gravel bedding in the depression. Both features were about 35 cm in diameter.

A mass of rocks in the base of stratum 2 along the south side of the unit was found to be resting on an area of discoloration and associated rodent holes in stratum 3. As stratum 3 was removed in this area, this discoloration began to look more and more regular, and by the time the surface of stratum 4 was reached, the area had resolved itself in the clear outline of a footing trench surrounding a line of circular postmold stains. The trench outlines extended eastward at right angles to the west wall. It had parallel sides and a rounded west end, stopping just short of the stone wall. Subsequent excavation of this trench as feature 10 showed that the trench was about 30 cm wide and 31 cm deep below the surface of stratum 4, with straight vertical sides. The clear trace of the mold of one of the posts could be seen extending from the bottom of the trench through stratum 3

to its top surface. A row of small, shallow depressions was found on the bottom of the trench, apparently the impression of the ends of the posts. The trench fill was a tan, sandy clay, with a paler yellow clay intermixed at the actual surface of stratum 4.

The artifacts in stratum 4 were found predominantly in the top 2 to 4 cm. At a depth of 8 cm, the red-brown clay changed to a darker, harder clay. A 50 cm^2 sampling pit was dug into this stratum an additional 10 cm; it was found to be sterile after the first centimeter. Artifacts in the lower portion of stratum 4 and on the surface of stratum 5 were localized into three small areas, each about 15 to 20 cm across. The general characteristics of these areas suggest that they were rodent disturbances.

Observations

The original occupation in this unit appears to have been on the surface of stratum 4. A considerable number of artifacts were pressed into this surface.

After a period of time the *jacal* wall trench was cut into this deposit. It cannot be determined whether the structure associated with this wall extended to the north or the south of it. The nature of the material deposited against the *jacal* wall in stratum 3 seems to indicate that it is the buildup from garbage dumping and fire hearth cleaning--a kitchen midden. At present it is assumed that this type of deposit is characteristic of a buildup outside a structure, near a doorway.

The top of stratum 3 apparently represents the destruction of the *jacal* and the cessation of occupation in this area, except for a possible short-term visitation represented by the thin ash and charcoal layer dividing stratum 1 from stratum 2. Strata 1 and 2 are predominantly recent soil and wall collapse debris.

UNIT 12

There was a gap in the line of rubble marking the west wall position, which was considered to be a gateway some 2 m wide. Unit 12, a 1 x 2 m unit with its long axis towards the north, was situated at the south edge of this opening. It was intended to examine the stonework at the edge of this gateway (if it were one) and to examine the cultural deposits in the gateway opening and against the outside of the west wall.

Stratigraphy

Stratum 1 in the south end of the unit was the usual stone robbed wall rubble found in most of the units situated against the wall. Random fragments of sandstone up to 10 to 12 cm across in a matrix of tan, sandy clay were piled against the surviving wall fragments; this overlaid a flat surface of tan, sandy clay; the ground surface at the time the wall collapsed or robbing began. This surface is ca. 5 cm below present ground surface at the face of the wall.

In the northern portion of the unit, no wall fall or equivalent stratum was seen.

Stratum 2 was a hard, tan, sandy clay with charcoal chunks of caliche mortar apparently from the bonding material in the wall, and some artifacts.

Artifacts became more scarce as the stratum was excavated. At 25 cm below the present surface this stratum bottomed onto a flat surface of brown loam.

This brown loam formed stratum 3. As it was excavated, no artifacts were found. The stratum was 10 cm thick, and overlaid a stratum of caliche, pebbles, and brown clay, which became more solidly caliche within the first 2 to 3 cm. This was stratum 4, and was also sterile.

The footing trench for the wall was found to have been excavated from the top of stratum 3, and was 25 cm deep below that surface, extending 15 cm into the stratum of caliche. The footing was well built and consisted of rough stone laid into a bedding of hard, light gray mortar which filled the trench. There were some charcoal fragments intermixed with the mortar.

The wall extended across the entire length of Unit 12 with no sign of any break.

Observations

The apparent gap in the structure of the west wall on the surface may be the result of extensive stone robbing or even bulldozing, but does not reflect the actual structure of the wall. The lack of any artifact deposition of note outside the wall is taken to indicate that no doorway or gateway was near this portion of the wall, and indicates that very little occupation occurred outside of the wall.

UNIT 13

A local informant indicated that a circular structure resembling a lime kiln had been found outside the north compound wall while the area around the site was being plowed. In an attempt to locate this structure, Unit 13 was placed outside the north wall near room 3 in a bowl-shaped depression of about 4 m in diameter.

Stratigraphy

Stratum 1 was an almost sterile hard tan clay, 10 cm in thickness. It overlaid a multiple-lensed stratum of silts and ash with charcoal, burned bone, and some ceramics, all excavated as stratum 2.

Beneath the zone of burned material and artifacts was a zone of almost sterile dark brown clay containing only a few bones. This zone was included with stratum 2. The total thickness of stratum 2 was 34 cm.

Stratum 3 was a lighter, sandy-brown clay with numerous bones and some ceramics. Some ash and charcoal were present. Several large bones were found in the southwestern corner of this stratum, including an almost complete bovine skull showing distinct butchering marks.

Stratum 3 ended on a yellow-white caliche surface which sloped steeply up from the southwest corner of the unit toward the northeast. The unit was too small to determine whether this surface was part of a man-made hole or a natural feature of the ground in this area.

Observations

It is possible that the feature found in the bottom of Unit 13 was a trash pit dug by hand or a dump into a natural depression or gully. The artifacts are not very concentrated, however, and a firm identification of the deposit must wait for further work in the area.

The bovine skull found in stratum 3 had been opened with an ax or butcher knife. The back of the skull is gone, implying that the brain was being removed. The flesh on the skull was not cooked off, since the skull was apparently still fully fleshed when it was dropped into the dump; several large fragments of the base of the skull were found broken free and separated from the rest of the bone but still approximately in place, apparently held in roughly the correct position by flesh.

This trash pit or gully was then covered by tan sandy clay until it had a level surface, and almost sterile soil was deposited above this as the lower component of stratum 2. Finally, a number of thin layers of ash, silt, charcoal, and some bone and other artifacts were collected on this surface. After this, most artifact deposition ceased, and stratum 1 formed as another layer of largely sterile clay.

UNIT 14

It was hoped that an area in the northern part of the state-owned property could be used as the visitors' center for the proposed work. To determine whether this area had any indications of a prior occupation, historic or prehistoric, a 1 m^2 unit was placed in the approximate center for the proposed location. An earlier surface survey indicated that very little cultural material was to be found in this area, but a deep test was necessary to check this conclusion.

Stratigraphy

No stratigraphy was observed, other than a slight change in color and texture at ca. 30 cm, probably indicating the bottom of the plow zone. The soil was a dark red-brown sandy clay. Four flakes of chert were found in the plow zone, but were considered to be plow fractures from the numerous large chert cobbles scattered through the soil. The excavation was taken 20 cm below the base of the plow zone with no further indications of cultural material.

Observations

No artifacts were found in the surface examination of the visitors' center area, and this, in conjunction with the complete lack of any cultural debris subsurface, indicates that there is no occupation on this hill, either aboriginal or historical.

UNIT 15

The location of the southwestern angle of the compound wall and the line of the eastern wall was known. Unit 15 was placed to establish the exact position of the south wall near the southeastern angle, and to examine the ground surfaces and stratigraphy outside the south wall.

Stratigraphy

Stratum 1 consisted of 2 to 4 cm of brown, sandy clay with a great deal of vegetal matter and some small rocks and pebbles.

Stratum 2 was a zone of wall debris with most of the large rock removed, as usual. The lower limit of the stratum was approximately level, while the top sloped upward to the remains of the wall. Larger rocks are found lower in the stratum. A large heap of debris and wall rubble lay along the inside of the wall line, and, in fact, is higher at its crest than the top of the surviving wall fragments.

Beneath the wall rubble was a thin lens of white mortar spilled or washed onto a rock-free soil surface. This strongly resembles the mortar between the stones of the wall, and probably represents a decay of the wall fabric or a spill of mortar during construction.

Stratum 3 below this thin white lens was a gray tan, with some charcoal and a few rocks and pebbles. Very few artifacts were seen in this stratum, and after ca. 5 cm it was decided to excavate only a 50 cm^2 quadrant in the southwest corner. This was taken to a depth of 10 cm below the top of stratum 3 with only one chert flake found.

Observations

The top of stratum 3 was ground surface when the wall was constructed. Virtually no occupation debris was found, indicating that there is a good probability that no doorway or gateway was nearby. The unit resembles Unit 12 in general characteristics of artifact deposition, and again indicates that very little occupational activity took place outside the compound at any time during the active life of the site.

THE ARTIFACTS

For the purpose of interpreting the history of the site occupation, the artifacts recovered in the test excavations at Las Cabras can be divided into two basic time periods. Those which are commonly found on 18th century sites in the San Antonio River valley (see Schuetz 1969; Scurlock and Fox 1977; Greer 1967.; Tunnell 1966; Gilmore 1974, 1975) are grouped together and considered to be of the Spanish occupation period. Artifacts which date to the late 19th and early 20th centuries can with confidence be attributed to later, sporadic visits by local hunters, picnickers, and treasure hunters. The following brief descriptions summarize the various types of artifacts found and, wherever possible, show the basis for dating each type.

REFERENCE

Santleben, August
   1910   A Texas Pioneer, Early Staging and Overland Freighting on the Frontiers of Texas and Mexico. Edited by I Dafflek, New York.

Mission Sites Archaeology

A DESCRIPTION OF THE STRATIGRAPHY,

FEATURES AND ARTIFACTS FROM AN ARCHEOLOGICAL

EXCAVATION AT THE ALAMO

By

John W. Greer

STATE BUILDING COMMISSION

ARCHEOLOGICAL PROGRAM

Report Number 3   March, 1967

INTRODUCTION

There has always been a great interest in the Alamo and in what lies buried below the surface in the vicinity. Early pipeline and foundation ditches which cut into the deposits on the Alamo property unearthed various types of materials. During construction of the buildings around the present Alamo Plaza, many interesting items were found. The excavation for the basement of the present Post Office (the location of the Indian houses during Spanish times) on the north side of the Plaza, reportedly unearthed many artifacts, especially Indian pottery, glass beads, and possibly Indian burials. One local resident reports that he was a young boy at the time of the construction of the Gibbs Building on the northeast corner of the Alamo Plaza, and he used to watch various things being uncovered. One interesting feature he recalled was a group of cannons buried, lying parallel. Today, no one knows what happened to these artifacts.

During improvements on the Alamo grounds in the spring of 1966, trenches were dug for electrical lines in parts of the north courtyard. Many artifacts were uncovered and collected. Since the possibility of recovering valuable information and specimens from the deposits seemed great, an archeological investigation was arranged. Excavation began on June 1, 1966, and continued for five weeks. Processing of materials, laboratory analysis and preparation of reports continued for several months.

The results of the archeological investigation of Mission San Antonio de Valero (The Alamo) are presented in three parts: Volume 1, The Historic Background, by Mardith K. Schuetz; Volume 2, A Description of Enameled Earthenware, by Curtis Tunnell; Volume 3, The Stratigraphy, Features and Artifacts, by John W. Greer.

Figure 1. Plan of the courtyard showing

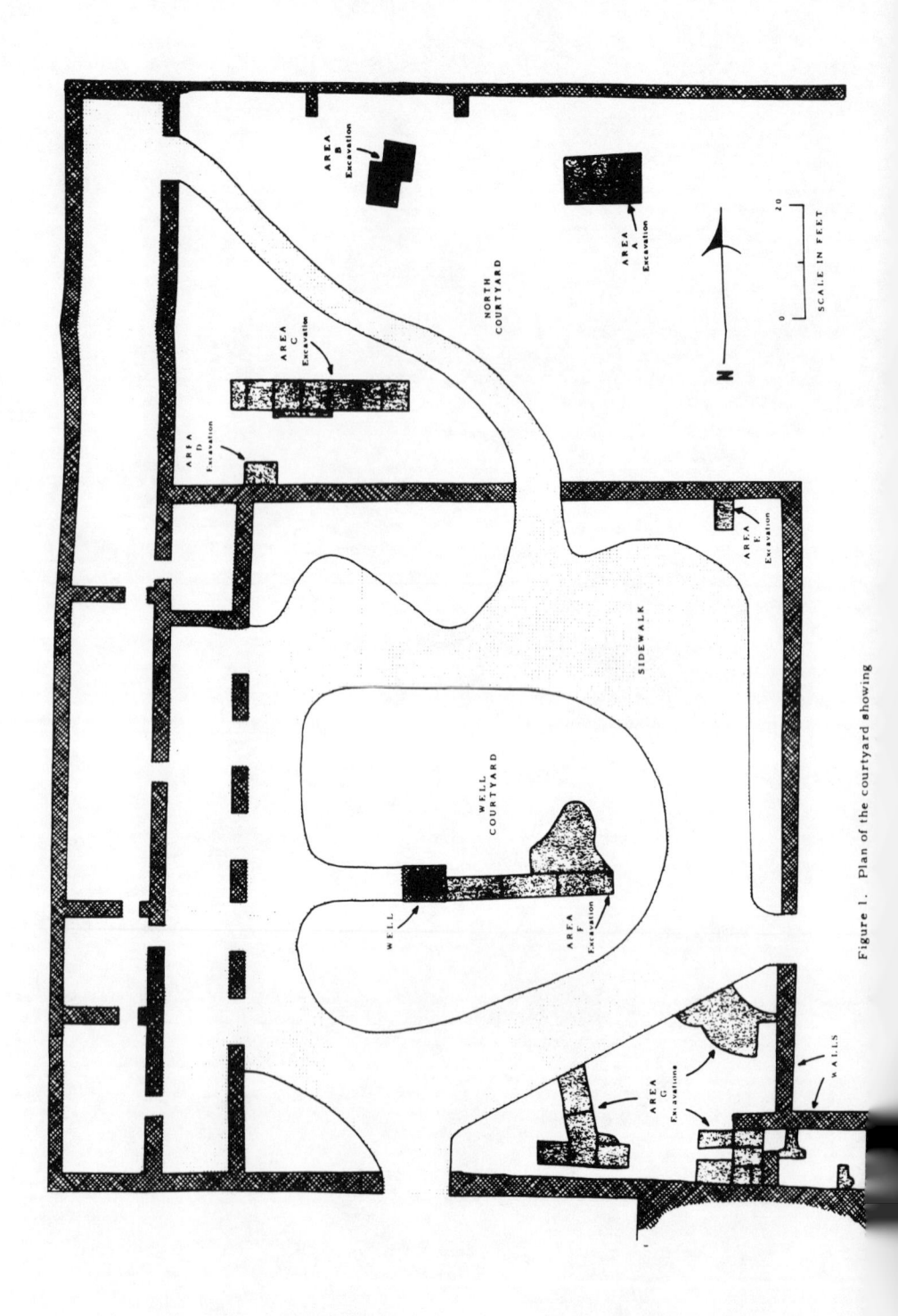

EXCAVATIONS

Excavations were begun on June 1, and lasted through mid-July, 1966, with work being completed during the normal working hours of a five-day week. The crew primarily consisted of three laborers, with an additional paid laborer for one week and always at least two volunteers. Standard archeological field techniques were employed. All excavated deposits were screened through one-quarter inch mesh hardware cloth, except for some layers of obviously recent fill dirt. All occupational materials except dirt, rocks, and charcoal were collected. These included all metal, pottery, glass, intrusive clay (for bricks), wood, trimmed stone, and recent materials (rubber, plastic). Artifacts were placed in labeled sacks and taken to the laboratory at the Witte Museum for processing. The artifacts were cleaned and labeled according to provenience.

Vertical control was maintained in relation to the present surface, as the surface elevation varied negligibly over the entire area. As an added control, elevations of the present surface around each square and at many of the zone contacts and features were also recorded in relation to the present surface of the sidewalk beneath the arch between the north courtyard and the well yard, which was assigned an arbitrary elevation of 100.00 feet.

Initial work began in the north courtyard in Areas A and C (Fig. 1). Area C was to be the primary testing area, and Area A was begun simply as a check of the stratigraphy in another corner of the courtyard. Area C was expanded with the hope of providing a large stratified sample of artifacts and work continued there until the end of the excavations. Area D (Square 5) was dug to check for possible rooms along the east-west wall and to check the depth of the original wall foundations. A test of Area B was started well along in the excavation period to check the findings in Area A, which was also expanded at that time.

In the well yard, a pit was excavated in Area E beside the north wall to check the similarity of the stratigraphy found here to that in Area D of the north courtyard. The grassy area near the well in the center of the courtyard was opened and a large adobe room was uncovered. Area G included three separate excavation units on the south side of the well yard (Fig. 1). One test was near the east gate; a

series of excavation units were beside the church in the southeast corner of the yard, and additional units were placed next to the church between the east wall and the south gate. A description of the results of the tests in each of the individual areas follows.

Area A

The first test in this area was near the present north wall of the north courtyard in Square 3. The fill of this square, composed almost entirely of large limestone rocks and lime mortar, was from about 1.5 to 5.5 feet deep. As this material appeared to be fill from a rubble wall, possibly the original north wall, a large square 10 by 15 feet was begun, incorporating the earlier Square 3. Although this unit reached a depth of only 2.5 feet, what appeared to be the outline of the rubble wall or foundation trench showed plainly in the floor of the square as a discolored area filled with large limestone rocks, brown dirt and caliche, and a small amount of mortar composed of white lime and yellowish sand. This feature was designated Feature 1 and was found to extend west into Area B.

While excavating the upper levels of Square 27 in Area A, three occupational surfaces were encountered. Each was a hard, black, clay-like surface with about 0.1 foot of ash and ashy material. In the fill and resting directly on the floor was a multitude of broken window panes and other types of glass, including broken bottle necks with wire clamps to hold the corks, metal bottle neck covers, square nails (and a few round nails), unidentified metal objects, and a few potsherds. The fill, especially on the lowest surface, was nearly pure cinders-- a sample of which was collected. These surfaces were labeled, from top to bottom, Features 3, 4 and 5. All probably represent debris from the Hugo and Smeltzer Store, and are present in both Area B and Area C. Similar buried occupation surfaces are also present in Area G.

Area B

Area B is the northwest corner of the north courtyard. The purpose of opening this area was to test the hypothesis that an old rubble wall ran east-west through Area A. A large unit of about 5 by 8 feet was excavated in what was estimated to be the area of the wall. The entire unit was dug by hand.

During the excavation of Area B, materials were encountered dating from recent times down through late Anglo-American, late Spanish Colonial, and possibly into earlier Spanish Colonial times (early eighteenth century). In the north central area of the unit was a well-defined feature containing early Anglo-American material with some of the earlier Spanish material mixed in.

In the upper levels, the burned surfaces (Features 3, 4 and 5) were present and contained more material than in other areas of the site. Data gained from the excavation of this unit supported our interpretation of the findings in Area A. Trimmed limestone blocks laid in a yellow, sandy mortar extended up into the bottom of the late Anglo (Hugo and Smeltzer) surfaces in the north part of the square. Below this, the construction changed to irregular, small limestone boulders (average ca. 1 foot in diameter) set in a brown dirt mortar, much like the south walls of the courtyard at Mission Espada in San Antonio. The wall foundation was apparently dug from the top of the late Spanish zones and extended down slightly into the sterile, hard clay underlying the early Spanish deposits. On the inside edge of the wall was a concentration of artifacts dating apparently to the early Anglo period, probably about 1836. The artifacts included almost all of the gun parts, musket and rifle balls, gun flints, early white-paste earthenware (such as the transferwares), and other materials from that time period. Also included were sherds and other artifacts dating from the Spanish period which had been turned up when the wall trench cut through the earlier Spanish zones. All evidence suggests that this wall was built and used during the seige of 1836. This would explain all of the materials dating from that period as well as all of the gun parts, cannon ball fragments, and possible bugle fragment found on the inside edge of the wall.

Area C

This area, consisting of a number of squares forming a long east-west trench, was the primary test excavation at the Alamo. The entire trench was dug by hand and screened. Whenever possible, the deposits were removed by natural zones rather than arbitrary six-inch levels for a better separation of materials.

Zones dating from all occupations at the Alamo were encountered. The upper zones consisted primarily of the burned surfaces (described previously) from the Hugo and Smeltzer store. Underlying these surfaces in the entire north courtyard (Areas A, B and C) was a zone about four inches thick of almost pure gravel,

Figure 3.   Profile of south wall of Square 1 (Area C).

→ W

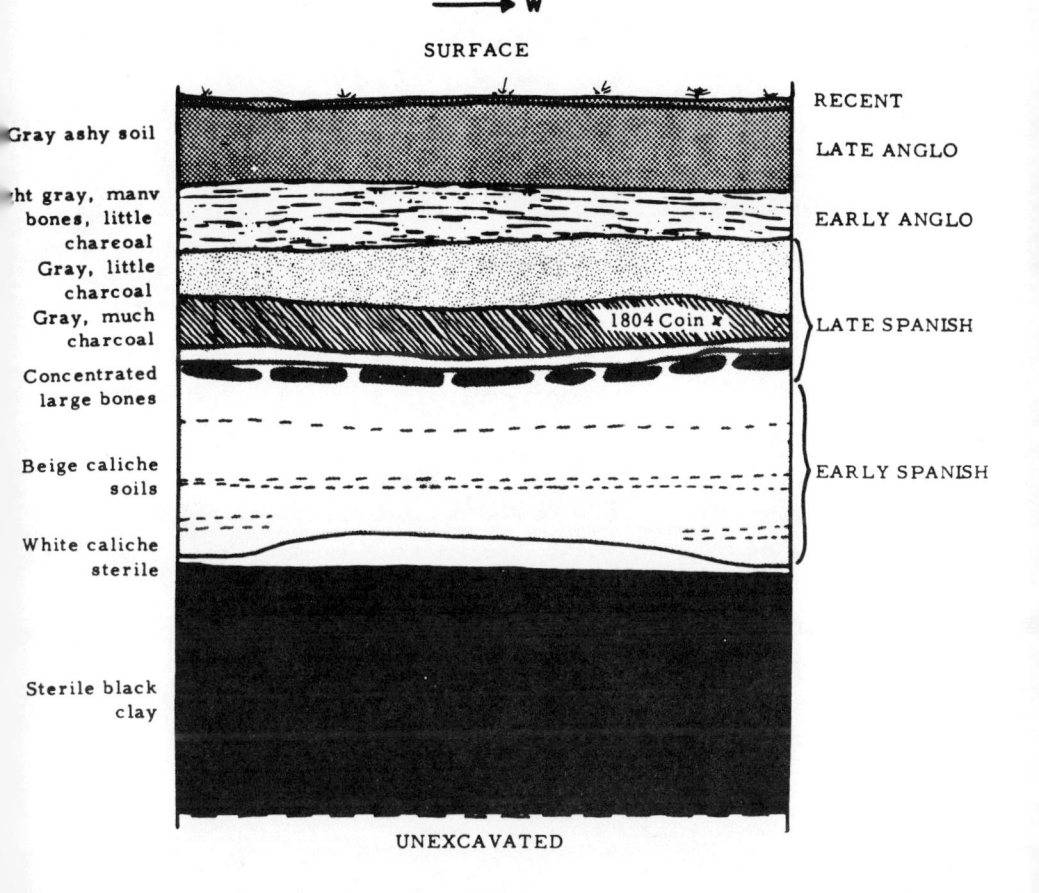

SURFACE

Gray ashy soil — RECENT / LATE ANGLO

ht gray, many bones, little charcoal — EARLY ANGLO

Gray, little charcoal
Gray, much charcoal — LATE SPANISH (1804 Coin)

Concentrated large bones

Beige caliche soils — EARLY SPANISH

White caliche sterile

Sterile black clay

UNEXCAVATED

0 — 2
SCALE IN FEET

Figure 4.   Profile of west wall of Square 2
            (Area C).

199

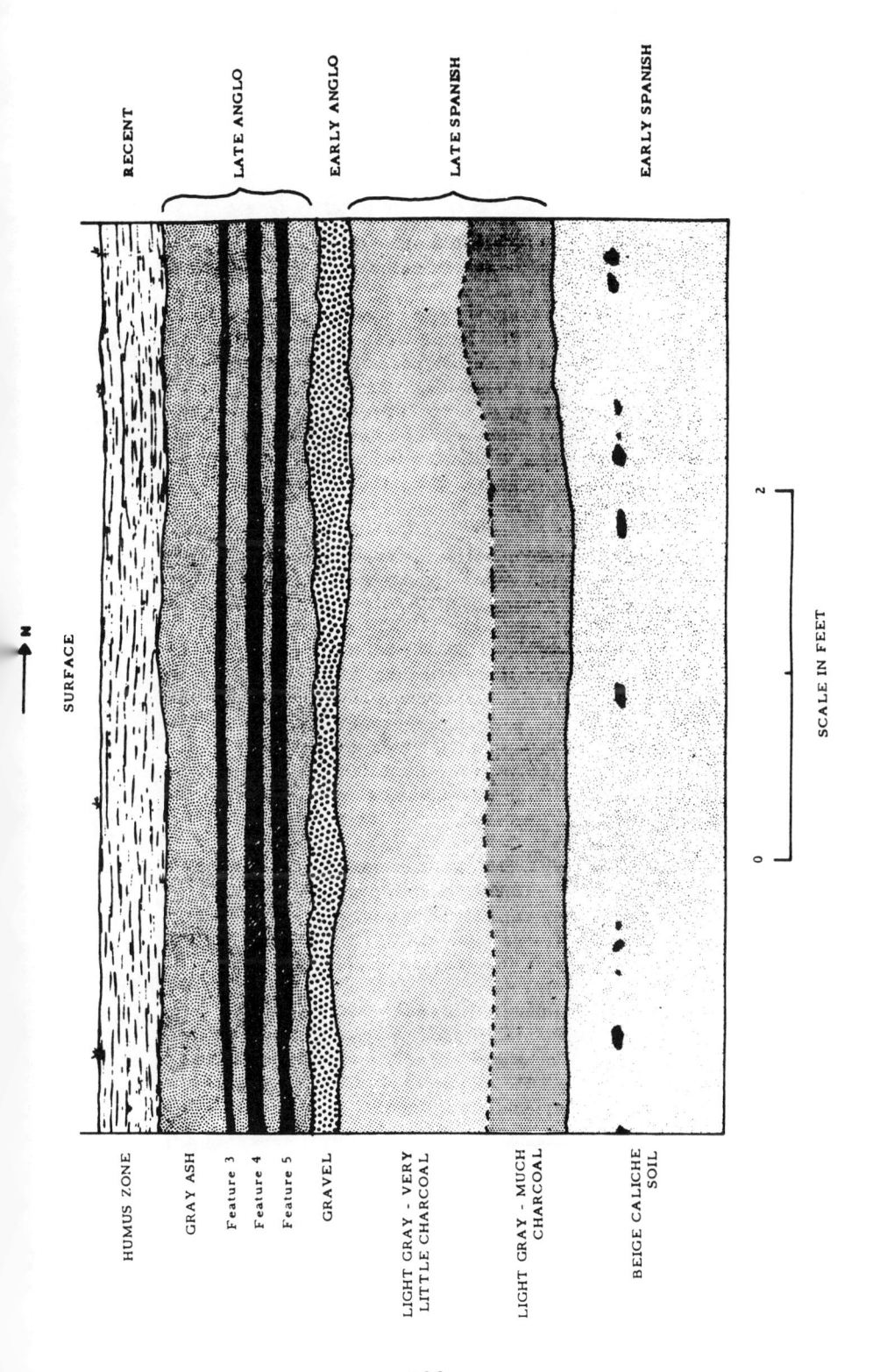

probably brought from a gravel deposit somewhere near the San Antonio River. This gravel may represent part of the improvements at the site by the U. S. Army during their occupation in 1848 and 1849. Below this gravel zone were layers dating to the Spanish Colonial period, which were in turn underlain by a very compact, sterile black clay.

A variety of features were encountered in various parts of the trench in Area C (Fig. 5). In the west central portion was a large trimmed stone and three juniper posts in line (Feature 6), dating probably to about 1900. This might have been a stepping stone, or more likely, the base stone for a large post or monument. The holes in which the stone and posts were buried contained mixed materials of the same types as found on the burned surfaces above. The holes also cut through the Spanish zones and extended almost down into the sterile black clay.

A large animal mandible (probably young horse; Feature 7, Fig. 5) was found in an upper Spanish zone near the west end of the trench. A partially restorable Majolica plate (blue-on-white) was found beside this bone.

Feature 8 was a floor of sandstone slabs in the west end of the trench. On top of the slabs was a layer one to two inches thick of charcoal and ashes, probably representing burned roof materials. These slabs date to late Spanish times and may represent the floor of a covered walkway. With the Majolica and lead-glazed Mexican earthenware on this floor was a Spanish coin minted in Mexico City and dated 1804 (Fig. 26, a-b).

Feature 9 was a caliche lens near the east end of the trench and dating well back into the Spanish occupation. This mound of caliche contained concentrations of bones, red brick fragments (Type I), Majolica sherds, and similar artifacts. The surrounding soil was relatively soft and grayish in color.

Near the caliche mound and deposited slightly later in time, but still within the Spanish period, was a portion of a stone slab wall (Feature 10). This consisted of only a few stones and very little mortar. Nothing definite can be said of its function, although it may have extended out perpendicular from the wall separating the two courtyards.

Areas D and E

Area D is in the southwest corner of the north courtyard and Area E is in the northeast corner of the well yard. This places both beside the wall separating the two courtyards. These two units were dug in order to determine whether any rooms once existed along the wall. Both units were fairly small and were dug by hand.

Most of the deposits in Area D were very light colored (beige) caliche containing very few artifacts. This test was dug deep into the sterile black clay. The single unit in Area E was also dug down into sterile clay. The upper levels contained burned surfaces much like those in the north courtyard (Features 3, 4 and 5). One of these surfaces contained large amounts of white lime, as if from a lime kiln. It is quite possible that this thin zone of lime dates from late Spanish times. No artifacts were found in the lime and the underlying materials were primarily Spanish. Artifact content for both of the areas beside this wall was quite small.

The primary feature (Feature 11) which showed up in both areas was a trench dug in 1917 by the State to find the original wall foundations during one phase of the reconstruction of the Alamo. These trenches were dug on both sides of the foundation (Fig. 6).

Area F

Testing in this area was begun to determine the stratigraphy of the central area of the well yard. This was to be a simple trench running east from the well. It was believed that this courtyard was an area of considerable activity, as the well would have been of primary importance in early days. The initial trench was dug by hand, but with the necessity for rapid removal of overburden and back dirt, a backhoe was eventually used for these chores.

The upper two feet of deposit in Area F was a very compact, black clay soil with lenses of clay. These layers probably dated, at least partially, to the Hugo and Smeltzer period. Beneath this were light caliche deposits which were primarily Spanish. Excavations reached a depth of about four feet, and although this was probably near the base of the occupational deposits, chipped flint tools and a musket ball were recovered from the deepest test (beneath the adobe room to be described later).

Figure 5.   Features in Area C.

203

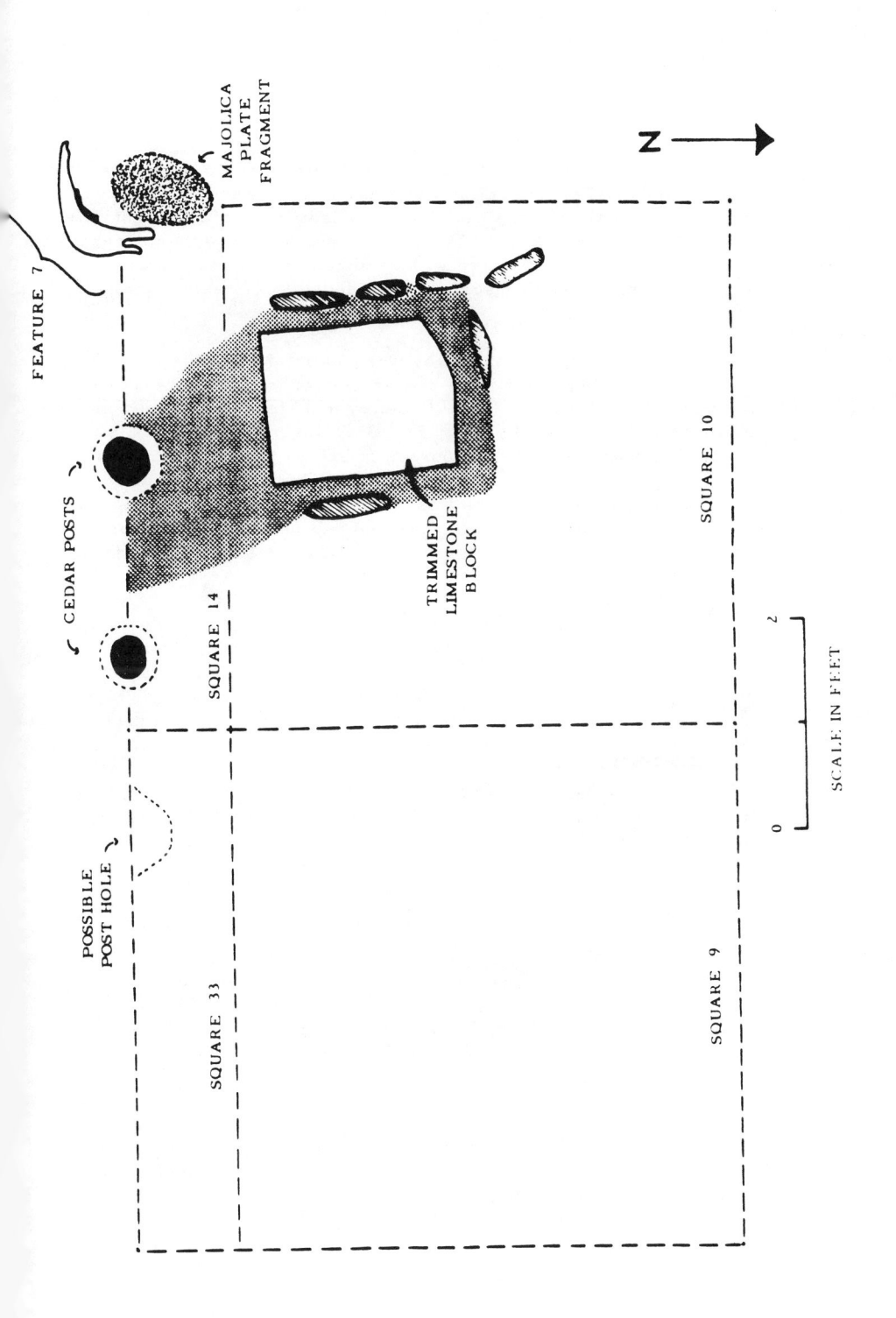

In the upper part of the caliche deposits was a packed occupational surface (Feature 12) on which lay at least one partially restorable creamware vessel. This would suggest that the surface might date to the middle 1800's. Slightly below this was another packed occupational surface (Feature 13) covered with sandstone slabs and containing a single posthole. On this surface were Indian and Mexican plainware sherds.

Below the sandstone slabs were walls of an adobe room (Feature 14). The walls were constructed of large caliche bricks (average about 1.80 feet by 0.76 feet by 0.37 feet) with a mud mortar of brown clay and caliche (Fig. 7). Only the bases of the walls were present, a maximum of two courses of bricks in thickness. The west wall and adjacent parts of the north and south walls were uncovered. The inside width of the room was about 13 feet, and the outside width (north-south) about 16.7 feet. The other dimension of the room could not be determined because it extended beneath a sidewalk. The floor was very thin and of puddled adobe.

It is interesting that this early Spanish structure was oriented about 45 degrees off north rather than north-south like the rest of the mission complex. From the thinness of the floor it appears that the structure was used very little. It is possible that this small room was built during the early Spanish period while the stone church was being built. Although work in this area stopped with the adobe room, a small hole dug through the floor yielded occupational material at least another nine inches into the dark clay. This underlying material is much like the sterile clay in the north courtyard and must be the deepest Spanish deposit in this part of the site.

Also found in the initial trench near the well was a cement-covered water pipe (Feature 15). This is probably relatively recent, most likely dating after 1900.

Area G

This is the area of the well yard near the church. This entire area also was dug by hand, but in some places the overburden (recent fill and part of the late Anglo deposits) was removed without screening. The excavated areas can be seen on the site map (Fig. 1).

In all excavation units the deepest deposits were of uncertain age. The upper zones were late Anglo and contained surfaces much like the ones in Areas A through E. Next to the small room in the

southeast corner of the yard and adjacent to the gate to the north, the deposits were probably Spanish, but the artifact sample was very small.

In Square 28, two burned occupational surfaces with cinders, window panes, etc., were uncovered. These surfaces were labeled Features 16 (upper) and 17 (lower). Both probably date between 1880 and 1900. A cement-covered sewer pipe (Feature 18) was found running almost east-west and possibly represents sewage facilities for the Hugo and Smeltzer store. Inside the pipe was a great deal of rust, broken glass, metal fragments, and cinders. Beside the pipe, in deposits cut through by the ditch holding the pipe, was a thin zone of artifacts, such as white-paste earthenware, rifle balls, and cannon ball parts. This might date to the destruction by the Mexican army in 1836. Below the pipe and on the south side was an articulated vertebra (Feature 19) of a large animal (probably a calf). Just below this was a small fragment of a wall of untrimmed limestone rocks set in a yellow sandy mortar. Inspection of the data showed that the ditch for this wall was dug from late Anglo times. Its purpose and extent are unknown.

In Square 11 was found a wooden water pipe (Feature 21) wrapped with heavy wire. The log was about ten inches in diameter with a central opening about four inches in diameter. This probably served as a water supply for the early store at this location in about 1870. At a later date an iron pipe was pushed through the wooden log, and recently the iron pipe was used as a casing for an electrical cable extending to the present water valve cover only a few feet to the west.

In Square 11, 12 and 13 was found an occupational surface (Feature 22) which was packed and burned. In Square 12, on this same surface, were four adobe bricks in place, as if for a floor. The light brown bricks had been laid on a coarse, gray, sandy mortar surface (Fig. 8) and then a light pink mortar was used between the bricks. After they had been laid, they were coated with a thick, dark red clay slip. All of the bricks of this type (Type IV) were handmade. This surface probably represents a paved walkway or patio area built during Spanish times.

In Square 16, also in this immediate area, very near the surface, was a row of four bricks (Feature 23) set on their sides and laid end to end. No mortar was used. These may have been placed here in recent years (since 1913) as a border around a flower garden.

Figure 6. Profile through wall between well yard and north courtyard. West wall of Square 6 (left) and west wall of Square 5 (right). Brown humus zone filling the trenches of 1913 on surface; sterile black clay at bottom, and miscellaneous caliche and ash lenses between the original foundation appears to rest directly upon the black clay.

N →

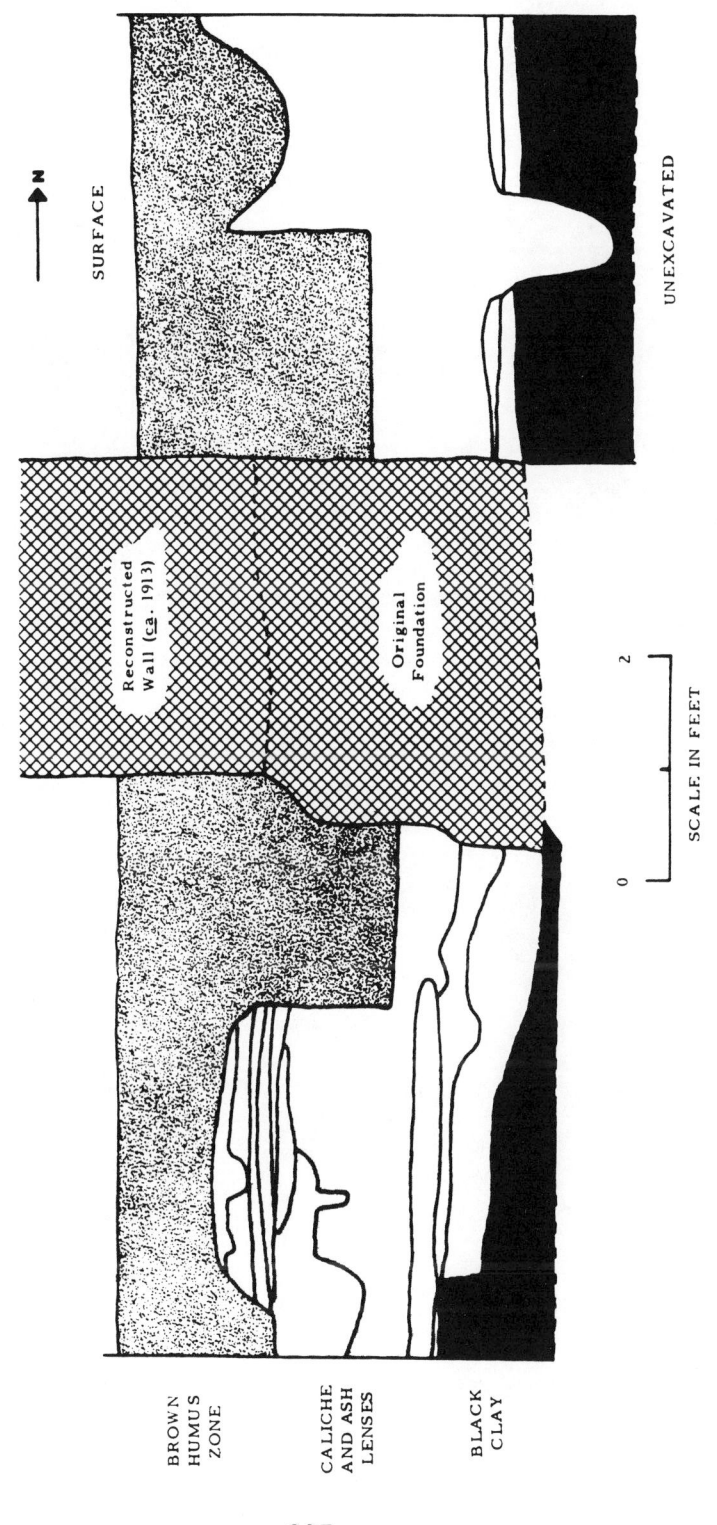

SURFACE

Reconstructed Wall (ca. 1913)

Original Foundation

UNEXCAVATED

SCALE IN FEET
0   2

BROWN HUMUS ZONE

CALICHE AND ASH LENSES

BLACK CLAY

Figure 7.   Feature 14 in Area F. Foundation made of adobe bricks in early Spanish Colonial deposits.

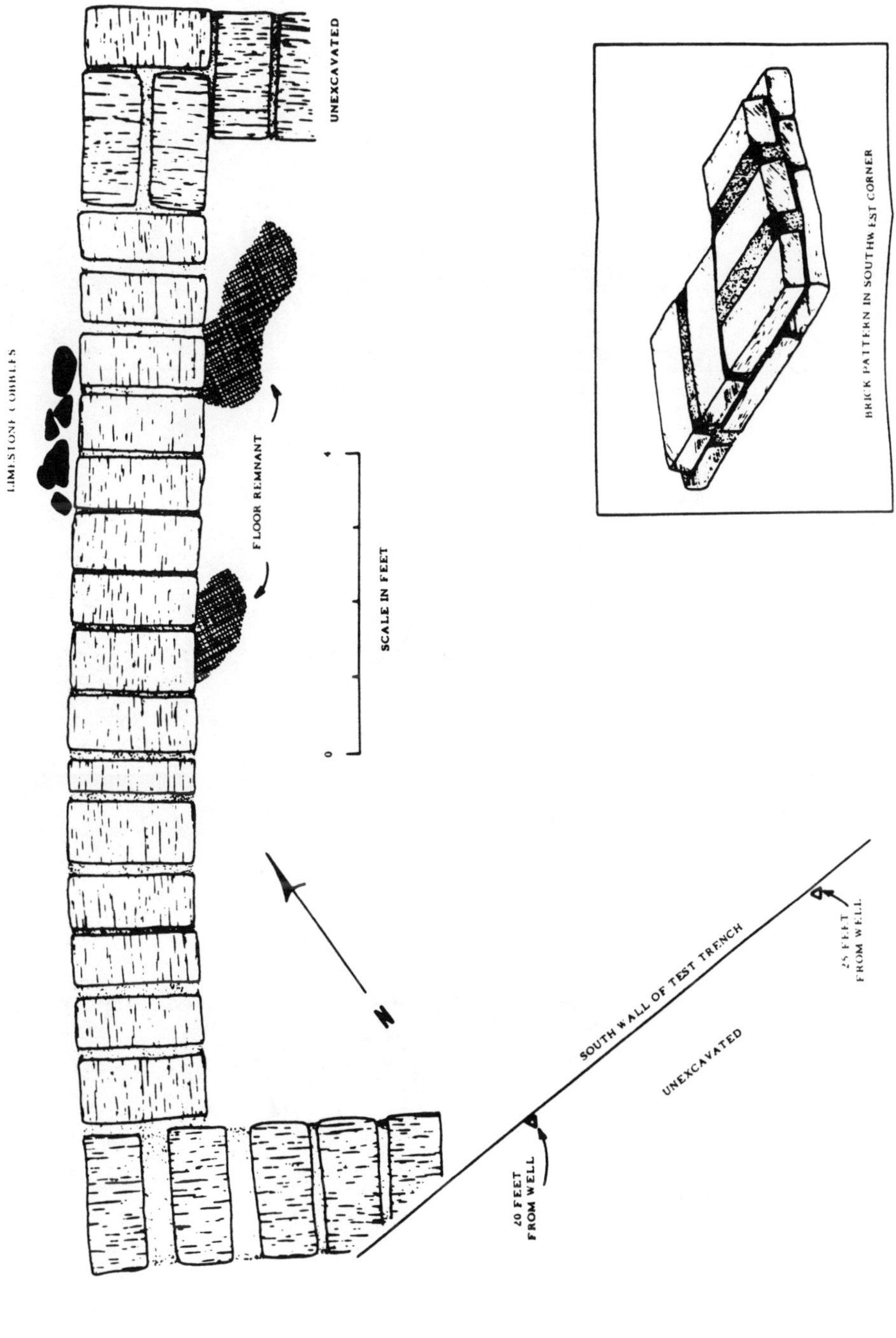
LIMESTONE COBBLES
UNEXCAVATED
FLOOR REMNANT
SCALE IN FEET
0
4
N
SOUTH WALL OF TEST TRENCH
UNEXCAVATED
20 FEET FROM WELL
25 FEET FROM WELL
BRICK PATTERN IN SOUTHWEST CORNER

Next to the church, in the squares on the west side of this area, another occupational surface was encountered. This also was hard-packed caliche and contained bottle fragments and other artifacts, dating to late Anglo times. In Square 22, on this same level, there were large amounts of wall debris consisting of limestone rocks set in a fine, white lime mortar, and white wall plaster, much of which contained portions of wall murals in red, yellow, and rarely, black. At this same level in Square 26, in the midst of the wall debris, the base of what was probably a wall buttress was uncovered. This is composed of very large limestone blocks fashioned into a square column about 3 feet wide. It is probable that the buttress and wall materials date to the Spanish occupation. The destruction of these rooms might be the result of the occupation of 1836.

Figure 8. Arrangement of adobe bricks on floor in Feature 22, Square 12 (Area G). Shaded bricks are those which were found in place.

0 1
SCALE IN FEET

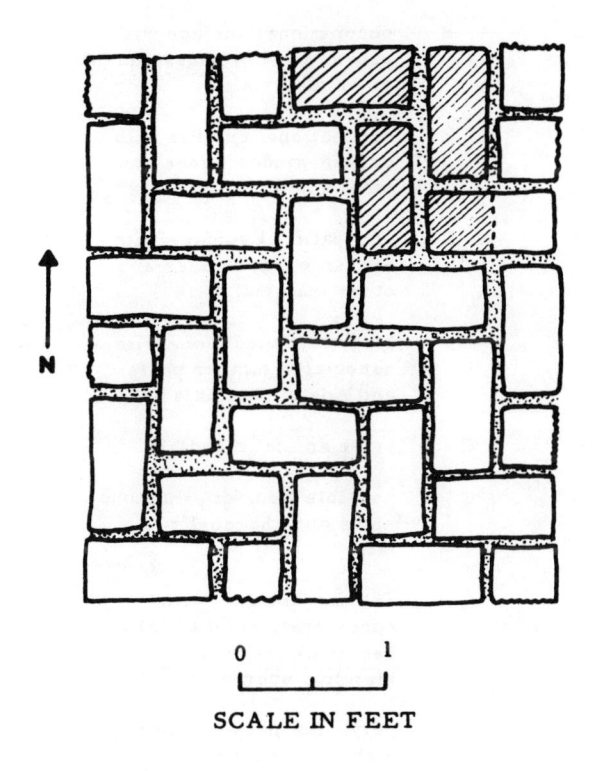

Table 1. Features Found in the Excavations

Feature Number	Courtyard	Area	Description	Approximate age	Square
1	North	A, B	possible E-W rubble wall with some trimmed stones	1836	3, 27, 17, 31
2	North	B	concentration of artifacts at inside base of Feature 1 (above) (Lot 257)	1836	17
3	North	A, B C	occupational surface with broken window panes and other material	1910	27, 17, 31, 2, 7, 8
4	North	A, B C	occupational surface with broken window panes and other material	1900	27, 17, 31, 2, 7, 8
5	North	A, B C	occupational surface with broken window panes and other material	1890	27, 17, 31, 2, 7, 8
6	North	C	large trimmed stone with associated juniper posts and Anglo materials	1900	10, 14, 33
7	North	C	large animal mandible	1810	14
8	North	C	possible floor of sandstone slabs and charcoal roof fall	1810	1, 32, 34
9	North	C	caliche "mound" with concentrations of bones, red brick fragments, Majolica sherds, etc.	1750	8
10	North	C	portion of possible stone slab wall in South profile of Square 8	1790	8

12

Table 1. Features Found in the Excavations.
(Continued)

Feature Number	Courtyard	Area	Description	Approximate age	Square
11	North & Well	D, E	1917 trench to find wall foundations during initial reconstruction.	1917	5, 6
12	Well	F	caliche occupational surface with creamware (Surface A)	1850?	18, 19 23
13	Well	F	occupational surface covered with sandstone slabs, 1 posthole, Indian and Mexican plain wares	1790	18, 19 23
14	Well	F	adobe room oriented northeast	1730	18, 19 23
15	Well	F	cement-covered water pipe	1930?	20
16	Well	G	occupational surface with window panes, etc.	1900	28
17	Well	G	occupational surface with window panes, etc.	1880	28
18	Well	G	cement-covered sewer pipe	1900?	28
19	Well	G	articulated large animal vertebrae	1800?	35
20	Well	G	possible wall fragment in a ditch	1890	28, 35
21	Well	G	wooden pipe wrapped with wire	1870	11
22	Well	G	surface with bricks in place in Square 12	1800-	11, 12 13

13

Table 1. Features Found in the Excavations.
(Concluded)

Feature Number	Courtyard	Area	Description	Approximate age	Square
23	Well	G	row of four vertical bricks	1920	16
24	Well	G	occupational surface and possible floor, wall breakdown with painted wall plaster, buttress base beside church	1880 (rooms, etc., from 1750)	21, 22, 24, 25, 26

THE HISTORY AND ARCHEOLOGY OF MISSION

SAN JUAN CAPISTRANO, SAN ANTONIO, TEXAS

VOLUME I (of two volumes)

Historical Documentation and Description of the Structures

By

Mardith K. Schuetz

STATE BUILDING COMMISSION

ARCHEOLOGICAL PROGRAM

Report Number 10   January, 1968

INTRODUCTION AND ACKNOWLEDGMENTS

The excavation of the Spanish Mission San Juan Capistrano in 1967 was prompted by the plans for the immediate restoration of some parts of the mission by the Archdiocese of San Antonio. Rooms in the northwest wall (Rooms 4 through 13 of Figure 1) were to be completely restored for two priests and a custodian. The church (Structure 17 of Figure 1) had developed a serious crack in the south wall and was to be reinforced. This necessitated placing tie-beams in the church and completely renovating the interior (which, incidentally, was last done in 1907). Present plans also call for refurbishing the parish hall (Structure 18 of Figure 1).

Our goals for the San Juan excavation were three-fold. The first was to recover a sample of artifacts that were unequivocally Coahuiltecan. Very little is known about the cultures of the numerous bands of Coahuiltecan speakers who roamed over south central Texas and northern Mexico. The missions of San Antonio, which were built for the benefit of these people, are the logical starting points from which archaeologists can work backward to reconstruct their origins. The second goal was to recover the remains of the Coahuiltecans themselves. They were extinct as far as racial identity goes in the early nineteenth century and there was not a Coahuiltecan skeletal series in the county. We set ourselves the goal of recovering 35 to

40 adult remains--or a large enough series that a physical anthropologist might describe the racial type and characteristics for a normal and healthy population. The third goal was to recover data on building techniques and the building sequence of the various parts of the mission ruins.

The first plan was to completely excavate some rooms and only test others in the northwest corner area just to recover building information. As time passed our goals became increasingly ambitious. The large volunteer labor force which turned out and the rewarding recovering of artifacts caused us to abandon mere testing in favor of the complete excavation of Rooms 4 through 13 before they were restored. The second goal, the recovery of Indian skeletons, was actually exceeded in five weeks spent in the complete excavation of about one-half of the old church and the baptistry (Room 26 of Figure 1). The work force provided by running a volunteer field school enabled us to excavate some rooms and to test others in the north and south walls as well. We were able not only to verify the number and locations of rooms recorded in Colonial documents, but also to locate several unexpected features and to establish a nearly complete building sequence for the entire mission complex.

The archaeological excavation of San Juan was undertaken jointly by the Catholic Archdiocese of San Antonio and the Texas State Building Commission through a contractual agreement with the Witte Memorial

Museum of San Antonio. His Reverence, Archbishop Robert E. Lucey, has been interested in the preservation of the local missions since he first arrived in San Antonio in 1941. Our heartfelt thanks are offered to his Reverence for granting us permission to excavate San Juan and salvage a wealth of information before restoration makes complete excavation impossible. Our thanks are also offered to The Reverend Charles Herzig, the Curator of Missions, for his support in our venture.

The Texas State Building Commission arranged the excavation as part of its archaeological research program. Curtis Tunnell, the State Archaeologist, has been a constant source of help and encouragement. He not only spent time at the site helping with mapping and burials, but arranged to have supplementary studies made by various specialists.

Sherry Humphries of Southern Methodist University has provided a preliminary analysis (Appendix C, Volume II) of the Coahuiltecan Indian burials, with a final report to be published later in this series. Mrs. Humphries' monumental task was supervised by Dr. Edward I. Fry, Professor of Physical Anthropology at Southern Methodist University.

Dr. Ernst Lundelius of the Department of Geology, The University of Texas, prepared the report on faunal remains (Appendix B, Volume II).

FIGURE 1

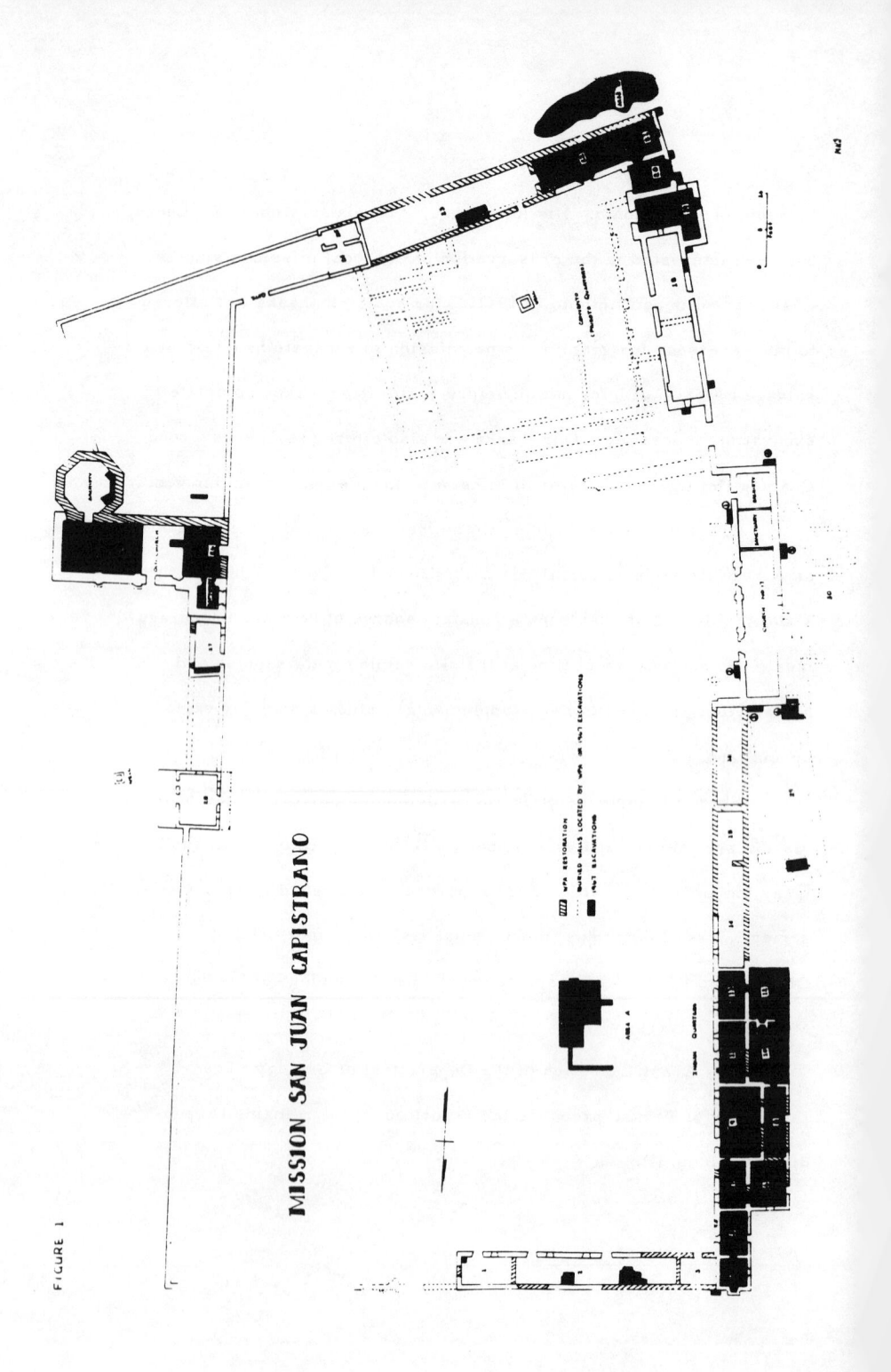

MISSION SAN JUAN CAPISTRANO

EXCAVATION PROCEDURES

For convenience in describing rooms and labeling artifacts, each room, or structure, of Mission San Juan was assigned a number, beginning with the first room west of what is now the driveway into the grounds in the north wall, and continuing counter-clockwise around the quadrangle to the stone and adobe house in the east wall given the number 28. Excavated areas bearing no relation to structures were given area designations (Fig. 1).

The rooms were first cleared of trees, brush, weeds, and garbage, and the surface exposed. All digging was done with hand tools and the dirt was removed by buckets to areas outside the mission walls where it was put through screens of either one-quarter or one-half inch mesh. A fine mesh screen was also used where concentrations of trade beads were suspected.

The fill was removed from the rooms in half-foot levels, using the room as the excavation unit. Not all rooms were excavated to the same depths. Some were dug deeper than others in order to expose the bases of walls, or to determine the depth of sterile soil upon which the wall foundations rested. A given level in one room cannot be absolutely equated with a particular level in another room. The highest point in each room was determined with a line level and a nail driven into a centrally situated stake at that level. All half-

foot levels were measured below this nail. Thus, in some cases, the first half-foot level was not continuous across the room because of sloping fill. The measuring stakes were left in place, supported by a pedestal of dirt, until excavation of the room and mapping was completed. This provided a convenient reference point in each structure, and all the vertical datum marks were related to a permanent site datum with a transit. The pedestals were later excavated by levels and the artifacts added to the room sample. The room descriptions below will note the variations in the top level and the maximum excavated depths.

Many rooms which were not fully excavated were tested for building information by small pits dug either inside or outside the walls. In these tests the dirt was not screened and artifacts retrieved in the digging or backfilling were cataloged only by room number.

For mapping purposes, a site datum point was first established on the windowsill of the southernmost window of Room 7 and given the arbitrary designation of 100.0 feet. Since restoration will be carried on over the next few years and survey marks will likely be plastered over, several 100 foot datum points were established. The first is located on the southeast, exterior corner of Room 1 on the second course of stone and at a height of 1.4 feet above the present surface. The second is on the northwest corner

of the baptistry of the old church at a height of 2.3 feet above the surface. The third control is the elevation of the top of the arch over the middle door into the present church which is 109.06 feet measured from the arbitrary datum.

All interior room measurements were recorded relative to the site datum. However, wall heights are recorded from the surface to the tops of the walls. The profile maps in this report are all drawn from the 100-foot arbitrary site datum.

There is not a single room at the mission that has not been disturbed by treasure hunters and one of the interesting facts we learned from the project is that treasure seekers expect Spanish gold to be found in the corners and the centers of rooms. All rooms, likewise, had evidence of burrowing animals and, indeed, during the first two weeks of work while the weather was still cold, we excavated several hibernating inhabitants of the ruins. Pot-hunting, burrowing, and root activity all account for some displacement of artifacts.

ARTIFACT PROCESSING PROCEDURE

All artifacts are labeled with the site number (41BX5) and the room and level number. Thus, an artifact with the provenience numbers 4-1 is from Room 4 and the 0.0 to 0.5 foot level, and an

artifact with the numbers 10-3 is from Room 10 at the 1.0 to 1.5 feet level. All measurements are expressed in feet and tenths of feet.

Many artifact categories are inventoried by weight rather than by count. Not only does this expedite the task of the inventory, but also is more meaningful in most cases. A glass bottle can be shattered into 200 pieces, all of which represent a single artifact. Another similar bottle may break into three pieces. A count of the two bottles would only becloud the inventory. Where weights are not given in a category, the weight is under one ounce.

Under each room heading below, the inventory of contents will be given in broad categories rather than specific ones, since these will be taken up in greater detail in Volume II. Thus, a category of "transfer printed" china might include several colors and patterns.

All artifacts are currently housed in the Witte Memorial Museum. However, a representative selection will be exhibited at San Juan Capistrano when a proposed museum is built within its walls.

In the room descriptions which follow, use is made of early nineteenth century documents from the Bexar County Archives. The inventory of these Mission Records, including some complete transcripts, are in Appendix A.

ROOM DESCRIPTIONS

ROOM 1

<u>Physical Description</u> (interior dimensions)

North Wall: 22.0 feet long, 3.0 feet high at west end to 7.2 feet high at east end, 2.1 feet thick.

East Wall: 11.2 feet long, 7.6 feet high, 2.0 feet thick.

South Wall: 22.0 feet long, 7.4 feet high, 2.0 feet thick.

West Wall: 11.2 feet long, 3.2 feet high, 2.0 feet thick.

Northeast-Southwest Diagonal: 24.9 feet.

Northwest-Southeast Diagonal: 24.9 feet.

The west wall was rebuilt by the WPA. Their plans do not show any ruin for the west wall which served as their guide, but the placement coincides with the dimensions provided in Mission Record 15 (Appendix A) and is essentially correct. Their plans show that no window existed in the east wall, therefore the beveled window there now was broken through at that time. The sill is 2.8 feet above the surface and the height from sill to lintel is 3.9 feet. The old plans indicate two walled-up, beveled openings in the south wall. The eastern one was opened as a door which is 4.4 feet wide on the inside and 6.3 feet high. The area 3.4 feet west of the door was opened as a window and is 3.2 feet wide and 2.5 feet high. The room was unexcavated except for a pit in the southeast corner

73

which showed that the east and south wall bases were 1.4 feet beneath the surface and rested on sterile brown clay.

Historic Documentation

The 1824 inventory of the mission describes Room 1 (number 4 of Figure 6) as a room eight varas in length with stone walls, a poor terrace roof and unusable door (Fig. 1). The owner of the room at the time was Manuel Granados. He petitioned for land and water on December 27, 1823 (Mission Record 5, Appendix A), and is listed as a property owner in Mission Record 15. Mission Record 27 (Appendix A), dated 1827, pinpoints his property as our room designation no. 1, even though they fail to list the room in the document. His ownership is clarified by describing him as the landowner east of Room 3 (Fig. 6 or Room 2 of Fig. 1). Granados is identified in Mission Record 5 (Appendix A) as a retired alférez (second lieutenant) of the Presidial Company of Bexar. The Saucedo plat, which supposedly shows ownership in 1823, is clearly in error in listing "Trevino" as the owner, since archival records contradict it (Fig. 5 A). Treviño was probably a later owner as were others listed in the Saucedo plat. The north wall rooms were apparently maintained through the nineteenth century. The Lungkwitz painting (Plate 1) shows the rooms to be roofed in the mid-1900's and the Corner plat (Fig. 5,B) indicates that the walls were still in good condition in 1890. None of our local informants reported habitation in north wall rooms within this century.

ROOMS 2 and 3

Physical Description (interior dimensions)

    North Wall: 87 feet long, 2.4 feet high, and 1.8 feet thick.

    East Wall: 11.2 feet long, 3.2 feet high, 2.0 feet thick.

    South Wall: 87 feet long, 5.4 feet high at east end to maximum of 7.0 feet high in the center, to 2.0 feet high at west end, 2.1 feet thick.

    West Wall: 12 feet long, 9.0 feet high, 1.6 feet thick.

What is today reconstructed as a single room (Room 2 of Figure 1) was two separate rooms and half of a third in the Colonial period (see Figure 6). Two test pits were dug against the north wall (Fig. 1) to find the original cross-walls. Room 3 of the Colonial period (Fig. 6), adjacent to Room 1 of Figure 1 (or Room 4 of Figure 6), was eight varas long, with stone walls, "cabezeras de adobe," and white-washed terrace. No definite trace of the west wall was encountered in the 5.0 foot by 2.5 foot pit excavated. The pit did, however, yield some data. The bottom of the north wall was found to rest on sterile brown clay at a depth of 2.2 feet below the present ground level. The first 1.2 feet of fill below the surface was a mixture of caliche and loam with artifacts. Below this zone was approximately one foot of caliche, bits of charcoal and rocks. A large firepit was encountered in the southwest corner of the pit at a depth of 2.2 feet beneath the surface. The firepit was not completely exposed but an area three feet west to east and two feet from north to

south was cleared. The test pit was dug to a depth of three feet beneath the surface but the bottom of the firepit was not reached.

The twenty-two foot area which corresponds to Room 3 of Figure 6 has a beveled door in the south wall which is 4.4 feet wide on the inside and is 6.2 feet from the east wall. A beveled window which is 4.3 feet wide on the inside is located 4.0 feet west of the doorway. The south wall is not reconstructed in the original height, so that window and door heights are not known. The middle 23.5 feet section of Room 2 was also shown as Room 2 on Figure 6. It was described as being eight varas in length with stone walls, "cabezeras de adobe," grass roof, and with a poor terrace and door. The westernmost test pit in Room 2 uncovered the original west wall of the room. This buried foundation is also the original east wall of Room 3 of Figure 1. This latter room was thirty-six feet in length in the Colonial period, instead of fifteen feet as reconstructed by WPA. The test pit which uncovered the old wall was excavated to a depth of 3.6 feet below the surface. The top two feet of fill was a mixture of caliche, loam, and rock underlain by a thin strata of caliche and loam, caliche with charcoal and ash, firm caliche, and an ash lens--all accounting for an additional foot of fill. At the three foot level, a firepit was encountered with dimensions of 4.8 feet on the east-west axis and 3.4 feet on the north-south axis. The depth of the north wall foundation and the soil upon which it lay were not recorded. The average width of the buried wall is

1.0 feet. A beveled window is located in the south wall, approximately 5.0 feet from where the east wall should lay. The window is 3.7 feet wide on the interior. A beveled door in the south wall is located 3.6 feet from the southwest corner of the room and 5.0 feet from the window. Height measurements of the door and window are again lacking since the wall is not complete.

The western twenty-two feet of Room 2 was originally the eastern half of Room 3 of Figure 1 (or Room 1 of Figure 6). The room was described in Mission Record 15 (Appendix A) as a house with ruined walls of thirteen varas in length. The WPA erected a wall at fifteen feet from Room 4 on the base of a buried wall. This wall must have been a later partitioning of the room. Our description of Room 4 notes the fact that the north wall of Room 3 rests on the present ground surface where it abuts the east wall of Room 4 and that the room was obviously built later than Room 4. The south wall has a square (unbeveled) door located 6.0 feet from each corner.

Historic Documentation

As was noted above, what are now Rooms 2 and 3 (Fig. 1) were Rooms 1, 2, and 3, according to the 1824 descriptions in Mission Record 15 (Fig. 6). Room 1 of Mission Record 15 was a house with ruined walls measuring 13 varas (about 36 feet) in length located east of what we have designated as Room 4. The owner of the property at

the time of secularization in 1793 was probably Francisco Cadena. Cadena petitioned for land on December 27, 1823 (Mission Record 13, Appendix A), by right of being a resident Indian. "Francisco" is also the name of the owner of this piece of property on the 1823 Saucedo plat (Fig. 5 A). Furthermore, Francisco Cadena is listed as a property owner in Mission Record 15. Mission Record 15, which is dated February 10, 1824, indicates that the house was sold to Gerardo Hernandez on that date. A plat showing the division of mission fields in 1847 (Fig. 7) shows Francisco Cadena as the owner of one and one-half suertes of land south of the mission.* This was probably the land granted to the Indian Cadena as a result of his December, 1823, petition (Mission Record 13, Appendix A). The act of possession was dated February 7, 1824, just three days prior to the sale of Room 1 to Hernandez (Mission Record 15). Cadena had apparently been the long-time resident of the room and probably moved to his land grant as soon as it was acquired, thus accounting for the sale of Room 1 in 1824.

Room 2 of Mission Record 15 was described as a room of 8 varas (22 feet) in length with stone walls, "cabezeras de adobe," grass roof, and with a terrace and door in poor condition. The term "cabezeras de adobe" defies identification--relating to architecture

---

*The suerte is not a fixed unit of measurement, but the suerte allotted each Indian family in 1794 measured 400 by 100 varas.

it can refer to the beginning or principal part, upper end, or the ends of a dwelling. None of these definitions are satisfactory since the room descriptions refer to stone walls. None of these north wall rooms are complete and certainly nothing made of adobes is now to be seen (although the "caliche" in the fill may represent melted adobes. Ed.) My own guess is that "cabezeras" was a local term for gable. The gables in Room 18 are of adobe brick and certainly some feature at head level is indicated by the word itself.

The owner of Room 2 in 1824 was Teresa Ximenes. She is listed as a landowner in Mission Record 15, and her property is pinpointed in Mission Record 27 (Appendix A), dated 1827, as being between Room 1, owned by Hernandez, and Room 3, owned by Luisa Ximenes (Fig. 6). Her ownership is further confirmed by the Saucedo plat of 1823 (Fig. 5, A).

Room 3 of Mission Record 15 was described as 8 varas long (22 feet) with stone walls, a white-washed terrace, "una cabezera de adobe" and a cheap door. The owner of the room was Maria Luisa Ximenes, who was identified as a widow resident for thirty-six years. She was the widow of Matias Ximenes of Mission Record 4 (Appendix A). Her stated residency dated back to 1787, six years prior to secularization. She petitioned for water rights on October 31, 1823 (Mission Record 7, Appendix A), and for land in the fields on November 15, 1823 (Mission Record 11, Appendix A).

Mission Record 15 lists her as a landowner and Mission Record 27 of 1827 identifies her room between Teresa Ximenes on the west and Manuel Granados on the east. The Saucedo plat (Fig. 5 A) shows ownership under the name of "Gil," but this is clearly an error for the year 1823.

The Lungkwitz painting (Plate 1) would seem to show Rooms 1 and 2 as being roofed and sound in the mid-nineteenth century. There is a separation between these rooms on the north wall, and the first roofed structure on the west wall which I interpret as Rooms 4, 5, and 7; therefore, it seems probable that Room 3 (Room 1 of Figure 6) was in ruins once again. The Corner plat of 1890 (Fig. 5 B) appears to confirm this interpretation and further shows that the wall separating Rooms 2 and 3 of the Colonial period had been removed sometime between 1827 and 1890.

Artifact Inventories: Rooms 1 and 2

Artifacts from Rooms 1 and 2 are from the test pits against the north wall of Room 2 and the southeast corner of Room 1. They were not unearthed by levels.

Potsherds:
5 transfer printed
2 stamped and painted edge
15 handpainted
8 Mocha
. . . .
23 Mexican lead glazed
4 Majolica

2 Flown Blue
23 crockery
47 unidentified white
4 green glazed

45 Indian

Glass:	7.5 oz. green glass	2 oz. amber glass
	12.0 oz. uncolored glass	8 oz. amythyst glass
Rusted Metal:	8 oz. unidentifiable metal	spur
	4 nails	bucket handle
	spike	harness ring
	two-tined fork	cinch band ring
Miscellaneous:	2 lbs 4 oz. animal bone	copper kettle handle
	1 lb. flint	glass marble
	shell: mussel and marine	slate fragment
	ocher	porcelain door knob
	lava-stone pestle	charred corn cob

ROOM 4

<u>Physical Description</u> (interior dimensions)

North Wall: 12.15 feet long, 9.0 feet high at corners, 14.7 feet high at apex of gable, 1.5 feet thick.

East Wall: 11.9 feet long, 9.0 feet high, 1.6 feet thick.

South Wall: 11.9 feet long, 9.0 feet high at southeast corner, 5.0 feet high at southwest corner, 1.57 feet thick.

West Wall: 11.8 feet long, 5.0 feet high at southwest corner, 9.0 feet high at northwest corner, 1.65 feet thick.

Northeast-Southwest Diagonal: 16.7 feet.

Northwest-Southeast Diagonal: 17.1 feet.

The north wall is built against the west wall. The east wall is built against the north wall, and the south wall is built between the east and west walls. The west wall and the north wall are built upon

footings which are 2.2 feet thick and these walls are carefully constructed at the bases. The bottom of the west wall lies 3.4 feet beneath the surface. The base of the north wall slopes from 1.6 feet beneath the surface at the east corner to 3.4 feet beneath the surface at the west corner. The foundation of the east wall is poorly constructed and this, together with the fact that some of the wall stone is oriented vertically, or on end, rather than horizontally, is evidence of post-Colonial wall repair. The base of the east wall is just 1.6 feet beneath the surface and that of the south wall is 2.0 feet beneath the surface. The west wall is built with a typical colonial sandy-lime mortar while the other three walls are laid with a muddy sort of mortar. The west wall also differs from the others in that it rests on a thin bed of tan sand which, in turn, lies atop the sterile brown clay. The other three walls rest on brown clay, although some slight mixture of caliche pebbles and bone occurs in the brown clay under the north and south walls. Several large rocks were unearthed in the northwest corner of the room between 1.5 feet and 2.0 feet beneath the surface. A possible explanation is that they were left over from the earliest building phase of the room and covered over with fill in the foundation trench rather than carted out (see Figure 9 for profiles).

  The north wall of Room 4 is the only one of these rooms in the northwest walls of the mission which retains its gable. The

ROOM 4: FIREPLACE

PLATE 3

ROOM 4: NORTH WALL

north wall has a lovely fireplace built flush against the interior wall with the back jutting out from the exterior wall. The fireplace is the usual colonial construction with a keystone in its lintel (Plate 3). The floor of the hearth is 2.4 feet above the surface of the room fill. The fireplace opening is 2.4 feet high and 3.2 feet wide. The thickness of the fireplace and chimney wall is 3.5 feet. A beveled window is located in the west wall and a straight-edged (non-beveled) door is in the south wall leading into Room 5. The walls still retain much of their plaster both inside and out. The northern exterior corners of Room 4 are finished in the colonial pattern of dressed stone blocks carefully laid one upon the other (Plate 11, D). It is obvious that the room which abuts it to the east was added later. A test pit measuring 4 feet long and 2 feet wide was dug at the exterior northeast corner to a depth of 1 foot. The foundation of Room 4 continued deeper than the trench while the wall of Room 3 was resting on the surface.

Historic Documentation

In 1824, Room 4 was described as a room measuring 7 varas long and 4 varas wide, with stone walls, but roofless. It appears under the inventory number of 27 (see Figure 6). There is no record of when the roof was replaced and the room reoccupied. The Lungkwitz painting of the mission dated in the mid-nineteenth

century shows a roof over what are probably Rooms 4, 5, and 7, and a roof over what I believe to be Rooms 11 and 13 (Plate 1). Chances are that the roof was repaired early in the century. The room, along with Room 5, must have been owned in 1823 by Maria Luisa de Luna, the widow of Vicente Travieso. The Saucedo plat of 1823 shows Travieso as owning the northwest corner of the wall (Fig. 5.A). These two rooms must have been kept in satisfactory repair since that period. The Corner plat indicates the soundness of the rooms in the northwest section of the mission walls in 1890 (Fig. 5 B), and the rooms were occupied until 1927. The late Louis Kunze, owner of the saloon at Berg's Mill from 1886 until 1928, was born in Room 4. His widow, Annie Kunze, is still a Berg's Mill resident. In fact, Annie Kunze's father, Mr. Graf, once owned and rented the rooms in the northwest corner.

Stratigraphy, Features and Artifacts

The surface of Room 4 was nearly level, so that Level 1 was continuous throughout the room. Nineteenth century artifacts were concentrated near the surface and thinned out toward the one-foot level where they were replaced by a concentration of bone and colonial artifacts. Loose bits of caliche were found between 1.0 and 1.5 feet, but in such a disturbed condition that it was not possible to determine whether it might have represented an early

floor. An Indian firepit filled with charred corn cobs was unearthed in this same level (see Figure 19). The top of the firepit was not distinguishable, but the rounded bottom of it was 0.3 foot lower than the 1.5 feet level. The diameter of this section of the pit was 0.8 foot. A few bits of burned rock were found near the pit, but in no pattern. A concentration of Mexican lead-glazed earthenware sherds came from around the pit. Cultural material beneath the 1.5 feet level was scant. The 2.0 feet to 3.5 feet level (Level 5) is represented only by the trench sunk against the west wall in order to expose the deeply buried footing.

Artifact Inventories: Room 4

Level 1

Potsherds:
  12 transfer printed   12 Mocha
   9 stamped and painted edge   5 Flown Blue
  42 unidentified white   6 crockery
  43 handpainted   1 yellow-green glazed
   2 gold-banded green
  ....
  27 Mexican lead glazed   5 Indian
   6 West Mexico polychrome
   4 Majolica

Glass:
  2 oz. aqua glass, patinated
  8 oz. uncolored glass, patinated
  6 oz. amber glass, patinated and clear
  5 oz. green glass
  1 oz. cobalt blue, patinated

Rusted Metal:
  1 lb. 13 oz. nails
  10 oz. unidentifiable
  wire
  unthreaded bottle cap

Miscellaneous:	12 oz. animal bone 4 oz. wood 1 oz. brick shell: mussel and marine flint	brass band from lead pencil copper buckle piece slate pencil 4 china buttons 1 pearl button

Level 2

Potsherds:	32 transfer printed 76 handpainted 7 stamped and painted edge 54 unidentified white	32 Mocha 1 Flown Blue 1 gold-banded green

....

	180 Mexican lead glazed 24 West Mexico polychrome 2 Mexican burnished black 19 Majolica 1 French Faience	53 Indian
Glass:	4 oz. amber, patinated 5 oz. green 4 oz. uncolored, patinated	5 oz. aqua, patinated cobalt blue
Rusted Metal:	1 lb. 7 oz. nails 5 pieces heavy metal medicine tube and cap	portion of scissors 2 bottle caps 2 pieces wire
Miscellaneous:	4 lbs. 5 oz. animal bone 5 oz. flint 2 lbs. 13 oz. plaster 6 oz. brick shell: mussel and marine 1 oz. charred corn cob piece copper	stoneware pipe 22 cal. rifle shell 2 copper buttons 1 bone button 2 china buttons Lincoln Head penny, 1919

Level 3

Potsherds:	4 transfer printed 7 unidentified white	4 Mocha 6 handpainted

....

	76 Mexican lead glazed 4 West Mexico polychrome 1 Mexican burnished black 3 Majolica	23 Indian

FIGURE 9: ROOM 4

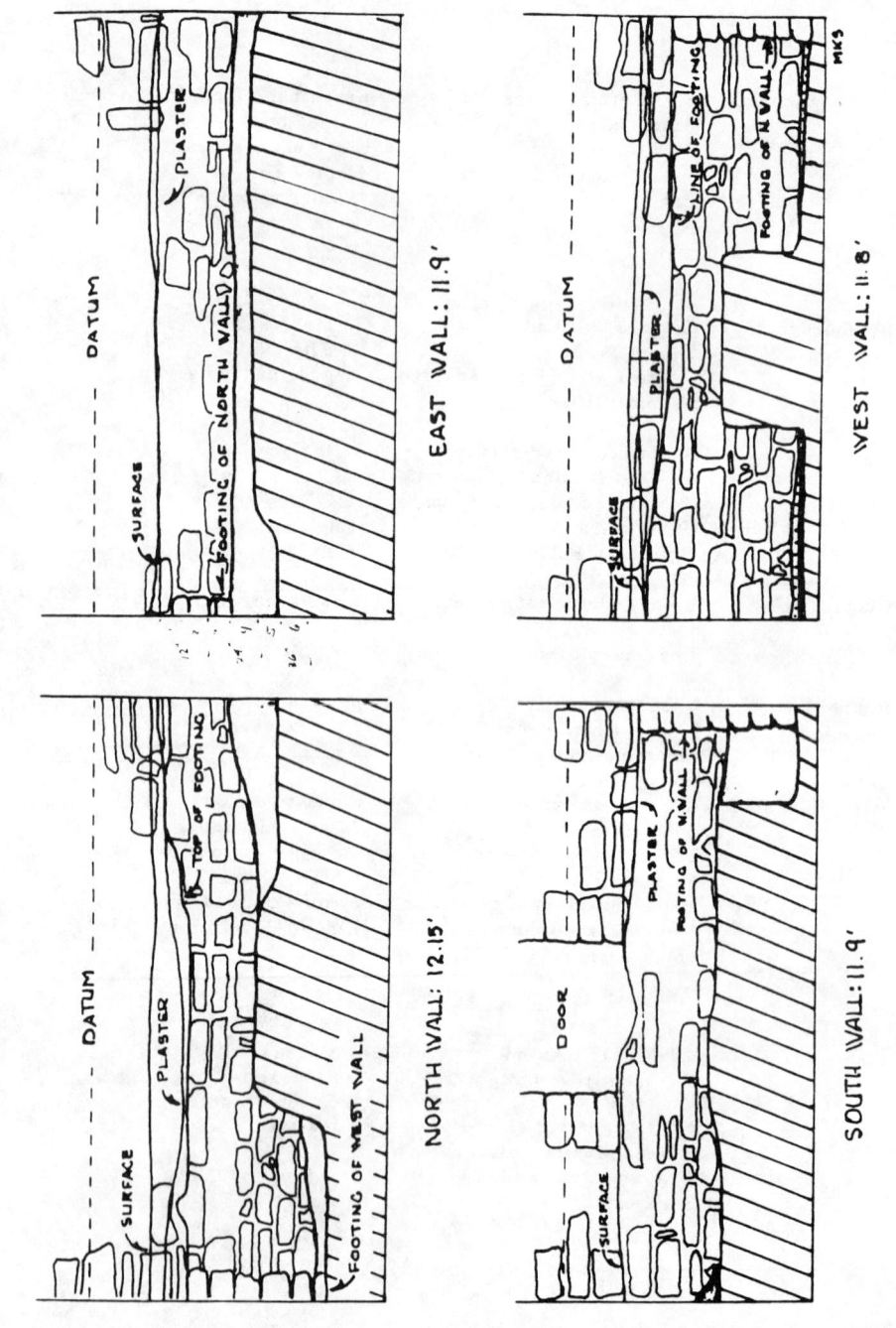

Glass:	amber glass, patinated green glass	uncolored glass, patinated window glass
Rusted Metal:	2 oz roofing tin 6 oz. nails 1 unidentified heavy metal 3 bottle caps	enamel pan (diameter approximately 9 1/2 inches, height approxi- mately 1 1/2 inches)
Miscellaneous:	2 lbs. 6 oz. animal bone 1 lb. 6 oz. corn cobs 7 oz. flint mussel shell quartzite scraper	faceted blue glass bead brass tack 1 china button 2 copper buttons

Level 4

Potsherds:	4 handpainted .... 11 Mexican lead glazed 1 Majolica	10 Indian
Glass:	1 oz. green glass uncolored glass, patinated amber glass	
Rusted Metal:	2 lbs 2 oz. roofing tin 6 oz. nails	
Miscellaneous:	5 lbs. 14 oz. animal bone 2 oz. plaster 4 oz. flint charcoal and wood mussel shell	piece cut bone carved brass sword hilt copper patch with rivet 1 bone button 1 china button

Level 5

Potsherds:	1 transfer printed 2 handpainted .... 3 Mexican lead glazed 2 Majolica	2 unidentified white 1 Indian
Glass:	amber glass green glass uncolored glass, patinated	

243

Rusted Metal: 5 oz. nails

Miscellaneous: 1 lb. animal bone   plaster
                  wood   flint
                  charcoal   fragment of cloth

ROOM 5

<u>Physical Description</u> (interior dimensions)

North Wall: 11.95 feet long, 9.0 feet high at northeast corner, 5.0 feet high at northwest corner, 1.57 feet thick.

East Wall: 18.4 feet long, 9.0 feet high, 2.3 feet thick.

South Wall: 11.65 feet long, 1.8 feet high, 1.6 feet thick.

West Wall: 18.45 feet long, 3.4 feet high on north side of door, 6.2 feet high on south side of door, to maximum of 9.0 feet near southwest corner, 1.6 feet thick.

Northwest-Southeast Diagonal: 21.95 feet.

Northeast-Southwest Diagonal: 21.9 feet.

The north and south walls are laid between (abutting) the east and west walls. The bases of the walls were not exposed. The west wall rests upon a footing that is 2.2 feet thick like the west wall foundation of Room 4. The door in the north wall, which leads to Room 4, and the door in the west wall are unbeveled, but the east door is beveled. Much of the plaster is retained on both interior and exterior walls (see Figure 10).

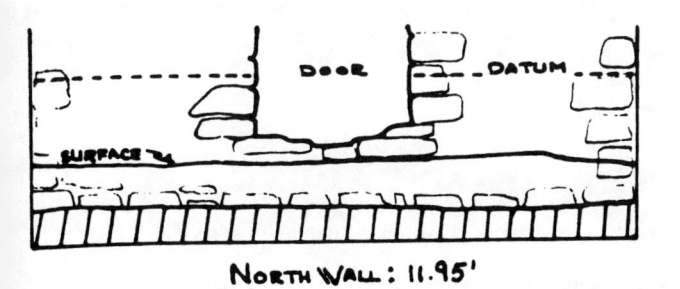

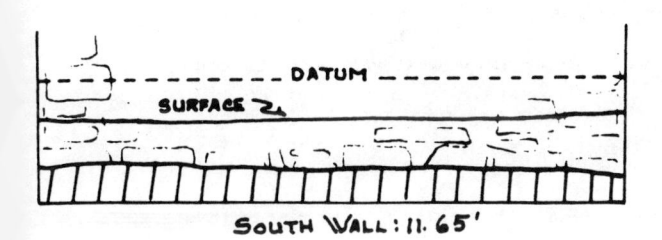

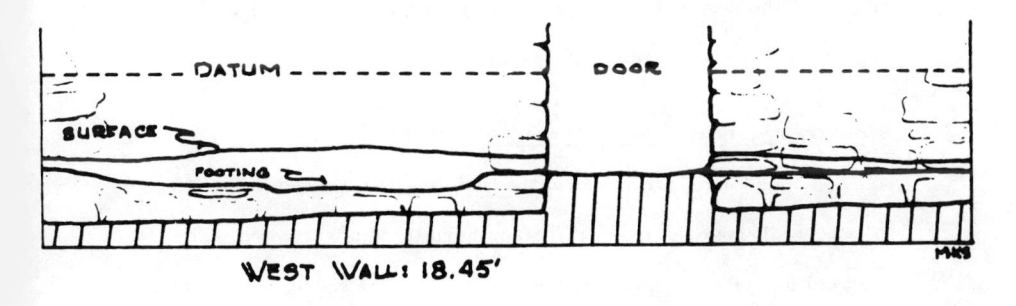

FIGURE 10: ROOM 5

Historic Documentation

According to the 1824 evaluation of mission property (Mission Record 15, Appendix A), Room 5 was described as being 8 varas long and 4 varas wide with stone walls and a grass roof. It appears as Room 26 in Figure 6. The apparent owner was Maria Luisa de Luna. She is listed as one of the individuals owning land and water at the mission in the same document, although exactly what each person on the list owned is not provided. Señora Luna was identified as the widow of Vicente Travieso when she petitioned for land in 1823 (Mission Record 9, Appendix A), and the Travieso property is identified as the northwest corner of the west wall in the Saucedo plat of 1823 (Fig. 5.A). The room was apparently kept in decent repair well into the nineteenth century. The Lungkwitz painting of the mid-nineteenth century (Plate 1), and the Corner plat of 1890 (Fig. 5.B) both indicate its soundness during the latter half of the century and the room was still occupied in 1927.

Stratigraphy, Features and Artifacts

A flagstone floor was encountered near the 0.5 foot level (Plate 4). It covered most of the northern third of the room with isolated pieces still *in situ* at the same level elsewhere in the room. The sandstone slabs were simply set into the fill of the room without benefit of a sand bed or use of mortar. A portion of flagstone

paving outside the rooms on the northwest section of wall was indicated on the old WPA maps. Upon excavating immediately outside the door to Room 5, it was found that the paving was at this same level below the surface. The actual elevation of the floor by instrument reading is 1.92 feet below datum.

Artifacts from the room were concentrated in the top foot of fill. In the 1.0 foot to 1.5 feet level a cedar post was uncovered. It lay on a north-south axis parallel to the west wall and in line with the west side of the door on the north wall (Fig. 19). It ran nearly the length of the room, although parts were missing because of pot holes dug through it. Apparently it was a roof beam which had fallen from the walls, although it does not appear to have been very thick (about 0.3 foot is the present diameter). The only puzzling factor is the direction in which it lay. By today's building pattern, the rafter usually spans the width, rather than the length of the room.

Artifact Inventory: Room 5

Level 1

Level 1 was continuous across the room since the surface was quite level.

Potsherds:	16 transfer printed	18 Mocha
	73 handpainted	1 Flown Blue
	4 stamped and painted edge	2 luster
	60 unidentified white	6 crockery
	3 blue Jasperware	1 gray stoneware

. . . .

	3 Mexican lead glazed 7 West Mexico polychrome 1 Mexican burnished red 3 Majolica	1 Indian
Glass:	1 lb. 12 oz. amber glass 1 lb. uncolored, patinated 12 oz. green glass	2 oz. aqua, patinated 8 oz. flint glass 4 oz. milk glass
Rusted Metal:	2 lb. 4 oz. nails 14 oz. roofing tin 10 pieces auto head gasket 32 pieces wire 4 unidentifiable pieces	side of toy gun washer piece spiraled metal 4 bottle caps rim of can part of pen knife

Miscellaneous:	1 lb. 5 oz. animal bone
	mussel shell
	flint
	22 cal. shell
	44 cal. shell
	1 glass marble
	2 clay marbles
	painted boot of porcelain
	  doll
	copper piece labeled
	  "Firth's Steel"
		2 unidentified modern
		  copper pieces
		metallic cap from wine
		  bottle
		metal tab-opener
		rubber shoe heel
		green plastic tube
		piece of cellulose
		1 copper button
		13 china buttons
		2 shell buttons
		1 ivory button
		American dime, 1843
		  or 1849

Level 2

Potsherds:	55 transfer printed 45 Mocha 60 handpainted 19 stamped and painted edge	100 unidentified white 2 luster 10 crockery 3 Ginger Beer

. . . .

10 Mexican lead glazed 20 West Mexico polychrome 3 Majolica	8 Indian

Glass:	1 lb. 2 oz. amber glass 1 lb. 4 oz. green glass 1 lb. 14 oz. uncolored glass	1 oz. window glass, patinated 6 oz. aqua glass painted milk glass
Rusted Metal:	1 lb. 4 oz. roofing tin 7 lb. 11 oz. nails 1 lb. 6 oz. unidentifiable 10 oz. wire	13 bottle caps 1 staple 1 can key 1 chain link 1 washer
Miscellaneous:	7 lb. 12 oz. animal bone charcoal mussel shell 8 oz. plaster 4 oz. brick gun flint 2 pieces copper brass clasp from chest pieces leather shoe heel piece of slate toy parrot on stand (metal, enameled) 16 guage shotgun shell 44 cal. shell 32 cal. shell	7 oz. flint 12 china buttons 4 bone buttons 5 pearl buttons 1 steel button 1 composition button 1 compound button 1890 Indian Head penny 1887 Liberty Head nickel 1867 Shield nickel

Level 3

Potsherds:	19 transfer printed 29 Mocha 77 handpainted 18 stamped and painted edge 104 unidentified white 2 unidentified, fire damaged	3 luster 2 handpainted porcelain 1 stamped black Jasperware (?) 1 crockery 4 yellow glazed 1 Japanese porcelain saki cup
	19 Mexican lead glazed 8 West Mexico polychrome 5 Majolica	14 Indian
Glass:	6 oz. uncolored glass, patinated 6 oz. green	2 oz. amber, patinated 1 oz. aqua, patinated

Rusted Metal:	10 oz. nails 1 lb. 4 oz. unidentifiable 1 jar cap 2 pieces heavy wire (one set through ring and bent for door latch)	piece light wire ring 3 bottle caps
Miscellaneous:	4 lb. 8 oz. animal bone 2 lb. 3 oz. brick 12 oz. plaster 6 oz. flint 2 oz. charcoal 4 oz. wood mussel shell bone tool flat piece lead 3 pieces copper brass curtain ring brass safety pin	slate pencil piece leather shoe heel 3 china buttons 1 pearl button 2 bone buttons 1 brass button 1 composition button

ROOM 6

<u>Physical Description</u> (interior dimensions)

North Wall: 15.4 feet long, 6.7 feet high east of window, 7.2 feet high west of window, 1.6 feet thick.

East Wall: 19.7 feet long, 3.2 feet high north of door to 9.0 feet high at northeast corner, 2.9 feet high south of door to maximum of 9.0 feet high in center and 4.3 feet high at southeast corner, 2.2 feet thick.

South Wall: 16.1 feet long, 4.0 feet high on east half, 1.9 feet high on west half, 1.7 feet thick on east half, 2.1 feet thick on west half.

West Wall: 19.8 feet long, 4.3 feet high north side of door, 1.6 feet high south side of door, 1.5 feet thick.

Southwest-Southeast Diagonal: 25.25 feet.

Northeast-Southwest Diagonal: 25.1 feet.

The bottom of the north wall is one foot beneath the surface. The northern section of the west wall and the entire north wall rest upon brown, sandy clay mixed with food bones and Spanish Colonial artifacts. The central portion of the west wall is underlain by the same deposit; however, it is mixed with the ill-laid foundation reconstructed by the WPA. It is also of interest to note that the mixed soil lies atop a plastered surface. The northern, unreconstructed segment of the west wall extends only 0.6 foot to 0.8 foot beneath the surface. The base of the reconstructed central portion of the west wall is 1.6 feet beneath the surface. The southern quarter of the east wall and the eastern quarter of the south wall rest upon a 0.4 foot thick bed of red-tan sand at a depth of about a foot beneath the surface. The remaining portion of the east wall rests on sterile brown clay, except for the three-foot segment south of the door where WPA reconstruction occurred. The bottom of the foundation of the east wall is almost a foot higher than the Room 7 side of the same wall. The sterile clay zone is traced under the sand bed and wall of the eastern half of the south wall. The western half of the south wall was not exposed because of extensive WPA reconstruction. A bed of plaster was put down by the WPA in

FIGURE 11

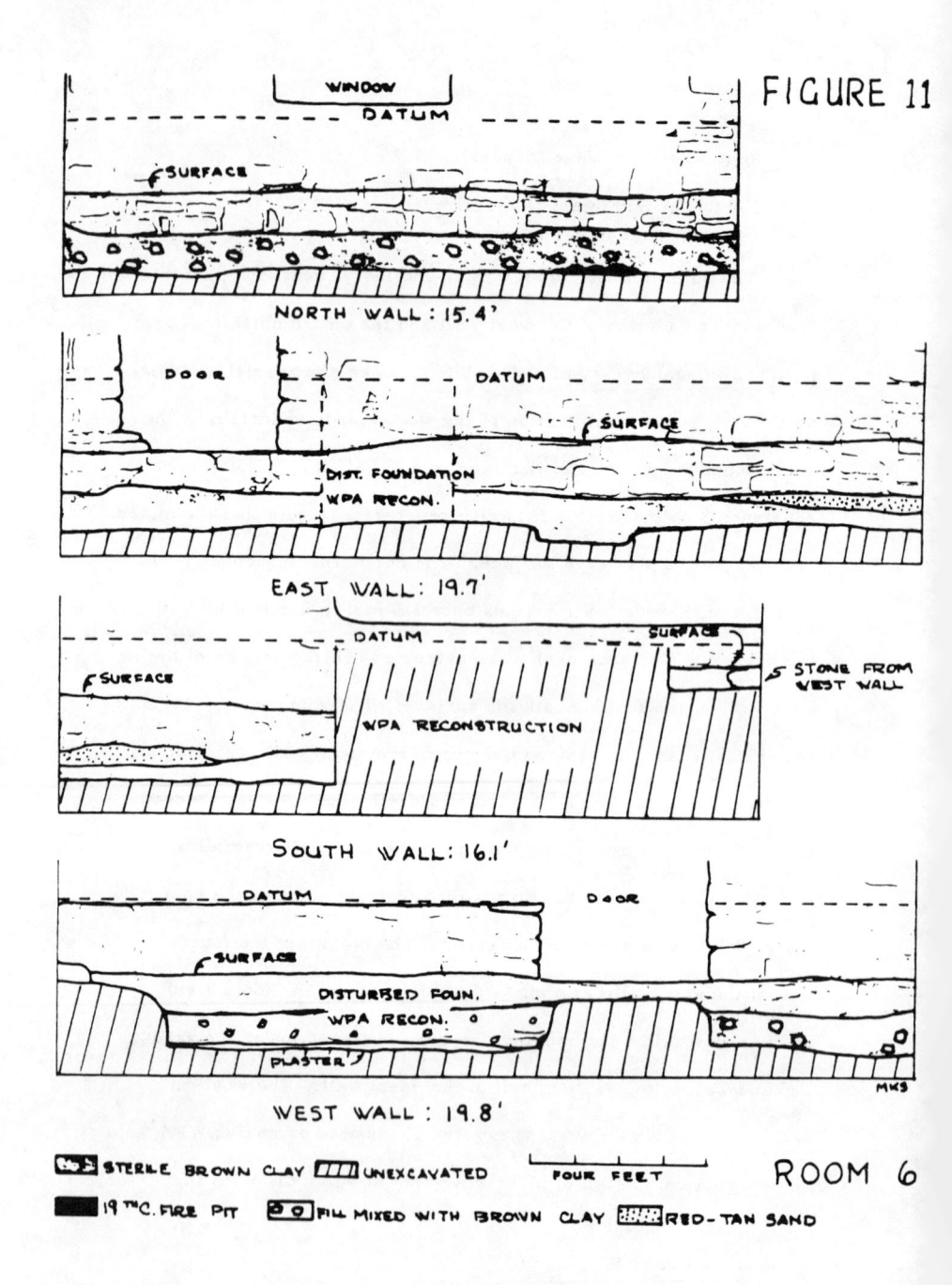

NORTH WALL: 15.4'

EAST WALL: 19.7'

SOUTH WALL: 16.1'

WEST WALL: 19.8'

STERILE BROWN CLAY   UNEXCAVATED   FOUR FEET   ROOM 6
19TH C. FIRE PIT   FILL MIXED WITH BROWN CLAY   RED-TAN SAND

reconstructing the fireplace outline on the south wall; however, it lies at a higher elevation than the plaster floor (which extends under the west wall) and there is apparently no connection between the two.

A beveled window is located in the north wall. The sill is 1.8 feet above the surface. A square (unbeveled) door in the east wall leads to Room 7 and a square door in the west wall leads outside. North and south walls abut east and west walls. Plaster remains only on the exterior face of the north wall (see Figure 11).

Historic Documentation

There is no historic evidence to pinpoint the date of the construction of Room 6. None of the outer rooms (Rooms 6, 8, 10, 12) had been built in 1827, the last date of Bexar County Mission Records. Two clues suggest a date in the final quarter of the nineteenth century. A firepit underlying the north wall had English china, nails, glass, and sawed steak bones of the late nineteenth century in the ash. The term "pit" is misleading, for the ash area was irregular in shape and appeared to have been nothing more than a garbage dump. The west wall of Room 9 was moved from its original location in line with all the eastern rooms, to its present location ~~about 1878~~ ca. 1835(?). The approximate dating is based upon the occurrence of Sponged Ware sherds in the trench of the original

wall. The stone from the original wall was apparently unearthed and reused in the new building phase. Sponged Ware was imported from England in great quantity about 1878. With these two considerations in mind, it is reasonable to assume that all this rebuilding occurred quite late in the nineteenth century. The Corner plat of 1890 (Fig. 5 B) includes the outer rooms. Room 6 was in use early in the twentieth century according to local informants, but the west and south walls were largely in ruin when the WPA did their repair.

Stratigraphy, Features and Artifacts

Colonial period artifacts were concentrated in Room 6 from the top level down. European material appeared only as a veneer and was concentrated along the east wall. The greatest colonial artifact concentration was from the center of the room through (and under) the northwest corner (Fig. 19).

The plastered floor area lay at a depth of 1.6 feet beneath the surface. It extended from the reconstructed area near the midpoint of the south wall, following a roughly circular course around the central measuring stake, to the south side of the door in the west wall (Fig. 19). The plastered layer continued under the west wall, but it was not exposed on the outside. No trace of it was encountered in Room 8.

Artifact Inventories: Room 6

Level 1

Potsherds:	20 transfer printed	5 stamped and painted
	21 Mocha	edge
	91 handpainted	3 luster
	100 unidentified white	1 Flint enamel
		1 yellow glazed
		9 Ginger Beer

....

	38 Mexican lead glazed	63 Indian
	5 West Mexico polychrome	
	1 Mexican burnished black	
	7 Majolica	
Glass:	11 oz. amber glass, patinated	10 oz. green glass
	1 lb. uncolored glass, patinated	10 oz. aqua glass
	2 oz. window glass, patinated	layered glass: green and white
Rusted Metal:	6 lb. 14 oz. nails	buckle
	1 lb. 6 oz. unidentifiable	can key
	22 bottle caps	strap hinge
	bridle ring	pin for hinge
		spike
Miscellaneous:	7 lb. 1 oz. animal bone	brass washer
	11 oz. flint	metal liner from bottle cap
	2 oz. charcoal	brass rivet
	6 oz. brick	brass bell clapper (?)
	wood	brass ball (?)
	white glass pony bead	steel backing of cufflink
	shell: mussel and marine	portion of leather shoe heel
	leg of stone metate	9 china buttons
	chunk of white granite	2 bone buttons
	section clay effigy pipe	3 pearl buttons
	midsection, unglazed porcelain doll	5 steel buttons
	7 clay marbles	3 compound buttons
	2 glass marbles	1885 Indian Head penny
	4 pieces slate pencil	1894 Indian Head penny
	piece of lead	1903 Liberty Head dime
	2 oz. copper	1918 Mercury Head dime
	brass clock wheel	(2) 1917 Lincoln Head pennies
		1918 Lincoln Head penny

Level 2

Potsherds:	12 transfer printed	6 stamped and painted edge
	14 Mocha	2 Flown Blue
	38 handpainted	3 luster
	75 unidentifiable white	

....

	45 Mexican lead glazed	179 Indian
	28 West Mexico polychrome	
	2 Mexican burnished red	
	20 Majolica	
Glass:	5 oz. green glass	amber glass, patinated
	8 oz. uncolored glass, patinated	aqua glass, patinated
Rusted Metal:	1 lb. nails	nut
	6 oz. unidentifiable	key can
	3 bottle caps	
Miscellaneous:	26 lbs. 6 oz. animal bone	bone handled knife
	3 lbs. 10 oz. brick	6 clay marbles
	corner dressed limestone	1 glass marble
	portion worked sandstone	piece slate pencil
	2 oz. shell: mussel and marine	cufflink: brass and glass
	incised mussel shell	white glass pony bead
	charcoal	handblown blue glass bead
	wood	cobalt-blue jewelry set
	3 oz. copper	(4) 22 cal. shells
	copper patch	unmarked cal. shell
	14 oz. flint	miniball
	brass band from lead pencil	7 china buttons
	copper clamp	3 pearl buttons
	copper cap from flat bottle	1 bone button
		1 steel button
		1 lead button

Level 3

Potsherds:	3 transfer printed	11 handpainted
	3 Mocha	25 unidentified white
	3 stamped and painted edge	

....

256

	117 Mexican lead glazed 1 Mexican burnished red 1 Mexican burnished black 16 Majolica	116 Indian
Glass:	2 oz. green uncolored glass, patinated	window glass, patinated amber glass, patinated
Rusted Metal:	8 oz. unidentifiable 11 oz. nails unidentified object	2 bottle caps staple
Miscellaneous:	43 lbs. animal bone 11 oz. flint piece quartzite mussel shell coal bone tool gun flint 2 oz. copper	copper spearhead piece brass chain metal seal from whiskey bottle 38 cal. shell unmarked cal. shell 4 china buttons 1 pearl button 2 brass buttons

Level 4

Potsherds:	3 transfer printed 2 Mocha 4 stamped and painted edge	20 handpainted 19 unidentified white 2 Ginger Beer
	41 Mexican lead glazed 2 Mexican red burnished 5 Majolica 1 French brown-bottomed Faience	52 Indian
Glass:	1 oz. green glass amber glass, patinated	2 oz. uncolored glass, patinated
Rusted Metal:	1 lb. 4 oz. nails 1 oz. unidentifiable center piece from single- tree blade of penknife	piece of hinge (?) bottle cap staple washer chain link

Miscellaneous: 33 lbs. 7 oz. animal bone   brass cog
                 1 oz. ocher   16 guage shell
                 1 lb. brick   22 cal. shell
                 1 lb. 6 oz. plaster   8 china buttons
                 6 oz. charcoal   2 shell buttons
                 mussel shell   1 steel button
                 12 oz. flint   1 bone button
                 2 gun flints   1 bronze button
                 piece copper with rivet   1891 Liberty Head
                 2 clay marbles   nickel
                 copper buckle (?)

ROOM 7

Physical Description (interior dimensions)

North Wall: 11.45 feet long, 1.8 feet high, 1.6 feet thick.

East Wall: 20.2 feet long, 9.0 feet high at north end to 8.0 feet high north of window, 5.0 feet high south of window, to 2.3 feet high at southeast corner, 2.0 feet thick.

South Wall: 11.5 feet long, 3.1 feet high at west end, 2.3 feet high at east end, 1.5 feet thick.

West Wall: 20.6 feet long, 3.2 feet high north of door to 9.0 feet high at northwest corner, 2.9 feet high south of door to maximum of 9 feet in center and 4.3 feet high at southwest corner, 2.2 feet thick.

Northwest-Southeast Diagonal: 22.95 feet.

Northeast-Southwest Diagonal: 23.85 feet.

The north wall rests on a layer of laminated gray, ashy soil mixed with charcoal and cultural material. The base of the foundation

is 1.4 feet beneath the surface. The eastern half of the south wall rests upon the same fill at about the same depth. The thickness of the ashy soil under the south wall is about 0.4 foot thick and rests upon sterile brown clay at a depth of 1.8 feet beneath the surface. The ashy soil underlying the south wall thins out at the middle of the wall and the foundation of the wall drops to a depth of 1.8 feet beneath the surface and lies directly on sterile brown clay. The east wall rests on sterile brown clay at a depth of from 1.4 feet to 1.8 feet beneath the surface. The west wall also rests on the sterile brown clay, but was set at least 0.5 foot into it. The base of the west wall is from 2.0 to 2.3 feet beneath the surface. The west wall is well built and unquestionably dates to the Colonial period--sandy-lime mortar is used in the lower portion of its construction. The east wall is not so well built, and in addition, shows a disturbed foundation near the southeast corner where the WPA converted what had been a door to the room into a window.

  A beveled window is in the northern half of the east wall and a square (unbeveled) door in the west wall leads to Room 6. WPA reconstructed an area of the west wall just south of the door. The base of the west wall is a foot lower in Room 7 than the base of the same wall on the Room 6 side. The trench into which the wall was laid was probably too narrow at the bottom

to accommodate the full two-foot thickness of the wall. Therefore, the building stones were laid with their long axes oriented north and south in the lower part of the foundation trench. North and south walls are laid between (abut) east and west walls (see Figure 12).

Historic Documentation

Room 7 was described in 1824 as a room of 8 varas in length and 4 in width, with stone walls and a grass roof. It is listed as property number 25 in Mission Record 15 (Fig. 6). In the mission property evaluation document of 1827, Angela Gonzales is recorded as the owner (Mission Record 27, Appendix A). The room is assigned the number "27" (Room 4 of Figure 1), but this is clearly in error for the room is described as 7 varas long (nineteen feet) which is close to its actual length of 20 feet, but is certainly nowhere near the twelve-foot length of Room 4 (or "27" of Mission Record 15). Furthermore, the document identifies Luisa de Luna as the owner to the north. The 1824 record (Mission Record 15) does not list Angela Gonzales as a property owner in that year, but she is listed as the owner in the 1823 Saucedo plat (Fig. 5.A). The Saucedo plat cannot be relied upon completely for the year of 1823 because Bexar County documents contradict it. Whether or not Angela Gonzales was the owner in 1823 is unclear, but she surely owned the room by 1827. I suggested in the section on Room 4 that that room,

together with Rooms 5 and 7, was in good repair in the mid-nineteenth century and was represented as one of the roofed houses in the west wall of the Lungkwitz painting (Plate 1). The Corner plat (Fig. 5.B) shows the room to have been habitable in 1890 and it was probably lived in up until 1927.

Stratigraphy, Features and Artifacts

Room 7 produced the most interesting assortment of nineteenth century artifacts. It was dubbed "the kindergarten" because of the quantity of toys. Artifacts reflecting post-Colonial occupation were concentrated to a depth of 1.5 feet. The 1.5 to 2.0 feet level was first thought to be sterile. The north half of the room was almost devoid of artifacts and the colonial period artifacts were concentrated in the south half of the room. It was necessary to dig to 2.0 to 2.5 feet to uncover the sterile brown clay throughout the room although it first appeared in the north end of the room at only about 1.7 feet beneath the surface. Some nineteenth century material was found at this level in the north end of the room and in the southeast corner, where the soil was very loose (probably from WPA reconstruction).

The second Indian firepit with charred corncobs was found in the 2.0 to 2.5 feet level (Fig. 19). Like the similar feature in Room 4, only the well-defined bottom of the pit could be traced.

It had a diameter of 0.8 foot and the rounded bottom was slightly deeper than 0.2 foot.

Artifact Inventories: Room 7

Level 1

Level 1 covered only the south half of the room.

Potsherds:	13 unidentified white	3 handpainted
	3 transfer printed	2 stamped and
	2 Mocha	printed edge
	....	
	2 Mexican lead glazed	16 Indian
	1 Majolica	
Glass:	9 oz. amber glass	green glass
	1 lb. uncolored glass, patinated	aqua glass
	window glass, patinated	
Rusted Metal:	4 oz. nails	bolt
	1 oz. wire	
Miscellaneous:	4 oz. animal bone	copper rim for
	1 oz. flint	screw cap
	mussel shell	lead washer
	clay marble	beer token
	glass button	

Level 2

Potsherds:	32 transfer printed	9 Mocha
	22 handpainted	9 Flown Blue
	29 unidentified white	2 luster
	2 cream glazed	1 crockery
	....	
	12 Mexican lead glazed	
	3 Majolica	

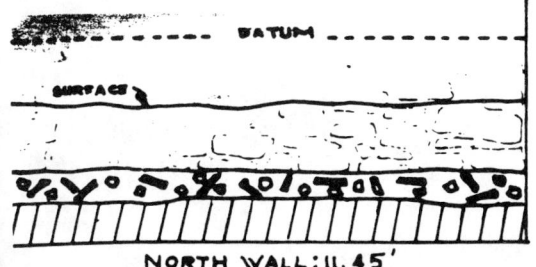

FIGURE 12: ROOM 7

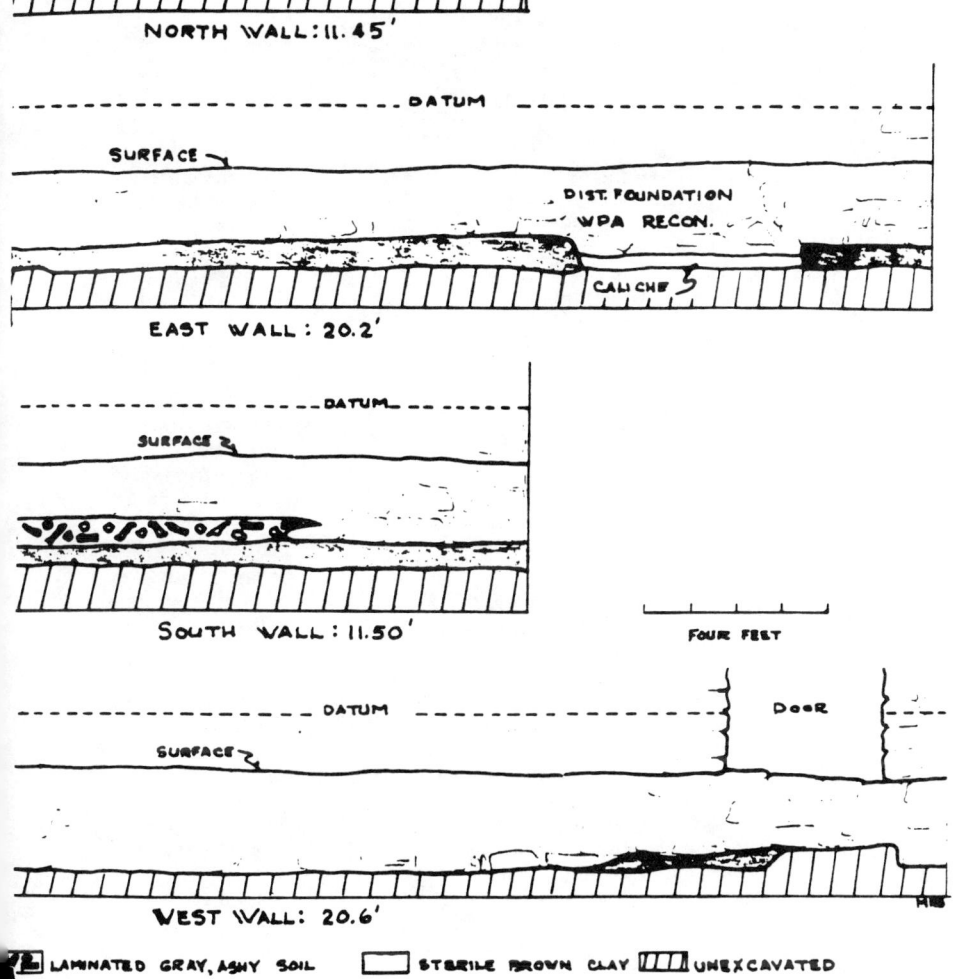

Glass:	4 lbs. 2 oz. uncolored glass, patinated 2 oz. window glass, patinated 3 lbs 12 oz. amber glass, patinated	2 oz. green glass 2 oz. aqua glass milk glass
Rusted Metal:	8 lbs. 5 oz. nails 1 lb. 4 oz. roofing tin 4 oz. wire 10 oz. unidentifiable blade from tractor sickle 17 bottle caps 2 jar caps railroad spike arrowhead	nut 3 staples latch hook chain link tin can fragments knife handle knife blade fork tines thimble
Miscellaneous:	1 lb. 3.5 oz. animal bone 12 oz. plaster 4 oz. flint 1 oz. shell: mussel and marine 4 oz. brick charcoal wood clay bead copper fragments copper decorative pin copper rivet copper ball (?) brass buckle and belt slide brass bottle cap 2 pieces brass from clock 2 links from brass chain 17 brass suspender slides 3 metal suspender adjustors top from salt cellar porcelain door handle portion of imitation tortoise shell double-comb aluminum whistle toy whistle 1907 Indian Head penny 1912 Lincoln Head penny	3 pieces slate pencil slate fragment 23 clay marbles 4 glass marbles porcelain forearm of doll hand from porcelain forearm upper arm, solid porcelain doll painted porcelain doll's shoe 26 china buttons 4 steel buttons brass military button 1 bone button 13 pearl buttons 1 copper button 3 compound buttons (6) 12 guage shells (2) 22 cal. shells (1) 44 cal. shell (1) 45 cal. shell 1 unstamped cal. shell 1 lead slug lead miniball

Level 3

Potsherds:	25 transfer printed	4 luster
	22 Mocha	1 yellow-glazed
	8 stamped and painted edge	1 cream-glazed
	3 Flown Blue	2 unidentified
	82 handpainted	2 handpainted
	101 unidentified white	porcelain
		3 crockery

. . . .

	9 Mexican lead glazed	34 Indian
	8 West Mexico polychrome	
	6 Majolica	
Glass:	1 lb. 3 oz. uncolored glass, patinated	4 oz. green glass
	9 oz. amber, patinated	7 oz. window glass, patinated
Rusted Metal:	4 lbs. 12 oz. nails	lock
	1 lb. roofing tin	spring
	4 oz. wire	button hook
	2 oz. unidentifiable	complete spoon
	6 bottle caps	bowls of 2 spoons
	part of scissors	fork tines
	part of branding iron	key
	buckle from cinch band	buckle
	ring from cinch band	nut
	blade from tractor sickle	spool (?)
	piece round mirror	staple
	tin can fragments	jar cap
	Prince Albert tobacco can	2 can keys
Miscellaneous:	2 lbs. animal bone	2 brass safety pins
	8 oz. plaster	brass wedding band
	4 oz. flint	copper thimble
	charcoal	brass pin
	brick	backing from earring
	ocher	white metal hairpin
	mussel shell	religious medal
	pieces copper	suspender holder
	fragments of slate	brass top of coin purse
	9 pieces slate pencil	handblown clear glass bead
	40 clay marbles	faceted yellow clear glass bead
	11 glass marbles	
	2 stone marbles	

copper wire
brass screw cap
2 brass clock wheels
ceramic doorknob
  (flintware)
white porcelain furniture
  caster
painted porcelain head
  from compound doll
painted head from solid
  porcelain doll
portion of forearm from
  compound doll, unglazed
  porcelain
portion of porcelain leg and
  foot with glazed boot
fragments of bisque headed
  doll
white porcelain sugar bowl
  from doll set
26 china buttons
1 bone button
4 steel buttons
16 pearl buttons
1 composition button
4 compound buttons

cap off lipstick tube
enameled metal ring
  (earring?)
brass curtain ring
2 brass bands from
  lead pencils
piece pencil lead
4 unidentified objects
  (metal)
cut leather from
  around lock
(5) 12 guage shells
(1) 16 guage shell
(1) 22 cal. shell
(3) 44 cal. shells
(1) 38 cal. shell
1 lead slug
1899 Liberty Head
  nickel
1909 Liberty Head
  nickel
1907 Indian Head
  penny
19 ? Indian Head
  penny
1916 Buffalo nickel
19 ? Lincoln Head
  penny
nickel slug
unidentified coin (size
  of early nineteenth
  century dime)
Thos. R. Dillon token

Level 4

Potsherds:
14 transfer printed
44 handpainted
46 unidentified white

6 Mocha
1 unidentified

12 Mexican lead glazed
7 West Mexico polychrome
8 Majolica

14 Indian

Glass:	2 oz. uncolored glass, patinated window glass, patinated aqua glass	2 oz. green glass amber glass, patinated
Rusted Metal:	6 oz. nails 3 oz. unidentifiable buckle bottle cap	jar cap connecting rod for automobile
Miscellaneous:	15 oz. animal bone 3 oz. flint corn cobs shell: mussel and marine 1 oz. plaster charcoal chunk building material calcite muscovite	brass thimble glass button slate fragment faceted blue glass bead 2 clay marbles 2 glass marbles 10 guage shell

Level 5

Potsherds:	12 transfer printed 21 handpainted 32 unidentified white	7 Mocha 1 stamped and painted edge 1 Flown Blue

. . . .

	2 Mexican lead glazed 2 West Mexico polychrome 2 Majolica	15 Indian
Glass:	2 oz. uncolored, patinated window glass, patinated	2 oz. green glass amber glass
Rusted Metal:	4 oz. unidentifiable metal several nails buckle	
Miscellaneous:	7 oz. animal bone 6 oz. flint 13 oz. brick 11 oz. plaster 1 oz. corn cobs brass hook for hook and eye 1 steel button	shell: mussel and marine round pebble for grinding ocher fragments of calcite tooth from comb 2 bone buttons

ROOM 8

<u>Physical Description</u> (interior dimensions)

    North Wall: 8.9 feet long, 1.9 feet high, 2.0 feet thick.

    East Wall: 29.65 feet long, 1.9 feet high, 2.0 feet thick.

    South Wall: 9.0 feet long, 1.9 feet high, 1.7 feet thick.

    West Wall: 29.45 feet long, 1.9 feet high, 2.0 feet thick.

    Northwest-Southeast Diagonal: 31.1 feet.

    Northeast-Southwest Diagonal: 30.9 feet.

The south and west walls were built directly on top of a one-foot thick layer of sandy soil mixed with ash and cultural material. The bases of the walls are only about 0.4 foot beneath the surface. The cultural zone rests upon sterile brown clay at 1.4 feet beneath the surface. The north wall, rebuilt by the WPA, rests upon an 0.2 foot layer of plaster which, in turn, rests upon the sandy soil. A trench along the north wall revealed sterile brown clay under the sandy fill at a depth of 1.4 feet beneath the surface (for a distance of three feet adjacent to the east wall). It is replaced by a thin layer of red sand overlying small red gravel, underlying the sandy fill for six feet adjacent to the west wall. Why the sand-gravel layer was brought in remains a mystery. The east wall foundation was set deeper into the fill than the other three walls, being about a foot beneath the surface at the north and south ends.

FIGURE 13 : ROOM 8

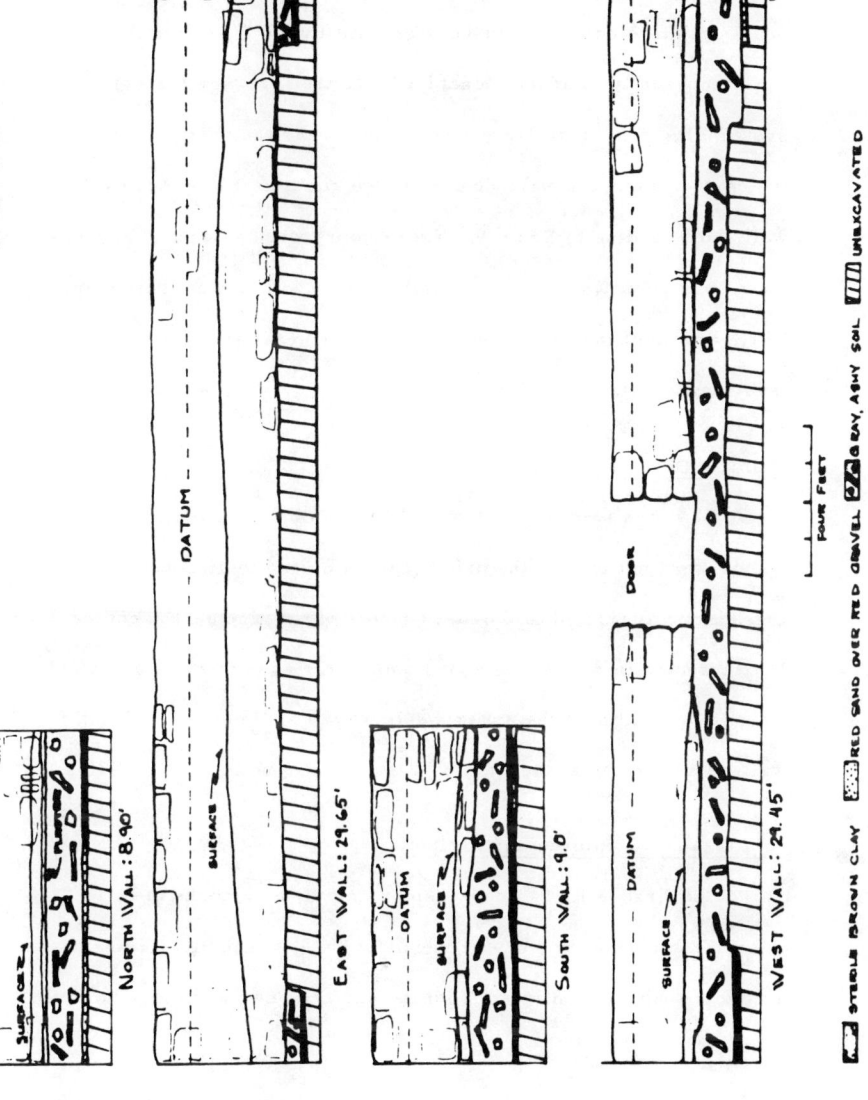

This wall rests upon only four-tenths of a foot of the sandy soil containing cultural material.

A square door (unbeveled) was built by the WPA into the west wall, apparently to accommodate a large tree growing through the spot. WPA plans indicate a beveled door near the north corner of the east wall and a square door near the south corner of the same wall, both leading to Room 9. These doors were filled in. A square door, now absent, in the south wall is also indicated on their map. North and south walls are set between (abut) east and west walls (see Figure 13).

Historic Documentation

What was said of Room 6 applies to Room 8 as well. These rooms were not part of the original mission and their construction can best be attributed to the last quarter of the nineteenth century. It also seems fairly certain that Room 8 was used for only a limited time because almost the entire western wall and most of the eastern wall were in ruins at the time of WPA reconstruction in the 1930's.

Stratigraphy, Features and Artifacts

The first level was represented only by hummocks of dirt in the center of the room--the result of WPA trenching. Colonial artifacts were concentrated from the surface down and the bulk of

the artifacts came from the south half of the room. In excavating Level 4, we encountered sterile, compacted, brown clay at 1.7 feet beneath the surface and subsequently stripped off only the 0.2 foot of fill lying on top of it.

Artifact Inventories: Room 8

Level 1

Potsherds:	6 transfer printed 6 Mocha 3 stamped and painted edge 1 blue Jasperware 1 unidentified	20 handpainted 38 unidentified white 7 crockery 2 Ginger Beer
	46 Mexican lead glazed 3 West Mexico polychrome 1 Puebla black luster 25 Majolica	50 Indian
Glass:	4 oz. green glass 2 oz. window glass, patinated	2 oz. uncolored glass, patinated 4 oz. aqua glass 2 oz. amber glass
Rusted Metal:	2 lbs. 5 oz. nails 2 oz. roofing tin 4 oz. unidentifiable bottle cap chain ring hook	2 washers buckle staple can key wire can
Miscellaneous:	11 lbs. 1 oz. animal bone 3 lbs. 12 oz. flint 1 oz. mussel shell and marine 3 shaped sandstones 2 oz. brick 1 lb. 5 oz. plaster portion doll's lower leg with top of boot, but foot missing, glazed porcelain white porcelain rim of doll dish	copper fragments bronze chapatone gun flint piece slate pencil unidentified object 8 china buttons 1 pearl button unidentified cal. shell

Level 2

Potsherds:
- 5 transfer printed
- 1 Mocha
- 9 handpainted
- 25 unidentified white
- 1 Ginger Beer
- 2 luster
- 1 unidentified

....

- 100 Mexican lead glazed
- 12 West Mexico polychrome
- 2 Mexican burnished red
- 63 Majolica
- 1 French Faience
- 142 Indian

Glass:
- 1 oz. green glass
- aqua glass
- 1 oz. amber glass
- window glass, patinated
- 7 oz. uncolored glass, patinated

Rusted Metal:
- 14 oz. nails
- 10 oz. unidentifiable
- 2 oz. roofing tin
- jar cap

Miscellaneous:
- 64 lbs. 6 oz. animal bone
- 5 lbs. 12 oz. flint
- 7 oz. brick
- 4 oz. plaster
- 10 oz. mortar and building material
- 2 blue glass trade beads
- blue glass set from jewelry
- 2 bone pins
- 2 unidentified bone tools
- 2 suspender parts
- copper rivet
- unidentified brass piece
- charcoal
- 2 oz. shell: mussel and marine
- 12 oz. coal
- 5 oz. ocher
- 2 pieces worked sandstone
- 3 gun flints
- 2 flint arrowheads
- bone spatula
- clay marble
- glass button

Level 3

Potsherds:
- 3 transfer printed
- 1 Mocha
- 5 handpainted
- 19 unidentified white
- 2 crockery

....

- 83 Mexican lead glazed
- 10 West Mexico polychrome
- 6 Mexican burnished red
- 60 Majolica
- 320 Indian

Glass:	2 oz. amber glass window glass, patinated 1 oz. green glass	cobalt blue glass aqua glass 2 oz. uncolored glass
Rusted Metal:	6 oz. nails 1 lb. 8 oz. unidentifiable	mule shoe nut
Miscellaneous:	86 lbs 11 oz. animal bone 4 lbs. 11 oz. flint 4 oz. shell: mussel and marine 12 oz. plaster charcoal 2 oz. copper lava-stone maul (?) pendant: copper with glass set chunk white porcelain unidentified ivory piece	bone spatula 2 bone pins shaped sandstone wood tool 3 Olivella shell beads 3 gun flints 6 flint arrowheads unstamped cal. shell 2 china buttons 1 bone button 1 compound button

Level 4

Potsherds:	4 handpainted	4 unidentified white 3 unidentified

....

	19 Mexican lead glazed 4 West Mexico polychrome 7 Mexican burnished red 14 Majolica	170 Indian
Glass:	green glass amber glass	uncolored glass aqua glass
Rusted Metal:	13 oz. unidentified metal several nails	
Miscellaneous:	33 lbs. 15 oz. animal bone 4 lbs. 3 oz. flint 1 oz. shell: mussel and marine plaster charcoal 5 flint arrowheads 1 glass arrowhead	copper fragment 2 gun flints blue glass trade bead portion rosary bead bone bead 3 bone pins

ROOM 9

Physical Description (interior dimensions)

North Wall: 17.8 feet long, 3.0 feet high, and 1.7 feet thick at west end, 3.1 feet high, to 2.3 feet high and 1.5 feet thick at east end.

East Wall: 30.1 feet long, 5.5 feet high, and 2.2 feet thick at northeast corner, 2.2 feet high south side of door, 3.7 feet high and 2.1 feet thick at south end.

South Wall: 17.8 feet long, 3.6 feet high and 1.4 feet thick at east end, 3.5 feet high and 2.0 feet thick at west end.

West Wall: 29.65 feet long, 1.9 feet high, 2.0 feet thick.

Northwest-Southeast Diagonal: 34.4 feet.

Northeast-Southwest Diagonal: 35.2 feet.

The bases of the walls were not exposed in Room 9; however, the trench dug perpendicular to the south wall suggests that they lie on sterile brown clay at an approximate depth of 1.5 feet beneath the surface. The original west wall was in line with Room 7 on the north and Room 11 on the south. Portions of its foundation were exposed just beneath the surface on both north and south walls (Plate 4). The 2.5 by 3.2 feet pit on the south wall showed that the original outer wall had been laid in a trench dug into sterile clay to an undetermined depth. The foundation for the western

extension of the south wall is poorly constructed and has the appearance of rubble dumped into a trench rather than carefully laid stone.

That part of the north wall lying between Rooms 9 and 7 is set between (abutted) west and east walls. The westward extension of the north wall abuts the new west wall. That part of the south wall between Rooms 9 and 11 abuts the west and east walls and the newer westward extension is set between the original and new west walls. The end of the old west wall was not refaced as it was on the north side of the room.

The east wall has a beveled door near the north wall. A second beveled door in the center of the same wall was converted to a window by the WPA and a second window south of it is adjacent to the south wall. Most of the newer west wall was rebuilt by WPA and a beveled door and a square door leading to Room 8 were walled-up at that time (see Figure 14).

Historic Documentation

Documentary evidence indicates that Room 9 did not exist as a room in the Colonial period. The 1823 Saucedo plat (Fig. 5 A) shows an entryway between property owned by Angela Gonzales, the owner of Room 7, and Dona Maria Calvillo, the owner of Rooms 11 and 13. The only reference to the ownership of this strip of land is in Mission Record 27 (Appendix A), where the residence of Angela

PLATE 4

ROOM 9: PORTION OF ORIGINAL WEST WALL SEEN AGAINST THE NORTH WALL

ROOM 9: PORTION OF ORIGINAL WEST WALL SEEN AGAINST THE SOUTH WALL

FIG. 5: 19th CENTURY FLAGSTONE FLOOR

VIEW OF NORTHWEST ROOMS ROOM 11 IN FOREGROUND, ROOM 4 AT FAR END WITH GABLE

Gonzales is defined as lying between the property of Luisa de Luna on the north and Bentura Quinones on the south. In all probability Quinones owned only a strip of land corresponding to the width of the room and extending to the San Antonio River on the west (the western boundary line of all privately owned property along the west wall). Quinones is not listed in Mission Record 15 as a land owner in 1824-- Mission Record 15 describes all the walls and structures of the mission in 1824, and every room in the west wall north of the chapel can be accounted for (both by measurements provided, and by owner) except for Room 9. There is simply no structure as long as thirty feet described. Archaeological evidence from these rooms indicates that the west wall of Rooms 4, 5, 7, 9, 11, and 13 was originally a rampart and that the concentration of Colonial Period material in Rooms 6, 8, and 10 can be explained as refuse dumped outside the old wall. Two middens seem to be involved. One was concentrated in the south half of Room 8 and the north half of Room 10. The other was in the north half of Room 6 and extended toward the north (Fig. 19). Both, of course, extend westward for unknown distances. Midden concentrations on both sides of an entryway into the mission compound is known from other Spanish Colonial sites. Room 9 therefore could correspond to an unoccupied space with an entranceway between the two roofed structures in the Lungkwitz painting of the mid-nineteenth century (Plate 1). I propose that

the property involved became Room 9 at the time that the west wall was moved in the last quarter of the nineteenth century (see Historical Documentation for Rooms 6 and 8). It was probably still occupied in 1890 when Corner drew his plat (Fig. 5 B). Local informants claim it was in use early in this century, but it was a ruin by the 1930's.

Stratigraphy, Features and Artifacts

The first level of Room 9 was limited to the center of the room and along the north wall. The upper three levels had nineteenth century materials. A concentration of Colonial period artifacts appeared only in Level 4 and these were clustered in the southwest quadrant of the room.

Artifact Inventories: Room 9

Level 1

Potsherds:	1 Mocha	1 unidentified white
	2 handpainted	3 crockery
	....	
	1 Mexican lead glazed	2 Indian
	1 West Mexico polychrome	
	1 Majolica	
Glass:	1 oz. aqua glass	window glass, patinated
	amber glass	green glass
	2 oz. uncolored glass	
Rusted Metal:	2 oz. metal including roofing tin and a few nails	

FIGURE 14 : ROOM 9

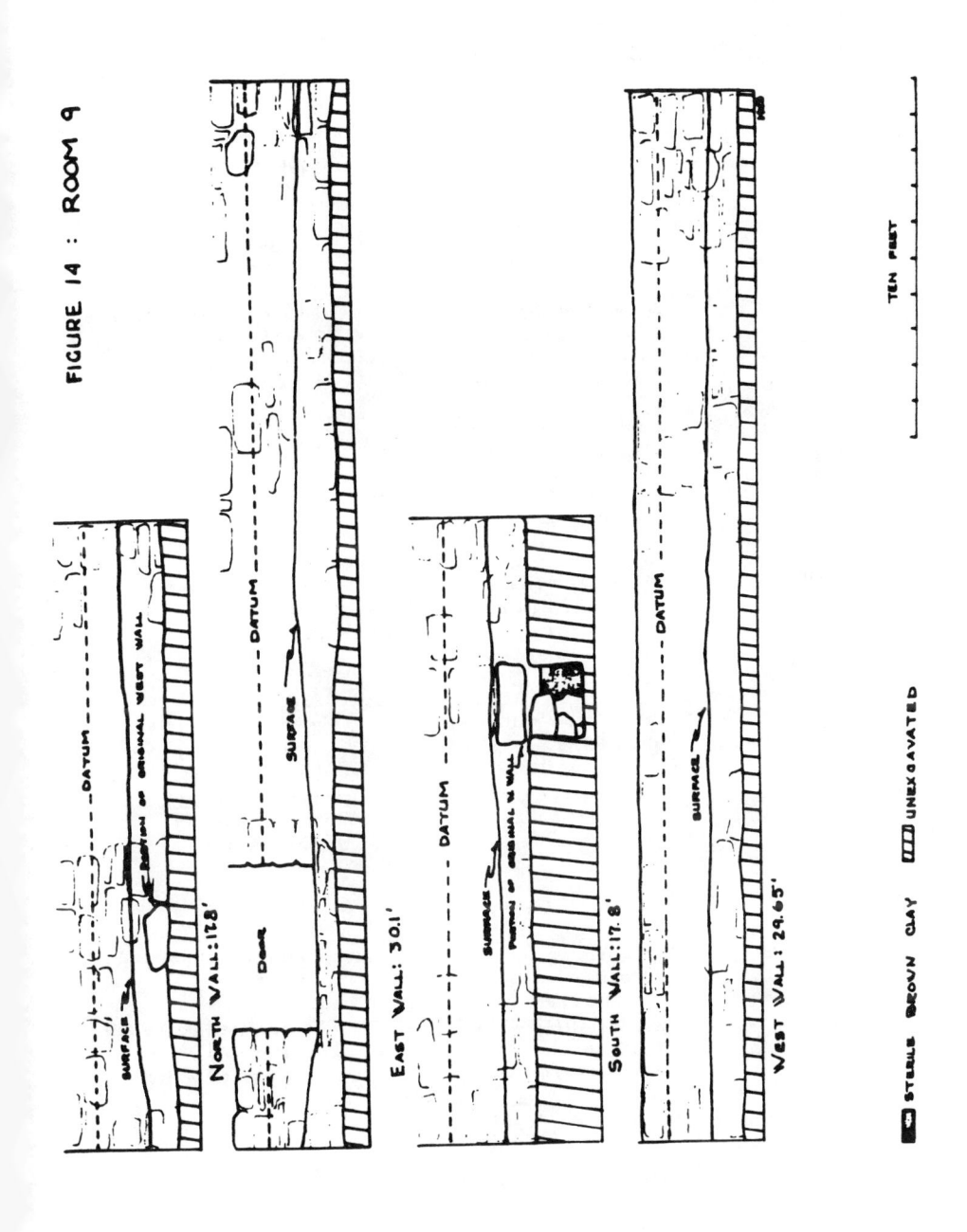

Miscellaneous: 12 oz. animal bone   glass marble
                    6 oz. flint   graphite from battery
                    mussel shell

Level 2

Potshards:
- 10 transfer printed
- 16 Mocha
- 2 stamped and painted edge
- 19 handpainted
- 3 yellow glazed
- 42 unidentified white
- 3 luster
- 1 handpainted porcelain
- 19 crockery

....

- 13 Mexican lead glazed
- 2 West Mexico polychrome
- 1 Mexican burnished red
- 10 Majolica
- 55 Indian

Glass:
- 12 oz. window glass, patinated
- 7 oz. aqua glass
- 4 oz. green glass
- 6 oz. amber glass
- 12 oz. uncolored glass

Rusted Metal:
- 1 lb. 8 oz. nails
- 10 oz. roofing tin
- 9 bottle caps
- handle of scissors
- heavy wire
- salt shaker cap
- tobacco tin
- can rims
- 2 unidentified pieces

Miscellaneous:
- 2 lbs. 6 oz. animal bone
- 1 lb. 3 oz. flint
- 6 oz. brick
- shell: mussel and marine
- 2 flint arrowheads
- shaped sandstone
- 2 pieces ceramic sewer pipe
- 4 glass marbles
- copper rivet
- brass screw cap
- copper button
- compound button

Level 3

Potshards:
- 36 transfer printed
- 13 Mocha
- 47 handpainted
- 86 unidentified white
- 70 crockery
- 22 yellow-green glazed
- 4 stamped and painted edge
- 3 Ginger Beer
- 5 handpainted porcelain
- 2 unidentified black
- gold-stamped white

most of 1 cup: stamped and transfer printed

....

- 48 Mexican lead glazed
- 5 West Mexico polychrome
- 3 Mexican burnished red
- 25 Majolica
- 2 West Mexico slip-painted
- 114 Indian

Glass:	15 oz. window glass, patinated 1 lb. green glass 11 oz. amber glass milk glass	1 lb. 2 oz. aqua glass 1 lb. 5 oz. uncolored glass cobalt blue glass
Rusted Metal:	4 lbs. 14 oz. roofing tin 11 lbs. 12 oz. nails portions of 2 horseshoes railroad spike piece of kettle (?) fused nut and bolt 6 bottle caps ring hook	chain link guncock tin cans staple washer nut wire
Miscellaneous:	7 lbs. 1 oz. animal bone 2 lbs. 10 oz. flint 2 oz. plaster brick charcoal 2 oz. shell: mussel and marine worked sandstone clear glass faceted bead green set from jewelry portion of aluminum comb 5 clay marbles 1 glass marble harmonica sounding board 11 china buttons 3 pearl buttons 1 bone button 1 steel button 2 brass clock wheels brass washer copper jar cap white metal boss	unidentified ceramic object portion flintware doorknob portion bisque doll, 1902 portion painted porcelain, hollow-headed doll portion unglazed porcelain forearm from composite doll shoulder button from composite, glazed porcelain doll, 1893 (2) 22 cal. rifle shells (1) 12 guage shell (1) 16 guage shell 1893 Liberty Head nickel

Level 4

Potsherds:	49 transfer printed 34 Mocha 122 handpainted 143 unidentified white 1 Flown Blue 1 luster 4 unidentified	23 stamped and painted edge 41 crockery 4 gold-stamped white 3 stamped and transfer printed 5 yellow glazed 2 painted porcelain

120

	73 Mexican lead glazed 24 West Mexico polychrome 18 Mexican burnished red 4 West Mexico slip-painted 56 Majolica	277 Indian
Glass:	1 lb. 4 oz. green glass 4 oz. window glass, patinated 11 oz. uncolored glass, patinated	5 oz. amber glass 11 oz. aqua glass cobalt blue glass
Rusted Metal:	4 lbs. 8 oz. nails 1 lb. 3 oz. roofing tin 4 lbs. 8 oz. unidentifiable bottle cap washer spear point frizzen portions of tin cans buckle and ring from cinch band	chain 3 buckles scissors spur bolt wire 2 spoon bowls bone handled knife fragment portion of key
Miscellaneous:	22 lbs. 8 oz. animal bone 5 lbs. 12 oz. flint 14 oz. plaster 10 oz. brick wood charcoal worked sandstone 4 oz. shell: mussel and marine 2 pebbles (for burnishing?) portion of fabric clay whistle bone bead clay bead copper crucifix 2 gun flints Montell dart point 3 flint arrowheads pieces copper portion stoneware doorknob slate pencil	fragment stone with green paint unidentified white metal 4 clay marbles 4 glass marbles 2 pieces lead brass hook from box 10 bone buttons 1 steel button 5 china buttons 9 pearl buttons 2 pieces from bisque doll painted porcelain head from compound doll (2) 22 cal. shells (3) 12 guage shells

Level 5
(trench perpendicular to south wall only)

Potsherds:	1 transfer printed	4 handpainted
	1 Mocha	8 unidentified white
	1 stamped and painted edge	

	5 Mexican lead glazed	6 Indian
	1 Mexican burnished red	
	2 Majolica	

Glass:	green glass	uncolored glass
	aqua glass	

Rusted Metal:	2 oz. nails

Miscellaneous:	shell
	flint
	brass filigree heart pendant

ROOM 10

Physical Description (interior dimensions)

North Wall: 17.5 feet long, 1.9 feet high, and 1.7 feet thick at west end, 3.5 feet high and 2.0 feet thick at east end.

East Wall: 25.6 feet long, 3.3 feet high, and 2.2 feet thick at north end, 4.7 feet high and 2.3 feet thick at south end.

South Wall: 11.2 feet long, 7.0 feet high, and 1.1 feet thick at west end, 9.0 feet high and 1.3 feet thick at east end, 4.0 feet thick on top of chimney.

Northwest-Southeast Diagonal (from the end of the west wall of Room 8): 31.1 feet.

Northeast-Southwest Diagonal: 30.0 feet.

Room 10 has no west wall and excavation provided no trace of one. The west end of the north wall, between Rooms 8 and 10, lies directly on the contemporary surface and is underlain by 1.2 feet of brown sandy clay mixed with food bones and other cultural debris. The eastern end of the north wall, shared with Room 9, rests on sterile brown clay at a depth of 0.4 foot beneath the surface at the center of the wall. This segment of the wall is built directly upon three large rocks. The eastern wall is based on sterile brown clay at a depth of 1.1 feet beneath the surface at the north end and 1.6 feet beneath the surface at the south end. The northern half of this wall was rebuilt by the WPA. The incomplete south wall is also resting upon sterile brown clay at a depth of 1.6 feet beneath the surface. The center of the wall projects about 2 feet into the room to accommodate the fireplace. The section of the south wall between the fireplace projection and the east wall rests upon a footing which is 0.5 foot wider than the top of the wall, or about 1.8 feet wide. The footing and the lower part of the adjacent section of the eastern wall are built of limestone blocks shaped in the early Spanish Colonial fashion. The fireplace wall might have been built on the remnants of a buttress supporting the original western rampart.

The fireplace hearth is 2.2 feet above the surface of the room and has an opening 3.3 feet wide and 2.9 feet high (Plate 3). The fireplace differs from those in Rooms 4 and 12 in that its lintel is

formed by a single large slab of sandstone laid flat instead of a series of dressed limestone blocks set with a keystone. The section of the fireplace from the lintel up appears to have been rebuilt and the original design may have been different (see Figure 15).

Historic Documentation

Whether Rooms 10 and 12 were ever completed is doubtful. They had not been built as late as 1830 for there is no description of them in the mission records of Bexar County. Doña Marie de Calvillo was the owner of Rooms 11 and 13 from 1810 to some time after 1847 (Mission Record 15 and Mission Record 27, Appendix A; Fig. 5, A and Fig. 7). Since the two unfinished rooms correspond to her holdings and share a common chimney, this suggests that she may have been responsible for this building phase. The Room 12 fireplace is built in the colonial style, but it has been pointed out that the Room 10 fireplace was probably rebuilt. Artisans skilled in the eighteenth century style of stone masonry were probably more prevalent in the early 1800's than in the later years of the century. There is not a trace of any western wall to the room and the south wall is not finished (its end may have been intended as the facing of a doorway between Rooms 10 and 12). Furthermore, the Room 10 fireplace shows no signs of having ever been used. The 1890 Corner plat does not depict the wall at all, although it certainly predates his map (Fig. 5,B).

Figure 15: Room 10

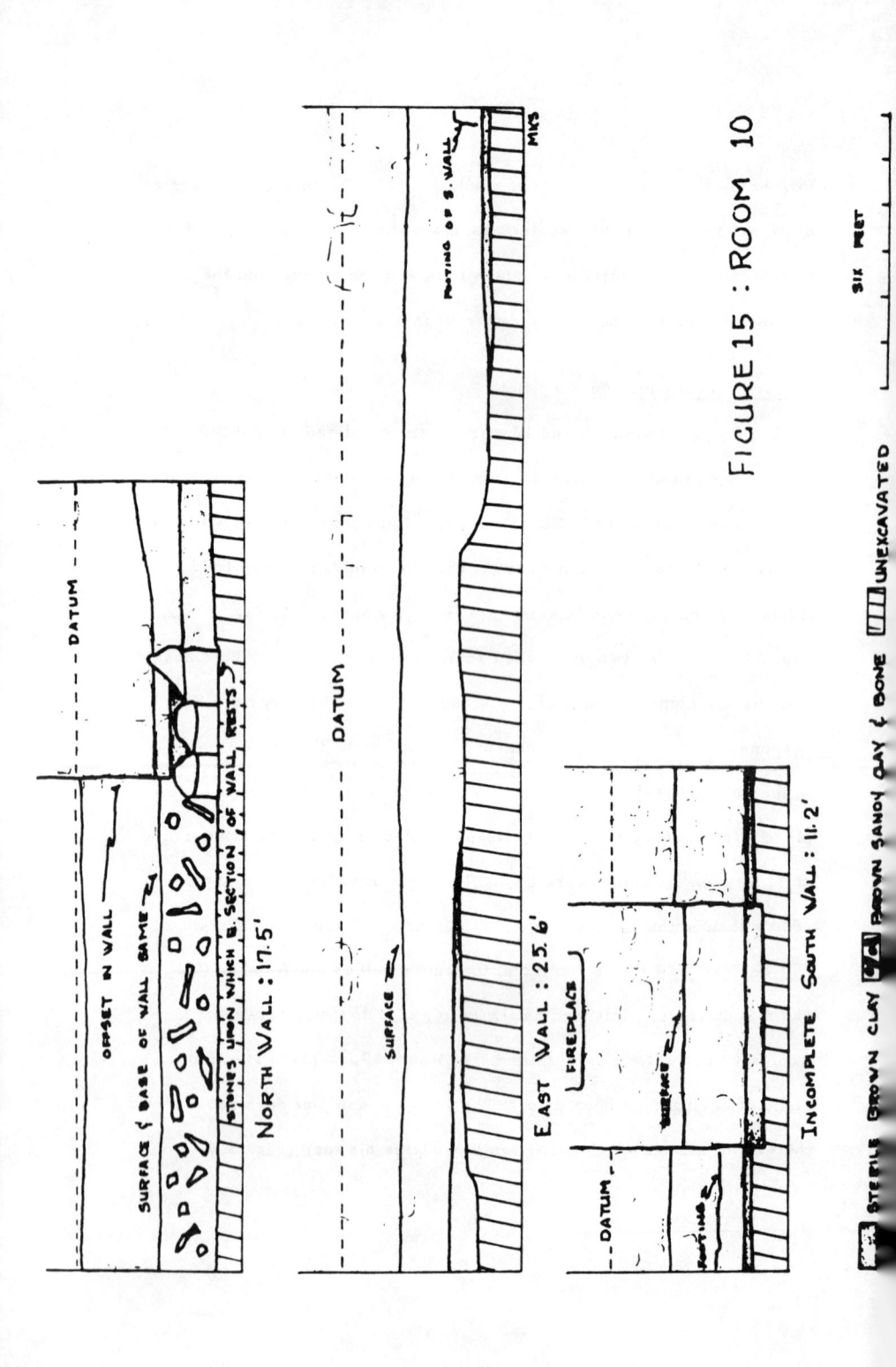

Stratigraphy, Features and Artifacts

Level 1 (0.0 - 0.5 foot) was represented by hummocks along the north wall, probably due to WPA trenching. Colonial artifacts in quantity were encountered from the surface down. Disturbed areas were located in the center of the room and in front of the fireplace, resulting in most of the mixture which occurred between nineteenth century and earlier artifacts. The bulk of the colonial artifacts and food bones were concentrated in the north half of the room, extending under the north wall to Room 8 and westward an undetermined distance. This midden material also extended southward into Room 12, although the deposit was not so thick there (Fig. 19).

A basin-shaped Indian firepit was located at a depth of 1.0 foot beneath the surface in the southeast quadrant of the room (Fig. 19). The diameter of the firepit was 1.3 feet and the depth from the one foot level was slightly over 0.3 foot. It was filled with charcoal, ash, and burned soil.

The fourth level (1.5 - 2.0 feet) was only partially dug when it was discovered that the only artifacts were in the west central part of the room. Some pieces of nineteenth century material were encountered at this level adjacent to the east wall, but their occurrence can be explained by the trenching connected with the reconstruction of the north half of that wall by the WPA. A concentration of plaster was uncovered at this level in the center of the room just

west of the measuring stake. It was carefully uncovered in the hope that it might reveal the outline of a jacal structure, but it seemed to be only spilled or dumped plaster, perhaps left over from the earliest plastering of mission structures.

In an effort to locate the western wall of the room, small trenches were initially dug out from the end of the north wall and the corresponding area of the south wall. The trenches were not dug by level, so that the artifacts from these areas are labeled separately. The trenches were so rich in artifacts, however, that the room was excavated for an additional two feet to the west. The extension was dug by levels and the artifacts recorded accordingly.

Artifact Inventories: Room 10

Level 1

Potsherds:
- 7 transfer printed
- 7 Mocha
- 3 stamped and painted edge
- 26 handpainted
- 1 Flintware
- 3 stenciled
- 52 unidentified white
- 1 luster
- 2 Ginger Beer
- 1 crockery

- 19 Mexican lead glazed
- 8 West Mexico polychrome
- 1 Mexican burnished red
- 13 Majolica
- 44 Indian

Glass:
- 8 oz. amber glass
- 4 oz. green glass
- window glass, patinated
- 15 oz. uncolored glass
- 14 sherds from glass cup

Rusted Metal:
- 4 oz. roofing tin
- 3 oz. nails
- bottle cap
- wire
- piece of heavy metal

Miscellaneous:	6 lbs. 6 oz. animal bone	blue glass trade bead
	8 oz. flint	copper pin with blue
	1 oz. wood	stone
	brick	river pebble
	mussel shell	2 gun flints
		(1) 12 guage shell

Level 2

Potsherds:	20 transfer printed	1 yellow-green glazed
	28 Mocha	1 Flintware
	10 stenciled	8 crockery
	12 stamped and painted edge	2 Ginger Beer
	71 handpainted	139 unidentified white
	2 Flown Blue	1 white with gold rim
	3 lusterware	

. . . .

	139 Mexican lead glazed	308 Indian
	5 West Mexico polychrome	
	2 Mexican burnished red	
	4 West Mexico slip-painted	
	56 Majolica	
Glass:	10 oz. amber glass	6 oz. aqua glass, patinated
	23 oz. green glass	2 lbs. 2 oz. uncolored
	3 oz. window glass, patinated	16 sherds from glass cup
Rusted Metal:	2 lbs. 8 oz. roofing tin	wire
	1 lb. nails	tin cans
	1 lb. 2 oz. unidentifiable	toy dish
	bridle fragment	ring
	wagon hub	knife
	scissor part	leaf-shaped spearhead
Miscellaneous:	125 lbs. 1 oz. animal bone	fragment of slate
	7 lbs. 12 oz. flint	2 glass marbles
	1 lb. 6 oz. brick	modern brass key
	2 oz. charcoal	lead pencil
	6 oz. shell: mussel and marine	brass band from lead pencil
	wood	harmonica vibrator
	9 gun flints	2 pearl buttons
	1 Abasolo point	1 copper button
	5 flint arrowheads	1 compound button
	Olivella shell bead	

127

2 copper crucifixes	(2) 45 cal. shells
mano fragment	1941 Mercury Head
brass handle from kettle	dime
5 fragments of copper	

Level 3

Potsherds:
4 transfer printed	19 handpainted
3 Mocha	37 unidentified white
2 stamped and painted edge	2 crockery
1 Flown Blue	7 Ginger Beer
1 porcelain with gold rim	8 stenciled
2 unidentified porcelain	

....

121 Mexican lead glazed	507 Indian
3 West Mexico polychrome	
6 Mexican burnished red	
unidentified clay object	
1 Puebla black luster	
75 Majolica	

Glass:
4 oz. window glass, patinated	8 oz. uncolored glass, patinated
5 oz. green glass	aqua glass
2 oz. amber glass	2 sherds from glass cup

Rusted Metal:
1 lb. 8 oz. roofing tin	bit
1 lb. 7 oz. unidentifiable	staple
6 oz. nails	piece of sword (?)
1 oz. wire	

Miscellaneous:
253 lbs. 12 oz. animal bone	4 Olivella shell beads
9 lbs. 12 oz. flint	2 other marine shell beads
1 lb. 2 oz. mortar and plaster	3 bird bone beads
12 oz. brick	2 glass trade beads
10 oz. ocher	black, faceted rosary bead
12 oz. shell: mussel and marine	bone tool
6 oz. charcoal	mussel shell with worked edge
2 smooth river pebbles	carved sandstone snail
6 pieces copper	4 gun flints
2 jeweled pendants	
handmade copper cufflinks	

128

	brass button glass button brass handle for lamp wick harmonica vibrator	15 flint arrowheads 2 dart points glass marble 2 plastic beads brass curtain ring aluminum lid

Level 4

Potsherds:	16 unidentified white crockery	Ginger Beer stenciled
	....	....
	5 Mexican lead glazed 7 Majolica	126 Indian
Glass:	green glass amber glass	window glass, patinated uncolored
Rusted Metal:	2 oz. total	
Miscellaneous:	30 lbs. 6 oz. animal bone 1 lb. 8 oz. flint mussel shell plaster charcoal	bird bone bead 4 glass trade beads 2 flint arrowheads 1 gun flint copper fragments

Level 5

Potsherds:	luster	
	....	3 Indian
Glass:	aqua glass	uncolored glass
Rusted Metal:	nail	
Miscellaneous:	2 Tortugas dart points piece asphalt flint mussel shell	

291

ROOM 11

<u>Physical Description</u> (interior dimensions)

North Wall: 11.5 feet long, 3.7 feet high and 1.3 feet thick.

East Wall: 26.3 feet long, 3.7 feet high and 2.1 feet thick at north corner to 3.7 feet high and 2.2 feet thick north of doorway, 5.0 feet high and 2.2 feet thick south of doorway, to 8.0 feet high and 2.2 feet thick north of window, 8.5 feet high and 2.2 feet thick south of window.

South Wall: 11.4 feet long, 5.0 feet high and 1.1 feet thick at east end, 4.5 feet high and 1.0 foot thick at west end.

West Wall: 26.5 feet long, 4.7 feet high and 2.3 feet thick at south end to 3.0 feet high and 2.1 feet thick at center, 3.3 feet high and 2.2 feet thick at north end.

Northwest-Southeast Diagonal: 28.6 feet.

Northeast-Southwest Diagonal: 29.0 feet.

The bases of all four walls lay at a depth of about one foot beneath the surface level of the room. The room was excavated only to the bases of the walls except for tests in the northwest corner and along the south wall which showed that those walls were lying directly upon sterile brown clay.

The east wall has a beveled door and a beveled window in it. The WPA plans show a niche in the wall between the door and the north corner which they apparently filled in. The WPA also rebuilt

FIGURE 16
ROOM 11

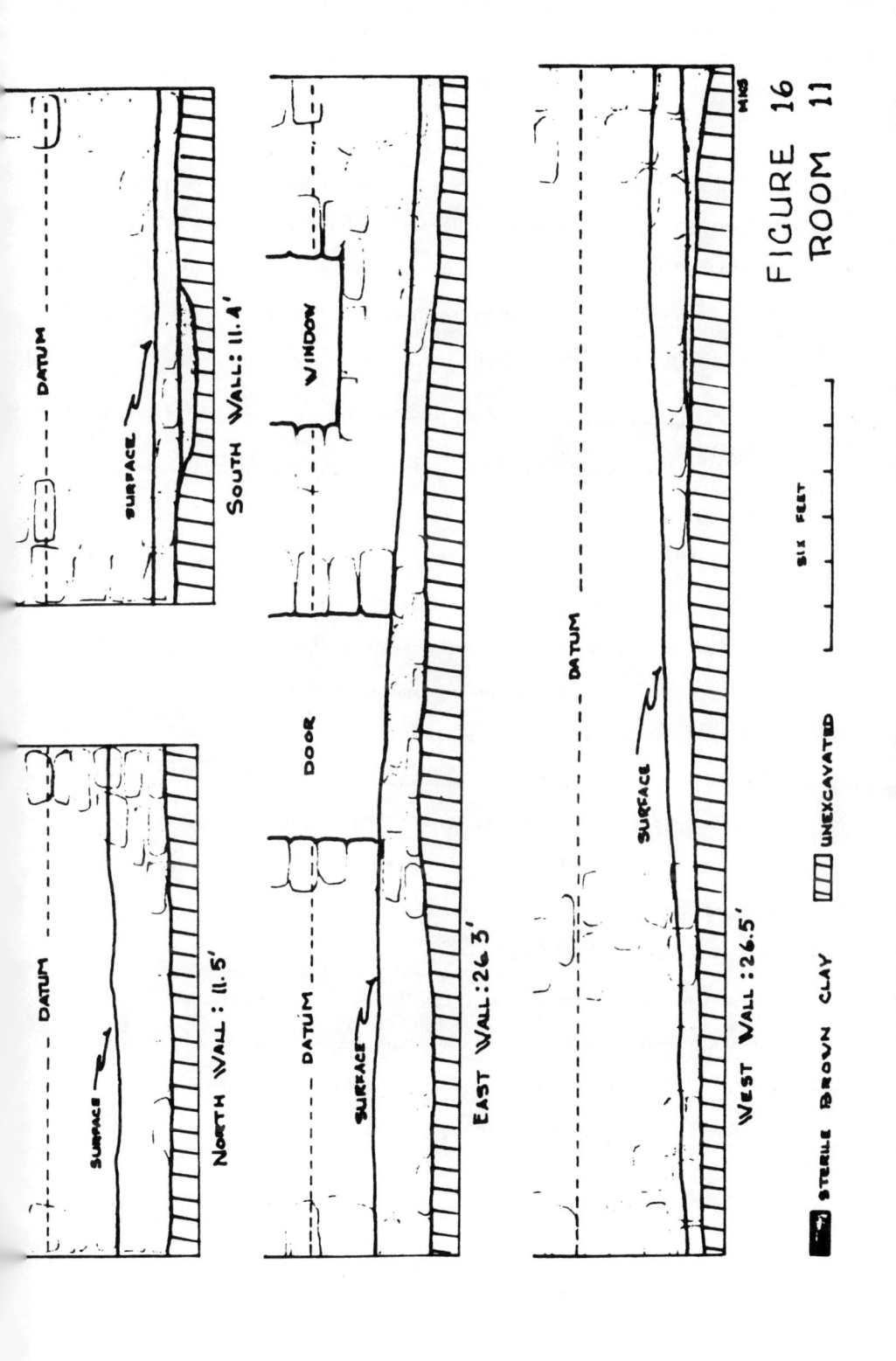

the northern half of the west wall. Room 11 retains plaster only on the exterior wall and it is thinner than that on the exterior wall of Room 13. The footing which underlies the south wall on the Room 13 side does not extend to the Room 11 side, indicating a rebuilding of the separating wall (see Figure 16) at some time.

Historic Documentation

In 1824, Room 11 was described as 9 varas long and 4 varas wide, with stone walls and a reed roof (Mission Record 15, Appendix A). Mission Record 6, dated December 27, 1823, is a petition for land and water by Maria del Carmen Calvillo in which she identifies herself as a resident of thirteen years and occupying a house which was built for the Indians and which she has completely restored. Maria Calvillo is also listed as a property owner in Mission Record 15. Neither document identifies her property, but Mission Record 27 (Appendix A), dated 1827, identifies her as the owner of Rooms 11 and 13 (Rooms 23 and 24 of Figure 6), and the Saucedo plat identifies her property as lying south of the gate and north of property owned by the Chaplain Maynes (Fig. 5 A). She still owned the property in 1847 (Fig. 7). Dona Calvillo's room (Rooms 11 and 13) is the second roofed structure shown in this section of the northwest wall in the Lungkwitz painting of the mid-nineteenth century (Plate 1). It had fallen into ruin by the time

Corner drew his map in 1890 (Fig. 5, B). He shows the west wall to be in ruins and since that was its condition when the WPA did its work, it was probably never rebuilt.

Stratigraphy, Features and Artifacts

Level 1 covered only the northern half of the room and Level 2 lay on sterile clay.

Artifact Inventories: Room 11

Level 1

Potsherds:	3 transfer printed	2 stenciled
	4 transfer and handpainted	90 unidentified white
	2 stamped and painted edge	8 crockery
	11 handpainted	2 Flintware
		1 yellow glazed
	....	
	8 Mexican lead glazed	1 Indian
	3 Majolica	
Glass:	1 lb. 14 oz. uncolored glass, patinated	9 oz. aqua glass
		2 oz. green glass
	12 oz. amber glass	cobalt blue glass
	1 oz. window glass, patinated	
Rusted Metal:	8 oz. nails	tin cans
	6 oz. roofing tin	nut
	2 railroad spikes	bottle opener
	3 bottle caps	wire
	unidentified pieces	lamp socket
Miscellaneous:	12 oz. animal bone	bone fork handle
	shell: mussel and marine	red plastic fragment
	8 oz. flint	wheel from toy
	4 oz. brick	body of porcelain doll
	hone (?)	(3) 12 guage shells
		(2) 16 guage shells
		1 unstamped shell case

Level 2

Potsherds:	21 transfer printed	8 stamped and painted edge
	25 Mocha	3 Flown Blue
	58 handpainted	1 yellow-green glazed
	229 unidentified white	1 yellow glazed
	11 Flintware	3 Ginger Beer
	15 crockery	5 fragments of flower pot
	4 lusterware	1 unidentified
	1 "Gaudy Japan"	

. . . .

	59 Mexican lead glazed	16 Indian
	2 Majolica	2 unidentified clay objects
Glass:	12 oz. aqua glass	3 lbs 12. oz. amber glass, patinated
	2 lbs. uncolored glass, patinated	1 lb. 5 oz. green glass
	4 oz. window glass	milk glass
Rusted Metal:	1 lb. 9 oz. nails	2 railroad spikes
	2 lbs. 8 oz. unidentifiable	2 bottle caps
	2 lbs. 8 oz. roofing tin	3 unidentified objects
	fragments of tin cans	nut
	buckle	wire
	chain link	fragment of window screen
Miscellaneous:	1 lb. 12 oz. animal bone	Flintware doorknob
	3 lbs. flint	2 china buttons
	2 lbs. 9 oz. plaster and mortar	handpainted stone jewelry set
	2 oz. mussel shell	harmonica vibrator
	2 worked sandstones	brass washer
	2 oz. brick	unidentified copper object
	charcoal	(3) 12 guage shells
	coal	(1) 16 guage shell
	copper fragment	

AN ARCHEOLOGICAL INVESTIGATION OF MISSION CONCEPCIÓN SAN ANTONIO, TEXAS

by Dan Scurlock and Daniel E. Fox

with appendixes by Viola Rawn and James Hoggins

Edited by Curtis Tunnell and Kathy Freydenfeldt

Office of the State Archeologist
TEXAS HISTORICAL COMMISSION

January 1977
Austin

Plan of Excavations and Map of Site

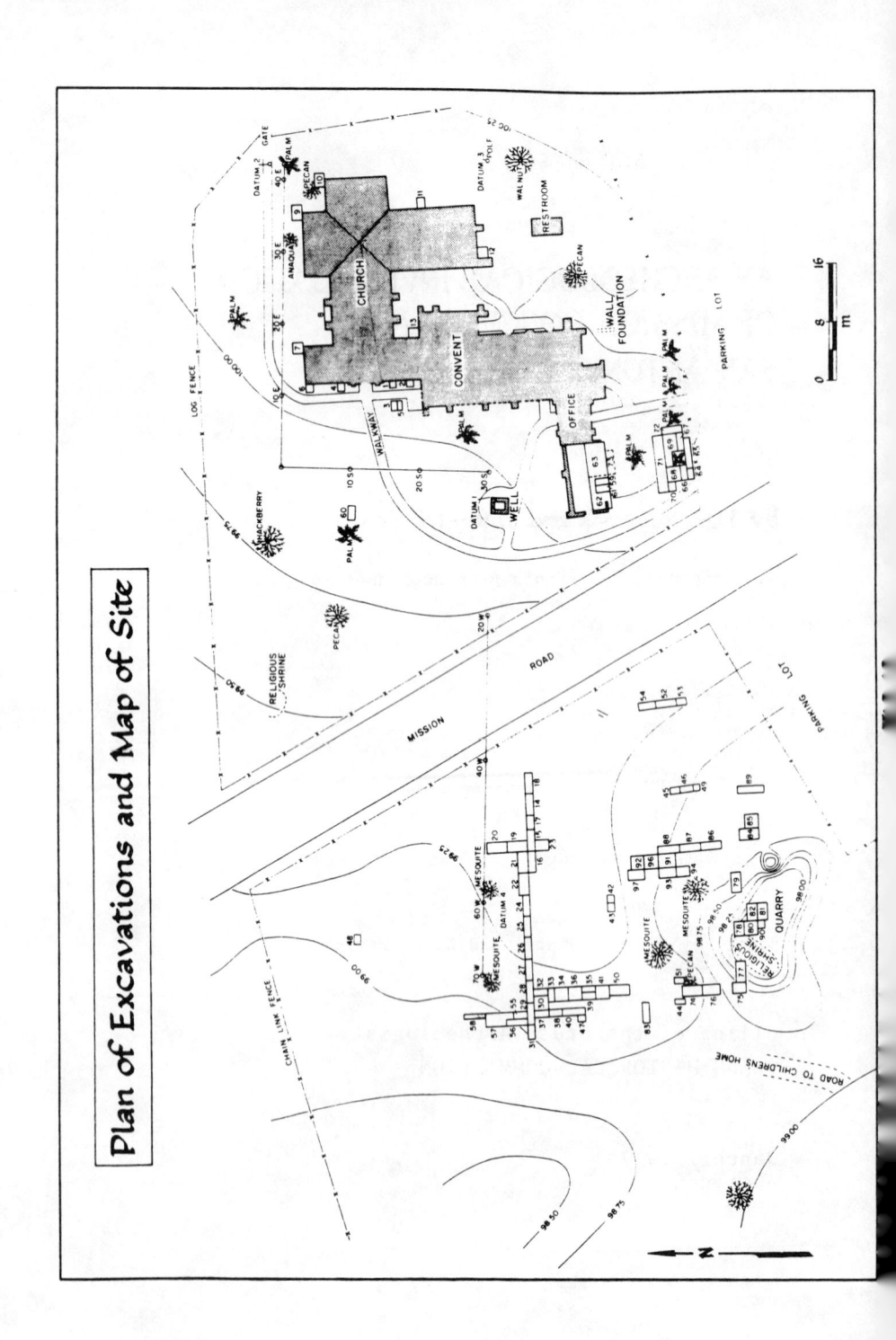

ARCHEOLOGICAL INVESTIGATION

Field Methodology and Laboratory Procedure

A primary purpose of the archeological investigations at Mission Concepción was to assemble information pertaining to foundation-moisture conditions of the extant structures at the site. A second purpose was to locate and study the remains of portions of the compound wall and other features west of Mission Road.

A week prior to initiation of the excavations on September 27, 1971, north-south and east-west base lines of wooden stakes were placed on the site with the aid of a transit. The "zero" or base stake was placed 12 m northwest of the northwest corner of the church (Fig. 10), and stakes were driven every 10 m along each line. These stakes were used as datum points in triangulating the location of extant structures, test pits and other features at the site.

Vertical control of the excavations was maintained with the use of a transit and stadia rod. The primary datum point was a large wire nail driven into the tufa limestone wall which forms the northeast corner of the surface enclosure of the well (Fig. 10). This datum was assigned an arbitrary elevation of 100.0 m. Three other datum points located at strategic points on the site also were established.

Test pits excavated during the fall of 1971 were located at selected points along the outside wall of the church to obtain foundation-moisture information. Other test pits were located west of Mission Road in search of the remains of the west compound wall. Additional testing was done in this area, and in and around the quarry, and between the parking lot and office on the south side of the site during March 1972 (Fig. 11). The size of each test pit was determined primarily by what type of information or feature was being sought, and in part by limitations imposed by obstacles such as walls, trees or walks. Most test pits were excavated in 15-cm or 30-cm levels; some were excavated by "cultural units," i.e., deposits between two prepared floors or materials associated with particular features.

Excavated soil was screened, for the most part, through quarter- or half-inch hardware cloth. The artifacts, bones, and soil samples from each excavation unit were placed in a bag labeled with the site name and number, horizontal and vertical provenience, name(s) of the excavator(s), and date excavated. Soil and charcoal samples were chosen at random, placed in plastic bags or aluminum foil, and labeled appropriately.

Excavated floor levels, cultural features and other data were recorded by standard archeological methods, involving the use of field notes, daily

Fig. 11. Excavating Test Pit 74 in west compound area

log, photographs, stratigraphic profiles, measured drawings, and detailed topographic maps. These records are on file at the Office of the State Archeologist, Texas Historical Commission, Austin.

The bags of recovered artifacts, bones, and soil samples were transported to the Austin laboratory to be cleaned, catalogued and inventoried. The bones were analyzed at the Vertebrate Paleontology Laboratory, Balcones Research Center, a part of the University of Texas at Austin. Some heavily rusted gun parts were cleaned at the Antiquities Conservation Laboratory at the Balcones Research Center.

Soils

Twenty-nine soil samples were collected during the excavation of test pits in the west compound and in the church areas. The following is the analysis and interpretation of these samples from Mission Concepción. Table 1 gives the provenience, color, horizon designation, and texture of each sample.

WEST COMPOUND AREA

The soils of the west compound area of Mission Concepción are characterized by shallow, weakly developed horizons riddled with travertine fragments from the nearby quarry. Accumulations of calcium carbonate are notable as is the lack of B horizon development. Profiles exhibit A-C horizon development which is indicative of young soils or soils rendered shallow by geologic, climatogical or other ecological factors. In the case of the compound area, the presence of travertine bedrock close to the surface acts as a retardant to soil development. Much of the limestone in the soil is a result of the decomposition of the travertine, a natural phenomenon that was accelerated by quarrying during the Spanish Colonial period and more recent times.

The soil of the compound area has been affected greatly by human habitation and use. Invariably, midden areas are characterized by a dark brown color, probably a result of organic enrichment (Fig. 12). Midden areas are included in the A horizon designation. Portions of the A horizon which do not exhibit midden characteristics are decidedly lighter in color. The soil also has received inclusions such as adobe brick and mortar fragments.

The quarry area shows evidence of extensive soil mixing and disturbance. At least some of the soil deposition can be attributed to erosion. In addition, quarrying practices undoubtedly have fostered the upheaval of the A horizon and increased the mixing (Fig. 13).

FIG. 12

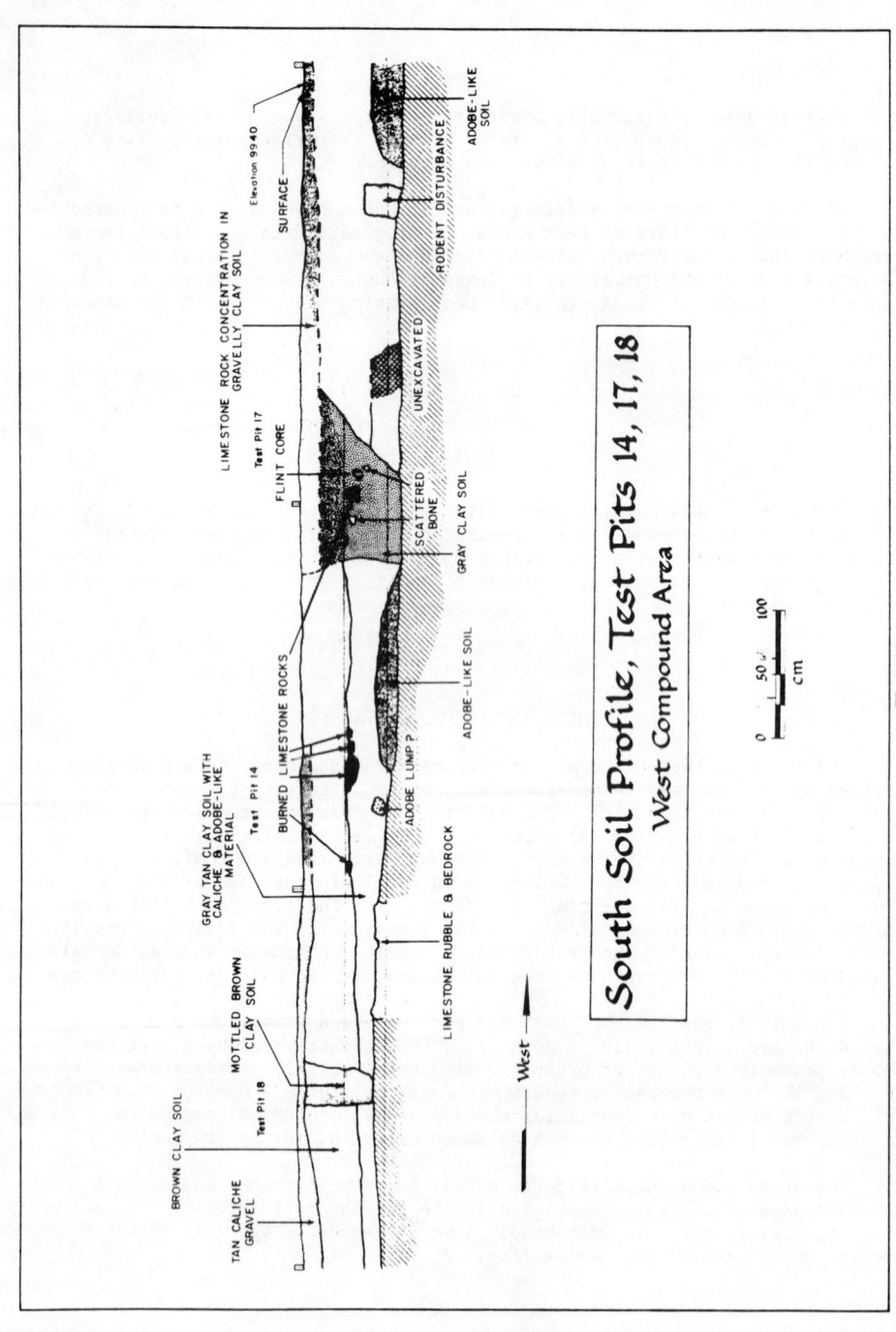

FIG. 13

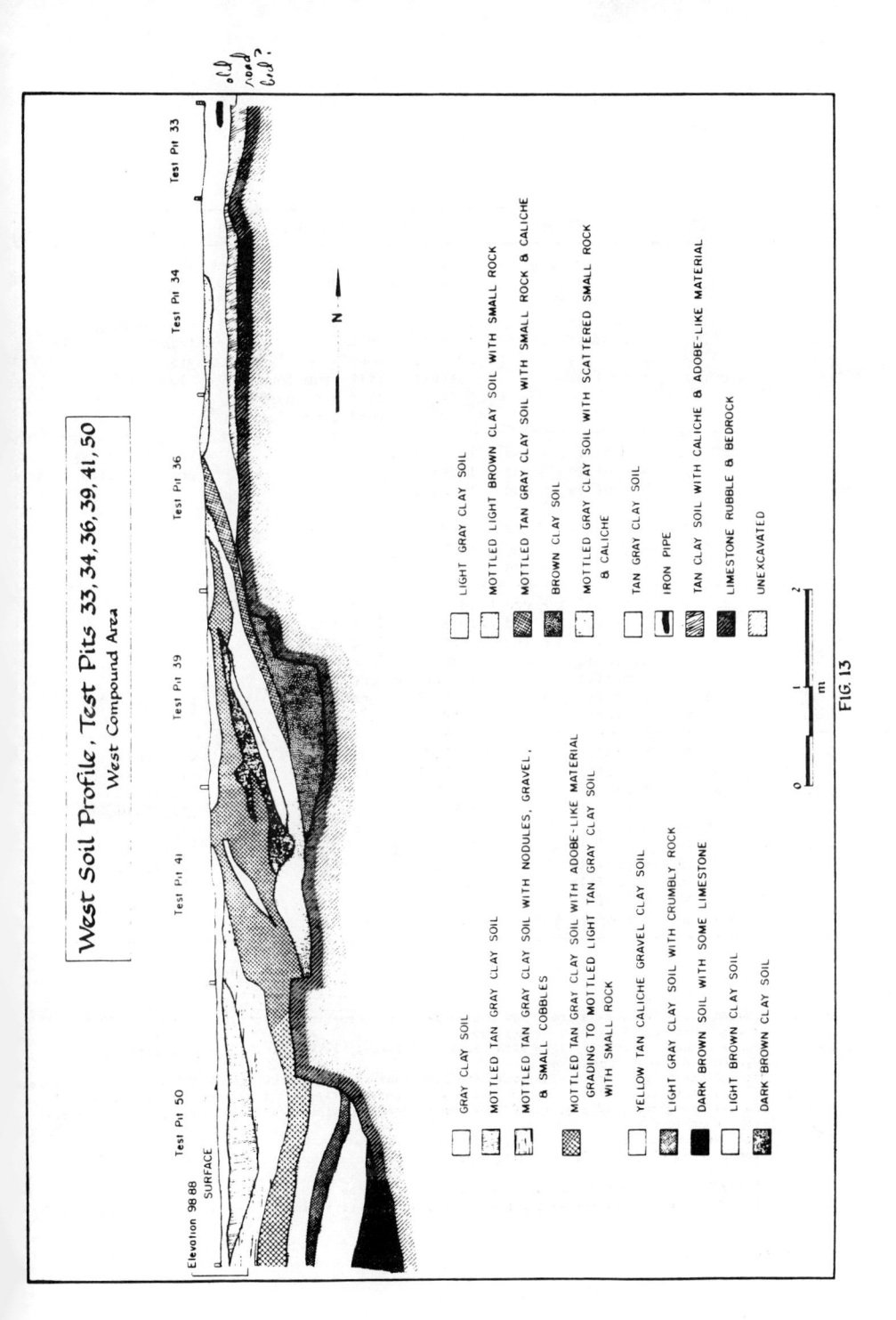

Table 1. Soil samples analysis.

T.P.	SAMPLE	ELEV.	PROVENIENCE	DRY COLOR*	HORIZON DESIGNATION	TEXTURE
11	1	100.40	north profile	10YR7/1	Zone 2	clay loam
11	2	100.29	n profile, upper pit	10YR6/1	Zone 2	clay loam
11	3	100.04	n profile	10YR7/2	Zone 2	clay loam
11	4	99.87	n profile	10YR7/1	Zone 6	friable, granular
11	5	99.58	n profile	10YR7/1	Zone 4	granular
11	6	99.54	n profile	10YR6/1	fill from foundation pit; possible Zone 2 origins	clay loam
19	1	99.39	w profile, s end	10YR7/1	Zone 4	friable, rocky
19	2	99.29	w profile, s end	10YR6/1	Zone 1	gravelly clay loam
19	3	99.17	w profile, s end	10YR6/1	Zone 3A	clay loam, granular, rocky
19	4	99.01	w profile, s end	10YR5/1	Zone 2 (midden)	clay loam
19	5	98.85	w profile, s end	10YR5/1	Zone 1	clay loam
19	6	98.72	w profile, s end	10YR6/1	Zone 2	clay loam
50	1	100.08	s profile, e end	10YR6/1	Zone 3	clay loam, rocky
50	2	99.93	s profile, e end	10YR7/2	Zone 3	clay loam, rocky
50	3	99.68	s profile, e end	10YR7/1	Zone 3A	clay loam, rocky
50	4	99.58	s profile, e end	10YR7/1	Zone 4	friable, gravelly
50	5	99.08	s profile, e end	10YR5/3	Zone 2	clay loam
50	6	98.68	s profile, e end	10YR6/1	Zone 4	friable, rocky
50	7	98.53	s profile, e end	10YR7/1	Zone 4	friable, rocky
82	1	98.96	s profile	10YR5/1	Zone 2	clay loam
82	2	98.86	s profile	10YR3/1	Zone 2	clay loam, gravelly
82	3	98.76	s profile	10YR5/1	Zone 1	clay loam
82	4	98.66	s profile	10YR4/1	Zone 2	clay loam
82	5	98.56	s profile	10YR6/1	Zone 2	clay loam
82	6	98.41	s profile	10YR5/1	Zone 2 (midden)	clay loam
82	7	98.19	s profile	10YR5/2	Zone 3A	rocky, caliche
82	8	98.06	s profile	10YR5/1	Zone 2	clay loam
82	9	97.91	s profile	10YR6/1	Zone 2 (midden)	clay loam
82	10	97.36	s profile	10YR5/1	Zone 2 (midden)	clay loam

Zone 1   Gray tan clay loam, relatively low concentrations of rock or caliche inclusions; 10YR5/2-10YR6/1 range; A horizon, area of root activity
Zone 2   Medium to dark brown clay loam with possible mottling; 10YR7/2-10YR5/1 range; midden areas exhibit dark brown hues; A horizon
Zone 3   Mottled tan to gray brown clay loam with limestone and caliche debris; 10YR7/2 to 10YR4/1 range; A-C transitional horizon. Zone 3A has higher concentrations of limestone and caliche inclusions
Zone 4   Tan caliche gravel; 10YR7/1 to 10YR5/2 range; horizon evincing weak calcium carbonate accumulation; C horizon
Zone 5   Light yellow tan adobe soil; culturally induced inclusions
Zone 6   Limestone rubble, very little soil; 10YR7/1; C horizon

Test Pit 11 samples illustrate a representative profile from the church grounds.
Test Pits 19, 50 and 82 are in the west compound area and are representative of the various profiles found in that area.

*Munsell Color Chart

CHURCH GROUNDS

Soil from within the area surrounding and immediately adjacent to the church is characterized by deeper profiles with thicker A horizon and considerable mixing in some units (Figs. 14-16). The most typical profile includes the A horizon, a medium to dark brown clay loam, underlain by a mottled A-C horizon which grows progressively lighter in color with depth. Less limestone rubble occurs in these profiles, but evidence of human activity extends deep into the profile.

At least one burial and several midden areas were encountered during excavation. Midden areas appear somewhat darker in color (Fig. 15), mirroring the situation in the compound area; however, the disturbed nature of the deposits has lessened the visual impact of such an association. Adobe inclusions are common as are areas of concentrated plaster fragments.

Features

For the purposes of this investigation, features are defined as any specific physical remains or soil modification which has resulted from human activity. Such evidence includes foundations, walls, burials, middens, post molds, hearths, and quarried limestone bedrock. In all, 17 features at Mission Concepción were recorded with photographs, drawings, notes and transit readings. Features will be discussed in the order in which they were encountered during the excavations.

FEATURE 1
(church foundation)

This feature was exposed in Test Pits 1, 2, 4, and 6-10 (Figs. 14, 15). The foundation is constructed of random rubble (unshaped) limestone varying from fist size to 50 cm in length, joined with lime mortar.(Fig. 16). The foundations project outward from the face of the main wall an average of 25 cm, except at the northeast corner and wall of the north bell tower where they protrude 70-85 cm. The depth of the foundation averages 1.12 m. In all but one location the foundation slopes slightly inward from top to bottom. Only in Test Pit 11, near the northeast corner of the apse, was there evidence of a foundation trench (Fig. 17).

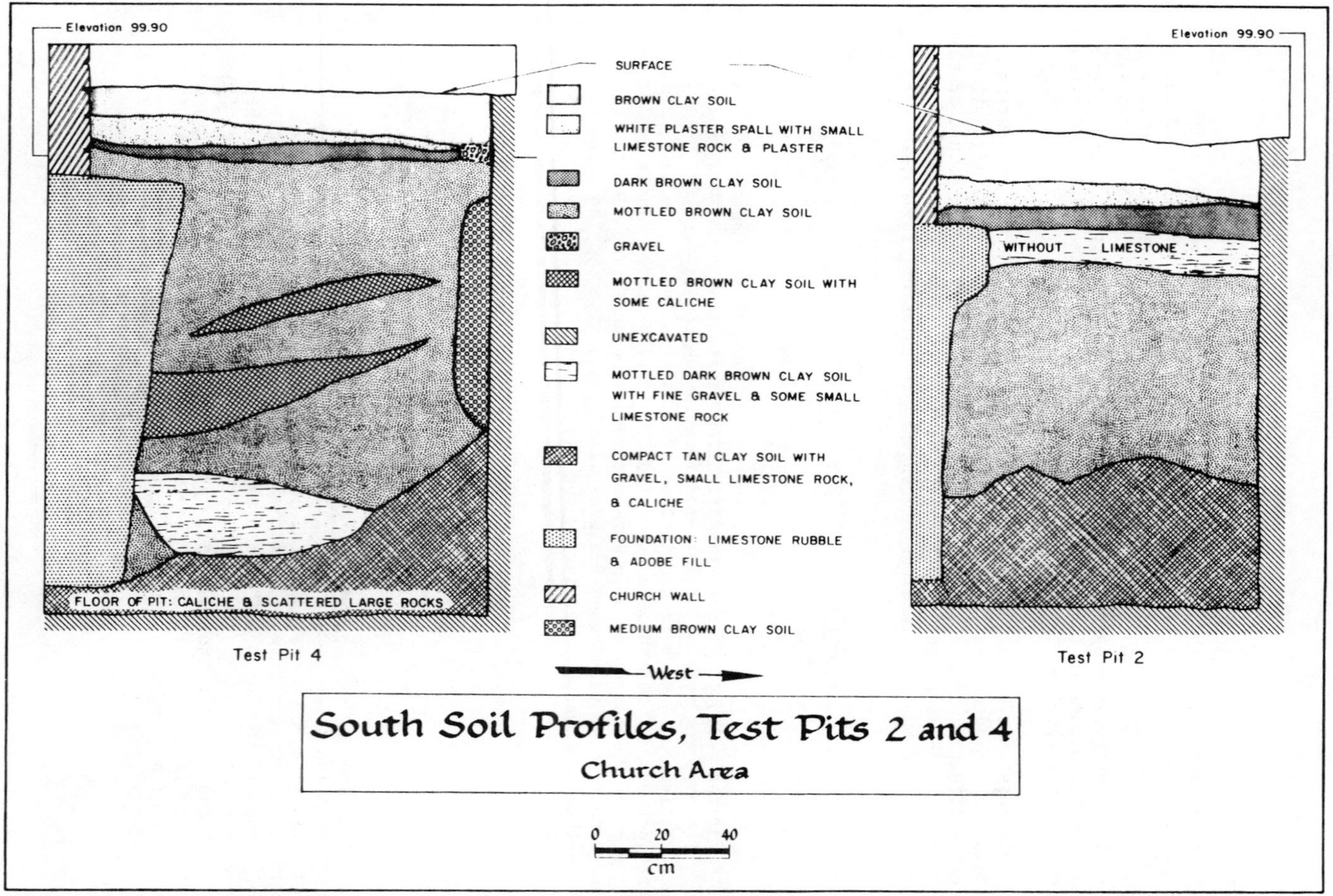

FIG. 14. South Soil Profiles, Test Pits 2 and 4, Church Area

FIG. 15. West Soil Profile, Test Pit 9, Church Area

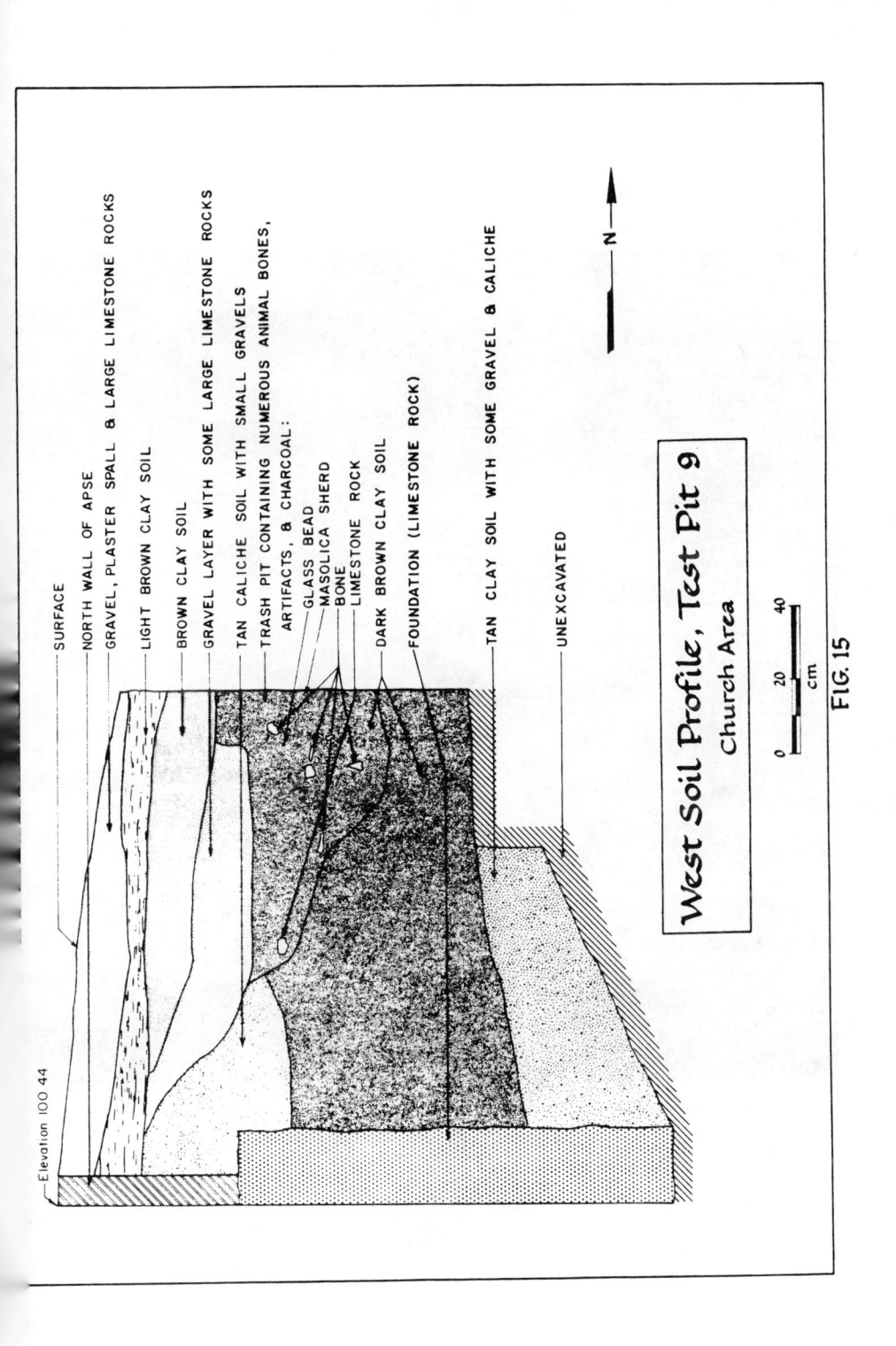

Fig. 16. Feature 1, church foundation, Test Pit 1

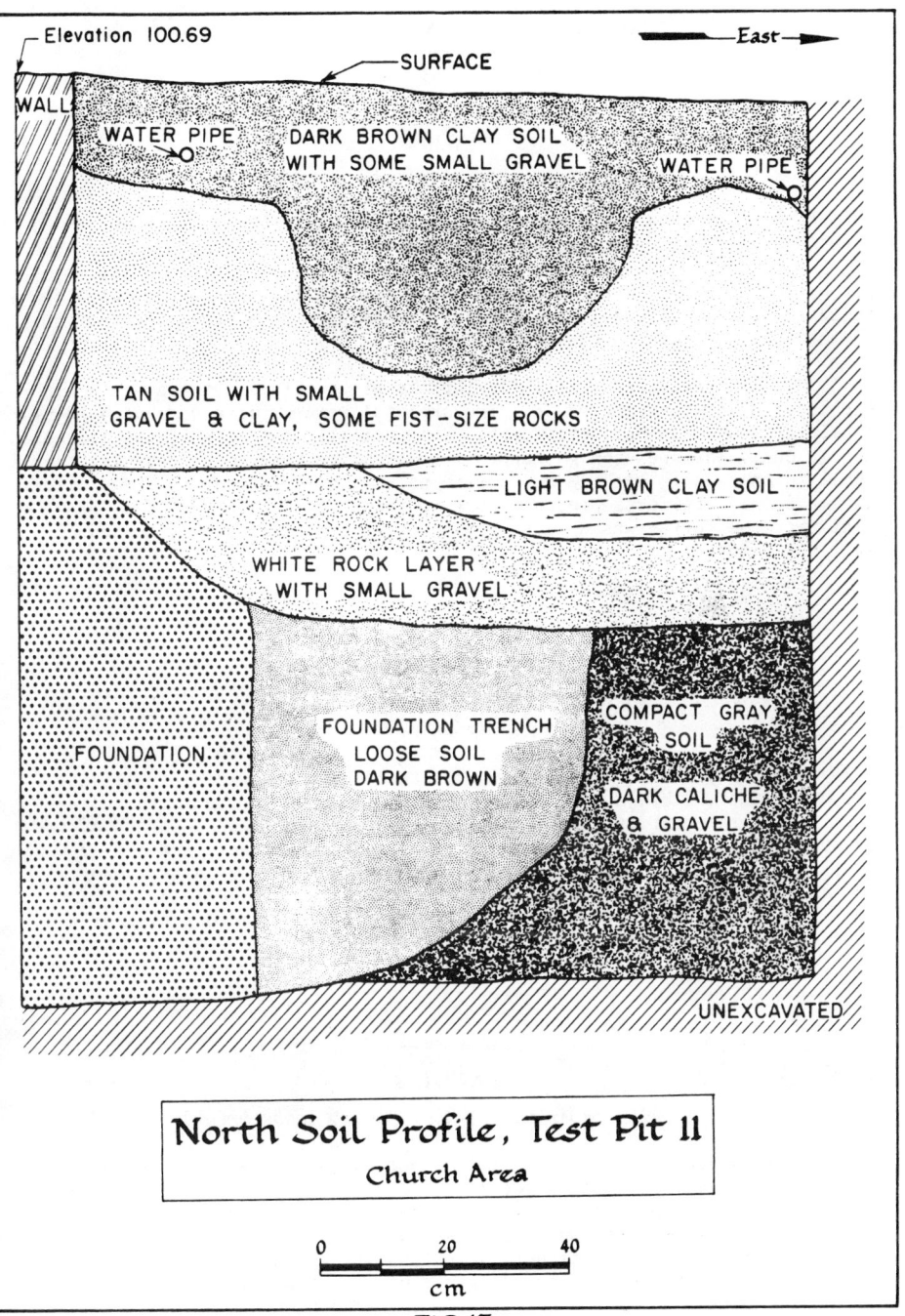

FIG. 17. North Soil Profile, Test Pit 11, Church Area.

FEATURE 2

(plaster floor and infant burial)

At elevation 99.77 in Test Pit 8, a light tan plaster floor was found between the two outside nave wall buttresses against the north side of the church. In the approximate center of this excavation unit was a rectangular pit with rounded corners and a brown clay soil fill. The purpose of a floor at this location is puzzling. Perhaps it was part of a structure built against the wall of the church.

The fill was excavated, following the pit outline, until a burial was encountered at elevation 99.36. The skeletal remains were very damaged by two large roots and had deteriorated substantially due to soil and moisture conditions. The skeleton was approximately 62 cm long, oriented with the skull to the west. Machine-cut coffin nails and a fragment of fired brick were the only artifacts present. Due to the condition of the bones and the fact that the burial was a late-19th-century Christian burial, the bones were not removed.

FEATURE 3

(midden)

This was perhaps the most concentrated midden excavated at the site. The dark, mottled brown clay midden soil is confined to the north and west sections of the test pit (Fig. 15), located at the northeast corner of the transept of the church. Among the artifacts recovered were two carved bone crosses, bone beads, majolica, lead-glazed earthenware, a large number of Indian earthenware sherds, and several arrowpoints. In addition, a large number of animal bones were retrieved. The midden extended from near the surface at elevation 100.44, to 99.54 elevation.

FEATURE 4

(possible post molds, clay floor, adobe brick)

In the south half of Test Pit 12, near the south wall of the sacristy stairwell, a clay floor and three possible post molds were found at elevation 100.19. To the north 45 cm was an adobe brick, approximately 40 cm long and 25 cm wide. The possible post molds vary from 10 to 17 cm in diameter. Several colonial artifacts were found, including two majolica sherds, two fired brick fragments, and fragments of two triangular arrowpoints, along with bone and mussel shell fragments. The elements of this feature might have been associated with the wall foundation found just to the south by the WPA excavations of the early 1930s (Fig. 3).

FEATURE 5
(midden and possible hearth)

An extensive concentration of artifacts and animal bones was found from the surface to 80 cm below ground level in Test Pit 13, located under the former stone stairway leading to the belfry of the south bell tower. In the northwest corner of the test pit, at 46 cm below surface, a concentration of charcoal, burned bone, and a single burned limestone fragment ca. 10 cm long were found. The concentration appeared to continue beyond the north wall of the test pit.

FEATURE 6
(midden and hearths)

Between 98.94 and 99.94 elevations in Test Pits 14 and 17 located in the compound area west of Mission Road (Fig. 12), a fairly dense concentration of European and Indian colonial artifacts was encountered. A hearth of concentrated burned limestone rock and river cobbles, 10-14 cm long, was present. Also noted in the north and south profiles at the junction of the two test pits was the outline of a ditch, possibly an acequia, or an erosional feature, filled with mottled gray clay. The midden deposit was of the characteristic brown clay soil.

FEATURE 7
(midden and hearths)

This midden, located in Test Pits 19, 20, and 21 (east end) a few meters north and northwest of Feature 6, is similar and conceivably could be part of the same midden. Two round hearths, dish-shaped in cross section, were found at 98.87 and 99.00 elevations, slightly overlapping horizontally. Burned limestone, bone and charcoal constituted each hearth. The brown clay soil type again was present in the midden. Artifacts dating from the colonial period, such as majolica, lead-glazed earthenware, Indian-made earthenware, and an arrowpoint, were recovered.

FEATURE 8
(midden)

A concentration of late-19th- and early-20th-century artifacts associated with several large limestone rocks was found in the west end of Test Pit 25 and the east end of Test Pit 26 at ca. 99.05 elevation. The soil was mottled gray clay with considerable ash scattered through the deposit. Located in the west compound area, this feature probably represents a refuse accumulation or dump site.

FEATURE 9
(limestone rubble concentration and travertine limestone bedrock)

In Test Pits 28-30 and 32-40 of the west compound area, between elevations 98.62 and 98.92, extensive limestone rubble and travertine bedrock were exposed (Figs. 13, 18, 19). The travertine is part of the same formation utilized in construction at the mission and obtained from the quarry located just south of Feature 9. The limestone rubble originated probably from quarrying activities. Artifacts associated with this feature are predominantly colonial—majolica, Indian earthenware and Indian lithic material.

FEATURE 10
(midden)

Just north of the quarry depression in Test Pits 42 and 43, from the surface (99.38) to 99.19 elevation, a distinct concentration of late-19th- and early-20th-century artifacts was encountered. The soil type was a mottled gray clay.

FEATURE 11
(midden)

The excavation of Test Pit 44, located a short distance northeast of the quarry depression, resulted in the recovery of several hundred animal bones and colonial and post-colonial artifacts from a mottled gray clay soil in the upper third of the test and from a brown clay soil in the lower portion.

FIG 18

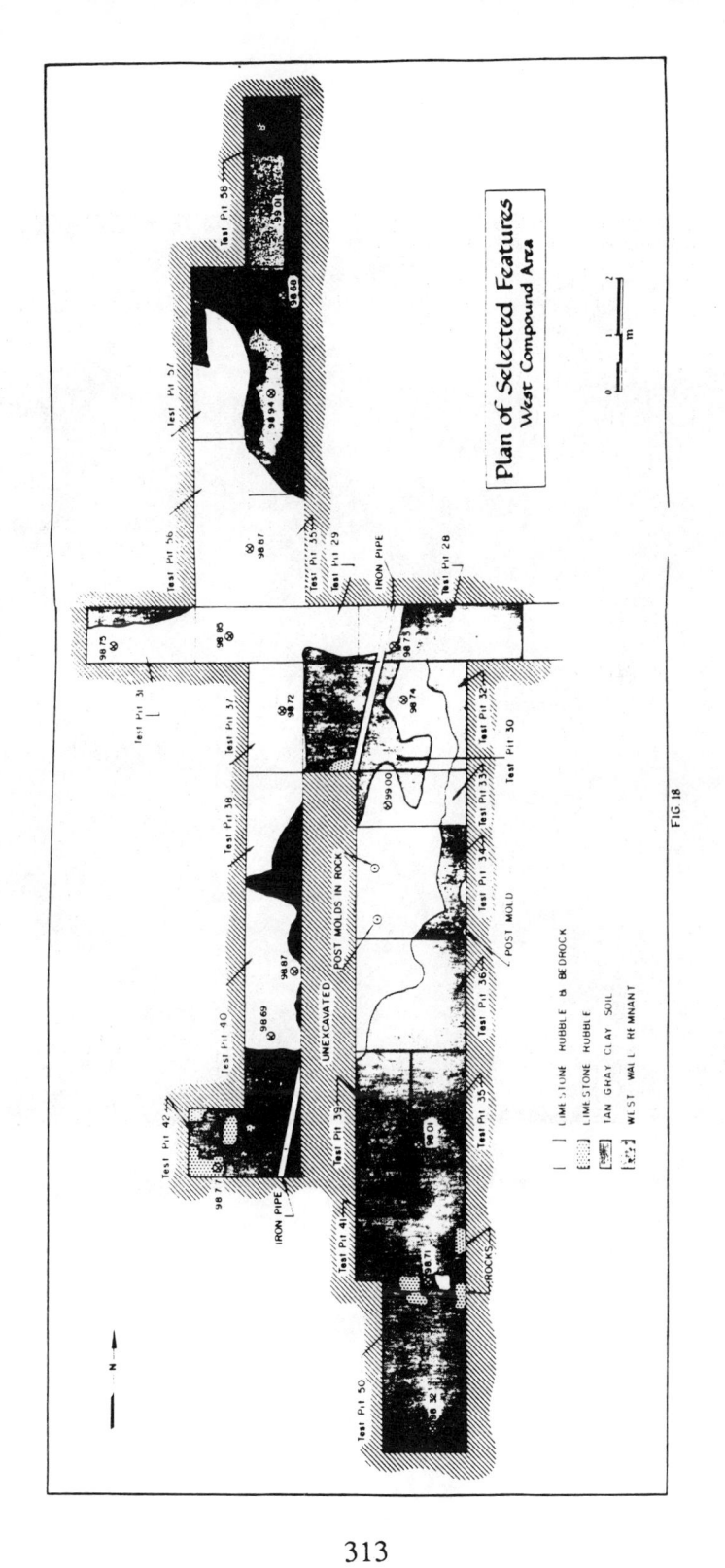

Fig. 19. Feature 9, quarry rubble, west compound area

FEATURE 12
(limestone wall remains)

Two aligned sections of a wall were found beneath the grass sod in Test Pits 57 and 58 in the west compound area (Figs. 18, 20). Respectively, one section 0.5x2.3 m and one 0.7x2 m were encountered at elevations 98.94 and 99.00. Construction material consisted primarily of large, flat, irregularly shaped limestone rocks. Associated with the wall remnants were a small number of colonial-period artifacts, predominantly Indian-made earthenware sherds. The wall alignment is located about 88 m west of the front of the church, only 30 ft more than the 250 ft estimated by Habig (1971:plan of square) to be the distance from the church to the west wall of the mission compound.

FEATURE 13
(adobe brick walls and plaster floor)

A section of a wall constructed of adobe or sun-dried bricks and associated with a plaster floor was found in Test Pits 59 and 61 (Fig. 21). These dark brown clay bricks, joined together by a contrasting tan mortar, were about 40 cm long. One complete specimen measured 20 cm in width. The west face of the wall was covered with a thin light tan plaster. Adjacent to this wall was a light tan plaster floor (elev. 99.98) and two adobe bricks abutting the north-south wall. Disturbances around this feature precluded definition of its original function, but probably it was the remains of an adobe structure dating from the early Spanish occupation of the site.

FEATURE 14
(limestone wall enclosure and burned area)

Located in the southwest corner of the ruined room which adjoins the west side of the present park office, excavation of Test Pit 62 encountered the lower remnant of an "L"-shaped limestone wall at elevation 98.88. The west side of this wall is aligned with the west wall of the ruin, while the second side, or north side of the feature, is situated at a right angle to the west wall, forming an enclosure from which a large number of late-19th- and early-20th-century artifacts were recovered, along with abundant ash and charcoal, between elevations 98.41 and 98.21.

Also within the enclosure, at elevation 98.31, was a dark, black orange, semicircular outline on a possibly plastered floor. This burned area may represent a corner fireplace.

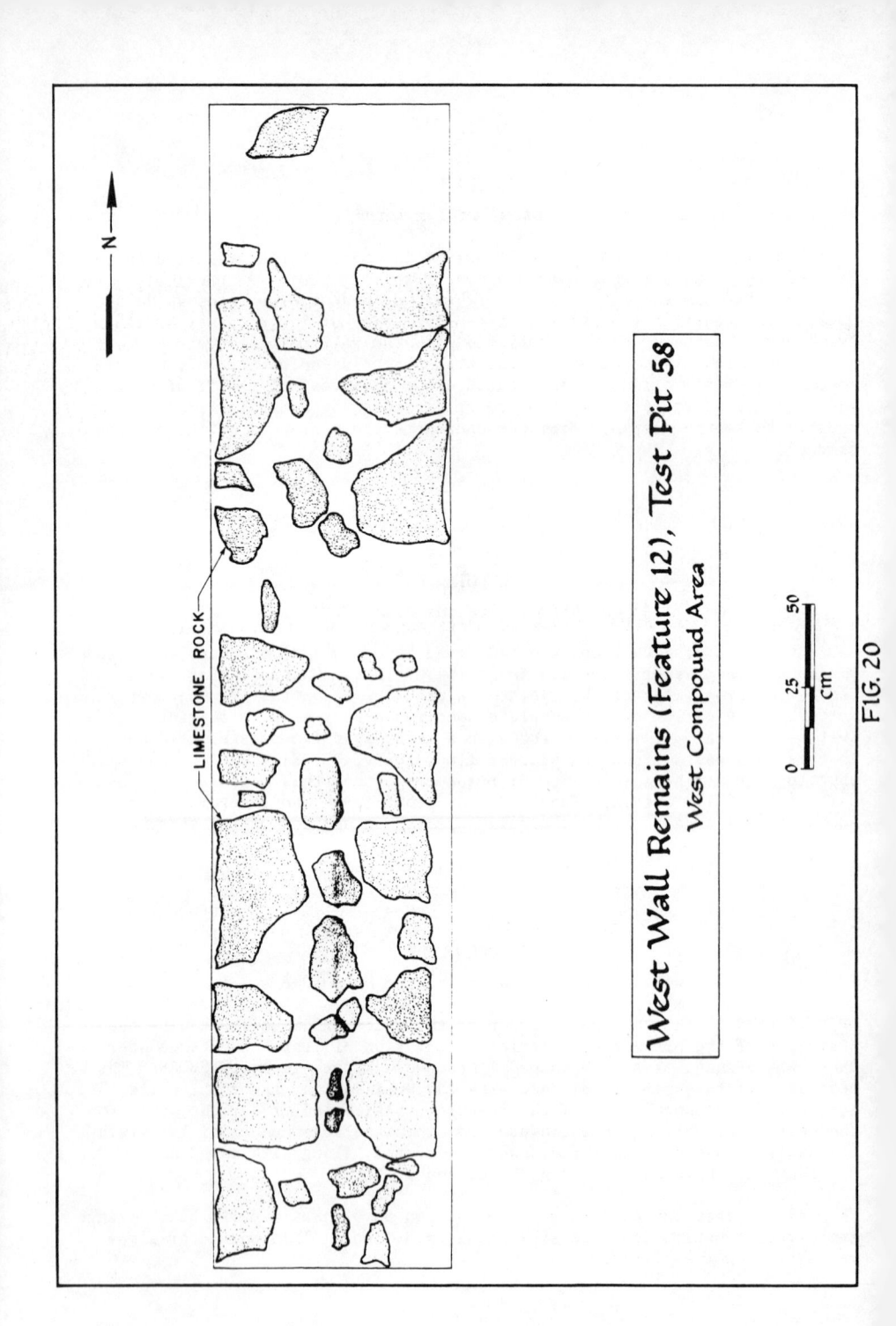

West Wall Remains (Feature 12), Test Pit 58
West Compound Area

FIG. 20

Fig. 21. Feature 13, adobe brick walls and plaster floor, office area

Along the west edge of this feature and beneath the present restored west wall of the ruin (next to the park office), an adobe wall or foundation was found at elevation 98.68, which extends the 2-m length of the test pit. Unfortunately, these features could not be associated with a particular cultural period because of the disturbed nature of the deposits within the limestone enclosure and the possibility of contamination by late Anglo-American refuse deposition.

FEATURE 15

(plaster floor, post support?)

These features were encountered at elevation 99.71 in the east portion of Test Pit 62. The floor consisted of a typical tan plaster. On the south edge of the test pit, a shallow depression ca. 15 cm in diameter was found in the plaster. It is possible that this depression and the plaster floor are associated with Feature 14, although there was a difference of 17 cm elevation between the floors of the two features.

FEATURE 16

(limestone wall and plaster floors)

A section of limestone wall and associated clay and plaster floors were uncovered in Test Pits 64-72 (Fig. 22), south of the park office and between the two sidewalks leading from the parking lot. The wall was oriented generally east-west and the floors were located south of it. The horizontal extent of the feature could not be traced by additional excavations because of obstructions such as sidewalks, trees, and a log fence. This same area was excavated by the WPA in the early 1930s and the foundations of a square structure were uncovered (Fig. 3). Two different tan plaster floors were found at elevations averaging 100.00-100.20. Generally, the artifacts associated with the upper plaster floor seem to date from the early to mid-19th century, while those from the lower plaster floor are primarily from the 18th century. The entire feature may have been part of the Indian quarters which lined the south side of the mission compound (Habig 1968:139).

South Wall Remains and Plaster Floors (Feature 16), Test Pit 71
Office Area

FIG 22

FEATURE 17

(quarry and associated middens)

Test Pits 75-82 and 90 were placed in the quarry depression located in the southwest portion of the mission compound area. The test pits were excavated to check the depth of the quarried bedrock, to study the cultural material deposited in the quarry, and to examine any existing tool marks to determine, it was hoped, the types of tools employed and the size of stone blocks removed.

In Test Pit 82, quarried bedrock was found at elevation 97.25; in Test Pit 80, it was reached at 98.19. At these locations the bedrock floor has an uneven surface, and a narrow, curving wall-like remnant of travertine has been sculptured out of the bedrock. The top of this feature was encountered at elevation 98.72.

Dark midden soils in Test Pits 78-82 and 90 contained colonial-period artifacts, while the upper levels (0-20 cm) yielded predominantly 19th-century and 20th-century cultural material. A typical cut in the travertine bedrock is illustrated in Figure 23. The quarry depression is roughly triangular in shape, about 28 m long at its greatest dimension.

Fig. 23. Cut in bedrock, quarry (Feature 17)

ARCHEOLOGICAL RESEARCH AT 41SA25,

MISSION DOLORES DE LOS AIS

1977

A Preliminary Report

submitted to

the Texas Historical Commission

by

James E. Corbin

Stephen F. Austin State University

Nacogdoches, Texas

ACKNOWLEDGEMENTS

All of the work detailed in the following report was made possible by significant contributions of interested Texans, both at the local and state level. The excavations would not have been possible without the permission and cooperation of the landowners, Mr. and Mrs. David Maxwell. Funding and services significant to the accomplishment of the tasks carried out were contributed by the citizens of San Augustine, Texas, the San Augustine Historical Society, the City of San Augustine, the Texas Historical Foundation, the Texas Historical Commission, Southland Paper Mills, the Stephen F. Austin Archeological Field School, the SFASU Anthropology Club, and the Nacogdoches Archeological Society. Of primary significance was the money ($7,000) raised by the citizens of San Augustine and donated to the San Augustine Historical Society to contract with the SFASU Anthropology Program for six weeks' archeological research in the summer of 1977. All of these contributors are to be commended for their interest and investment of time, effort and money.

ARCHEOLOGICAL RESEARCH AT 41SA25, MISSION DOLORES DE LOS AIS
1977

During 1976, student volunteers from Stephen F. Austin State University conducted cursory excavations at the supposed site of Mission Dolores de los Ais. This work comprised approximately 8 working days at the site. As a result of this work, a number of facts became evident. First, there was indeed some sort of Spanish colonial site in the vicinity of Mission Hill. Secondly, there were more archeological remains pertaining to this occupation than was believed from earlier archeological work (Gilmore 1976), which had concentrated on the area of the hill north of FM 147. On the basis of the weekend work, a $2,000 grant ($1,000 from the San Augustine Historical Society, $1,000 from the Texas Historical Foundation) was obtained to begin the highly important research into contemporary Spanish documents. This research is being carried out by the Old Spanish Missions Research Library in San Antonio; the first reports indicated a very limited amount of new data are being uncovered.

At this point, it was felt that more exploratory archeological research was needed before more time and money could or should be allocated to the project. With this in mind, the SFASU Archeological Field School agreed to excavate for ten days at the site, with the option to continue if sufficient archeological remains were uncovered. Within the allotted time period, it was soon evident that more work would be advantageous to the project. Thus the field school continued excavations for the remainder (four weeks) of their schedule. As a result, a number of archeological features pertaining to the Spanish occupation of the site were uncovered and thousands of artifacts were recovered, washed and catalogued. This work showed that much more archeological work needed to be done at the site in order to have a more complete understanding of the nature of the Spanish occupation, the plan, if possible, of the mission settlement, and the structural aspects of the building walls, etc., which most certainly occurred at the site. To this end, the citizens of San Augustine raised $7,000 to continue excavations for six more weeks.

A preliminary report (Corbin 1976) of the weekend work at 41SA25, detailed the archeological assessment at that point. The following sections will describe the results of the six-weeks' excavation by the SFASU Archeological Field School (1977) and the subsequent six weeks of excavation at the site funded by monies raised by the citizens of San Augustine.

The 1977 Excavations

The first portion of the 1977 field season was conducted under the auspices of Stephen F. Austin State University as an archeological field school (Ant. 440). Thus the primary focus of this session was teaching archeological field methods. Nevertheless, we feel that archeological field schools should also be designed to contribute to general archeological data, and the preservation of our historical and cultural resources. Therefore, general excavation strategy was designed to locate archeological features associated with the presumed location of the Spanish Colonial Mission Dolores de los Ais. The preliminary work in 1976 had indicated that a portion of Mission Hill (south of FM 147), heretofore only cursorily examined, contained archeological data (numerous artifacts and what appeared to be trash pits) which supported the contention that Mission Dolores de los Ais had indeed been located on the hill. By the end of the first two weeks, the field school excavations had yielded enough data to warrant spending the remainder of the six-weeks' session at the site. The area in the vicinity of N100/W100 (Fig.1), known as the French Area, was producing hundreds of artifacts on what appeared to be the floor of a structure. Other field school participants had uncovered a large trash pit and portions of a second. As the field school excavations progressed, portions of a jacal wall, a well, and the subsurface remains of what appeared to be two structures were revealed. It soon became apparent that this portion of the site was rich in archeological remains of the Spanish Colonial activity associated with what had to be Mission Dolores de los Ais. It was also apparent that an extended field season was highly desirable, particularly in terms of more fully exploring the features uncovered by the field school participants.

A proposal was submitted to the San Augustine Historical Society, and the citizens of San Augustine, for six more weeks of excavation. The money was raised within two weeks, and, utilizing students trained in the field school, the excavations continued without a break. The second half of the 1977 season concentrated on expanding our knowledge of several important archeological features discovered in the exploratory phase carried out by the field school. This subsequent work revealed no new features, but did confirm our earlier interpretations. By the end of this second six weeks there was no question that Mission Hill was the site of Mission Dolores de los Ais. This conclusion is based primarily on the presence of archeological remains of structures and other cultural features in direct association with thousands of Spanish Colonial period artifacts.

The Archeological Features
Although the thousands of artifacts recovered during the excavations suggested that Mission Hill was a significant

archeological site, it was the presence of subsurface features which indicated we were dealing with a significant Spanish Colonial presence. These features are the archeological remains of structures and other cultural activity which suggest strongly that Mission Hill was something more than an occasional camping spot along El Camino Real. Significantly, the features were non-Indian (i.e., this is not the site of a historic Ais Indian village) and in fact duplicated features uncovered at other Spanish Colonial sites in Texas.

The Refuse Pits (Figs. 1, 4, 5, 6)
One of the first tasks of the field school exploration was to profile the ditch wall that paralleled FM 147. It was hoped that this would reveal concentrations of cultural debris and features which might be related to the Spanish occupation. This profile revealed what appeared to be portions of two refuse pits. A test pit (1976) (Fig. 4) a few meters to the south of this part of the ditch had also indicated that this general area was rich in cultural debris. Expanded excavations in the vicinity uncovered a third refuse pit as well as a portion of one of the pits revealed in the ditch profile. The third trash pit (F-8) and the remainder of a second (F-18) were completely excavated. They contained large rocks, animal bone, and hundreds of artifacts which dated the pits to the period of the mission occupation. Pits of this type also occur at the site of Los Adaes (Robeline, La.), which was the capital of Texas during the period Mission Dolores was occupied, and other Spanish Colonial sites in Texas.

A fourth refuse pit, Feature 34, was uncovered while investigating the well (see below) on the west end of the site. This pit (Fig. 1), more elongated than the other pits, differed from those described above in that it contained no rocks and almost no bone. In addition it contained much more ashy material, large Indian sherds (as well as European goods), and a lot of charred organic remains, primarily corncobs. At this point the relationship between this pit and the well are uncertain, but it is felt that the pit was excavated after the well had been filled by its users.

The Jacal Wall (Feature 25)
Near the end of the field school season, three small post molds were discovered near the west end of a one-meter wide trench (Fig. 1) that paralleled the ditch profile. Using the alignment of the post molds as a guide, additional units were excavated to see whether there were other post molds in that line. These excavations revealed the post molds were associated with what had been a narrow trench oriented in the line of the post molds. Subsequent excavations uncovered other segments of the trench and associated post molds (Fig. 1, 7, and 10). This feature is aligned NE-SW and, at present, is approximately

12 meters long. The configuration of this feature suggests
a wall of jacal-type construction. The size of the elements
and the length of the feature also suggest this was a perimeter
wall rather than a wall associated with a building. Fired clay
fragments and charcoal indicate that the wall was plastered and,
at some time, had burned.

The Well (Feature 13)
    The field school reopened the backhoe trench (Fig. 1)
excavated by North Texas State University in 1973 to further
investigate trash pits reported, but not excavated. The new
trench was started further north and excavated deeper than the
previous trench. This work revealed that one trash or refuse
pit was in fact the upper portion of a filled well. The artifacts from the "pit" safely date the well to the Spanish occupation.
    The well (Fig. 5, 8) is ca 2 meters in diameter at the top
and then steps down to ca 1.5 meters. The backhoe trench and
additional probing revealed that the well extends to a depth of
at least 3.3 meters (ca eleven feet). After the well was
originally filled, several additional fill episodes were necessary as the fill settled and compacted in the well. The last
filling was primarily refuse. A similar well was uncovered at
the site of Los Adaes (Gregory, personal communication).

Feature 32
    This feature is a concentration of what appear to be frag-
ments of adobe bricks, post molds and portions of a wall-setting
trench. The wall-setting trench (Fig. 11) and associated clay
wall-footings (and/or adobe blocks) were discovered while pro-
filing the west wall of the backhoe trench. Schnitting of the
ground surface to the west of the trench revealed large, amorphous
concentrations of clay similar to that in the setting trench.
A portion of this area was then excavated, in 1.0cm levels,
revealing some large fragments of what appear to have been adobe
blocks. At approximately 6.0cm below ground surface, the associated post molds were discovered.
    At this point it is difficult to interpret this feature.
Similar clay material occurs for at least 3 meters south of the
excavated area. Additional material is present in portions of
the east wall of the backhoe trench opposite that on the west
side of the trench. The maximum extension of this feature to
the east, west and south is not known. At present it is hypo-
thesized that Feature 32 is the remains of a substantial structure which was constructed of large vertical posts and adobe
brick. Numerous Spanish and French artifacts as well as
presumed construction type and material suggest this feature was
definitely a significant part of the mission complex.

Feature 17 (Fig. 1, 9)
   This feature is a series of post molds (Features 17, 44, 45, 46, 48, 50, 61, and 62) and associated fragments of charred posts which appear to have been associated with a small rectangular structure (?) adjoining the well. Most of the large post molds were preceded (stratigraphically) by horizontal or near-horizontal sections of charred posts. Significantly, the post mold alignments are parallel and perpendicular to the line of Feature 25, the jacal wall, indicating that it is part of a general architectural plan. The probable function of this feature is a mystery at this point since almost no artifacts were found in its vicinity. In fact the 3x4-meter unit (Fig. 1) to the east of F-17 was almost totally devoid of artifactual material, which is in stark contrast to most areas of the site that have been excavated.

Feature 6 and the French Area
   The original SFASU excavations (Fig. 2) were begun in this area of the site. It was here that Spanish colonial, French and aboriginal artifacts were found eroding from the ditch face early in 1976. The original ditch profile revealed a shallow ash lens (F-6), and excavations from ground surface produced numerous artifacts. Expanded excavations during the field school season revealed the ash lens to be rectangular in shape. The original size and shape of the lens is unknown since some portions of the feature were probably destroyed when the ditch was constructed. The lens is associated with a shallow (3-4cm) but extensive concentration of generally small fragments of artifacts and bone. This area has the appearance of a living (working) surface (centered around the ash lens?) which has had bits of cultural refuse trampled into it. No artifacts were recovered from in or under the ash lens, indicating it was in use (as a fireplace?) when the surface containing the artifacts was in use. At this point the true nature of this feature is not understood. Since the majority of the French faience sherds and a number of gunflints were recovered from this feature, it may relate to French trading activities at the mission.

The Artifacts (Figs. 12-20)
   During the excavations, nearly all of the matrix from the excavations was passed through ¼"-mesh screen. This allowed the recovery of several thousand artifacts. The most numerous ceramic artifacts are sherds from vessels of Indian manufacture (Fig. 12) Although analysis has not begun, field inspection has identified the types similar to Patton Engraved, Natchitoches Engraved, and Y'Barb Incised, all of which have been recovered in historic contexts in East Texas. Of the non-Indian ceramic types, French faience (Fig. 13) is the most common, followed by Chinese porcelain (Fig. 14), Mexican majolica (Fig. 15) and English salt-glazed stoneware and creamware. Glass artifacts

(Fig. 16) are primarily bottle sherds and trade beads. The most common metal artifacts are hand-forged iron nails (Fig. 19) but many articles of brass (Fig. 18) and lead (Fig. 20) also occur. Artifacts of stone (Fig. 17), including three small triangular arrowpoints (common at mission sites), gunflints, and a leg fragment from a basalt metate, also occur. With the exception of a few beer bottle sherds, barbed wire and staples, recent artifacts are conspicuously absent. All in all, the artifacts recovered make a nice package of data, all relating to the Spanish colonial period.

Summary and Conclusions
    Archeological investigations carried out under the auspices of the SFASU Archeological Field School (Ant. 440) and the Anthropology Program at SFASU have succeeded in uncovering archeological remains associated with the Spanish Colonial site of Mission Dolores de los Ais. This identification is based on the association of Spanish Colonial and other artifacts with architectural remains typical of frontier missions of this period of Texas history. In addition, the location of these remains fits the general description of the location of the mission derived from contemporary Spanish documents. It is significant to note that this is the first of the five known Spanish Colonial missions in East Texas to be so identified and placed on the National Register of Historic Places.
    As can be seen from the excavation plan (Fig. 1), much more archeological work needs to be conducted before we can know more about this important historic Texas site. Placement on the National Register of Historic Places will facilitate matching fund grants which will allow this work to be continued. Although Federal monies for 1978 are not available, a matching fund grant proposal is being prepared for 1979. In the meantime, the SFASU Archeological Field School plans to conduct its 1978 season at the site to continue this very important research into Spanish colonialism in East Texas.

FIGURE 1 Excavation plan of 41SA25, Mission Dolores de los Ais.

333

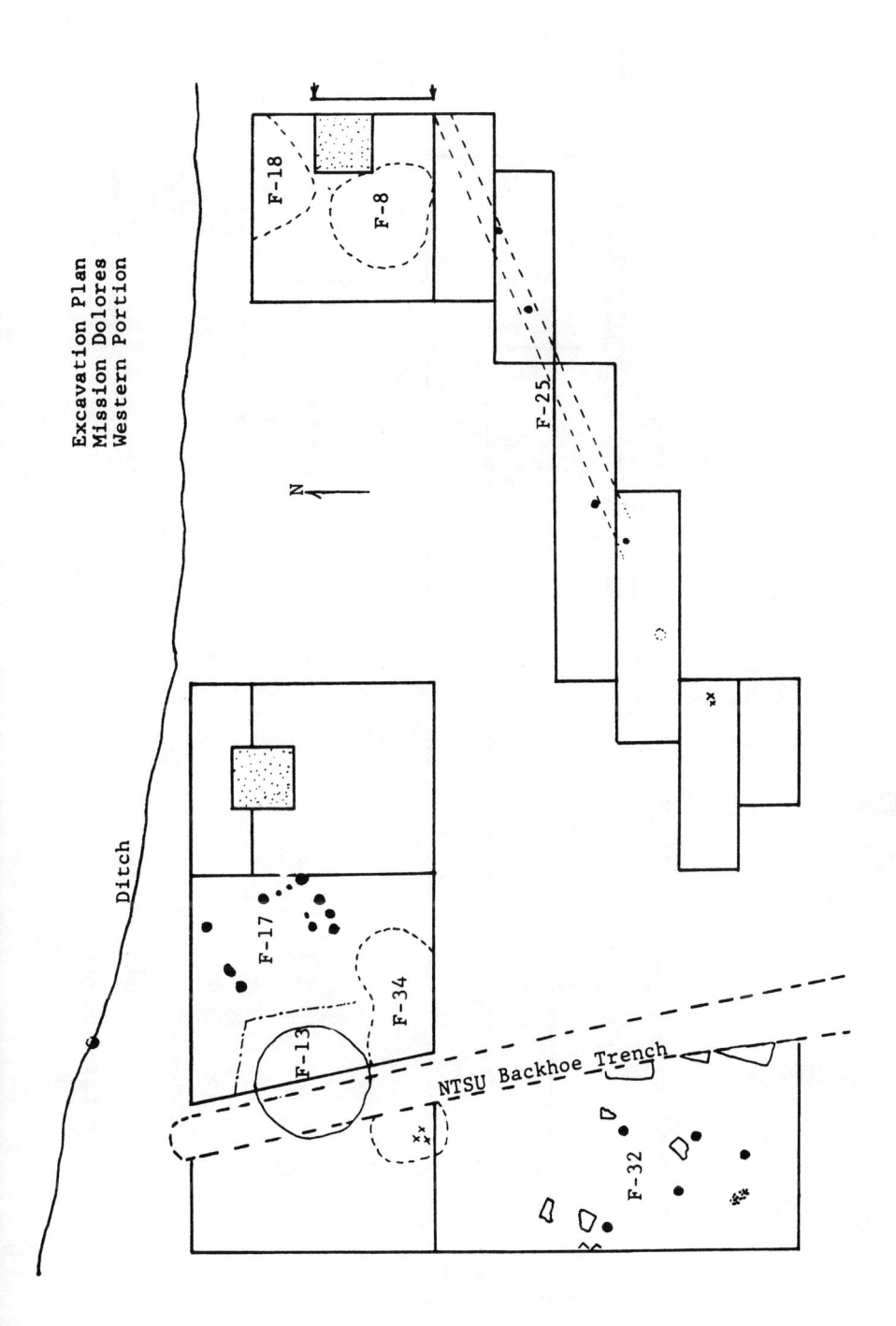

334

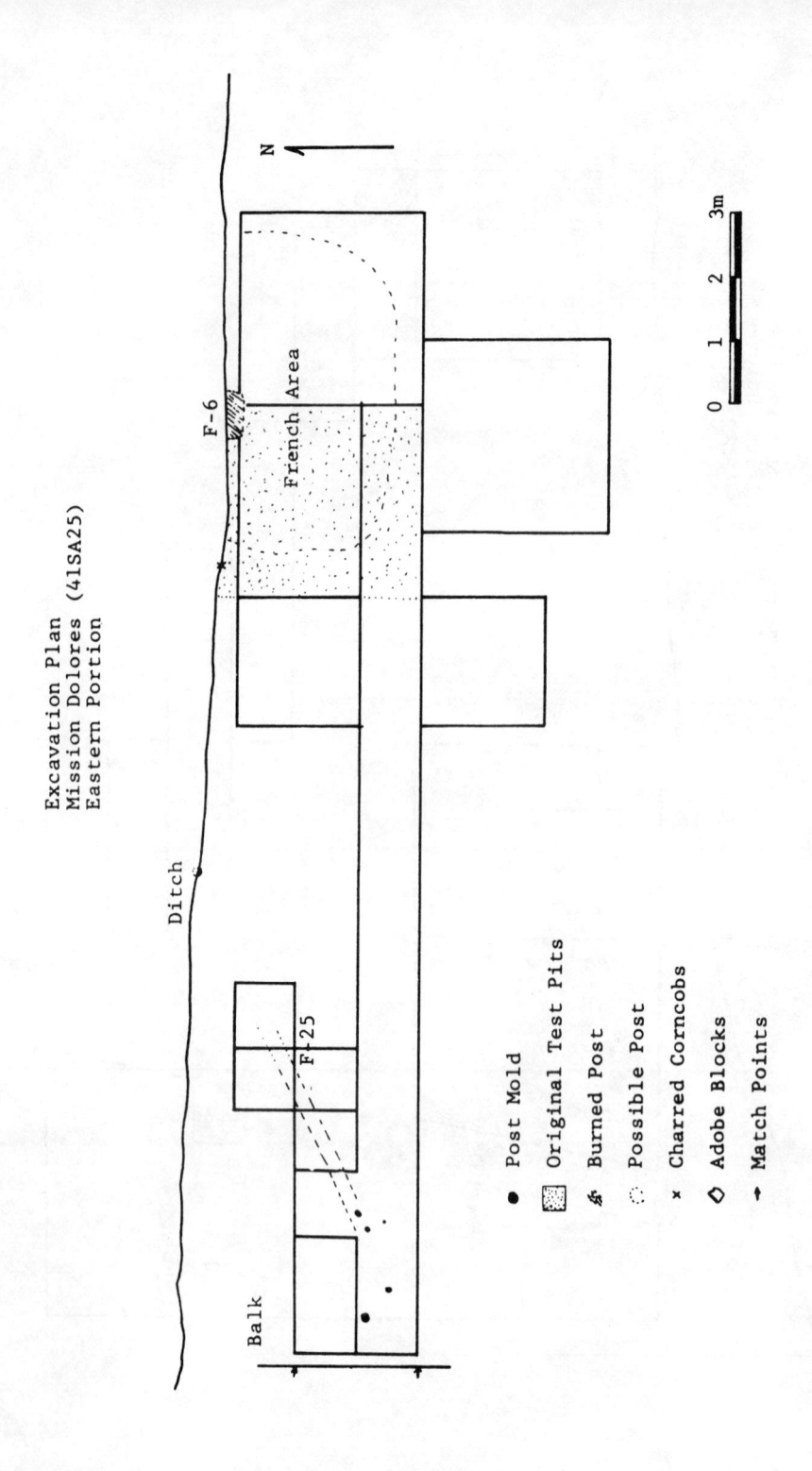

FIGURE 2 View of site area, looking south, showing initial excavations by SFA and Nacogdoches Archeological Society in area along ditch where Spanish colonial artifacts were eroding. F-6 is a shallow rectangular ash "lens" which is believed to be the base of a fireplace. Because of the predominance of French trade goods in this immediate vicinity, this area is referred to as "the French area". The area exposed is 3x5m.

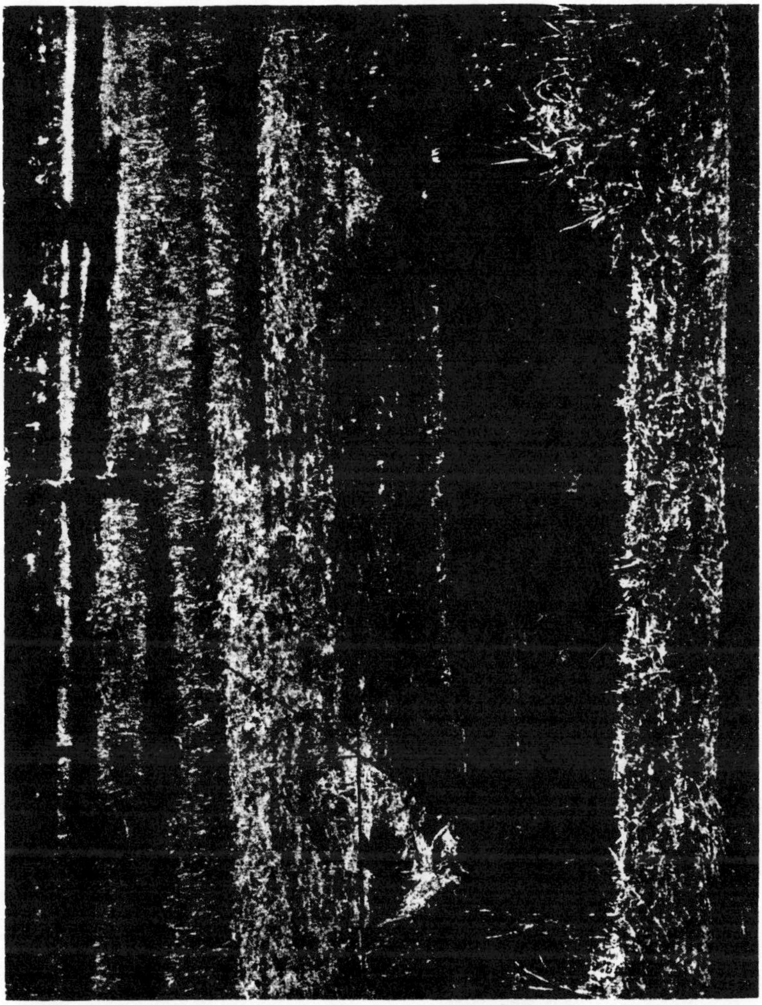

FIGURE 3 View of site area, looking southwest, at the beginning of the 1977 summer field season.

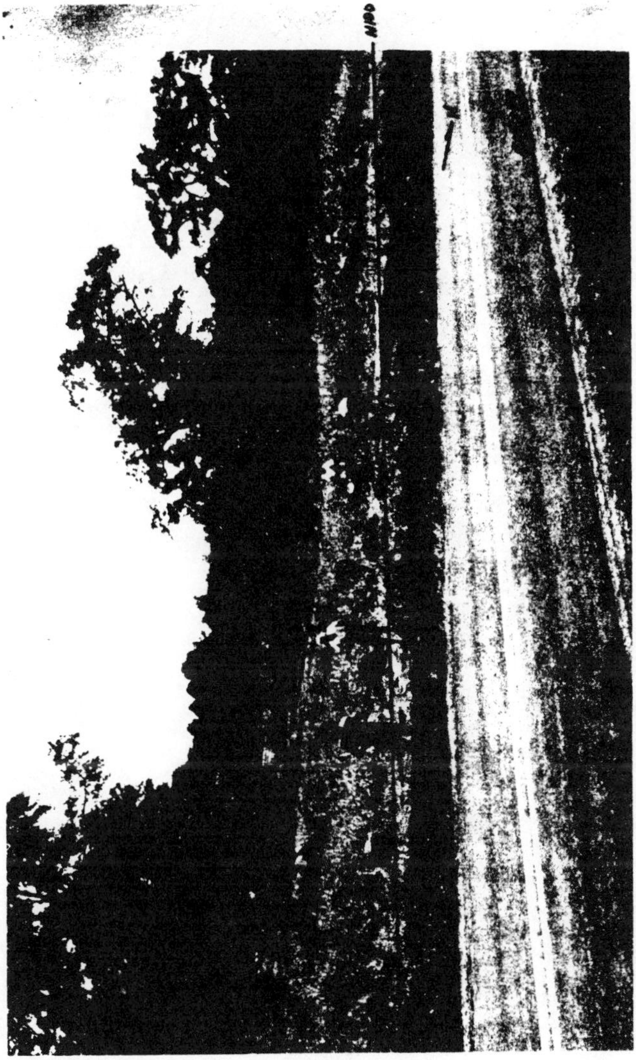

FIGURE 4 View of site area, looking northeast, at the end of the first six weeks' excavation, 1977.

Legend:

F-8   trash pit, showing stones in bottom of pit
F-18 about half of this pit has been excavated; the remainder is in the balk between the excavation units and the ditch.
----- the line of F-25, the jacal wall

→   locate some of the first post molds found in association with the wall trench

A   one of the original 1976 SFA test pits

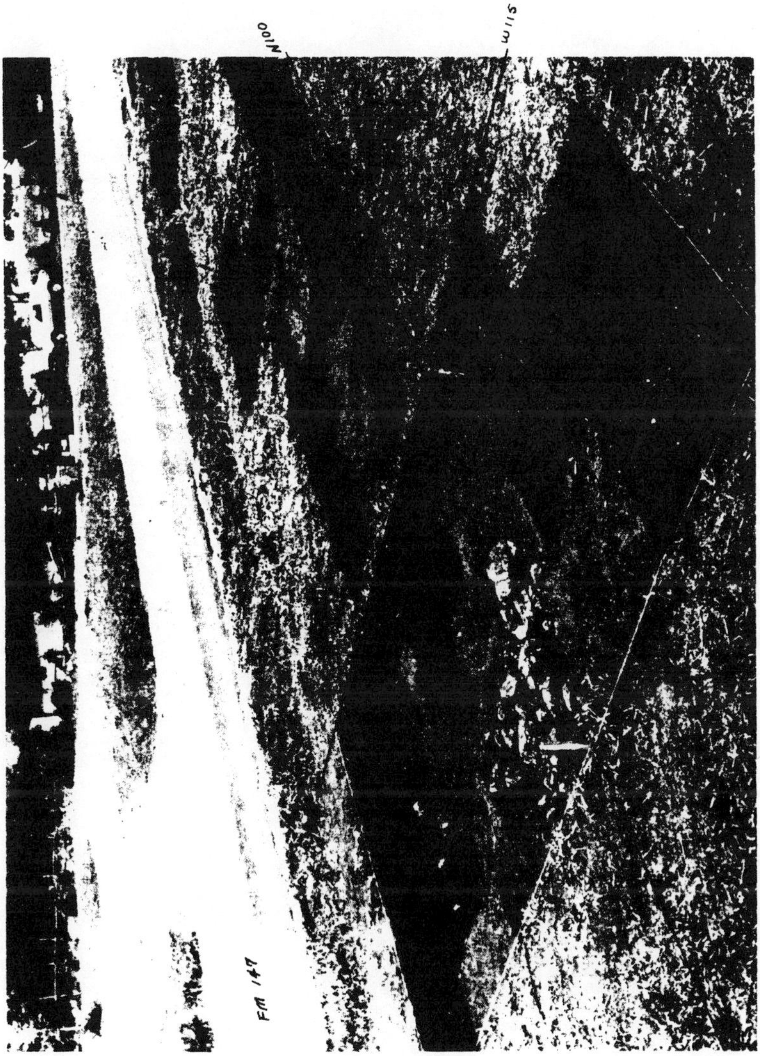
N100
W115
FM 147

FIGURE 5   View of site, looking west, at the end of the first six weeks of excavation, 1977.

Legend

F-8   trash pit

F-13   filled well

F-17   small rectangular structure (?)

F-32   adobe structure (?)

·······   NTSU backhoe trench

- - - -   line of F-25, the jacal wall, at ground surface. It should be noted that the post mold alignments in F-17 and F-32 parallel this line.

→   post molds in F-25

x   postholes which belong to a fence we believe may mark boundary of the original Quinalty-Quirk survey. This boundary line followed approximately the line of El Camino Real as of ca 1827.

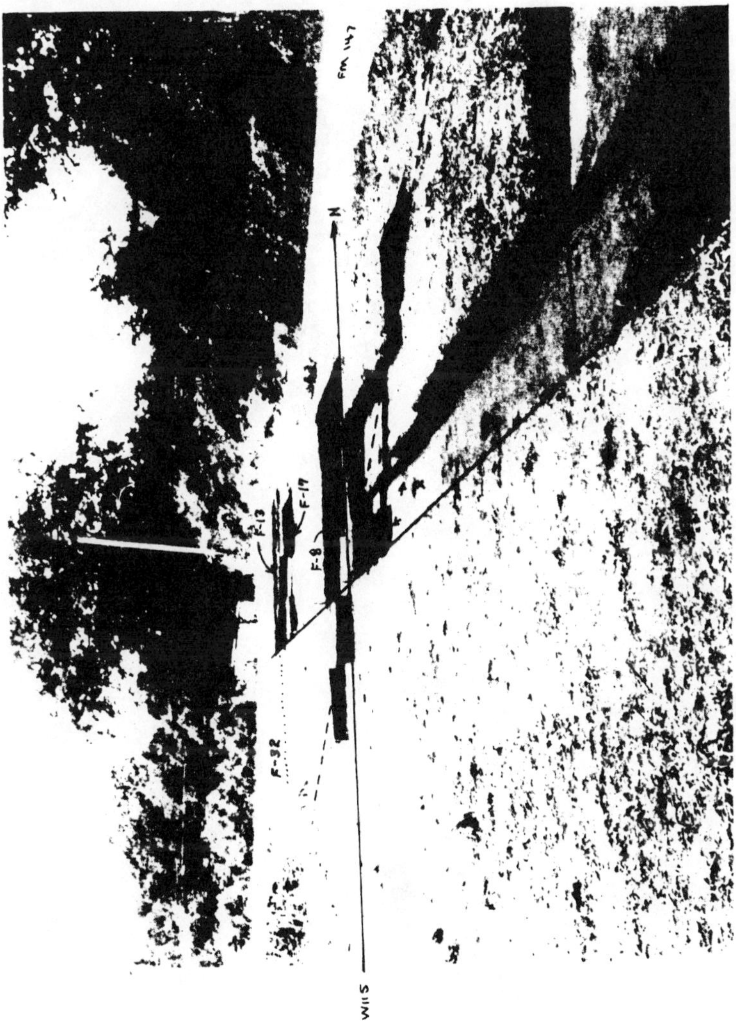
N
F-13
F-19
F-8
F-32

FIGURE 6 Excavation of Feature 8, a large trash pit,
in progress (looking approximately south).
The pit contained primarily bone and rocks.
Many ceramic, glass, and metal artifacts
of the Spanish colonial period were, however,
also recovered.

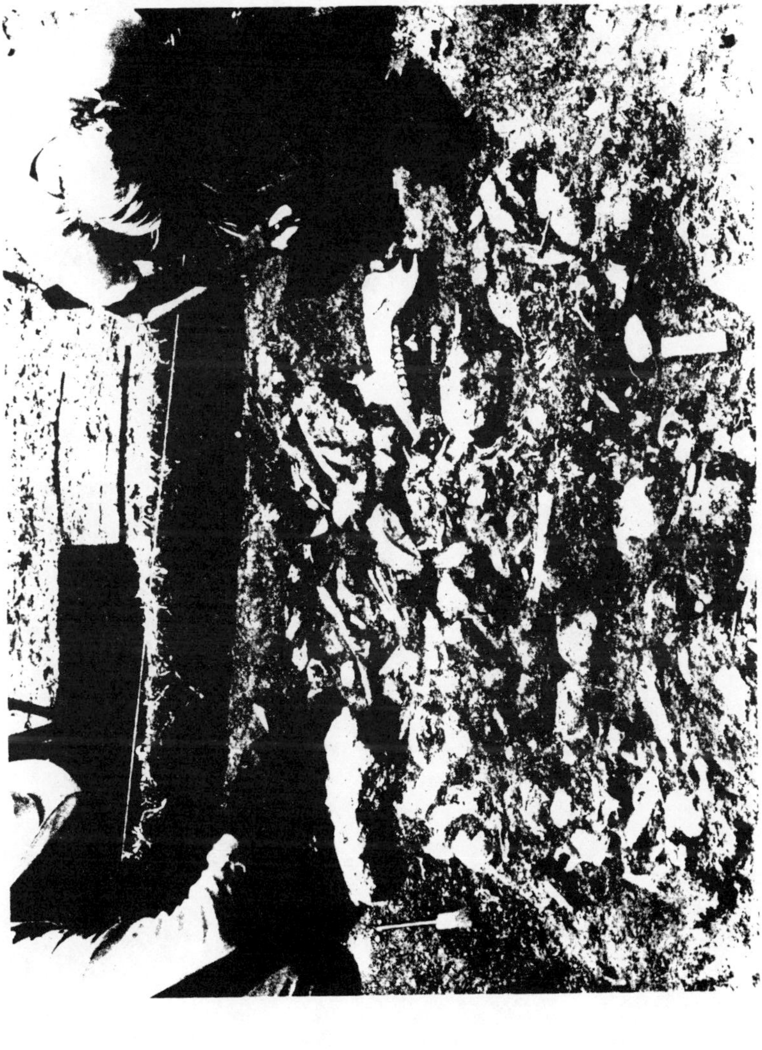

FIGURE 7 Typical tapering post mold in Feature 25, the jacal wall (see Fig. 10).

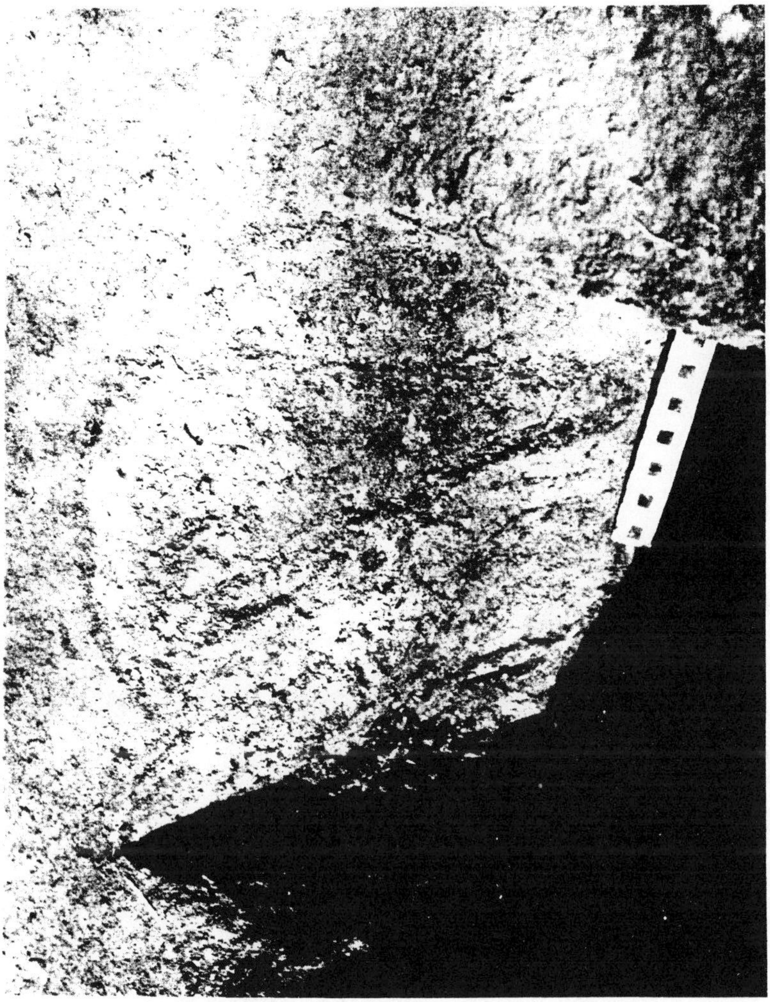

FIGURE 8 Profile of F-13, filled well.

PROFILE OF FEATURE 13, A FILLED WELL
East Wall, NTSU Trench

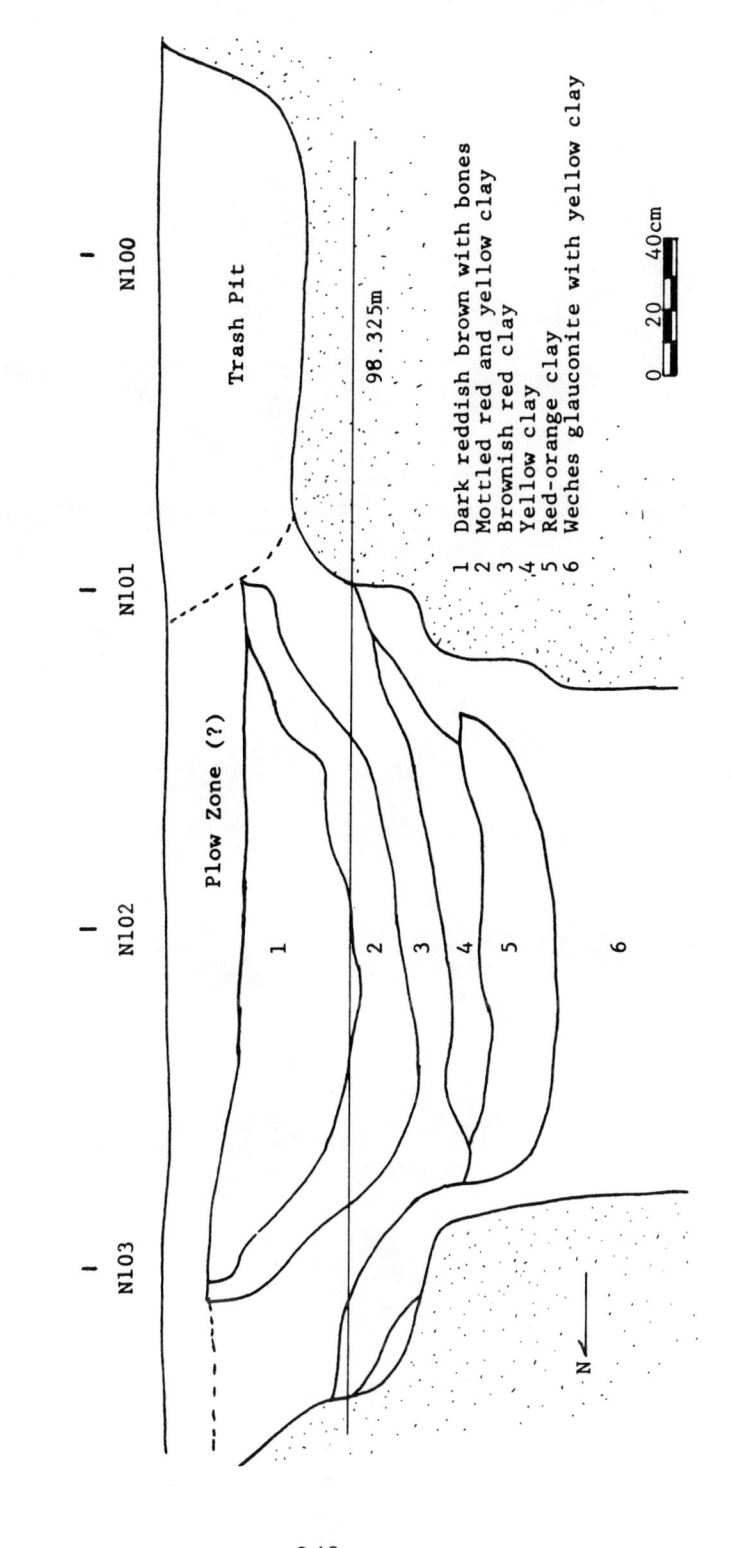

1 Dark reddish brown with bones
2 Mottled red and yellow clay
3 Brownish red clay
4 Yellow clay
5 Red-orange clay
6 Weches glauconite with yellow clay

FIGURE 9 Plan and profile of F-17, structure

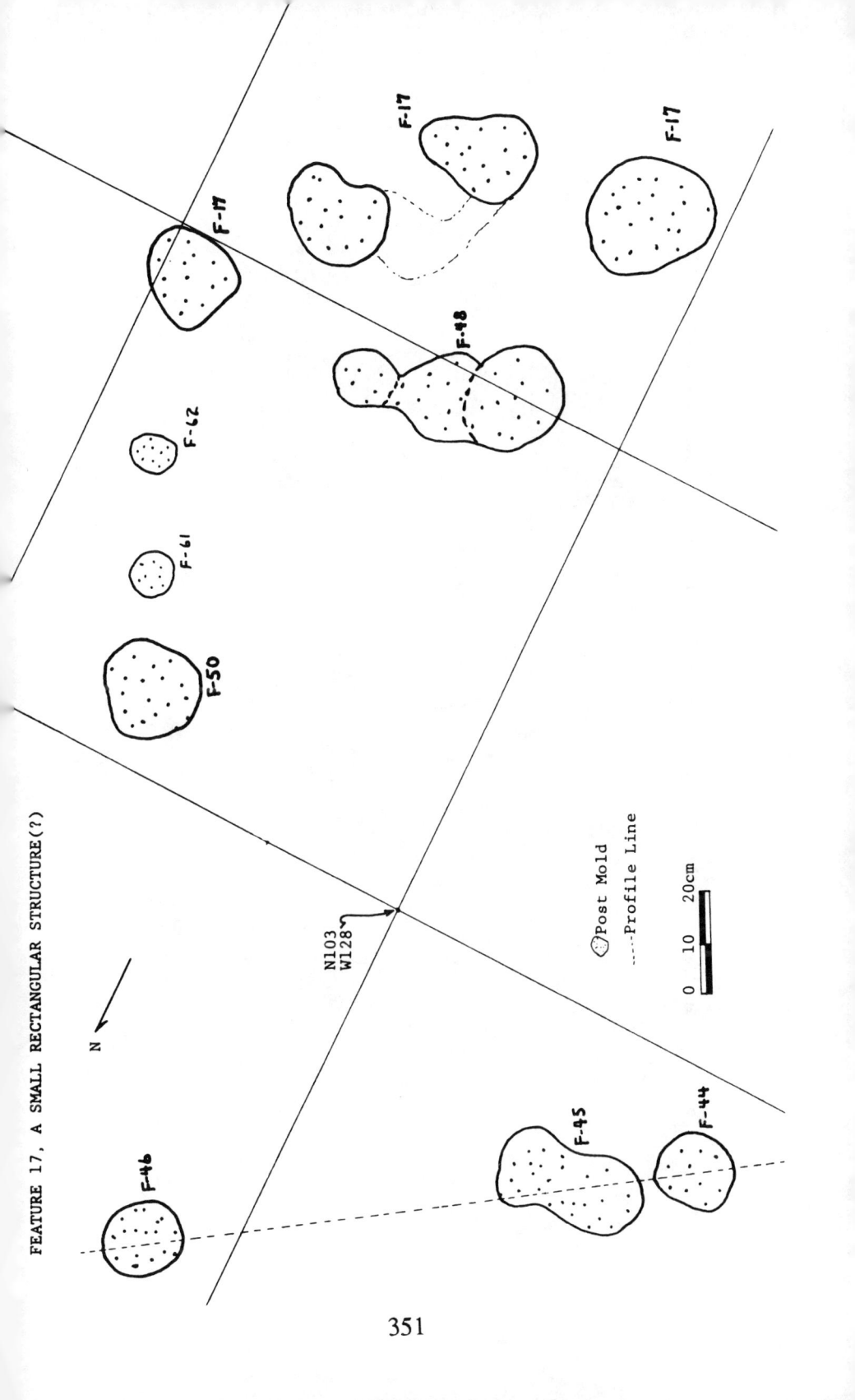

FEATURE 17, A SMALL RECTANGULAR STRUCTURE(?)

PROFILE OF THREE POST MOLDS IN FEATURE 17, A SMALL RECTANGULAR STRUCTURE (?)
(See Plan Map)

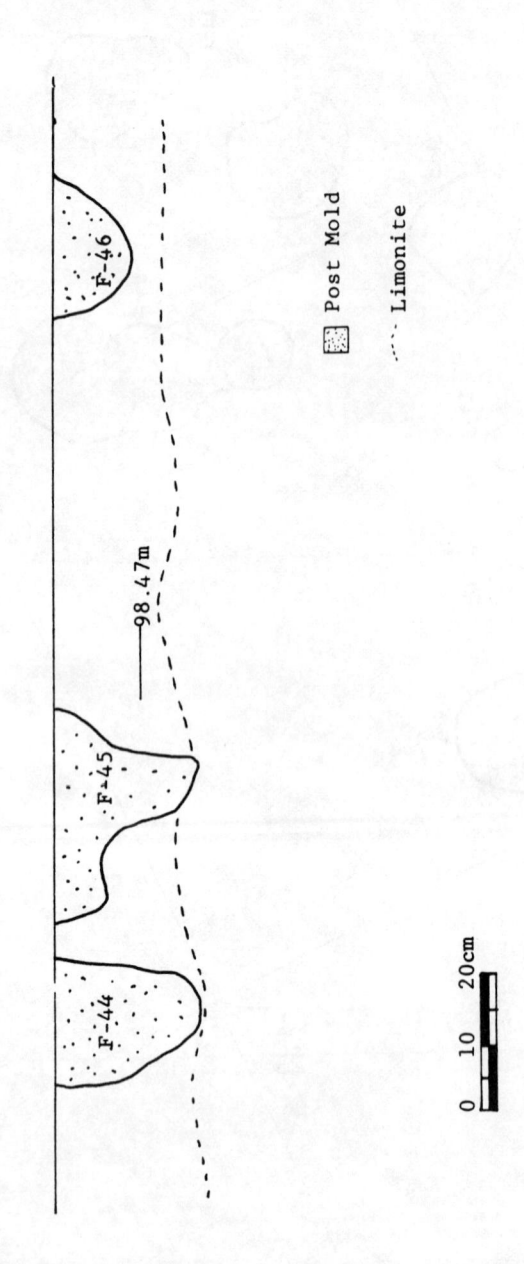

FIGURE 10 Plans and profiles from F-25, jacal wall

PLAN AND PROFILE OF A PORTION OF F-25, A JACAL WALL TRENCH (WITH POSTS)

Post Profile

98.61m

N99 W118

N98 W118

Floor Elevation--98.73m

98.93m

Wall Trench, West Profile

N

0 10 20cm

Wall Trench, East Profile

98.74m

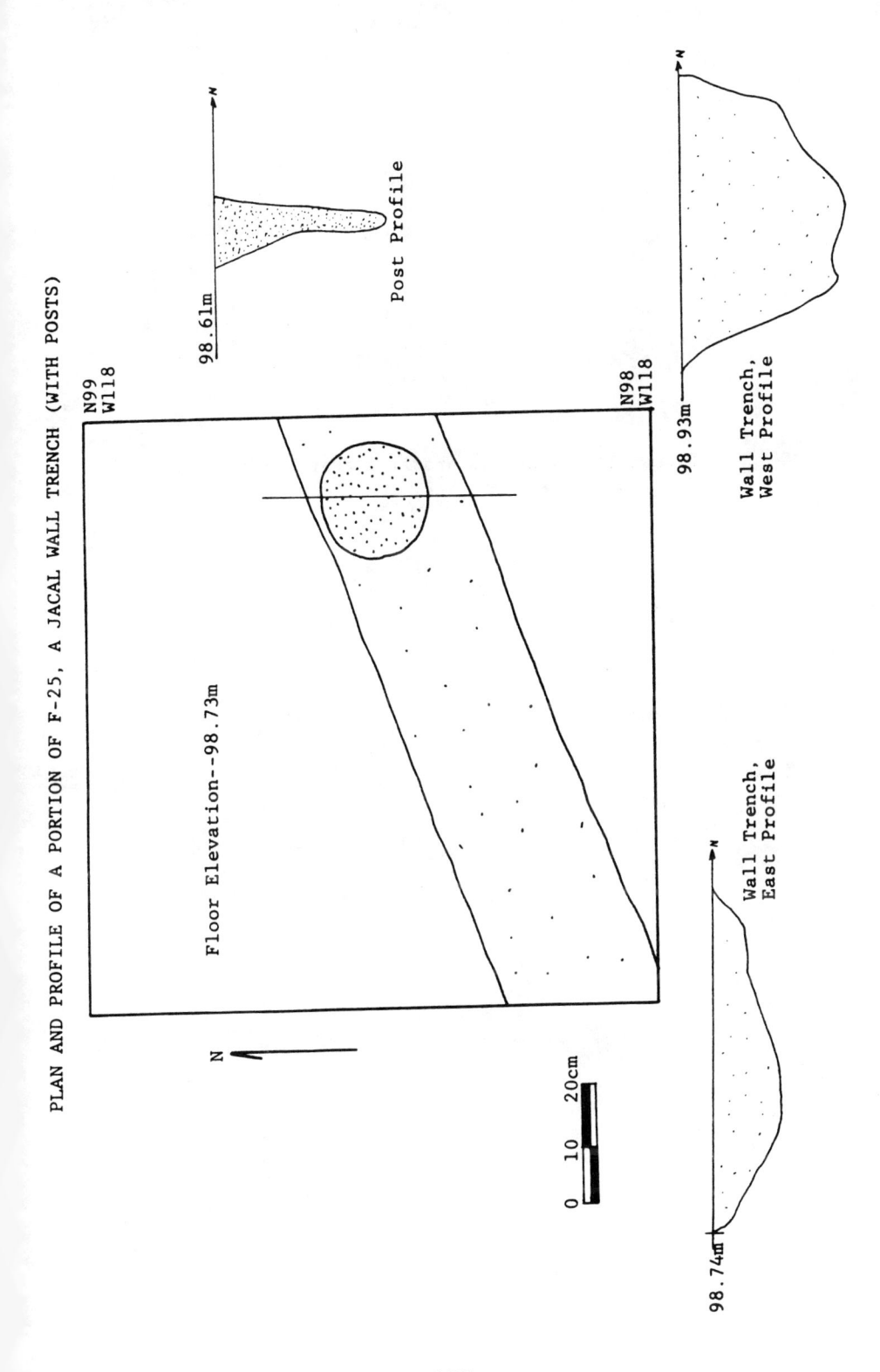

355

FIGURE 11 Plans and profiles from F-32, adobe
          structure (?)

PLAN OF FEATURE 32, REMAINS OF ADOBE STRUCTURE (?)

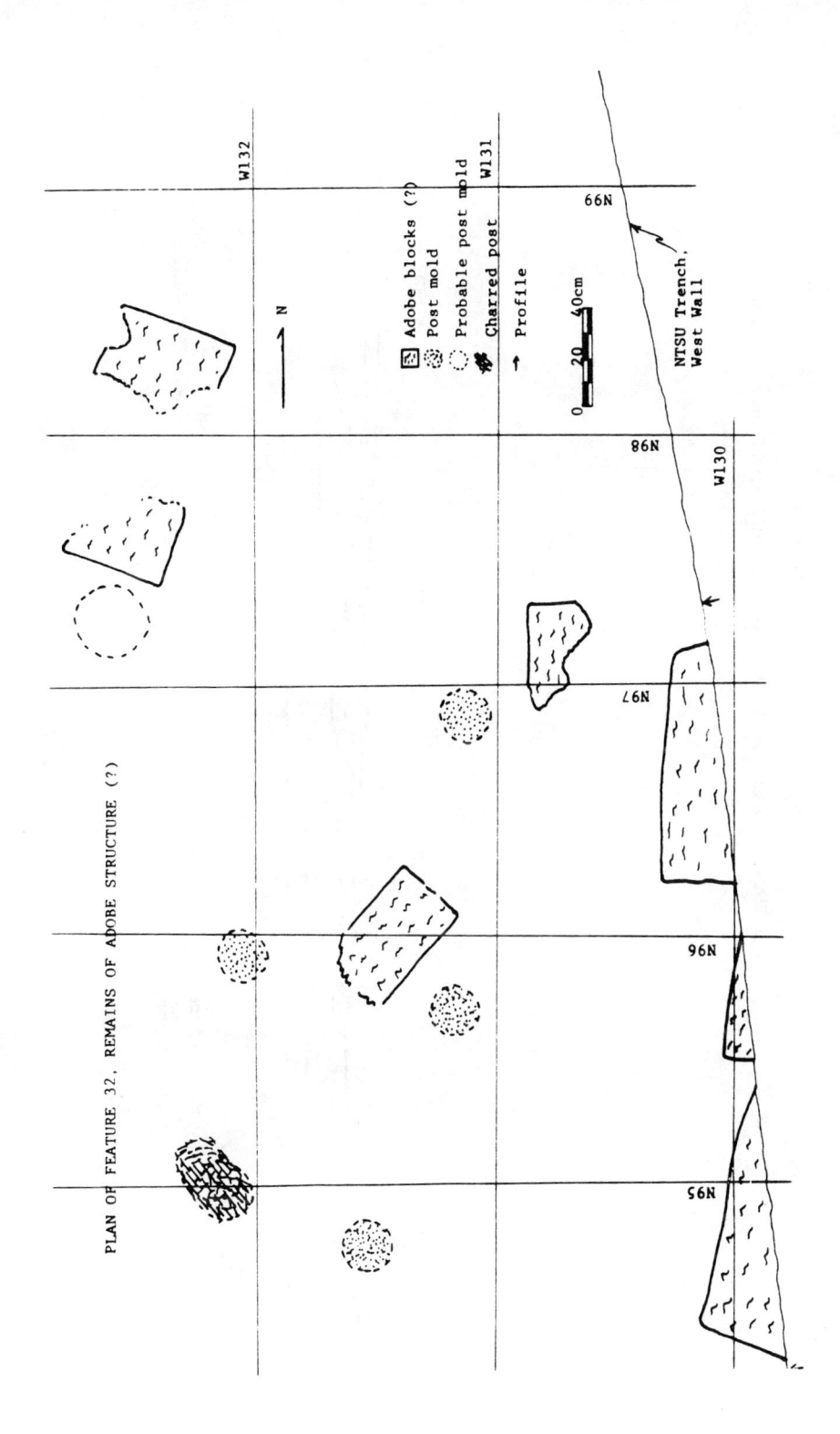

WEST PROFILE OF NTSU TRENCH SHOWING WALL-SETTING TRENCHES AND ADOBE (?) BLOCKS

Feature 32

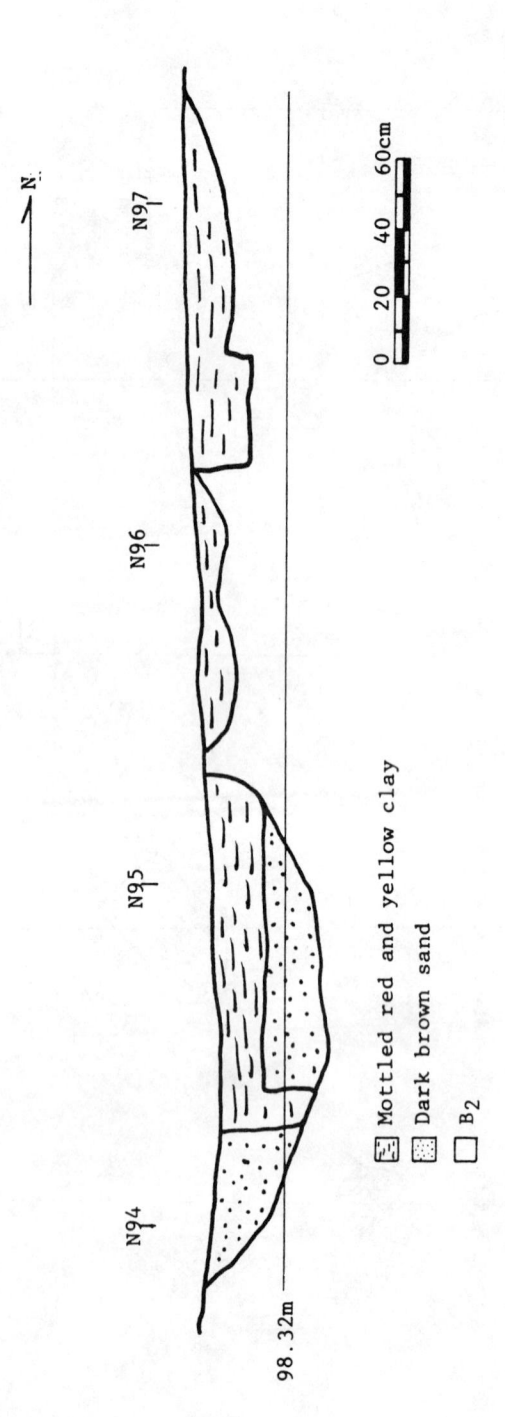

FIGURE 12 Typical Indian ceramics from the site of Mission Dolores. Bone tempering is the rule. Many sherds exhibit small fused silica particles. This can occur at low temperatures (ca 800°F) when iron and silica are present in a reducing atmosphere. Sherd 1 is from fill in F-13, the well. The design execution of the Patton Engraved Sherds (2, 3) is exceptional. All of the design elements pictured are duplicated in the collection from the site of Los Adaes in Louisiana. The punctations on sherds (4, 5, 6) are on a raised ridge. This design element is very common at Mission Dolores and Los Adaes.

FIGURE 13 Typical French faience from Mission
Dolores. Most of the designs are typical of French export faience of the
period 1725-50.

0 10 20mm

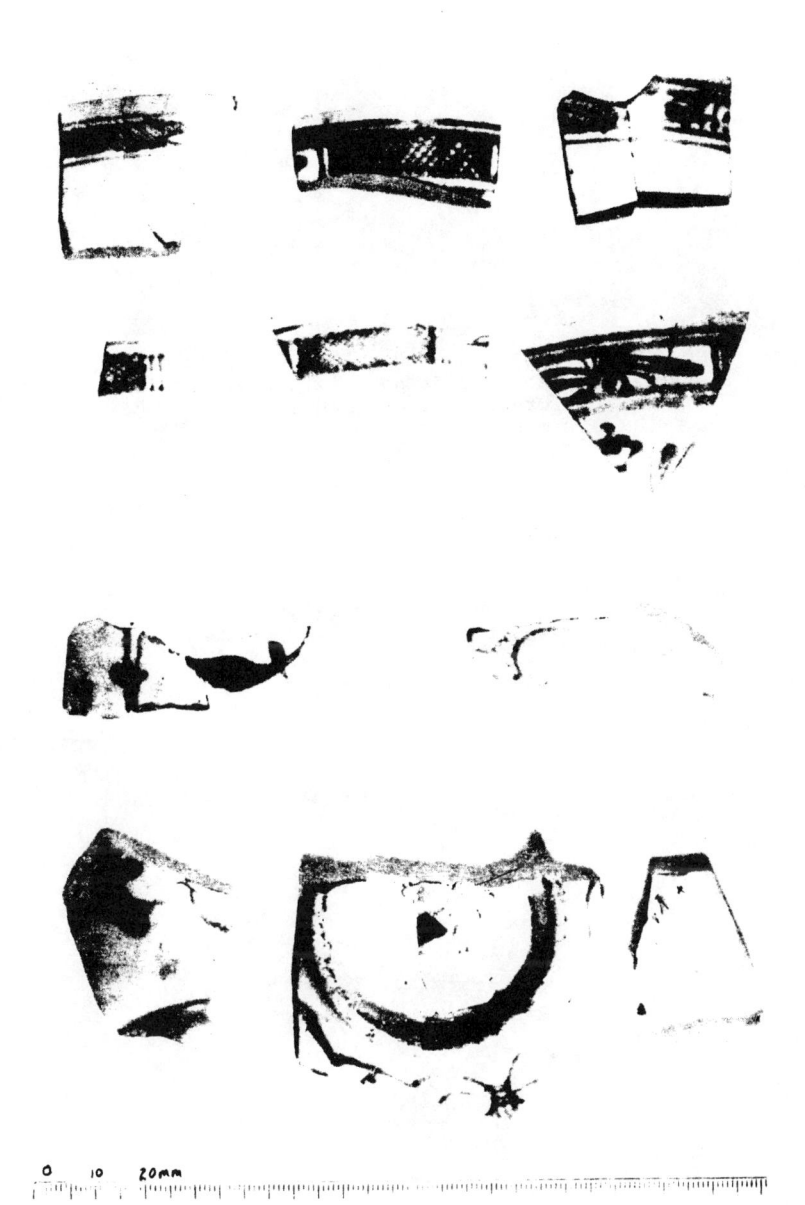

FIGURE 14 Chinese trade porcelain from Mission
            Dolores. All fragments appear to be
            from small, footed bowls.

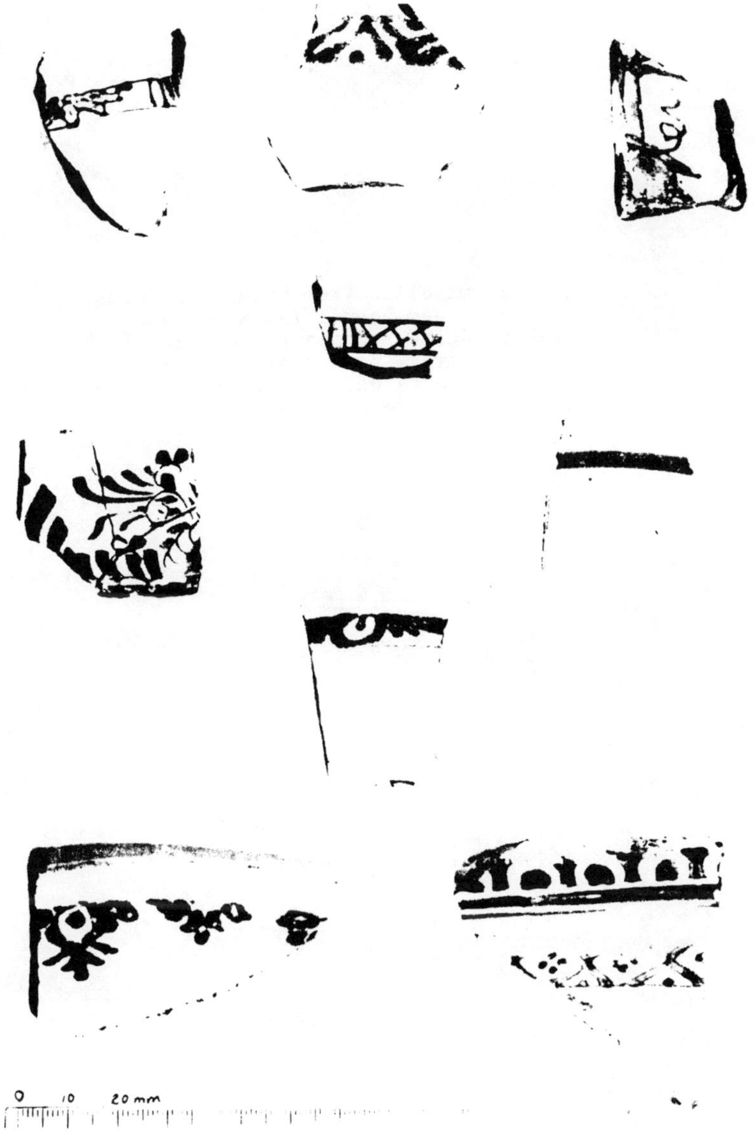
0 10 20 mm

FIGURE 15 Mexican majolica from Mission Dolores.
Most has been identified as Puebla
Blue on White. Compare the size of the
majolica fragments (the largest) with
that of the faience, aboriginal pottery,
and the Chinese porcelain.

0 10 20 mm

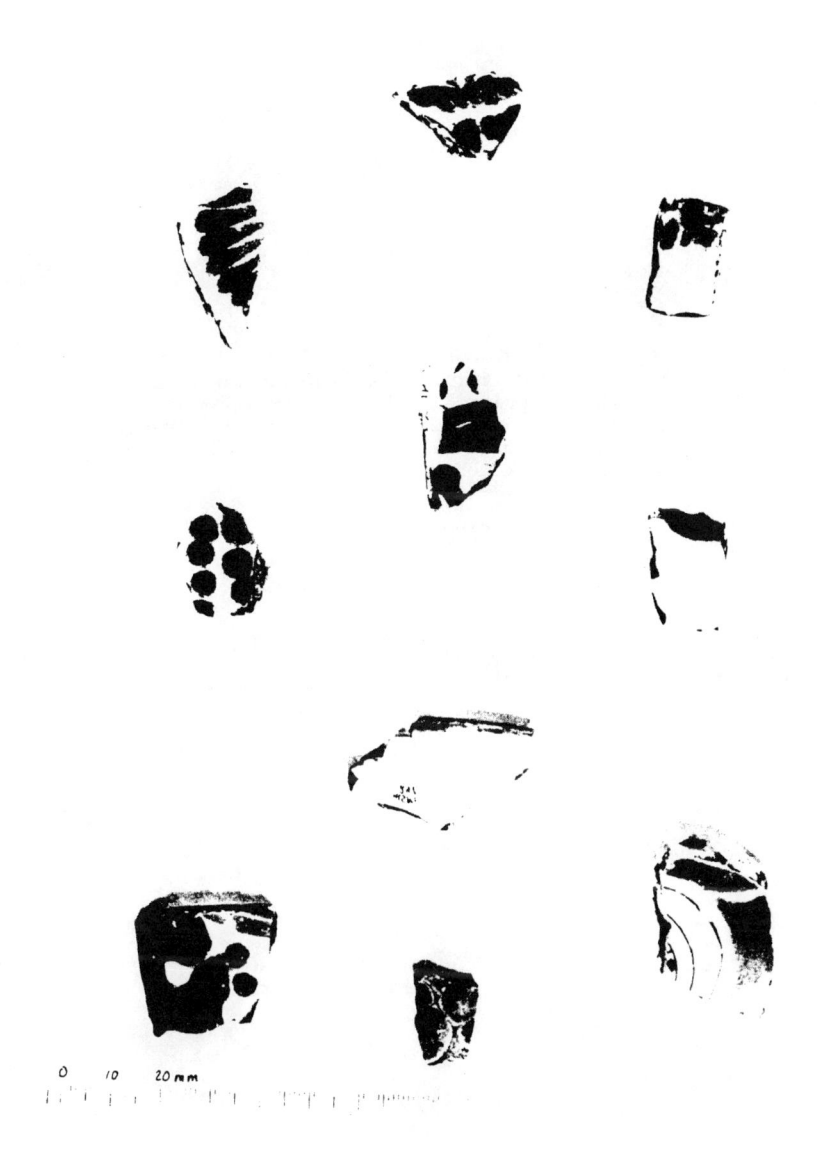

FIGURE 16 Glass artifacts from Mission Dolores.
The spherical beads are blue-green,
the cylindrical bead is red. The typical
bead from the site is smaller (ca 2-3mm)
and black.

0 10 20mm

FIGURE 17 Stone artifacts from Mission Dolores:
a-g are gun and/or strike-a-light flints;
i-j, arrowpoints; k, a <u>fica</u> carved from jet;
and l, a basalt metate leg fragment.
The jet <u>fica</u> is a Spanish artifact associated with the Pilgrimage of St. James. The metate fragment and most of the gunflints were recovered in the "French area" near F-6.

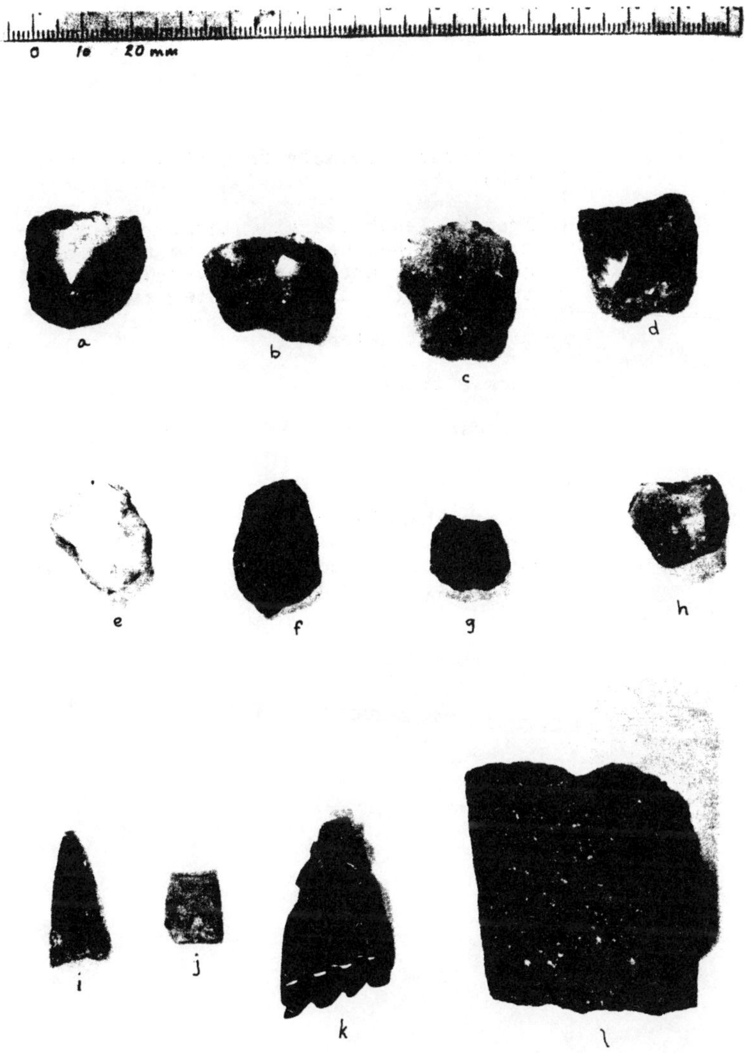
0 10 20 mm
a
b
c
d
e
f
g
h
i
j
k
l

FIGURE 18 Brass/copper artifacts from Mission Dolores.

a, French claspknife sideplate. The uppermost edge has been ground to a sharp edge. This artifact recovered while troweling the ditch profile near F-17.

b-c, copper tinklers

d, buckle fragment

e-f, brass trigger guard fragments

g, spoon

h, scissor handle

i, handle; recovered in Feature 8, a large trash pit

373

FIGURE 19 Iron artifacts from Mission Dolores.

        a-e, hand-forged nails. This is a very common artifact at the site, surpassed only by aboriginal ceramics. Many have been clinched

        f-g, <u>Ficas</u>. Both are incomplete.

        h-i, small, spoon-shaped "dangles"

        j, large spur rowel fragment

375

FIGURE 20 Lead/pewter artifacts from Mission Dolores.

a,e   flattened shot

b,   unidentified object

c, d, f,   small lead seals (?)

g,   pewter (?) handle

h-k, shot/musket balls

l,   lead hide-bale seal. Various unidentified inscriptions occur on both surfaces

m-n, lead pieces, probably from molding musket balls or shot. A number of these items were found in (next to) a small portion of F-25, the jacal wall.

0   10   20mm

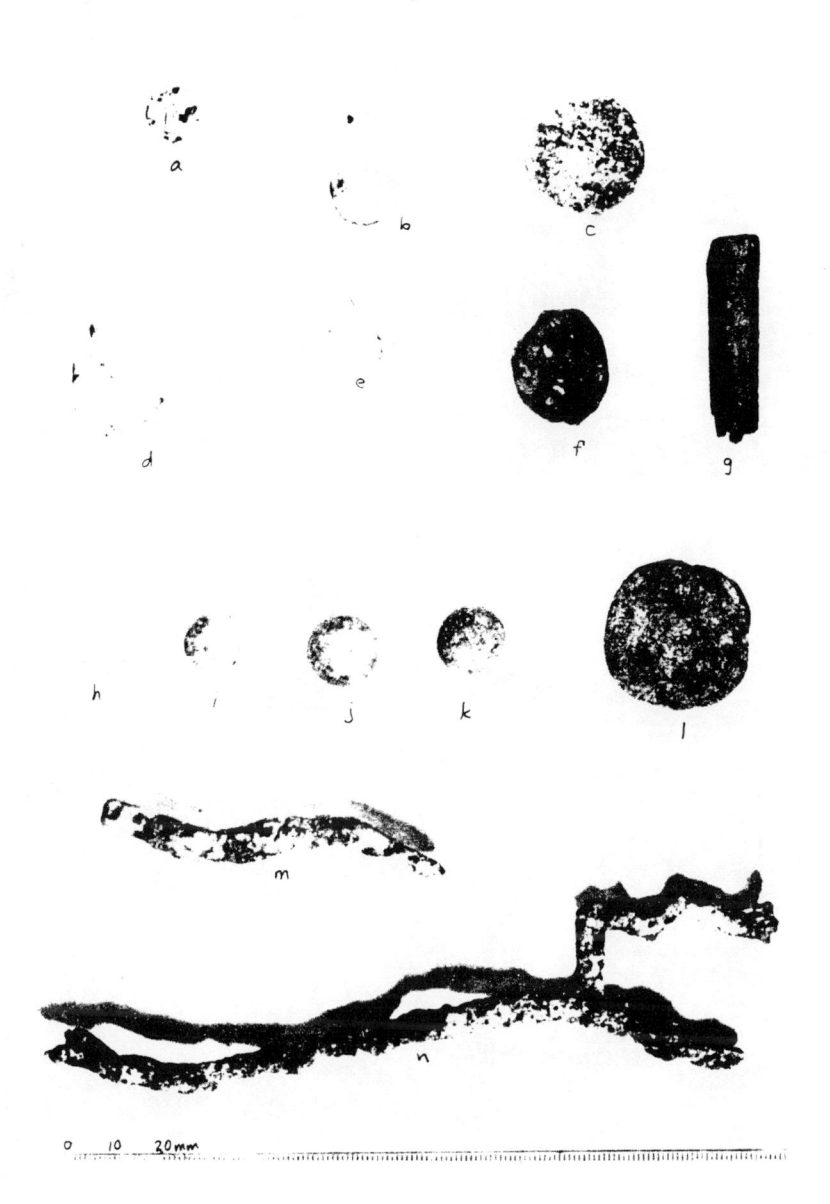

Titles in the Series

1. The Idea of Spanish Borderlands
   Edited by David J. Weber
2. Native American Demography
   Edited by Clark Spencer Larsen
3. Ethnology of the Alta California Indians
   I: Precontact
   Edited by Lowell John Bean and Sylvia Brakke Vane
4. Ethnology of the Alta California Indians
   II: Postcontact
   Edited by Lowell John Bean and Sylvia Brakke Vane
5. Ethnology of the Baja California Indians
   Edited by W. Michael Mathes
6. Ethnology of Northwest Mexico
   Edited by Randall H. McGuire
7. Ethnology of the Texas Indians
   Edited by Thomas R. Hester
8. Ethnology of the Indians of Spanish Florida
   Edited by David Hurst Thomas
9. The Native American and Spanish Colonial Experience in the Greater Southwest
   I: Introduction to the Documentary Records
   Edited by David H. Snow
10. The Native American and Spanish Colonial Experience in the Greater Southwest
    II: Introduction to Research
    Edited by David H. Snow

11. The Hernando de Soto Expedition
   Edited by Jerald T. Milanich
12. Earliest Hispanic-Native American Interactions in the American Southeast
   Edited by Jerald T. Milanich
13. Hispanic-Native American Interactions in the Caribbean
   Edited by William F. Keegan
14. Documentary Evidence for the Spanish Missions of Alta California
   Edited by Julia G. Costello
15. The Archaeology of Alta California
   Edited by Leo R. Barker and Julia G. Costello
16. The Spanish Missions of Baja California
   Edited by Robert H. Jackson
17. The Spanish Missions of New Mexico
   I: Before 1680
   Edited by John L. Kessell
18. The Spanish Missions of New Mexico
   II: After 1680
   Edited by John L. Kessell and Rick Hendricks
19. The Jesuit Missions of Northern Mexico
   Edited by Charles W. Polzer, Thomas H. Naylor, Thomas E. Sheridan, and Diana W. Hadley
20. The Franciscan Missions of Northern Mexico
   Edited by Thomas E. Sheridan, Charles W. Polzer, Thomas H. Naylor, and Diana W. Hadley
21. Archaeology of the Spanish Missions of Texas
   Edited by Anne A Fox
22. Documentary Evidence for the Spanish Missions of Texas
   Edited by Arthur R. Góme
23. The Missions of Spanish Florida
   Edited by David Hurst Thomas
24. Pedro Menéndez de Avilés
   Edited by Eugene Lyon
25. America's Ancient City
   Spanish St. Augustine: 1565–1763
   Edited by Kathleen A. Deagan
26. Native American Perspectives on the Hispanic Colonization of Alta California
   Edited by Edward Castillo
27. Hispanic Urban Planning in North America
   Edited by Daniel J. Garr